The Cinema of Ann Hui

Global East Asian Screen Cultures

Global East Asian Screen Cultures showcases cutting-edge scholarship on East Asian screen practices and cultures in local, regional and global contexts. Titles in the series take "East Asia" as a focus, a nodal point interlinked with other regional screen cultures, and a method to reorient the global screen-culture cartography. The series embraces screen studies focused on geographic East Asia as well as work exploring mobility, migration and hybridity as mediated through screen media production, textuality and reception that traverse East Asia and its diasporas.

We welcome proposals that intersect with these areas of investigation. Please direct initial enquiries to series editors Mark Gallagher and Yiman Wang at doctorgalaga@gmail.com and yw3@ucsc.edu.

Published and Forthcoming Titles:

Contemporary Chinese Cinema and Visual Culture: Envisioning the Nation
By Sheldon Lu

Contemporary Art Cinema Culture in China
By Xiang Fan

Fighting Stars: Stardom and Reception in Hong Kong Martial Arts Cinema
Edited by Kyle Barrowman

Producing Chinese Reality Television: Power, Precarity and Working Cultures
By Tianyu Zhang

The Cinema of Stephen Chow
Edited by Gary Bettinson and Vivian P.Y. Lee

The Cinema of Ann Hui: Aesthetics, Gender, and Displacement
Edited by Zhaoyu Zhu, Weiting Fan and Xueyan Cheng

Exploring Isekai: Mapping Worlds through Anime and Manga
Edited by William B. Ashbaugh and Shintaro Mizushima

The Cinema of Ann Hui

Aesthetics, Gender, and Displacement

Edited by

Zhaoyu Zhu, Weiting Fan, and Xueyan Cheng

BLOOMSBURY ACADEMIC
LONDON • NEW YORK • OXFORD • NEW DELHI • SYDNEY

BLOOMSBURY ACADEMIC
Bloomsbury Publishing Plc, 50 Bedford Square, London, WC1B 3DP, UK
Bloomsbury Publishing Inc, 1359 Broadway, New York, NY 10018, USA
Bloomsbury Publishing Ireland, 29 Earlsfort Terrace, Dublin, 2, D02 AY28, Ireland

BLOOMSBURY, BLOOMSBURY ACADEMIC and the Diana logo are
trademarks of Bloomsbury Publishing Plc

First published in Great Britain 2026

Cover design: Ben Anslow
Cover image: Director Ann Hui, on set of *Boat People*, (aka TAU BAN NO HOI), 1982.
(© International Spectrafilm / courtesy Everett Collection / Alamy)

A catalogue record for this book is available from the British Library.

A catalog record for this book is available from the Library of Congress.

ISBN: HB: 978-1-350-51444-7
PB: 978-1-350-51443-0
ePDF: 978-1-350-51446-1
eBook: 978-1-350-51447-8

Series: Global East Asian Screen Cultures

Typeset by Integra Software Services Pvt. Ltd.
Printed and bound in India

To find out more about our authors and books visit www.bloomsbury.com
and sign up for our newsletters.

Contents

Illustrations

Contributors

Yiran Ai is an independent scholar based in the UK. She completed her PhD, "What Makes a Film Feminist? Gender Perspectives of Directors of Westernised and Hong Kong Cinema Between 1990 and 2000," at the University of Birmingham. She subsequently held a postdoctoral research position in Literary Theory at Shanghai University. Ai's research interests include the representation of diverse gender identities in cinema, as well as issues surrounding postcolonialism and postmodernism. Her writing has appeared in *Asian Cinema*.

Gary Bettinson is Senior Lecturer in Film Studies at Lancaster University, UK. He is the author of *The Sensuous Cinema of Wong Kar-wai* (2nd edition, 2025) and co-editor of *The Poetics of Chinese Cinema* (2016), *Hong Kong Horror Cinema* (2018), and *The Cinema of Stephen Chow* (2024). He is the editor-in-chief of the journal *Asian Cinema*.

Jessica Ka Yee Chan is Associate Professor of Chinese Studies at the University of Richmond, USA. She is the author of *Chinese Revolutionary Cinema: Propaganda, Aesthetics, and Internationalism, 1949–1966* (2019). Her articles have been published in the *East Asian Journal of Popular Culture*, *Inter-Asia Cultural Studies*, the *Journal of Chinese Cinemas*, *Modern Chinese Literature and Culture*, and *The Opera Quarterly*.

Siao-Yun Chen is Adjunct Assistant Professor of the Graduate Institute of Taiwan Literature and Transnational Cultural Studies at National Chung Hsing University, Taiwan. Her research fields include Hong Kong literature, Taiwan literature, Sinophone cinemas, and cultural studies. She has published numerous articles in journals such as *Chung Wai Literary Quarterly*, *Thought and Words: Journal of the Humanities and Social Science*, *Cultural Studies Quarterly*, and *Film Appreciation Academic Journal*. She is also the author of *Trans-Border Imagination: The Construction of Hong Kong Literature in the 1980s* (2025).

Xueyan Cheng is a Ph.D. candidate at the National University of Singapore in the Cultural Studies in Asia Programme. Her research focuses on contemporary Chinese cinema and Southeast Asian cinema. She is also a film critic.

Weiting Fan is Assistant Professor at Chongqing University Meishi Film Academy, China. She received her PhD in film theory and film philosophy at King's College London. She studied comparative literature at the University of Hong Kong in her undergraduate years. Her research interests include East Asian cinema, Chinese film theory, and Chinese intellectual histories.

Han Li is Professor of Chinese and Chair of the Department of Modern Languages and Literatures at Rhodes College, USA. Her research interests include the global transplantation of "Chinese-ness" as well as contemporary Chinese cinema and media, and she has published widely in scholarly journals. In addition to her academic work, she has given media interviews on East Asian topics for outlets such as *Time*, *VOA China*, *Sixth Tone*, and the *South China Morning Post*. She is currently working on a monograph that examines the representation of rural children in Chinese post-socialist film and media.

Gabriel F. Y. Tsang is Assistant Professor at Hong Kong Baptist University, Hong Kong. He holds a PhD in Comparative Literature from King's College London, UK. He has served as President of the British Postgraduate Network for Chinese Studies and has conducted research at Stanford University, the National University of Singapore, the University of Copenhagen, and Sun Yat-sen University. His work has been published in peer-reviewed journals such as the *Journal of Narrative Theory*, *World Literature Studies*, and *Asian Studies*. He is also the author of the monograph *Chinese Educated Youth Literature: Ambivalent Bodies and Personal Literary Histories* (2025).

Raymond Tsang is Lecturer in the Department of East Asian Languages and Cultures at the University of Southern California, USA. He received his PhD in Cinema Studies from New York University. His research interests include martial arts cinema, leftist film and literature, and revolutionary transmedial practices, such as photographers traveling in Thailand and Vietnam, opera artists visiting North Korea, and mobile film units in rural Hong Kong. His work has appeared in *The Routledge Companion to Asian Cinemas* (2024) and in peer-reviewed journals, including the *Journal of Chinese Cinemas* and the *Journal of Chinese Film Studies*.

Chenfeng Wang is a PhD candidate in Cultural Studies at the University of California, San Diego, USA. She holds a BA in Chinese Literature from Tsinghua University and an MA in East Asian Languages and Civilizations from the University of Pennsylvania. Her research focuses on film and media in contemporary East Asia, with particular attention to gender, technology, and transcultural practices in the context of globalization and shifting media ecologies. Her work has appeared in leading journals in film and media studies.

Hui Faye Xiao is Professor in the Department of East Asian Languages and Cultures at the University of Kansas, USA. She is the author of *Morning Sun in the Tiny Times: Youth Economy, Crisis, and Reinvention in Twenty-First Century China* (2020) and *Family Revolution: Marital Strife in Contemporary Chinese Literature and Visual Culture* (2014) and co-editor (with Dr. Ping Zhu) of *Feminisms with Chinese Characteristics* (2021). Currently she is working on a third monograph tentatively titled *The Hen Cackles in the Morning: Gendered Soundscape and Female Leadership in Modern Chinese Literature and Cinema.*

Suk Man Yip teaches Hong Kong cinema, Chinese contemporary history, and Cantonese in Sinology at the University of Heidelberg, Germany, where she earned her PhD in 2026. Her research interests include East Asian history, Chinese art and literature, Hong Kong culture, and media studies. Her doctoral research investigates propaganda by the CCP and KMT in the British colony of Hong Kong during the Cold War (1960s). During her studies, she received several paper awards, including the "Best Student Paper Award" at the International Graduate Conference (2022) and the "Excellent Paper Award" at China's Digital Humanities Conference (2022).

Dailin Zhao is a PhD candidate in the Department of Film Studies at King's College London, UK. She holds an MA from the School of Liberal Arts at Renmin University of China. Her primary research project focuses on the intersection of film philosophy, Buddhist philosophy, and the cinema of King Hu. Her research interests include the intermediality of film and other art forms, comparative film theories and philosophies, and Chinese and Sinophone cinema. Zhao's articles have been published in *Minzu yishu yanjiu* [National Art Studies], *Dianying pingjie* [Film Review], and the *Journal of Chinese Film Studies.*

Zhaoyu Zhu is a Teaching Fellow in Communication and Cultural Studies in University of Nottingham Ningbo, China. He received the Katherine Singer Kovacs Essay Award from the Society of Cinema and Media Studies in 2022. His publications can be found in Screen; Journal of Chinese Cinemas; Continuum; Animation: An Interdisciplinary Journal; Asian Cinema; Transnational Screens; Journal of Youth Studies.

Introduction

Zhaoyu Zhu, Weiting Fan, and Xueyan Cheng

Revisiting Ann Hui

Ann Hui On-Wah has been one of the most important figures in the Hong Kong film industry. She started film production in 1979 with the film *The Secret*. Her early films marked the beginning of the Hong Kong New Wave, which was distinct from the genre of gangster and crime films that was popular in Hong Kong. Her work consistently delves into Hong Kong's identity by portraying the lives of migrants and women, while reflecting the historical transition from a British colony to post-handover Hong Kong. In recognition of her four-decade contribution to both Hong Kong and international cinema, she was awarded the Golden Lion for Lifetime Achievement at the 77th Venice International Film Festival in 2020. However, aside from Audrey Yue's monograph *Ann Hui's Song of the Exile*, there are few book-length projects dedicated to studying Hui's cinema within English-language academia.[1] Her prolific career, spanning more than forty years, provides scholars with valuable resources to investigate the historical changes in Hong Kong and Chinese-language film production.

Given her extensive and diverse oeuvre, it is insufficient to approach Hui solely through a single lens that overly emphasizes the filmmaker's association with a distinct style and aesthetic. Hui herself prefers to view her films not as confined to a specific style but rather as adaptable to various styles.[2] On one hand, Ann Hui's contributions to cinema extend beyond the boundaries of the Hong Kong New Wave movement. Prior to her career in film production, Hui had already established herself in television film production. Following her graduation from the London Film School, she joined Television Broadcasts Limited (TVB) as a scriptwriter-director, where she worked for documentaries and short dramas such as *Wonderful* and *C.i.D.* Subsequently, she directed several television dramas for the Independent Commission Against Corruption (ICAC). Among her notable television works is *The Boy from Vietnam* (1978), one of three episodes she directed for Radio Television Hong Kong's documentary series *Below the Lion Rock* (1978). This episode is widely regarded as the inception of her Vietnam trilogy. This early television production laid the foundation for Hui's focus on realism in her narrative feature films and also influenced her subsequent documentary productions, such as *As Time Goes By* (1997) and *Elegies* (2023).

On the other hand, Hui's film production encompasses a diverse array of film genres, extending beyond her realist portrayals of Vietnamese migrants and Hong Kong locals. Her debut film, *The Secret* (1979), is a horror film infused with crime elements, inspired by the actual Double Corpse Murder Case that occurred in 1970s Hong Kong. Subsequently, she ventured into the production of cinematic adaptations of literature, directing works based on the martial-art novels of Louis Cha Leung-yung, including *The Romance of Book and Sword* (1987) and *Princess Fragrance* (1987), as well as adaptations of modern novelist Eileen Chang's fictions, such as *Love in a Fallen City* (1984), *Eighteen Springs* (1997), and *Love After Love* (2020). This attention to literary masters is also reflected in her adaptation of the story of the exiled female writer Xiao Hong during the war in *The Golden Era* (2014).

Until now, scholars have generally recognized two common themes in Ann Hui's films. The first theme is the gender issues and female subjectivity addressed in her films. Although Hui personally usually distances herself from feminist movements, her career represents a successful strategy for female filmmakers to secure a unique position within the Hong Kong mainstream cinema which is predominantly led by male filmmakers.

> Women filmmakers generally lack long-term visibility in the mainstream Hong Kong film industry. Ann Hui however succeeds most persistently in the mainstream playing field, with a clear grasp of box-office expectations and a few runaway hits to her names. More importantly, she also maintains critical anticipation and creative visibility among her New Wave contemporaries and resists being limited by set themes or genres expected of a women filmmaker.[3]

Even though Hui often adopts a compromise in her films to meet the commercial needs of the film market, she still preserves a female perspective to explore local Hong Kong life in her works. Elaine Ho analyzes the transformation of female representation from her early films to the films produced in the 1990s and understands "a perceptible shift in her stance on women as agents of change."[4] In early productions like *The Secret* and *Princess Fragrance*, the female characters struggle in bearing the ethical ideals within the Chinese patriarchal familyhood and even become the defeated victims. However, turning to the 1990s, films like *Song of the Exile* (1990) and *Summer Snow* (1995) show the women's self-determination and self-transformation to "enable the reparation of disrupted kinship and social bonds."[5] When analyzing *Summer Snow*, Erens comments on the film as "an homage to the strength of Chinese women, especially those past middle age."[6] Hong Zeng examines the translocal female subjectivity in the film *The Golden Era*. She understands that Ann Hui's construction of the bodily experiences and personal feelings of Xiao Hong reinforces the theme of feminist writing that "the private is political."[7]

Another prominent theme is migration and displacement. Hui, originally from Anshan in Northeast China, relocated to Macau during her childhood. Subsequently, she and her family moved to Hong Kong where she received her education until she completed her postgraduate studies in comparative literature at the University of Hong Kong. Her familial background is characterized by multiple diasporic elements: she is part of the mainland Chinese diasporic community in Hong Kong, while her mother is of Japanese descent and was raised in Manchuria. Her own and her family's intricate diasporic experience is inscribed in the themes of her films. As Audrey Yue argues, "diaspora are signature sites in the films of Ann Hui."[8] Since the Vietnam trilogy, her films not only feature the migration between different places but also represent varieties of conditions of the people in migration. This is particularly reflected in the film *Song of the Exile*, where "the multiple journeys of migration are central."[9] The film reenacts Hui's real migration experience into the main character Hueyin's journey between Britain, Hong Kong, Macau, and mainland China. The film captures Hueyin's travel with her Japanese mother, Aiko, who worked in Manchuria during the war and resettled in Hong Kong, as they return to Aiko's hometown in Japan. The film examines the hybrid identities of its characters, which are influenced by their ongoing experiences of border crossing. It critically analyzes and questions the concepts of homeliness and belonging, which are often linked to a stable hometown and native language.

Following the existing discussions on Ann Hui's cinema, this edited collection aims to be a comprehensive anthology, gathering cutting-edge academic writings on Hui's oeuvre. While this book focuses on a film auteur, the edited collection does not intend to establish a closed loop between a filmmaker and a fixed system of aesthetic style and representation. Instead, it explores Ann Hui's cinema as an open-ended, multifaceted entity to enhance our understanding of the evolution of Hong Kong and Chinese-language cinema, the representation of women in film, and the reshaping of Hong Kong's identity through the works of a globally recognized filmmaker.

At the same time, Hui's open-ended work and her unique position within Hong Kong, Chinese, and international film cultures also lead us to revisit the concept of auteur. If traditional auteurism risks reducing a filmmaker to a fixed style, a reconceptualized approach to auteurship may instead highlight the multiple, intersecting historical, cultural, and industrial contexts that shape Hui's practice. The following section focuses on the theoretical conundrum of auteurship, examining how Ann Hui can be studied as an auteur without foreclosing the openness and diversity of her cinema.

Auteur: A rhizomatic reconceptualization

To organize an anthology of research that focuses on the study of Ann Hui's cinema, it is inevitably necessary to address the theoretical conundrum of auteurship. What does it mean to consider Ann Hui as an auteur? Why is it still necessary for us to treat Ann Hui as an auteur? Though Dudley Andrew has reassured us that "[a]fter a dozen years of clandestine whispering, we are permitted to mention, even to discuss, the auteur again," we still cannot take the concept of auteur for granted.[10] David Gerstner and Janet Staiger have offered us solid reasons for the discussion of authorship to be still relevant and even indispensable in the academic realm of film studies. For Gerstner and Staiger, while Roland Barthes' declaration of the author's death is merely a rhetorical "attempt to make a place for the reader," to persist with the name of the author is to hold on to a "pragmatic" and "enabling tool" that can still function for "social actions" and "agency for minority production."[11]

For this anthology, it is precisely because Ann Hui's filmography can serve as the textual locus for our encounter and engagement with the historical and sociopolitical reality of minority groups, such as women and immigrants living in the postcolonial Hong Kong, that Ann Hui should be studied as an auteur. Hui is the only female Hong Kong director whose filmmaking career runs through the contemporary history of Hong Kong cinema, from the Hong Kong New Wave to the post-handover, mainland–Hong Kong joint-production era, with her films constantly keeping a keen eye on marginalized communities and neglected histories. As noted by Song Hwee Lim in 2007, rather surprisingly, unlike the much more mature scholarship concerning Japanese auteurs, the majority of book-length publications on Chinese cinema tend to bypass auteur-based research, with "very few English language book-length publications on auteurs from Chinese cinema."[12] Lim hence suggests that the time has come "for scholars researching on Chinese cinemas to focus more attention on acclaimed directors and embark on auteur studies on a larger scale."[13] However, with nearly two decades having passed since Lim's proposition, there is still hardly any book-length publication dedicated solely to the study of Ann Hui as an auteur. Our anthology aims to fill this lacuna, together with the intent to refresh the paradigm of auteur studies in Chinese cinema.

As Lim has warned us, our revisiting of auteur theory should never "take the auteur as a self-evidential, unproblematic category of analysis."[14] Rather, in response to Barthes' replacement of the dead author with the birth of the reader, Lim has proposed a redefinition of auteurs as readers themselves, particularly in the sense that auteurs can be studied as cinephiles who passionately engage with other auteurs' work intertextually through their creative work.[15] To a certain extent, we can also reconsider Ann Hui's auteurist signature as resulting from her being a passionate reader of history in general instead of film history itself. In other words, to study Ann Hui as an auteur never means to treat her as the god-like figure who leaves individualistic fingerprints all over her works, nor to read her oeuvre as a flawlessly coherent entity differentiated and isolated from other auteurs' artistry. Intertextuality emerges from Hui's work not as a cinephilic attachment to previous auteurs but as the respectful sharing of the same sociohistorical context with others.

Therefore, by considering Ann Hui as an auteur, this anthology suggests a rhizomatic reconceptualization of auteurship. In *A Thousand Plateaus*, Gilles Deleuze and Félix Guattari offer us an alternative paradigm to understand the author by differentiating three types of writing: roots, radicles, and rhizomes. For Deleuze and Guattari, the first type of writing symbolized by the image of the roots is dictated by binary logic and operates in the subject/object dichotomy.[16] It can hence be paralleled with the classical or structuralist understanding of the dichotomous relationship between the author and their works: either the dominance of the author over their works or their replacement—the death of the author and the birth of the text. Nevertheless, as suggested by Deleuze and Guattari, what this binary thinking truly assumes is still a "signifying totality," "a strong principal unity" that rejects real multiplicity.[17] In other words, as it secretly reaffirms a unified textual meaning, this dichotomous understanding of the author–text relationship can never really lead to the death of the author's totalizing authority and the text's proliferation.

The second type of writing is described by Deleuze and Guattari as the radicle system, featuring mostly "an immediate, indefinite multiplicity" that is meant to destroy and abort the signifying totality of a text yet unfortunately is incapable of doing so. As argued by Deleuze and Guattari,

> [T]he folding of one text onto another, which constitutes multiple and even adventitious roots (like a cutting), implies a supplementary dimension to that of the texts under consideration. In this supplementary dimension of folding, unity continues its spiritual labour. That is why the most resolutely fragmented work can also be presented as the Total Work or Magnum Opus.[18]

Deleuze and Guattari use modernist authors, such as James Joyce, to illustrate this type of writing. For them, the stream of consciousness's intentional shattering of the "linear unity of the word" is merely a form of "typographical, lexical, or even syntactical cleverness," while it creates a text "all the more total for being fragmented."[19] Therefore, the totalizing limitation of authorship still cannot be resolved in this radicle system that suggests textual fragmentation.

The true answer lies in the third type of writing proposed by Deleuze and Guattari: a rhizomatic system that breaks from both structured binary thinking and chaotic fragmentation. As Deleuze and Guattari put it: "[a] rhizome ceaselessly establishes connections between semiotic chains, organizations of power, and circumstances relative to the arts, sciences, and social struggles."[20] That is, the rhizomatic thinking values the interconnectedness between entities, even though certain entities, like the author, used to be considered a totalizing authority, or in Deleuze and Guattari's words, as the source of stratification and territorialization. As specifically clarified by Deleuze and Guattari, "every rhizome contains lines of segmentarity according to which it is stratified, territorialized, organized, signified, attributed, etc., as well as lines of deterritorialization down which it constantly flees."[21] This is because, for them, "movements of deterritorialization and processes of re-territorialization" must be constantly "relative, always connected, caught up in one another."[22] Deleuze and Guattari even warn us that we need to maintain a "meticulous relation" with any totalizing authority (such as the idea of authorship) instead of wildly destroying and collapsing them, as this behavior will mostly "bring them back down on us heavier than ever."[23]

Therefore, this anthology insists on not simply forsaking Ann Hui's auteurship but suggesting a rhizomatic reconceptualization of Ann Hui as an auteur, one that reilluminates the interconnectedness between Hui as a filmmaker herself and her cinematic works, as well as among the diverse filmic texts she has made across her long and fruitful career. The anthology indeed follows certain "lines of segmentarity," being organized into four thematic parts: literary adaptation, storytelling, representations of Hong Kong females, and displacement and homeland. At the same time, each chapter also addresses multiple issues that cross the boundaries of the set framework. For instance, while some chapters focus on Hui's storytelling techniques, they also engage with her interest in literary adaptation. Some chapters foreground her representation of Hong Kong women yet situate these depictions within aesthetic, sociocultural, and transnational contexts. Some chapters are dedicated to the study of her signature portrayal of the diasporic experience but also engage deeply with the intersectionality of gender, class, and ethnography.

In this light, the anthology contributes to the study of Ann Hui as an artistically accomplished filmmaker and a gateway to further understanding the cinematic representation of Chinese femininity and postcolonial Hong Kong. Her films are considered not only aesthetically and philosophically intriguing artworks but also cultural productions that contribute to the making and altering of social discourses. In this manner, this edited collection does not intend to complete a coherent and close-ended narrative of Ann Hui's entire oeuvre and then triumph over the individualism of traditional auteur theory. It reconsiders the issue of auteurship not simply as an expression of personal voice but as a critical tool that can be juxtaposed with other frameworks, such as national and transnational cinema, to open up further innovative approaches to cinematic research.

Outline of the book

Following a rhizomatic approach, the editing of this book began with a global call for papers, inviting scholars to produce works under the theme *The Cinema of Ann Hui*. The editors did not want to impose restrictions on the contributors during the editing process; instead, this book intends to offer a broad scope and a profound vision through the contributors' independent and free reflections on Ann Hui's filmography. The book maintains a keen focus on the four most crucial topics based on the twelve essays collected. However, during the editing process, it is impossible to ignore the probable overlap and intersections among these four themes. The edited collection acknowledges these intersections but, at the same time, tries to accommodate diverse and innovative research approaches to Ann Hui's filmography in the structured form of a book. This book also covers a wide range of Ann Hui's repertoire in her career, from Hui's early televisual works to her most recent feature narrative film *Love After Love* (2020).

Part One, titled "Literary adaptations: Aesthetics and historical context," comprises three chapters that explore how Ann Hui adapts the texts and spirits of the literary classics to her cinematic works. Chapter 1 by Hui Faye Xiao examines how Ann Hui adapts the *wuxia* (martial arts/chivalric) spirit to the historical realist cinema in the form of *wen xi wu pai*, which means taking a martial-spirited approach to shooting a non-martial-arts film. The chapter attempts to explore how Ann Hui incorporates the martial arts spirit from Chinese literature into the female figures of her historical realist films, showcasing how they survive and resist in the manner of martial arts amid the changes of the times. Xiao's chapter presents an adaptation that transcends certain texts. It uncovers the Chinese literary traditions and cultural context supporting Ann Hui's works and fully demonstrates that the martial spirit still holds enduring social significance in delivering the gendered voices of the marginalized women in their social reality and articulating a resistant, progressive stance against the masculinist world order.

Chapter 2 by Dailin Zhao analyzes Ann Hui's inspiration from classical paintings in her adaptation of Eileen Chang's novella *Love in a Fallen City* (1984). Through comparing the composition in films and traditional paintings, Zhao argues that the traditional painting of women, narrative scrolls, and images of ruins largely affect how Ann Hui designed the relationship between characters and space. She argues that this stylistic borrowing from traditional paintings mirrors the spiritual temperament of Chang's novella.

In Chapter 3, Gabriel F. Y. Tsang displaced Ann Hui's adaptations of Eileen Chang's novellas within the sociopolitical context of Hong Kong during their respective releases. Tsang elucidates the ways in which Hui has both visually and textually reconstructed the fictional landscapes of the 1930s and 1940s. He argues that Hui's adaptations of Cheung's works resonate with notions of identity, belonging, and cultural commentary. Hui's trajectory of adaptations also reflects an evolving cultural landscape where Hong Kong cinema increasingly seeks to define itself amid the broader context of mainland influences.

Part Two, titled "Storytelling: Media forms and social change," follows Part One in understanding Ann Hui's narrative strategies. However, this section envisions Ann Hui as an innovative storyteller challenging the generic form of film narration and forming a powerful social intervention in the social reality. This section starts with Raymond Tsang's contextual reading of Hui's early televisual production *The Boy from Vietnam* (1978). Tsang's chapter delves into the shift toward realism within the context of the Hong Kong television wars in the late 1970s. Instead of romanticizing the struggles of oppressed individuals or championing revolutionary ideals, Hui shines a light on the mundane settings and tangible realities that shape fragmented histories and cross-border experiences in the late Cold War. Through a close reading of the theoretical and historical context of Hong Kong television production, Tsang argues that Hui's contribution is not merely a humanistic depiction of Vietnamese refugees in Hong Kong; rather, she seeks to reclaim the essence of humanism itself in a postrevolutionary world where notions of absolute subjectivity and grand narratives are increasingly put to the test.

Following on from Chapter 4, Gary Bettinson's chapter explores the stylistic minimalism in Hui's cinematic narratives, using *The Way We Are* (2008) as a specific case study. He finds that although Ann Hui tries to minimize the story's dramatic sense with scattered plots, Hui keeps the viewers hooked as this film strongly engages with spectators' cognitions of the real world and people's understanding of the genre conventions in both Cantonese *wenyi pian* (letters-and-arts film) and Hollywood melodrama. Through this narrative analysis, Bettinson argues that Hui's storytelling indicates that local filmmakers did not capitulate to globalizing pressures from mainland China and Hollywood in the post-handover era characterized by cultural disappearance.

Han Li's chapter frames the everyday representation of ordinary women in Hui's *Our Time Will Come* (2017) within the broader context of mainland–Hong Kong geopolitics. This film suggests that narratives of women can serve as an alternative trope for nationalist resistance stories. However, Han also argues that the alteration of narrative focus and the use of anticlimactic storytelling in this film intentionally diverge from the generic conventions of the neo-main melody films, which often glorify revolutionary heroism and grand narratives, in contemporary Hong Kong films. The pseudo-documentary style appears to evoke a sense of historicity, drawing attention to the "constructed" nature of historiography through its conspicuous theatricality.

Continuing on from the discussion by Han Li, Part Three, titled "Visualizing Hong Kong females," casts light on how Ann Hui's filmography reflects the female subjectivity of Hong Kong local females as sociocultural and historical constructions channeled through her creative agency as a female auteur. Yiran Ai focuses on the identity of a Hong Kong middle-aged woman in the film *The Summer Snow*. She employs the concept of "in-betweenness" as a critical framework and finds the female protagonist May's struggle highlights the complexities of patriarchal culture, personal autonomy, and the broader sociopolitical environment of postcolonial Hong Kong.

Weiting Fan focuses on the representation of female bodies in Ann Hui's Tin Shui Wai diptych, including *The Way We Are* and *Night and Fog* (2009). Through a close analysis of these two films, this chapter seeks to integrate the Daoist concept of qi with two poetic notions from Chinese culture—*shuqing* (lyricism) and *youyu* (melancholy) to explore a gaseous embodiment that is emancipated from the concrete form of the female body. With a philosophical inquiry, the exuberant and elusive cultural experience of Hong Kong females dissipates the concrete form of the body itself as a political and ethical effort to de-classify and de-essentialize the female body.

Jessica Ka Yee Chan's chapter examines the character of Amah, a Cantonese migrant domestic servant, in *A Simple Life* (2011) to discuss challenges of the medical welfare system and nursery system in Hong Kong after the handover. Chan argues that this film presents various conceptualizations of home, family, and community as interrelated domains of care, illustrating the simultaneous articulation of postcolonial, national, and transnational notions of home and belonging within the framework of the Closer Economic Partnership Arrangement (CEPA) between mainland China and Hong Kong.

Finally, Part Four, "Displacement and homeland," addresses the recurring theme of people's displacement from their homeland in Hui's cinema. This feeling of displacement is not necessarily limited to physical migration but encompasses all forms of struggle and confusion related to identity within colonial and/or postcolonial contexts. Siao-Yun Chen's chapter interrogates the mediating position of Hong Kong in Hui's Vietnam trilogy—*The Boy from Vietnam* (1978), *The Story of Woo Viet* (1981), and *Boat People* (1982). This chapter innovatively employs the theoretical framework of new materialism. Chen posits that objects and props play an active role in reflecting on Hong Kong's role within the Chinese diaspora and its significance in shaping the imagination of Hong Kong identity.

Suk Man Yip's chapter critically examines the concept of homeland by drawing parallels between *Song of the Exile* (1990) and *My American Grandson* (1991). Yip examines how Ann Hui represents the contemporary Chinese diaspora, while also exploring the implications of the concept of homeland and the intergenerational connections that arise within this context. The last chapter by Chenfeng Wang presents a reinterpretation of *The Golden Era* (2014) as a deliberate reflection on the modern Chinese female writer Xiao Hong's life in exile. This is achieved by comparing Xiao's experience of displacement, as depicted in the film, with Hui's own diasporic experience as a Hong Kong filmmaker. Through the film's nonlinear, multi-perspective narratives, Hui uses the alienation effect to call attention to the constructedness of the biopic form.

She explores the life and work of Xiao Hong in a way that highlights the temporal and spatial instability and the importance of individual freedom.

This edited collection aspires to enhance the scholarship on Ann Hui, while simultaneously providing a pathway to a deeper comprehension of the sociocultural implications of her cinema. In this context, her films are regarded not only as aesthetically and philosophically compelling works of art but also as cultural productions that play a role in shaping and transforming social discourses. Consequently, this edited volume does not seek to present a cohesive and definitive narrative of Ann Hui's complete body of work to celebrate the individualism associated with traditional auteur theory. Instead of elevating the expression of a singular personal voice, the concept of the auteur is reconceptualized as an open-ended discourse that can incorporate alternative frameworks, including national and transnational cinema, feminist filmmaking, and postcolonial cultural studies.

Part One

Literary adaptations: Aesthetics and historical context

1

A lonely woman warrior

Sounding the book and sword in Ann Hui's historical cinema

Hui Faye Xiao

From the very beginning of her filmmaking career, Ann Hui has cultivated a close affinity with martial arts (*wuxia*) cinema, one of the most visible genres in the Hong Kong film industry. Meanwhile, Hui has long been acclaimed as a prominent New Wave director with strong humanist concerns for diasporic groups and lower-class struggles in local Hong Kong communities. While the gaps between fantasy and reality and between genre film and realist cinema seem vast on the surface, a closer look at Hui's works reveals that the central allegory of the book and sword threads through her entire oeuvre, serving as the bridge connecting her fascination with the martial arts world and her realist inclination and deep concern for the grassroots communities of Hong Kong.

Ain Ling Wong once characterized such a dialectic relationship between the dual tracks of Hui's cinema as *wu xi wen pai*, i.e., taking a *wen* (civil, cultured, literary, humanist) approach to shooting a martial arts film.[1] Building on Wong's insight, I propose that a parallel stylistic trademark is *wen xi wu pai*, i.e., taking a *wu* (militant, martial-spirited) approach to shooting a non-martial arts film. This *wu* approach exhibits itself less through flaunting the visual spectacles of muscles and violence than her persistent cinematic exploration of a haunting motif of the book and sword that can be found in Hui's works in a wide array of genres including crime thrillers, historical dramas, biopics, war epics, and political cinema. As perennial tropes in Hui's repertoire, the book is presented as the cinematic remediation of Chinese literary traditions, while the sword goes beyond the confines of the martial arts genre to signify a highly fluid fighting spirit, rebellious impulse, adventurous transgression, and social intervention at the core of political activism and individual resistance against different forms of oppressions and injustices. Moreover, rather than standing in opposition to each other, the book and the sword are interdependent and mutually complementary. While the book provides aesthetic and ethical grounds for the sword, the fighting spirit of the sword materializes through applying the book's knowledge to social engagement and intervention.

This chapter starts with an overview of the tradition in martial arts fiction and its profound influence on Hui. It then turns to study her *Ordinary Heroes* (1999) and *Our Time Will Come* (2017). Neither of the films can be comfortably squeezed into the box of martial arts films. However, a closer reading of both films reveals Hui's innovative *wen xi wu pai* strategy as her unique way of engaging with and problematizing the long tradition of book and sword. In analyzing these two films, I focus on examining the ways in which Hui's cinema documents the gendered voices of women warriors and activists in sounding out a resistant female genealogy, which contests the masculinist book and sword tradition that has been dominated by patrilineal narratives revolving around sworn brotherhood, male fellowship, father–son and master–apprentice descensions and transmissions.

Despite the expanding body of critical works on Hui's works in the past few decades, one aspect of Hui's cinema that has remained understudied is the gendered soundscape in her films.[2] Her fascination with the acoustic elements of the cinema stems from her training in and passion for literature that is centered upon the written (words) and verbal (sounds) transmissions of the linguistic signs. Scenes of characters reciting poems and literary works appear in nearly all her cinematic works, sounding out her cherished literary memories through the remediation of the film, which culminates in her most recent documentary *Elegies* (2023). In addition to conveying audible literary aesthetics, women's sound-making practices in Hui's cinema also transmit resistant energies that transgress and unsettle the boundaries of everyday order. More specifically, Hui's particular emphasis on the voices and sounds of women's everyday conversations and their constant interactions with other acoustic elements in a mundane environment full of rich life details and sound events diverts audiences' attention from the visual spectacles of masculinist violence and physicality. Rather than simply expanding the book and sword tradition to allow women to barge in as ersatz warriors, the fluid soundscape not only counters the hegemony of the male gaze by reasserting the importance of the often-overlooked gendered acoustic elements in the cinematic medium but also breaks down the epic and the mundane binary structure by revealing the epistemological elision of the political significance of women's everyday pursuits and sound events that are shaped by and shaping the communal lifeworld, affective networks, and local history.

The masculinist tradition of the book and sword

In his book *The Development of Chinese Martial Arts Fiction* (*Qiangu wenren xiake meng*), Chen Pingyuan explores martial arts fiction's cultural and social significance at different historical junctures. Rather than dismissing it as a fast-food cultural product to entertain poorly educated city folks, he argues that martial arts fiction is a literary projection of Chinese literati's ideals of battling oppression and injustice in the wake of social upheaval and political turmoil. Such a sublimated fighting spirit is embodied by the imagery of the sword that abounds not only in martial arts fiction but also in classical poems and essays for its ethical and aesthetic connotations. In comparison to other traditional combat weapons, swords in martial arts fiction and film are styled as the essential, and sometimes exclusive, means of achieving the ultimate goal of social justice. According to "The Forging of Swords" (*Jian zhi ming*) in *Rites of the Elder Dai* (*Dadaili*), "Wear it [the sword] like clothing, when you act, you must do so morally, acting with morals rings victory, violating morals brings destruction."[3] Chen pinpoints this passage as "the origin of the belief that, in *wuxia* novels, swords must be returned to the compassionate, the moral and the righteous."[4] As Chen contends, "the 'sword' is not simply a tool to kill people; it is an emblem of the spirit of the *xiake*, a symbol of strength of character and even of cultural traditions. In this context, the 'sword' cannot be without the 'book.'"[5]

Endowed with such a significant moral and affective power, the sword is often paired with the book to convey traditional Chinese male literati's yearnings for a flawless mastery of both *wen* (civility) and *wu* (martial arts) masculine skills to achieve their high ideals of fixing social ills, battling injustices, and restoring proper order to a chaotic world. Therefore, the moralized chivalric figure of a roving warrior should equip himself with both sword and book to be the perfect persona exemplifying male literati's romantic imagination of the model gentleman who embraces the heroic martial spirit and sublime masculine virtues simultaneously to fulfill his core missions of self-cultivation and social intervention. This book–sword dyad of masculinity was embraced by nationalistic male elites at the turn of the twentieth century as the ideal model for strengthening Chinese citizens who could, in turn, save the crumbling homeland plagued by imperialist invasions, economic crisis, and sociopolitical turmoil.[6] During his teenage years, Lu Xun adopted pennames such as Swordsman (*jia jian sheng*) and Scholar Warrior (*rong ma shu sheng*) to show his admiration for the chivalric and militant spirit of the knight errant.[7] As Lu Xun's pennames indicated, the scholar-warrior persona became "a masculine ideal with mastery of both words (writing) and swords (violence)."[8] While resorting to military prowess to upend the old imperial order, revolutionaries also picked up their pens to promote their political agendas and celebrate the sworn brotherhood and pledged loyalty among nationalistic comrades who cultivated heroic qualities and masculine virtues to fulfill their commitment to the national cause.[9] In reform-minded intellectuals' plans of national rejuvenation, as Jun Lei has pointed out, "[t]he specific references ... to the key roles of sons and husbands and to the literati tradition indicate a strong association between masculinity, patrilineality, and national identity."[10]

A similar trend of inscribing "the assertion of nationalism" on the heroic body of the Chinese swordman can be found in postwar Hong Kong's martial arts fiction and film.[11] As a staple constituent in martial arts cinema, particularly its swordplay subgenre, the book and sword tradition has often been rendered as "a mere vehicle for cultural nationalism."[12] Connecting such a masculinized nationalist discourse with the fable of the book and sword, Jin Yong, one of the most widely read Hong Kong-based *wuxia* writers in the Chinese-speaking world, named his very first martial arts novel *The Romance of Book and Sword* (1955–6). Having received funding from the Sil-Metropole Organization (*Yindu jigou*), Hui adapted Jin's martial arts epic into a two-part film *The Romance of Book and Sword* and *Princess Fragrance*, both of which were released in 1987.

Hui has been a zealous fan of martial arts fiction from a young age. Jin Yong has long been one of her favorite writers, whose literary rendition of the romanticized tradition of the book and sword has exerted its profound influence on her cinema. In the documentary *As Time Goes By* (*Qu ri ku duo*, 1997), Hui reveals her inferiority complex as a Chinese in the British colony and her aspirations for materializing the Chinese moral ideals through drawing from the fantastic power of martial arts (*wuxia*) fiction. In addition to her longtime fascination with the popular literary genre, Hui started her career working for King Hu, whose martial arts classics have been appreciated for their masterful fusion of the rich elements of *wen* and *wu*, book and sword, in traditional Chinese culture. Although she has never been commercially successful with her endeavors on this front, Hui stands out as one of the few women filmmakers, most likely the only woman filmmaker, who has ever directed martial arts films. Later on, when the male-dominated Hong Kong *kung fu* cinema turned to the "macho Chinese nationalism," with its emphasis on visual spectacles of masculine violence and physicality,[13] Hui took a different approach to reinventing the spirit of the book and sword in her realist-spirited early works through resorting to her dual strategies of *wu xi wen pai* and *wen xi wu pai*.

While working at Radio Television Hong Kong in the 1970s, she produced *Boy from Vietnam*, an episode in the TV series *Below the Lion Rock*, to shed light on the struggles of Vietnamese refugees in Hong Kong. Her later films *The Story of Woo Viet* (1981) and *Boat People* (1982) continued with her persistent concerns for the "boat people," or the Vietnamese diasporic communities at the center of *Boy from Vietnam*. In both films, the male protagonists are portrayed as chivalric (*xia*) figures who make selfless sacrifices to help those in need. In addition to their heroic deeds, these diasporic men are also endowed with scholarly qualities. For example, the title character in *The Story of Woo Viet* appears to be valorized as a modern *xia* figure with his combat skills and adamant determination to protect the less fortunate ones. The fact that the episodic film narrative unfolding in different times and locations is pieced together through a series of letters that Woo Viet has written to Leee Lap-quan, a Hong Kong social worker who provides aid for Vietnamese refugees, adds the *wen* qualities to the warrior persona. "Our generation of Chinese is destined to an eternal fate of exile," a melancholy line in one of Woo's letters makes him a self-reflexive intellectual figure who observes, experiences, and documents the shared pains and collective struggles of diasporic communities.

Demarginalizing women in the book and sword continuum

This earlier trend of masculinizing the book and sword spirit took a different turn in Hui's later works. Commenting on Hui's film *Ah Kam* (1996), Gina Marchetti argues that this film portrays a stuntwoman's (Michelle Yeoh) everyday struggles on the production site of martial arts films to reveal the mounting challenges facing women filmmakers in the Hong Kong film industry that has been dominated by male filmmakers who still embrace the traditional patrilineal apprentice system.[14] Enoch Tam Yee Lok also contends that Ah Kam can be seen as the cinematic avatar of Hui, a lonely woman warrior (*duxingxia*) struggling to leave her mark on Hong Kong cinema.[15]

Although *Ah Kam* was received poorly by audiences and film critics, Hui continued her cinematic exploration of women's fighting spirit and directed *Ordinary Heroes* (1999), which further problematized the masculinist tradition of the book and sword. Set in 1970s and 1980s Hong Kong and based on real-life social activists' life stories, this ambitious work interweaves two threads of episodic narratives to create a rich mosaic about a piece of forgotten local history. The main plotline revolves around the loss and recovery of a young social worker Sow Fung-tai's (Loletta Lee) memory. A secondary thread is a loose assemblage of fragmented installments taken from a multi-act street performance by Augustine Chiu-yu Mok (Mo Zhaoru), a dramatist who "seeks to excavate the history of the activist Wu Zhongxian."[16] Wu (Ng Chung-yin, 1946–94) is a real-life historical figure who started his eventful political career in Hong Kong's student-led social movements and youthful counterculture in the 1960s and 1970s.[17] In the 1980s, after being arrested briefly by the Chinese government and accused of treachery by his comrades in Hong Kong, he turned to commercial media and helped found the Chinese version of *Playboy*.[18]

Such a complicated film bordering on historicity and fictionality is represented in a vibrant visual language: on the one hand, the use of handheld cameras and the frequent insertions of newspaper reportage, black-and-white historical photos, and archival footage reenact the unsettling time period in the style of cinéma-vérité; on the other hand, this semi-documentary style, heavily influenced by Hui's earlier televisual work experience, is often disrupted by a slew of dramatized scenes of intense emotional and social conflicts that remind film audiences of the fictionality of the melodramatic narrative focused on diasporic subjects' interpersonal relationships and everyday struggles. Going along with the highly experimental visual style, the film's soundtrack is equally complex and dynamic, weaving together multiple layers of voices and sound practices. A central thread of the polyphonic soundscape is the earth-shattering sound wave of revolutionary slogans and speeches shouted out aloud by leftist social activists under the leadership of Yau Ming-foon (Tse Kwan-ho), a main character whose creation is obviously inspired by Ng Chung-yin's political career.

Starting from his college days, Yau has worked as a leading figure in a radical leftist group that consists of left-leaning college students, social workers, and Father Kam (Anthony Wong), who is based on a real-life figure, Reverend Franco Mella, an Italian Catholic priest who is also an adamant Maoist social activist. The first time Yau appears in the film is when multiple boats at the Yau Mai Tei dock are burned in a fire that causes heavy casualties among the boat people community. Holding up a loudspeaker, Yau gives a powerful political speech to mobilize boat people for a protest movement: "We shouldn't be afraid of officials who have two mouths (*guan zi liang ge kou*). We should speak up to make legitimate requests and have our voices heard." The proverb *guan zi liang ge kou* means that the Chinese character *guan* (official) has two mouth radicals, an etymological reference to bureaucrats' exclusive possession of political power as well as enunciative power with their control of administrative institutions, signifying systems, and communication venues. Challenging the colonial authorities' monopoly of political and enunciative power, Yau urges boat people to assert their rights to speech and to self-advocating for their legal rights. Then he leads the group to shout out aloud their collective petitioning to the

British government: "Let boat people live on land! Equal rights for boat people and land residents (*Shui lu pingdeng*)!" Their angry voices amplified through the loudspeakers disturb the calm surface of the water with radical political messages that clash with the mundane sounds of Buddhist monks' mantra reciting, traditional instruments playing, and boat people's crying at funerals held simultaneously in the backdrop. While the explosive fury and massive agitation indicate a rising fighting spirit against social inequalities, the sorrowful sounds of traditional funeral rituals and people's mourning infuse a profound sense of loss and melancholy that envelops the entire film.

After the protest, Yau came to visit boat people living in Yau Ma Tei and talked to Sow Fung-tai who was a teenage girl. When Sow asked why he would help them, Yau told her: "Ignorance is a sin, but it's even more sinful to keep silent after you've acquired the knowledge!" This grave statement indicates Yau's self-reflection upon his own elite intellectual positionality and underscores the central significance of speaking in revealing the truth about the world and effecting social changes. It speaks to Yau's firm belief in the power of words and intellectuals' sublime moral mission in aligning the book with the sword, or in applying book knowledge to social engagement and intervention. Not unlike the highly moralized symbol of the sword, knowledge becomes a powerful weapon of resisting and mobilizing that brings together people of different backgrounds to take up organized social action in upending the old order and ushering in a new world. Yau's statement on speaking up about diasporic and disadvantaged communities' unspoken struggles could also be heard as Hui's meta-cinematic comment on the functionality of the cinematic medium as a practical tool for political engagement and social changes.

However, rather than repeating the earlier narratives of chivalric heroes saving helpless women in *The Romance of Book and Sword*, *The Story of Woo Viet*, and *Boat People*, the film chooses to focus on the ways in which grassroots women's voices and affective labor empower marginalized groups and grapple with social injustice like a sword. In comparison to Yau's elite position, the female protagonist Sow is born and raised in an impoverished working-class family residing within the boat people (*Danjia* or *Tanka*) community that has long been banished to the margins of mainstream society. Reminiscing about her childhood, Sow recalls that she often falls asleep when helping her mom to make plastic flowers. In postwar Hong Kong, the labor-intensive industry of manufacturing plastic flowers and other products for export had played a key role in developing the local economy and providing an essential means for working-class families to make a living. The escalating capital–labor conflicts in one of the biggest plastic flower factories was the direct trigger of the 1967 riots.[19] Although the terror of the riots is not directly visualized in the film, the transnational capital's relentless exploitation of gendered labor is laid bare through Sow's bitter words recounting the fading memories of her past. Having witnessed and lived through the structural inequalities in postwar Hong Kong, Sow joins the group of social workers under Yau's leadership to help the socially disadvantaged groups gain their rights and have their voices heard.

Social workers have remained a staple persona in Hui's cinema since the very beginning of her career. In her early TVB years, Hui produced documentaries about younger generations' political protest and social activism, including two episodes of *Social Worker*: "Boy" (1976) and "Ah Sze" (1976). Social workers also occupy the center stage of her early films, including *The Story of Woo Viet* and *Starry Is the Night* (1988). Moreover, these social workers appearing in Hui's cinema are often gendered female. This cinematic documentation of the significant social agency of women who are tasked with crafting and articulating strategies in curing social ills, organizing events, and initiating changes is also prominent in *Ordinary Heroes* through the audiovisual representation of Sow's gendered labor and sound-making practices.

Different from those well-educated social workers who enjoy a middle-class lifestyle in *The Story of Woo Viet* and *Starry Is the Night*, Sow's working-class background and Tanka identity position her at the margin of the margins of the mainstream. This doubly marginalized positionality makes Sow more vulnerable in comparison to her male or middle-class peers. However, precisely due to her physical and emotional proximity to other disadvantaged women in the grassroots community, Sow has developed more creative tactics out of her local knowledge and cultural empathy to establish better bonding with those in need of social services.

Following the action of supporting boat people's fight for their rights to residence on land, Yau launches a new campaign to help their wives, many of whom are from mainland China, stay in Hong Kong legally. These mainlander wives are labeled *wu zheng mama* (literally, undocumented moms or moms with no papers), a term revealing that the proper boundaries of the domestic site are so closely monitored and controlled that government-issued papers are required for one to play the role of mother legitimately. Joining Yau and other cohorts, Sow participates in street demonstrations, sings revolutionary songs, writes slogans for rallies, and helps organize rallies and press conferences. On top of all these organizational activities, she is shown as the only social worker among the male-dominated group who has ever engaged in frequent daily interactions

Figure 1.1 Sow helps an "undocumented mom" make plastic flowers on the boat. *Ordinary Heroes* (1999), directed by Ann Hui.

with these "undocumented moms" and their young children. When helping one "undocumented mom" make plastic flowers, a labor practice resonating with her childhood memories as reminisced in Sow's voiceover, she hears that the mainlander woman has never set foot on the land of Hong Kong for fear of being arrested and deported. Sow volunteers to take her and her young child to venture into the city to eat at a McDonald's (see Figure 1.1).

Eating in a fast-food chain restaurant seems a trivial and mundane everyday activity. Yet it remains a privilege out of reach for the diasporic group from the mainland due to their unrecognized immigrant status. The shaky handheld camera used in shooting this sequence further externalizes the mainlander's anxiety and fear over her uncertain existence in the colonial urban space (see Figure 1.2). At the sight of a patrolling police officer, the frightened "undocumented mother" immediately turns around, attempting to go back to her home on the boat. Sow keeps encouraging her to continue with their small adventure: "Don't be afraid. Just act like normal. He wouldn't notice us." Having experienced the pain of being exiled from the urban space as a member of the underprivileged "boat people" herself, Sow uses her words to turn the policed street into a space of marginalized women's mutual empathizing and collective exploration for tactics in finding their positionality in the colonial city. With her calm demeanor and skillful guidance, the small group navigates the labyrinthine city and finally reach their destination to enjoy a happy meal at McDonald's. Accompanied by the traffic noise of the

Figure 1.2 Exiled women's public appearance when navigating the colonial urban space. *Ordinary Heroes* (1999), directed by Ann Hui.

busy city, a lingering medium shot through the restaurant window shows the three of them sitting together, eating, and chatting cheerfully, like a happy yet unconventional family consisting of two maternal or sisterly figures and a young child. With her affective labor and sound practices, Sow effectively applies Yau's abstract political speeches and slogans into community-based everyday practices that open a sisterly space where the existence of exiled women could be legible and a female genealogy outside of the surveillance of the patriarchal family state could be imagined and forged. No longer "an uncertain, shadowy kind of existence" that remains hidden and soundless, women's individual everyday experiences are de-domesticated and de-privatized through Hui's cinematic storytelling to become an inerasable public appearance that constitutes the social reality, which "comes from being seen and heard."[20]

Countering "main melody" with the soundscape of female genealogy

A similar cinematic practice of destabilizing the masculinist book and sword tradition through salvaging gendered memories and voices in grassroots communities is also prominent in Hui's later historical drama *Our Time Will Come*. Set at the onset of the Pacific War, the film recounts another piece of forgotten Hong Kong history: East River Column's anti-Japanese resistance between 1942 and 1944. The East River Column consisted of ordinary villagers from the New Territories of Hong Kong as well as overseas Chinese from Singapore, Vietnam, Malaya, the Philippines, Thailand, and Macao. Most guerrilla soldiers, including their general commander Zeng Sheng, were Hakka. They received substantial "material and kinship support from other Hakka in Southeast Asia and … from the East River region in south Guangdong" with the help of senior Chinese Communist cadres in Hong Kong, including Liao Chengzhi who made successful fundraising efforts with his extensive social networks.[21] These ordinary folks turned guerrillas remained "the only 'flicker of active resistance' after well-equipped British troops dropped weapons and surrendered to the invading enemy."[22] In addition to rescuing "about 100 British, American Air Force personnel, Indian soldiers, and other non-Chinese prisoners," they also helped more than 2,000 cultural and political figures, including Mao Dun, Zou Taofen, and Mei Lanfang, to escape from occupied Hong Kong.[23] In his memoir, Mao Dun painted a glorious picture of the masculine heroism of local outlaws (*Jianghu dage*) who helped with the rescue mission, which seems to provide abundant material for a mainstream male-oriented martial arts film.[24] Invested by the mainland-based Bona Film Group and released on the twentieth anniversary of Hong Kong's handover to mainland China, *Our Time Will Come* is often seen as a "main melody" blockbuster (*zhu xuanlü dapian*) that is tasked with packaging a patriotic leitmotif in the lucrative genres of war epics and action cinema. However, shaking off the bindings of the masculinist political and commercial "main melody," Hui chooses to deliver a gendered account of an ordinary Hong Kong woman Fong Lan, whose characterization is loosely based on a historical figure who took on a leadership position in the East River Column. At the beginning of the film, Fong Lan is an elementary school teacher who is passionate about modern Chinese literature. Coincidentally, Mao Dun, a leftist literary icon, rented a room in Fong and her mother's house during his sojourn in Hong Kong after 1936. Sitting in front of Mao Dun, Fong recites the excerpts of his poetic essay "Dusk" (*Huanghun*, 1934). A lingering long shot matches a visual close-up of Fong's face with an acoustic close-up of her voice during her recital:

> The wind has gone with the manifesto of the setting sun.
> As if they have melted suddenly, the myriad golden eyes of the sea have been flattened into a big, dark-green face.
> There is a sad and solemn sound of a nomad flute from afar.
> The black canopy of the night is going to fall and yet to fall.

> The wind that travelled elsewhere has suddenly returned; this time as if it is drumming: Bellow! Bellow! No, not only wind, there is also thunder! Wind has come with thunder!
> Waves are roaring in the choppy sea. Rumbling! Rumbling!
> The storm has come to the sea at night![25]

Comparing the unsettling natural sounds made by the unpredictable movement of the wind, rain, and waves in the chopping sea to the sad and solemn sounds of drums and flutes, the recited excerpts capture the rising tensions and uncertainty in the air when the historical thunderstorm strikes the city. The horror of the surreal visual imageries of "myriad golden eyes" and the flattened "big, dark-green face" is dispersed by the roaring sounds that gather the momentum to penetrate the black canopy of the night like a sword of fury. Zhou Xun, a mainland Chinese actress who plays Fong Lan, has often been mocked for her low-pitched hoarse voice that is considered "unfeminine" according to mainstream standards in gendered acoustic aesthetics. In this film, nonetheless, the acoustic close-up of her deep-voice and slow-tempo utterance injects an unusual theatrical strength and grave beauty into the reciting, conveying the profound intensity of her psychological repercussion stirred up by the literary projection of an impending stormy change, which naturally leads to her bold decision to help Mao Dun and other leftist intellectuals to flee the Japanese-occupied Hong Kong in the next scene. Living precariously with her mother in occupied Hong Kong, Fong yearns to do something to change the suffocating reality. Thus, her recital of Mao Dun's essay is presented as a transformative performance and an acoustic manifesto of her urgent yearning to connect herself with the revolutionary impulse of the leftist literary and political movements, which serves as a prelude to her commitment to the anti-Japanese cause at the historical moment.

Such a transmedial practice invested in the experimental interplay of the literary and the cinematic through the acoustic close-up of the female voice is not uncommon in Hui's cinema thanks to her dual training in comparative literature and film production. *The Golden Era* (*Huangjin shidai*, 2014), her previous film based on the legendary woman writer Xiao Hong's life story during the Second World War, is also such a literary-cinematic crossover work that features Xiao's frequent acts of writing and reciting of her own literary works. Similarly, Hueyin's recital of classical poetry in Hui's semi-autobiography *Song of the Exile* is also a prominent acoustic reenactment of gendered memories at the center of the retrospective narration. In *Our Time Will Come*, the scene of Fong's recital unfolds in the mundane space of a cramped Hong Kong apartment with soiled walls and tattered furniture. Then Fong reminisces about teaching literary works to her young students, which resonates with the director's personal memories of reading leftist literature at a young age.[26] All these different layers of gendered literary memories and lived experiences on and off the screen domesticate and transmute a seemingly staged literary scene amid the terror of the war into an organic part of Hong Kong's local history and women's daily lives. Bridging the poetic and the everyday, this localized sound event breaks down the boundary between literary imagination and historical event.

Later, with the help of Darkie Lau (Eddie Peng Yuyan), a swordman-type guerrilla sniper with superb martial skills, Fong joins the East River Column and takes on a leadership position.[27] Not unlike the social activists in *Ordinary Heroes*, Fong puts her bookish ideals into practice by refashioning her identity from a Chinese literature teacher to a resistance army leader. Connecting discourse and praxis, her act of recital is not merely a linguistic performance. Rather, it carries the power of political acts to do things, to create new community-based organizations and networks, and to bring about social changes. Fong's metamorphosis as a scholar-turned-warrior who transforms her literary romanticism into the revolutionary practice in the resistance army appears to connect the swordswoman (*nü xia*) tradition in Hong Kong cinema with the patriotic "main melody." Two parallel subplots depicting Darkie Lau's (based on the real-life commander of the Sai Kung Detachment of the Column) and a former Chinese literature teacher Lee Gam-Wing's (Wallace Huo) military and espionage activities seem to bring the film closer to the book and sword tradition that celebrates swordsmen's sublime mission of saving the nation in crisis. However, deviating from both formulaic swords(wo)man films and "main melody" revolutionary biopics, *Our Time Will Come* chooses to deploy a series of acoustic close-ups of networking gendered voices to centralize a female genealogy as a challenge to the masculinist book and sword tradition that tends to create a patrilineal generational descension and transmission between father and son, between master and apprentice, and between (sworn) brothers. Even some of the most unforgettable figures of women warriors ranging from Gold Swallow (in King Hu's *Come Drink with Me*, 1966) to Qiu Moyan (in Raymond Li's *New Dragon Inn*, 1992) are still more or less embedded in such a patrilineal narrative. They wander in a mystified *jianghu* (martial arts) world and commit themselves to serving as courageous yet loyal aides fighting to help accomplish the masculinist deeds of their heroic fathers, brothers, or lovers. By contrast, Hui's female genealogy is remapped in everyday spaces that are de-territorialized from such patrilineal structures and made tangible and poetic through the cinematic representation of minuscular details and quotidian senses, particularly an enriching gendered soundscape of (self)exiled women's voices, speeches, communications, and interactions. Luce Irigaray problematizes the meaning of genealogy as "male and female genealogies are collapsed into a single genealogy: that of the *husband*."[28] In a society of "intermale bondings," Irigaray contends, "[t]he daughters are separated physically and culturally from their mothers when they have to move into their husbands' families and male institutions."[29] Therefore, centralizing the mother–daughter relationship is significant in order to redefine the concept of genealogy that has always been gendered male with an exclusive focus on the father–son relationship at the core of the patriarchal family and patrilineal kinship based on heterosexual marriage.

The mother–daughter relationship has been a recurring theme in Hui's oeuvre that is marked by her meticulous cinematic portrayals of women's day-to-day lives, struggles, and interactions. Similarly, this unusual war epic also flaunts Hui's signature everyday aesthetics through zooming in on a series of domestic scenes set at dusk when Fong Lan and her mother (Deanie Ip Tak Han) sit together to have dinner (see Figure 1.3). Their gendered labor of cooking and sharing food together and their intimate conversations on everyday concerns serve as the essential sound bridge between different generations in building up the female genealogy outside of the patrilineal-heterosexual matrix. At a dinner scene, Fong Lan suggests her mother go back to the countryside to reunite with her father as Hong Kong is occupied by the Japanese. Fong's mother immediately rejects this idea as she hates to live together with her husband's primary wife (*da ma*). She then assures her daughter that they are still self-sufficient with the harvest of pumpkins and yams she grows on the rooftop. This intimate conversation reveals Fong's mother's marginal positionality as a concubine in the patrilineal polygamy system. The outbreak of the war lends her a ready excuse to exile herself from the oppressive patrilineal family where she can never hold an equal status with her husband and his primary wife. Refusing to surrender to the heteropatriarchal power structure, she chooses to hold on to an unconventional mother–daughter family structure. Such an alternative ethical and affective network of (self)exiled women is reminiscent of a similar female genealogy in Hui's earlier film *The Way We Are* (2008). In both films, women's voices in their everyday conversations and interactions serve as the firm acoustic and affective infrastructure on which a female genealogy could be built and sensed.

Figure 1.3 Fong and her mother at the dinner table. *Our Time Will Come* (2017), directed by Ann Hui.

Compared to *The Way We Are* set in contemporary Hong Kong, *Our Time Will Come* highlights how the terror of the war threatens to disrupt the female genealogy and casts shadows over their daily lives. At dinnertime, one topic that is repeatedly brought up is the lack of food that threatens Hong Kong residents' subsistence. On top of the risk of starvation, women are also faced with the danger of being sexually violated by the Japanese army. Instead of visualizing upfront the violence of the war, Hui deploys offscreen sounds to attack audiences' ears with the noises of the war machine. One evening, the sudden crashing sounds of gongs striking interrupt Fong's conversation with her mother. Upon this, Fong's mother immediately turns off the light and whispers angrily: "Those monsters! Snatching girls again!" This unexpected eruption of the acousmatic noises immediately occupies audiences' auditory senses with its explosive energy, reminding them of a vast chaotic offscreen space outside of the frame. Here I allude to Michel Chion's idea of acousmatic voice, or the voice whose source of the sound cannot be seen within the visual frame.[30] Such an acousmatic voice in cinema often suggests a mysterious, omniscient, and even supernatural force attached to the disembodied sound and puts its owner in a position of unquestionable power. With the fading visuals immersed in the dark, the thunderous sounds of the gongs are further reinforced. Alluding back to Fong's reciting of "Dusk," this evening scene reenacts the linguistic description of the fearful, yet shapeless, canopy of the night, revealing the hidden emotions of fear and anger that agitate to find an outlet. Hence, the acoustic close-up transforms the objective sonic elements that transpired as part of the local sensory history into subjective sounds emanating from a gendered point of listening and feeling.

Citing women's recollections of occupied Hong Kong, historian Lu Yan identifies that, for women, the most horrifying noise of the war is not that of machine guns and bullets but the "sound of heavy boots of enemy soldiers" because it was the sound signal of the approaching dangers of sexual violation and gang rape.[31] In order to counter the "Sacred Noise" of army boots, or the acoustic signal of Japan's aggressive "sound imperialism," Hong Kong residents invented a "passive way of defense" by "beating gongs, wash basins, and kerosene tins" to warn people of Japanese soldiers' intruding into their neighborhood.[32] With Ann Hui's acute gender perspective and skillful reenactment of the wartime soundscape to bridge the personal and the historical, the literary and the cinematic, the darkened domestic space of invisibility is turned into a public space of appearance in which acoustic close-ups translate the wartime turmoil and its gendered trauma into shocking soundwaves reverberating in the air of the besieged city. Hence, the trauma and impact of the war are manifested as a bitter struggle of conflicting sounds and noises that bombard the eardrums of the film audiences.

The emotional impact of the violent disruption and even destruction of the female genealogy reaches its peak toward the end of the film. After Fong moves out of the home to serve as the captain of the Urban Detachment of the East River Column, her mother also starts to assist the resistance guerrillas. Their place becomes an underground station for Fong and her assistant Ah Si to stop by on their trips to gather intelligence. Treating Ah Si as her own daughter, Fong's mother cooks for her, looks after her, and helps her collect intelligence. The old house is transformed from a physical shelter for the mother and daughter exiled outside of the patrilineality to a fluid site where a new type of female genealogy connecting the personal and the political is grown. Not based on blood ties, this female genealogy between Fong's mother and Fong Lan as well as Ah Si materializes through these exiled women's resistance against heteropatriarchy in its militant and everyday forms. Countering the deafening noises of destructive masculinist forces such as sirens, gongs, and bombs, the persistent intimate sounds of women's everyday conversations and Fong's mother's wooden clogs when she navigates Hong Kong's labyrinthine streets to run errands and complete her missions stand out as the acoustic index of such a developing "political sisterhood" forged through locally grounded practices of grassroots women of different ages and backgrounds.[33] Traditionally filtered out from the official records as trivial feminine noises, these gendered sounds serve as local women's essential means of immaterial labor that facilitates the construction of the social networks of active resistance. Hence, sound-making/listening is not only a sensory experience, a narrative device, but a bodily enactment of politics that catalyzes changes in people's life program, interpersonal relationships, and social practices.

Once, when assisting Ah Si to deliver an urgent message, Fong's mother is captured and detained at the Japanese police headquarters. Trying to protect Ah Si, she is severely beaten by the Japanese. To Ah Si's question "Does it hurt badly?", she responds: "Not as badly as when I gave birth for the first time." Comparing physical torture with women's reproductive pain and suffering, this conversation lays bare the gendered dimension of violence during wartime that also exhibits itself in a different form in women's everyday sufferings and sacrifices. After much internal struggle, Fong decides to call off the action of rescuing her mother that puts the lives of many guerrilla soldiers at risk. Accompanying a long shot of Fong's lonely figure sitting still in a darkened room, her earlier recital of "Dusk" is played again in the soundtrack (see Figure 1.4). The second recital of the essay transforms the male-authored piece celebrating the impending outbreak of the revolution into a feminine poetics of memorizing and reenacting the female genealogy between mother and daughter as well as between two women fighting shoulder to shoulder against the heteropatriarchal oppressions in its different forms during war and peace. Intensive emotional investment in the second recital gives new affective meanings and aesthetic values to the linguistic articulation. Woman's voices, amplified in this recurring acoustic close-up, serve as a bridge between past and present, as well as between the personal and the revolutionary.

Such a gendered soundscape of a poetic female genealogy subverts the masculinist book and sword tradition and highlights exiled women's agency, bonding, and voices in reconstructing collective memories of the war. The last

Figure 1.4 The lonely woman warrior thinking of her mother. *Our Time Will Come* (2017), directed by Ann Hui.

close-up of a female voice appears toward the end of the film. Although the war is nearly over, no loud noises of celebration appear in the soundtrack. Instead, the film ends on a note of quiet farewell in the dark. Dressed in a Tanka outfit, Fong Lan bids farewell to Darkie Lau who leaves to join the North Canton front. Fong tells him: "My real name is Hung Sau-Fong. I will turn twenty-seven at the end of the year. Remember my name, and you will be able to find me." Again, the acoustic close-up is happening in the dark. Both actors remain motionless, allowing audiences to concentrate their sensory energies on capturing Fong's sound waves. The only difference is that this scene is unfolding in the outdoor space. Accompanied by the soft ambient sounds of water gurgling, grass leaves rustling, and crickets chirping, Fong's calm voice interweaves with an intimate soundscape of Hong Kong's night. Her black attire in the style of local Tanka fisherwomen blends into the black canopy of the night that is penetrated by the acoustic close-up of her hopeful voice full of anticipation for creating a better future with their persistent efforts and sacrifices. Although talking to Lau, she seems to address the audience directly, reminding them not to forget Hong Kong's past, particularly the communal history constituted and transmitted by a myriad of nameless grassroots women like Fong and her mother. Following her voice, a panning shot moves horizontally from the right to the left of the screen, revealing a compressed temporal change: the darkened silhouette of the rippling water and mountains gradually fades into the glamorous skylines of a bustling modern Hong Kong.

Connecting the sensory realism of the martial arts cinema with postwar Hong Kong's rapid modernization, Man-Fung Yip draws upon Ackbar Abbas's famous observation of Hong Kong's "culture of disappearance" that identifies the former colony as "a space of perpetual dislocation and displacement closely associated with speed."[34] Going against this trend of sensory realism built upon masculinist strength, speed, and visual spectacles in martial arts cinema, the ending sequence speaks volumes about Hui's ambition in countering the visual disappearance with acoustic remembrance. While the visual signal in this sequence underscores Hong Kong's culture of displacement and disappearance as a result of the city's disorienting speedy modernization and mutation in a compressed time-space, Fong's voice, through the conduit of the cinematic soundtrack, acts as an essential vehicle for remembering the past and conveying hope for the future, which remedies the woman warrior's absence in the visual panel to create an acoustic space of appearance that preserves the suppressed memories and fighting spirit of many unrecognized "ordinary hero(in)es" like her for today's audiences.

Conclusion

Through her adept interweaving of the *wu xi wen pai* and *wen xi wu pai* tactics, Ann Hui alluded to the *wuxia* cinema to infuse the *xia* spirit into her realist historical cinema. Rather than amplifying and celebrating the visual spectacles of swordsmen's superb martial skills and male fellowship that are essential to "the imagination of an exclusively male order,"[35] Hui rewrites the masculinist book and sword tradition with her cinematic engagement with women's interweaving voices and narratives of their everyday experiences of and social struggles against inequalities at the intersection of gender, class, age, and ethnicity. Her constant exploration of and experimentation with the cinematic medium's unique capacities of archiving the history, documenting people's lived experiences, and making tangible the mundane details and senses of the city's everyday lifeworld transform her films into a space of appearance that makes appear the disappearing historical events, social movements, and communal memories, particularly those often-forgotten women activists and leaders from groups exiled out of the official records.[36] Only with the continuous narration and action of women characters on the screen and women filmmakers off the screen can memory be preserved, and our time will come one day when the silenced stories of ordinary heroines will be recognized publicly and talked about openly.

Acknowledgments

Thanks to the Honorary Visiting Fellowship provided by the Chinese University of Hong Kong (CUHK), I spent a fruitful semester conducting research on this project at the Institute of Chinese Studies (ICS) at CUHK. During my fellowship period, I gave talks on different aspects of my ongoing research at CUHK, Hong Kong Baptist University, Hong Kong Lingnan University, and the University of Hong Kong and received invaluable comments and suggestions from audiences. Moreover, I have benefited enormously from the volume editors' and anonymous reviewers' constructive feedback, and from inspiring conversations with the following colleagues and friends: Tani E. Barlow, Chen Jing, Poshek Fu, Ge Liang, Gu Yixin, Gong Haomin, Maciej Kurzynski, Lai Chi Tim, Leung Shuk Man, Lin Pei Yin, Qi Xiangu, Miriam Serger, Flair Donglai Shi, Song Geng, Tan Jia, Max Xiaobing Tang, Gabriel F. Y. Tsang, Wang Ding Kun, Alvin Wong, Zhang Chen, Zhang Hongsheng, Zhang Yu, and Zhu Ping.

2

Women, space, and ruins

Chinese painting aesthetics in Ann Hui's *Love in a Fallen City*

Dailin Zhao

As the first film adaptation of Eileen Chang's fiction, *Love in a Fallen City* (1984) is often overlooked in Ann Hui's oeuvre. Although this film was Shaw Brothers Studio's last major production before its closure in 1986, it was not widely acclaimed on release. *Love in a Fallen City* was once regarded as Ann Hui's "worst performance as a director."[1] Some critics argued that Hui added too many commercial elements to the film's sets, props, and dramatic scenes for market considerations, leading the film to run counter to Eileen Chang's original style.[2] However, when we pay attention to the adaptation process of *Love in a Fallen City*, which is hostage to the operation of Hong Kong's film industry and commercial mechanism, we should also note that Ann Hui has been striking a difficult balance between business and art. In her own words, she is pulled between the two tendencies:

> I was really surprised because I had to face a choice: between commercial and artistic achievement. Halfway through, I cut out what I thought was commercial, but not thoroughly enough. Because if you start as an experiment or a very religious attempt, you shouldn't think about pleasing the audience … But now because I've had a lot of changes in the middle, it wasn't artistic enough for the critics and wasn't commercial enough for Miss Fong (Yihua Fang, the producer of *Love in a Fallen City*). But in the end, I'm already on the artistic side, so I'm quite happy already.[3]

It can be observed that despite the constraints imposed by the market and investments in film production, Ann Hui ultimately accomplished her artistic expression of Eileen Chang's works through this film. This chapter aims to underscore that the emulation of Chinese painting techniques constitutes one of the crucial means through which this expression was realized. Eileen Chang's affinity for painting is evident from her early exposure to art education under the influence of her mother and aunt. She also authored a series of art critique articles. For Eileen Chang, the impact of artistic expression through painting inevitably permeated her literary concepts and creative endeavors. Similarly, the film *Love in a Fallen City* demonstrates a continuation of traditional painting aesthetics in the construction of style and the expression of meaning. This chapter does not intend to prove that Ann Hui intentionally imitated ancient Chinese paintings during filming. Instead, it attempts to point out that, driven by familiarity with Eileen Chang's works and a desire to faithfully restore Chang's artistic style, *Love in a Fallen City* exhibits visual patterns reminiscent of traditional painting in the process of translating from fiction to film. These patterns, as a cinematic restoration of the text, present Eileen Chang's special aesthetic perspectives.

Moreover, it is important to note that Hui has consistently demonstrated a deep interest in exploring female perspectives throughout her directorial career. Her films frequently examine women's lived experiences and the expression of their delicate emotions within specific sociocultural contexts. In *Love in a Fallen City*, this interest is prominently expressed through her use of the *meiren* painting. This technique not only captures Eileen Chang's exploration of female identity but also offers a deeper insight into the complex emotions and psychological depth of the protagonist, Bai Liusu. The visual patterns drawn from *meiren* painting highlight Liusu's journey of self-reflection, her negotiation with societal expectations, and her quest for autonomy within a patriarchal family structure. Hui's framing and composition effectively evoke a sense of Liusu's inner world and show how it is both intertwined with and often constrained by her spatial surroundings.

Building on this, the theme of space is further developed as the narrative transitions from Liusu herself to the domestic realm she navigates. Drawing inspiration from Chinese narrative scrolls, Hui employs fluid camera movements and interconnected scenes to reflect Liusu's experience through family obligations. This spatial technique captures the instability and fluidity of Liusu's world, while fragmented shots, such as her encounter with an ancestral portrait, introduce moments of temporal dislocation and ambiguity. This approach not only highlights the constraints Liusu faces but also echoes Eileen Chang's literary concept of "desolation."

Finally, the imagery of ruins plays a critical role as the narrative expands beyond the confined domestic setting into the chaotic landscapes of wartime

Hong Kong. Drawing on the imagery of ruins from Chinese painting, Hui uses the modern ruins created by war as a prominent visual element in the film, which highlights the tension between the eternal and transient. Furthermore, through framing the collapse of civilization as the backdrop to Liusu's emotional narrative, the film depicts how emotional relationships and personal identity are forged among the ruins of a disintegrating world and creates a dialogue between historical trauma and individual modes of existence. This approach not only aligns with Eileen Chang's desolate worldview but also situates the film within a broader exploration of Hong Kong's colonial history.

In other words, the visual elements and aesthetic expressions inherent in these painted models themselves contribute rich dimensions to the film's interpretation of meaning. As Andre Bazin articulates: "In no sense is the film 'comparable' to the novel or 'worthy' of it. It is a new aesthetic creation, the novel so to speak multiplied by the cinema."[4] Through the film adaptation of Eileen Chang's fiction, Ann Hui forms a juxtaposition of two mutually reflective texts. By borrowing compositional and layout principles from traditional paintings such as portraits of women, narrative scrolls, and depictions of ruins in the visual representation, *Love in a Fallen City* constructs an intermedial "middle ground." This realm amalgamates three distinct aesthetic origins—fiction, paintings, and film imagery—in a subtly discernible manner. It serves as a platform for Ann Hui to manifest her subtle concern for female emotions and reflections on modern civilization. Additionally, it offers an interpretation of the "desolation" aesthetic style attributed to Eileen Chang.

Visual fragments and environmental systems: The emotional space of female characters

When categorizing *Love in a Fallen City* as a failed adaptation, many critics have highlighted the film's shortcomings in the portrayal of the characters' psychological depth. For instance, He Xing believes that Eileen Chang's intricate portrayal of the psychology of men and women is challenging to translate into visuals, causing the film to downplay the emotional fluctuations presented in the original work.[5] However, it is worth noting that Ann Hui, when discussing her understanding of the original work, continues to place the focus on the inner lives and emotions of characters, particularly women. In a speech, Ann Hui pointed out that the most captivating aspect of *Love in a Fallen City* lies in how the upheaval of the times inadvertently fulfills the love story between a man and a woman. This ironic emotional relationship between men and women, vividly depicted by Eileen Chang, is "written very vividly, simultaneously offering insights into the status of women at that time."[6] Although the distinctive qualities of Eileen Chang's fiction pose challenges in adaptation, Ann Hui's admiration for Eileen Chang's works and her sensitivity to the plight of women enable the film to exhibit a concern for female emotions and consciousness. By visualizing the patterns of traditional beauty portraits implied in Eileen Chang's fiction through the medium of imagery, *Love in a Fallen City* constructs a space within the visual narrative for the expression of the female psyche and emotions. This utilization of classical painting references contributes to the film's nuanced portrayal of female characters, offering a visual dimension to the emotional and psychological aspects of Eileen Chang's literary creations.

To begin with, as we delve into the original text of *Love in a Fallen City* and scrutinize the characterization, it becomes evident that Eileen Chang's choice of expressions and narrative style in shaping characters reflects a pronounced inclination toward a return to classical Chinese literature. For instance, in the initial stages of introducing major characters in the narrative, the fiction often adopts the perspective of an observer, providing meticulous delineations of their appearance, attire, and immediate surroundings to establish a comprehensive readerly impression. This is prominently exemplified in the fiction, particularly in the scene depicting Bai Liusu's introspective moment before a mirror following a dispute with relatives at home:

> Liusu cried out, covered her eyes, and fled; her feet beat a rapid retreat up the stairs to her own room. She turned on the lamp, moved it to her dressing table, and studied her reflection in the mirror. Good enough: she wasn't too old yet. She had the kind of slender figure that doesn't show age—her waist eternally thin, her breasts girlishly budding. Her face had always been as white as porcelain, but now it had changed from porcelain to jade—semitranslucent jade with a tinge of pale green. Once, her cheeks had been plump; now they were drawn, so that her small face seemed smaller yet, and even more attractive. Her face was fairly narrow, but her eyes were set well apart. They were clear, lively, and slightly coquettish. Out on the balcony, Fourth Master had once again taken up his *huqin*. The tune rose and fell, and Liusu's head tilted to one side as her eyes and hands started moving through dance poses. As she performed in the mirror, the *huqin* no longer sounded like a *huqin*, but like strings and flutes playing a solemn court dance. She took a few paces to the right, then a few to the left. Her steps seemed to trace the lost rhythms of an ancient melody. Suddenly, she smiled—a private, malevolent smile; the music came to a discordant halt. The

huqin went on playing outside, but it was telling tales of fealty and filial piety, chastity and righteousness: distant tales that had nothing to do with her.[7]

In this passage, Eileen Chang does not explicitly delineate Liusu's psychological activities. The subtle emotional transitions, from a sudden and disoriented exclamation to a private, malevolent smile, are accomplished through Eileen Chang's precise portrayal of Bai Liusu. What makes this passage distinctive is its resemblance to the character embroidery illustrations found in ancient popular fiction, imparting a high degree of visual and pictorial qualities to the scene. The action of "looking at oneself in the mirror" turns the "mirror" into a visual element within the text, functioning as a frame and serving as the medium through which Bai Liusu creates a self-portrait. Simultaneously, the reader, while engaging with the text, becomes the viewer of this portrait, experiencing her emotional fluctuations as the visual subject, achieving a synesthetic harmony between text and image.

Bai Liusu's appearance and actions constitute a female image imbued with classical charm, aligning with Eileen Chang's consistent interest in female figures in traditional art. In her prose *A Chronicle of Changing Clothes*, Eileen Chang personally illustrated illustrations depicting women in late Qing dynasty attire, creating a visual contrast with the accompanying text. Moreover, the cover painting for the expanded edition of the fiction collection *Legends*, which includes *Love in a Fallen City*, borrowed from the late Qing painter Wu Youren's painting *In Praise of This Evening* (*Yiyong jinxi*). The painting depicts a woman "quietly playing *gupai*, accompanied by a nursemaid holding a child, evoking a scene of ordinary family life after dinner."[8] Therefore, it is plausible for us to seek the visual prototypes of the female characters in *Love in a Fallen City* from the female images in traditional paintings.

In Chinese fine arts, the depiction of women as the subject of paintings can be traced back to the Song and Yuan dynasties. By the mid-Ming dynasty, a popularized *meiren* painting pattern gained popularity, swiftly integrating into contemporary culture and becoming a subject of mass visual consumption. These pictures either showcased individual female figures or presented collective activities of multiple women, becoming significant content in fiction and theatrical illustrations. As the genre of *meiren* painting matured during the Ming and Qing periods, the construction of beauty images became increasingly formalized and detailed. Xu Zhen, a prose writer of the Qing dynasty, authored *A Catalog of Beauties* (*Meiren pu*), listing thirteen aspects of a beauty's "appearance" and twelve aspects of her "adornments." Wei Yong, in his book

Pleasant Appearance Compilation (*Yuerong bian*), commented on the living environment and activities that an exemplary woman should engage in. This highly itemized and systematic discourse on the standard of beauty gradually resonated with the construction of beauty images in *meiren* paintings.

According to Wu Hung, these *meiren* paintings, in their portrayal of characters' posture, attire, actions, and environment, do not create a continuous narrative effect. Instead, they form fragmented pieces for the appreciation and evaluation of the "deconstructed fragments of the beauty's body, face, and attire."[9] The women in the paintings are not seen as complete individuals but are incorporated into a space composed of elements such as the environment, objects, and appearance. Consequently, the exact identity of the women in these pictures is often blurred. The paintings attempt to establish a symbolic system without specific referentiality, and the female image serves as a collection of these symbolic rules.

When we reexamine the original text of *Love in a Fallen City*, we find that Eileen Chang almost transcribes the visual composition of *meiren* paintings into words. In the abovementioned text, Eileen Chang's description provides readers with a viewing experience similar to observing *meiren* paintings: visual fragments connected by Bai Liusu's figure, facial features, movements, and expressions. The inclination to restore scenes from the fiction leads the film adaptation to similarly leverage the composition and expressive methods of traditional *meiren* pictures. Through imagery, the film reconstructs and visualizes the feminine space in Eileen Chang's original work. There is an episode in the film in which Bai Liusu, having been scorned by her relatives, turns to her elderly mother for solace. However, the aged mother can only advise her to endure as much as possible. Disheartened, Bai Liusu is left with no choice but to retreat to her own room alone. The camera first captures a close-up of Bai Liusu's face, with Fourth Sister's sarcastic remarks about her divorce coming through as off-screen dialogue. As Bai Liusu says, "I can't stay in this family anymore," she cries and lies on the bed. The film then switches to a full shot, providing the audience with a fixed view of the environment: Bai Liusu lies on a bed covered with layers of curtains, a lamp is lit on her right, and behind the lamp are dressing accessories and a vanity. In this shot, the curtained bed becomes the visual centerpiece, forming another layer of framing in the image (see Figure 2.1).

It confines Bai Liusu within this layered space and readily evokes a visual parallel with the female figure in *meiren* painting. One example can be found in Qiu Ying's *Spring Morning in the Han Palace* (*Hanggong chunxiao tu*), where a woman is shown reclining indoors at the center of the composition, enclosed

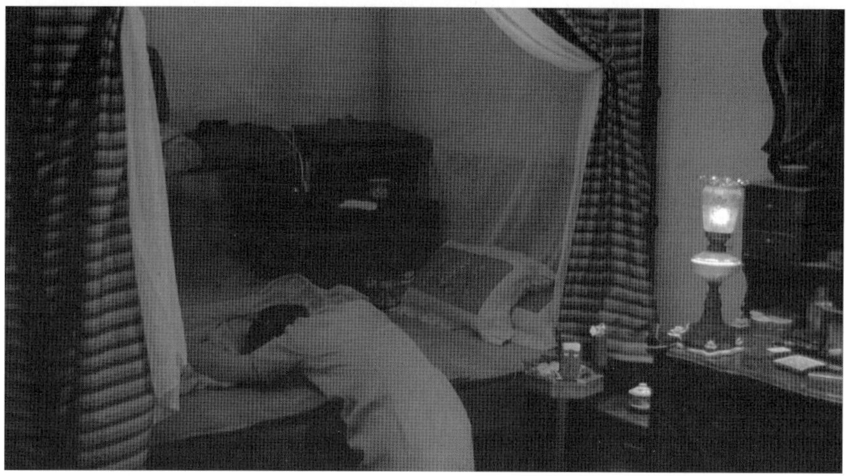

Figure 2.1 Bai Liusu lying her head on a curtained bed. *Love in a Fallen City* (1984), directed by Ann Hui.

by architectural walls and foliage. Jonathan Han has described the aesthetic of constructing inner spaces in Chinese painting and architecture as "a wrapped space." Beds in women's bedrooms are often enveloped in multiple barriers to ensure greater privacy.[10] In this scene, the layered curtains "wrapped" Bai Liusu, creating another internal demarcation within the film frame. Utilizing the compositional method of traditional paintings, the space is internally folded, adding to its inherent privacy. The bedroom becomes a place resistant to malicious external voices, a space for expressing personal emotions, possessing both lyrical and private qualities. The lighting and dressing items in the room, while enhancing the richness of the image, further reinforce the feminine significance of the space. Subsequently, Ann Hui inserts a scene not exhaustively described in the original work, where the young Liusu stands in the bustling city center, crying and incessantly calling for her mother. The camera then cuts back to a close-up of Liusu in the room, implying that she is recalling a childhood trauma, experiencing a similar sense of helplessness (seeking help from her mother in vain) in the current situation. This sudden flashback segment has a distinct stylistic difference from the preceding narrative. It departs from the present reality, entering a hazy, poetic, and fragmented stream of memory. The visual pattern of the "boudoir space" in the bedroom bestows Bai Liusu with the position of a female subject. This space, with its lyrical and private qualities, provides an entry point for the flow of Bai Liusu's emotions, allowing her to break free from suffocating familial ties and engage in introspection and solace.

Furthermore, another crucial scene in the film involves the presentation of Liusu's "self-reflection in the mirror," as depicted in Eileen Chang's original work. Ann Hui employs more environmental details to recreate this visual pattern from the fiction. In a full shot, Bai Liusu rushes into the room, and on the walls on either side behind her hang two paintings featuring female subjects. One portrays a woman contemplating at a table, while the other illustrates two women leisurely seated in a domestic setting. These two *meiren* paintings become distinct visual symbols, hinting that this is a space imprinted with the private emotions of women. As Liusu moves, the camera follows suit, panning to focus on Liusu's self-examination in the mirror. Behind Liusu in the mirror is the bed with a mosquito net, and she, accompanied by the sound of the *huqin*, scrutinizes herself, performing theatrical gestures. The stationary camera perfectly captures this entire process (see Figure 2.2).

The visual motif of "self-reflection in the mirror" can be traced back to the Southern Song painter Su Hancheng's *Lady Adorning Herself Before a Mirror* (*Zhuangliang shinv tu*), where a woman sits before a dressing mirror, slightly extending her head and neck, carefully observing her own reflection. Through the mirror, the viewer's gaze is directed toward two closely connected but not entirely identical subjects: appreciating her body in front of the mirror and seeing the appearance in the mirror, imagining her inner world based on this. Leo Ou-fan Lee believes that Liusu's act of dancing in front of the mirror is not

Figure 2.2 Liusu's self-examination in the mirror. *Love in a Fallen City* (1984), directed by Ann Hui.

only the request for a new marriage prospect but also seeking her own identity as a woman torn between two worlds.[11] The film accomplishes this nuanced psychological translation through the visual motif of the beauty painting. The mirror serves as a medium for the Liusu images in her two worlds to meet. When the audience's focus simultaneously includes the character in front of the mirror and the reflected image, they are drawn into Liusu's dialogue with herself, discovering the trajectory of her psychological activities and feeling the desires and emotions contained within this female space.

In its formal significance, *Love in a Fallen City* seamlessly integrates the simulation of the *meiren* painting pattern with Eileen Chang's traditional literary style, thereby infusing the entire film with a poetic aesthetic ambience. However, in its symbolic meaning, this imitation expresses a rebellion against *meiren* paintings, leading to Ann Hui's own focus on women. *Meiren* paintings meticulously dictate women's activities and living environments, attempting to perfect the systematic impression of "beauty," yet the true identity of the figures in the paintings is often blurred, with "beauty" remaining merely a general aesthetic perception in people's minds. James Cahill also points out that as the techniques of *meiren* painting mature, "intensifying the erotic appeal of the image, making it for male viewers a more overtly effective icon of the courtesan-concubine ideal. For female viewers, we can speculate, much was lost in that process."[12] In her construction of the *meiren* painting motif, Ann Hui creatively allows the female figures within this space to break free from the status of a generalized object of desire. Through meticulous depiction of the scenes and Liusu's interactions with her surroundings, Hui ensures that she is not confined to a passive role. The use of layered compositions and symbolic props does not simply frame Liusu as an object of beauty; rather, Liusu's gestures, expressions, and engagement with her environment collectively convey her thoughts, desires, and inner conflicts, which enables her to escape the constraints of traditional family and moral expectations. In this way, Hui subverts the *meiren* painting's tendency to objectify women, instead granting Liusu agency and subjectivity. Ray Chow once pointed out Eileen Chang's utmost emphasis on sensory experiences in her analysis of *Affinity of Half a Lifetime* (*Bansheng yuan*) and *The Golden Cangue* (*Jinsuo ji*). She believes that this deliberate emphasis reiterates the private emotional structure of women, placing female characters at the center of the narrative mode. Through the depiction of their trivial actions, the narrative manifests the traditional position of women. Chang's nuanced and meticulous attention to women disrupts the identity association between characters and progressive rhetoric such as "new nation" and "modernity" in the mainstream literary tradition since the May Fourth period.[13] The treatment of characters in the film *Love in a Fallen City* follows a similar path. Through the segments where Bai Liusu reminisces in the bedroom and gazes at herself in the mirror, these two "self-loving" sequences break the link between divorce and the degradation of women. Liusu isolates herself from societal norms such as loyalty (*zhong*) and filial piety (*xiao*) that demand women's self-sacrifice. In this new female space generated by the *meiren* painting motif, Liusu's personal feelings take an absolutely dominant position. Through the comprehensive arrangement of objects, characters, and activities, this space guides Liusu beyond the constraints traditionally imposed on women within cultural and ethical orders.

Scroll narratives and detail focus: The desolate feeling of everyday life

The application of Chinese painting aesthetics in *Love in a Fallen City* is not confined merely to using *meiren* painting techniques to capture the complexity of female subjectivity. Building on this foundation, Ann Hui expands her visual narrative by incorporating elements of Chinese scroll painting to further explore the spatial dynamics within *Love in a Fallen City*. While the *meiren* painting outlines Liusu's inner world, the use of scroll painting techniques in the spatial arrangement of film scenes extends the film's focus to the broader familial and public spaces inhabited by the characters.

The narrative of *Love in a Fallen City* unfolds initially within the confines of a secluded mansion, known as the "Bai family mansion," described by Eileen Chang as an old-style large family where "Ten o'clock to them was eleven to everyone else."[14] It represents a bygone era of extended family living, spanning multiple generations, with a flourishing population. Despite being situated in contemporary society, the prevalence of these traditional kinship ties makes it challenging for the characters to possess individual spaces similar to those of modern individuals. The boundaries between individuals often blend and intertwine, forming a network structure based on blood ties. In the cinematographic treatment of *Love in a Fallen City*, efforts are made to restore this traditional family form. Lu Weili pointed out the distinctive nature of scene handling in this film: "Ann Hui pays close attention to the lives of people in different spaces. In her other films, we can see her using the layout of the montage to construct the reality of space. But in this film, the treatment of communal space often involves mise-en-scene, which is an attempt."[15] This commentary accurately summarizes the visual characteristics of *Love in a Fallen City*. Through the dialogues and interactions of various characters within the Bai family, the film establishes multiple narrative spaces. These narrative spaces, however, are not independent; instead, they are interconnected and interact through the movement of the camera, constructing complex relationships between characters. Lu Weili attributes this style to Ann Hui's imitation of Cantonese films from the 1950s. But if we further trace the artistic origins of this aesthetic style, we will find similarities between Ann Hui's spatial treatment and the structural aspects of traditional narrative paintings.

In Chinese fine arts, handscroll paintings often serve as a medium for narrative expression by artists. The process of depicting objects and events in these paintings typically possesses a strong sense of sequence and fluidity, resembling the narrative flow found in modern comics. Instead of simply recording a single scene, handscroll paintings construct a complex spatial system and a continuous series of images. While each individually framed image is distinct, narrative handscrolls often lack a centralized visual focus, accommodating a diverse array of scene details. Viewers are free to select and focus on the elements that interest them within the composition. David Hockney once used a camera to film the contents of a long handscroll titled *Kangxi Emperor's Southern Inspection Tour* (*Kangxi nanxun tu*). He noted that this visual form places the audience within a space where their gaze can roam freely, ensuring that the narrative continues to organically unfold through unrestricted perspectives.[16]

The unique format and layout principles of handscroll paintings are also employed in *Love in a Fallen City* to facilitate the composition of character relationships and spatial dynamics. Ann Hui once discussed her observations in an interview:

> The original work has a very distinctive and interesting structure. It spends a considerable amount of time and intricate detail describing the scenes that take place in the mansion at the beginning. However, as the story progresses, the transitions between scenes become increasingly intricate.[17]

She interpreted this structure as "echoing the theme of the ancient world in the story collapsing due to war."[18] By emulating the spatial arrangement of traditional narrative paintings, these scenes that continually circulate within the mansion are connected, visualizing Eileen Chang's depiction of the fragmented old-fashioned family structure in ancient China. Early in the film, the audience is presented with life scenes within the Bai family: Bail Liusu's fourth brother (Fourth Master) attempts to persuade Bai Liusu to attend her ex-husband's

Figure 2.3 The spatial arrangement in the Bai family's mansion. *Love in a Fallen City* (1984), directed by Ann Hui.

funeral. In this mid-shot, Fourth Master stands in the foreground, the messenger delivering the news in the middle, and the Fourth Mistress, positioned in the background, attentively observes their conversation (see Figure 2.3).

As Fourth Master moves to the right toward Bai Liusu, the camera pans horizontally, revealing the furnishings of the entire living room. Fourth Master sits beside the table in the center of the living room, while the two children play on chairs in the background. On the wall behind, a calligraphy scroll reads, "Respect the father as the sky, respect the mother as the earth; your descendants shall also do likewise." Fourth Mistress then reenters the scene, standing in the middle of the frame behind Fourth Master. In response to Liusu's refusal:

> Are you saying that those legal proceedings were empty nonsense? You can't fool around with laws!

Fourth Master retorts:

> The law is one thing today and another tomorrow. What I'm talking about is the law of family relations, and that never changes! As long as you live you belong to his family, and after you die your ghost will belong to them too!

Within this stable shot, the actions of the characters interconnect, gradually unfolding the space along with their movements, ensuring the completeness and coherence of the narrative. The different positions of the characters also echo the admonitions in the calligraphy scroll, collectively forming a traditional family network representing the moral principles and ethics emphasized by Fourth Master. Through this layout reminiscent of traditional narrative paintings, the audience's gaze follows the extension of space, experiencing the tightness and stability of this community structure: a space continually expanding in rich actions, exerting pressure on Liusu, who desires to escape from the family.

As the narrative gradually unfolds, *Love in a Fallen City* once again employs the compositional pattern of traditional narrative paintings to depict this space. When Bai Liusu sits alone in the room crying, Mrs. Xu comes to console her, advising her not to be disappointed and encouraging her to find a good marriage. Initially focusing on the conversation between the two, the camera gradually zooms out, shifting from the bedroom to the empty living room in Liusu's home, revealing its furnishings. With Liusu's sigh, "Auntie, of course you know the situation. Would a family like mine ever let us go out and meet people?," the camera performs two horizontal pans, sequentially presenting the table in the middle of the living room, the chairs on the left side, and the portrait of late Qing dynasty figures hanging in the background. In terms of visual composition, this scheduling method avoids spatial isolation, providing a seamless viewing experience. Simultaneously, Liusu's voiceover leaves clues in this space, propelling the narrative forward. Her life circumstances and destiny struggles are intertwined with the mundane household environment through this handscroll-like progression method.

In the dynamic spatial movement, *Love in a Fallen City* draws inspiration from traditional painting aesthetic methods, amalgamating diverse perspectives to shape a flexible and shifting viewing rhythm. Simultaneously, Ann Hui visualizes Eileen Chang's literary philosophy by interrupting this fluidity. Eileen Chang proposed the renowned theory of "desolation":

> I do not like heroics. I like tragedy and, even better, desolation. Heroism has strength but no beauty and thus seems to lack humanity. Tragedy, however, resembles the matching of bright red with deep green: an intense and unequivocal contrast. And yet it is more exciting than truly revelatory. The reason desolation resonates far more profoundly is that it resembles the conjunction of scallion green with peach red, creating an equivocal contrast.[19]

In Eileen Chang's perspective, "tragic" is a form of stimulation, laden with clear significance yet resistant to prolonged contemplation, while "desolation" serves as a "contrast." As a managed, imbalanced state, it is closer to a realistic system and aligns more closely with Eileen Chang's literary aesthetics. Therefore, Eileen Chang prefers to populate her fiction with seemingly unrelated life details. In her view, these details can generate a "desolate" feeling in "contrast" to the dramatic narrative, reconstructing the foundation of real life and revealing simple truths. In her essay "Demons and Fairies," she wrote:

> It is doubtless owing to this agnostic tendency that Chinese literature is pervaded by a great sadness. It finds joy only in materialistic details, which explains why traditional fictionists dwell so tirelessly on the un-abridged items in meals and love-making (complete menus are often given for no specific purpose). The details can be gay and distracting whereas the theme is invariably pessimistic. All generalizations on life point to nothingness.[20]

In Chang's opinion, "details" symbolize the intricate and vivid texture of life, and the isolation of these trivial aspects in themselves represents a detachment from the broader world, redirecting the significance of dramatic narrative toward emptiness. It is the tension between these two aspects that constitutes the source of the desolate feeling. As a devoted reader of Eileen Chang's works, Ann Hui sensitively captures this aesthetic inclination and translates it into special attention to visual details in the film.

Therefore, in the spatial concatenation brought about by the transition of the camera, *Love in a Fallen City* deliberately disrupts this fluid visual experience by inserting fragmented captures of details. This approach adds tension and variation to the visual content, bringing the film closer to Eileen Chang's own expression of aesthetic philosophy. The scene where Liusu says goodbye to Mrs. Xu serves as a typical example. The camera continues to follow the two characters as they move from the stairs to the living room. With the swaying movement following Mrs. Xu's departure, it then fixes on Liusu once again. However, the continuous flow of this scene is abruptly interrupted the next moment. The shot switches, following Liusu's gaze to the ancestral portrait hanging on the wall, seamlessly transitioning to a close-up of the pattern on the woman's clothing. Upon seeing these patterns, Bai Liusu seems to awaken from a dream, stumbling back to her room. In this seemingly abrupt segment, the figure dressed in traditional attire, fixed within the portrait, also constitutes another metaphor in line with Eileen Chang's essay "A Chronicle of Changing Clothes":

> You would move down the path between bamboo poles, flanked by walls of silk and satin—an excavated corridor within an ancient palace buried deep under the ground. You could press your forehead against brocades shot through with gold thread. When the sun was still out, this thread was warmed by the light, but now it is cold.
>
> People in the past went laboriously about their lives, but all their deeds end up coated in a thick layer of dust. When their descendants air these old clothes, that dust is shaken out and set dancing in the yellow sunlight.[21]

The details of the clothing serve as a kind of corporeal presence in absence. The camera's gaze on the clothing undoubtedly disrupts the stability conveyed by the traditional family structure in the scroll-like image construction, guiding the viewers and Bai Liusu into a "punctum moment." These details provide fragments of the past, bringing about a juxtaposition of the old and the new, resulting in a temporal dislocation. However, despite the vastly different lifestyles of generations, their predicaments are remarkably similar: the issue of finding a way out in the context of the extended family. This close-up shot, which abruptly interrupts the visual flow, transports Liusu into a shared temporal cycle with her ancestors. The fiction describes Bai Liusu's emotions in this way:

> Time grinds on, year after year, and the eyes grow dull, the minds grow dull, and then another round of children is born. The older ones are sucked into that obscure haze of crimson and gold, and the tiny flecks of glinting gold are the frightened eyes of their predecessors.[22]

Within the confines of the traditional family, the conventional way to attain a sense of security was to conform to family rules, allowing each generation to smoothly propagate. However, Liusu does not place her hopes on this path. Therefore, in the film, when Bai Liusu sees the pattern on the clothing, a panicked and disoriented expression appears on her face. She realizes the passage of time yet simultaneously remains trapped in the same predicament. Consequently, this moment becomes a blurred zone where the "present" and "history" coexist. The shadows of the past linger in the traces of the present. The linear distinctions between the "old" and the "new," the "now" and the "past," become blurred in this temporal space. This ambiguity, chaos, and the reversal of order introduce an uncertainty that disrupts the previous sense of order in visual composition, bringing about the aesthetic experience of "emptiness" that Eileen Chang keenly perceived. Through the appropriation and disruption of traditional painting structures, the film achieves a visual interpretation of this temporal framework, realizing the kind of "equivocal contrast" mentioned by Eileen Chang. This allows the love story to further respond to and deepen the theme of "desolation."

Past recollections and identity confirmation: The genesis process of modern ruins

While the previous section focused on how Hui employed the techniques of Chinese scroll painting to depict the interconnectedness of characters within the Bai family mansion, this aesthetic sensibility is carried into the chaotic landscapes of wartime Hong Kong and connects personal experiences with broader historical forces. If the portrayal of the female psychological world and the spatial arrangement of domestic settings in *Love in a Fallen City* shape the style of everyday life through the lens of traditional painting aesthetics, the extensively depicted scenes of wartime in the film showcase the unique states of life during periods of turmoil. The production cost of *Love in a Fallen City* reached a staggering HKD 6.5 million. Due to Shaw Brothers Studio's commercial demands for the film, Ann Hui incorporated numerous war scenes not detailed in the original fiction. One of the major scenes depicting wartime chaos—the reconstruction of the Repulse Bay Hotel—was being undertaken at the time. Ann Hui spent more than HKD 3 million to construct balcony sets within Shaw Brothers Studio and devoted a quarter of the film's duration to emphasize the realities of war and the chaotic aftermath.[23] While this decision was primarily driven by market considerations, aiming to attract audiences with visual spectacle, it cannot be denied that Ann Hui attempted to use the emphasis on war to complete the film's unified aesthetic system. In doing so, she sought to resonate and contrast with the spiritual temperament of Eileen Chang's fiction. We can find the visual model for the wartime chaos scenes in *Love in a Fallen City* within the traditional painting trope of "ruins."

"Ruins" is a frequently recurring imagery element in ancient Chinese literature and art. Wu Hung has pointed out that the Chinese concepts of *qiu* and *xu* collectively constitute the notion of ruins. In traditional painting, they often refer to the location of past structures where the main architectural form has disappeared. Therefore, ruins manifest a state of "emptiness." Chinese perception of ruins depended on the notion of erasure: frequently it was the "void" left by a destroyed timber structure that stimulated a lament for the past.[24] Ruins often refer to the "emptiness" left by vanished wooden structures, and it is precisely this "emptiness" that evokes a sense of sorrow for the past. Therefore, even though the depiction of ruins in paintings may be associated with a specific location, its purpose is not to illustrate the historical stories that happened there but to evoke a stirring emotional response from the viewer. Wu Hung further cites the tenth-century master Li Cheng's painting *Reading the Stele* (*Dubei tu*) as a typical scenario of a ruins image. In this painting, a man and his servant stand in front of a stone stele in the wilderness, gazing at its blank surface without any inscriptions. In Wu Hung's opinion, this stele does not seek to portray specific experiences or individuals but is "more likely a general situation, in which a traveller feels that he is encountering an anonymous past."[25] The visual representation of ruins in traditional painting embodies the tension between the fleeting and the eternal, the transient and the existent.

In the film, Ann Hui portrays war as the creator of modern ruins, showcasing the devastation caused by war through numerous scenes of crumbling walls and ruins. At the film's conclusion, Liusu and Fan Liuyuan are already married. Liusu, waking up from a dream, leans thoughtfully on the sleeping Fan Liuyuan. Subsequently, the film overlays her face with a panning overhead shot, revealing the ruins of the Repulse Bay Hotel during the war. The once magnificent hotel is now covered in shattered debris, with wounded soldiers scattered on the ground. As the camera moves, the original ending is superimposed on the scene:

> Hong Kong's defeat had brought Liusu victory. But in this unreasonable world, who can distinguish cause from effect? Who knows which is which? Did a great city fall so that she could be vindicated? Countless thousands of people dead, countless thousands of people suffering, after that an earth-shaking revolution.

Unlike the poetic mood created by the images of ruins in traditional paintings, these clips more realistically show the devastation caused by the war, evoking a heavier sense of trauma. Hong Kong film critic Shi Qi believes that the extensive rendering of war scenes in this film is Ann Hui's record and reenactment of the historical period when Hong Kong fell under Japanese occupation during the Pacific War.[26] Undeniably, the display of war scenes shows the importance of Hong Kong's history in Ann Hui's mind. However, the ending shot seems to point this trauma to another form of "emptiness," that is, the trauma is not the visual subject of the entire frame but yields to the inner monologue of Bai Liusu presented in written form. Therefore, the perspective of the camera can be seen as the perspective of Liusu, who transcends the narrative imagery to reflect on the past. The extensive presence of ruins in the visual narrative provides a barren backdrop, and it is precisely this authentic and vast barrenness that rationalizes Liusu leaning against Fan Liuyuan in the previous shot. The "ruins" signify a world that was once solid and stable, now shaken, and it is the collapse of this old order that makes the emergence of love possible. By establishing the visual trope of modern ruins, the film constructs a classic juxtaposition, exploring the relationship between a moment of solid meaning and infinite emptiness, continuing to echo the "desolation" theme of Eileen Chang's love stories.

In addition, one of the most significant symbols in Eileen Chang's original work, "the grey brick retaining wall," has been transformed by Ann Hui into a visual trope more closely aligned with the visual representation of ruins in traditional paintings. In the story, Bai Liusu and Fan Liuyuan stand in front of a stone wall during a conversation. In this scene of the film, the presence of the wall is also highly apparent. While Liusu and Fan Liuyuan converse, the stone wall becomes the sole backdrop of their spatial setting. Fan Liuyuan says to Liusu:

> This wall makes me think of the old sayings about the end of the world. Someday, when human civilization has been completely destroyed, when everything is burned, burst, utterly collapsed and ruined, maybe this wall will still be here. If, at that time, we can meet at this wall, then maybe, Liusu, you will honestly care about me, and I will honestly care about you.

Later, in front of the wall, he talks about his past experiences:

> When I arrived in China I was already twenty-four. I had such dreams of my homeland. You can imagine how disappointed I was. I couldn't bear the shock, and I started slipping downward.

After the outbreak of the war, Liusu and Fan Liuyuan walk together on a deserted road in the mountain surrounded by vast and barren landscapes. Their figures appear tiny in the distant shot of the continuous mountain ranges. In the fiction, Fan Liuyuan's background is quite turbulent. After his father's death, he faces challenges in legally confirming his identity, leading to a life of exile in England, where he has to go through several hardships to obtain the right of inheritance. As they progress, the camera once again pans through the withered trees and barren rocks around them. Liusu gazes at the rising wisps of smoke on the beach and says, "That wall … I don't know if it still exists." The sturdy stone wall has vanished without a trace, only appearing in the characters' dialogue. The disappearing stone wall, along with the hills and ridges, jointly forms a symbol of "emptiness" in the mode of ruins paintings. Both their lives and identities become precarious within this visual mode. This also aligns with Eileen Chang's perception of the zeitgeist:

> Our whole era is being pushed onward, is breaking apart already, with greater destruction still coming. Our entire civilization—with all its magnificence, and its insignificance—will someday belong to the past. If the word I use most often is "desolate," it's because I feel, in the back of my mind, this staggering threat.[27]

What emerges from Eileen Chang's doubts about the future of civilization is a nightmare similar to that of the Ruined World. This also resonates with Ann Hui's own attitude toward history and the present. In her autobiographical documentary, *As Time Goes By*, Ann Hui explores her reflections on traditional Chinese and colonial cultures:

> You feel sorry for not recognizing things about your homeland. But if you don't quickly learn about the culture of this colony, you won't keep up with the times, and you won't survive in this society. … So if I say I have a feeling, a kind of unspoken nostalgia for this colonial life, it may not be right, but you can't be without this feeling.

Due to the release of *Love in a Fallen City* on the eve of the signing of the Sino-British Joint Declaration, He Xingfeng considers Ann Hui's "imagined retrospection" of colonial Hong Kong.[28] However, if we consider that Ann Hui poured a significant amount of attention into Hong Kong and nostalgia for colonial history in this film, then the visual trope of ruins in the film directs this attention to a more profound insight: skepticism and criticism of the view of civilization's progress. The vibrant colonial Hong Kong portrayed in the film and the civilization envisioned by Fan Liuyuan as the "real China" have both been lost. What remains are the ruins brought about by war, and the passage of time is visualized as a sensory experience within space. The sense of desolation serves as both a retrospective reflection on the irretrievable colonial history of Hong Kong and a rupture of temporal constraints. The perpetual existence of ruins makes the feeling of desolation belong not only to this era but to all eras. Therefore, the ruins in the film transform the passage of time into a spatial sensory experience, providing a visual metaphor for the perception of people's lives: civilization begins from a wasteland only to return to it. The film's solution is affirmed in the departing silhouette of Liusu and Fan Liuyuan: grasping for the most basic things in the ruins of civilization to confirm their existence. Grounded in this present moment, love and self-affirmation paradoxically come to fruition in the apocalypse. In *Love in a Fallen City*, ruins become a crucial medium, allowing individuals to understand the inexplicable world before them in the collapsing civilization. It serves as a means for confirming one's subjective identity and mode of existence, something otherwise unattainable.

Conclusion

Through the incorporation of traditional paintings of women, narrative scrolls, and images of ruins, *Love in a Fallen City* continues Ann Hui's focus on the female subject, establishing interwoven relationships between multiple characters and spaces, while also reflecting on the history and civilization of Hong Kong. The translation from still images to moving images not only infuses these visual tropes with meaning within the cinematic context but also triggers further expansion and interpretation of the cinematic meaning of these images. This translational process not only visualizes crucial plot points from the source material but also mirrors the spiritual characteristics and aesthetic principles of Eileen Chang's fiction. Therefore, the adaptation of *Love in a Fallen City* incorporates diverse aesthetic systems from literature, film, and painting. This interactive convergence allows Ann Hui to subtly integrate her artistic expression, showcasing a multifaceted and nuanced presentation. Through the integration and collision of various elements, the film adaptation has sparked a more intricate and enriched aesthetic experience that visual imagery can offer to the audience.

3

Beyond failed adaptation

A postcolonial contextual rereading of Ann Hui's film adaptations of Eileen Chang's fiction

Gabriel F. Y. Tsang

Eileen Chang (1920–95) started out as a popular fiction writer in 1943 with well-received short stories and novellas, such as "The Golden Cangue" ("Jin Suo Ji"), which earned critical recognition from Fu Lei.[1] A few years after failing to please her Shanghainese audience in 1947 with the film *Long Live the Missus!* (*Tai Tai Wan Sui!*), for which she was the scriptwriter, Chang moved to Hong Kong and then the United States, where she stayed until her death.[2] Over her career Chang became increasingly obsessed by the Sinophone world and was acknowledged in C. T. Hsia's *A History of Modern Chinese Fiction* (1961),[3] in which she is credited as a literary figure in the same vein as Lu Xun, Mao Dun, Lao She, Shen Congwen, Qian Zhongshu, and others. With Chang's diasporic experiences across the East, within a Westernized colony, and in the West, her transmedia writing from fiction to script, and her reception as an icon of both serious literature and popular literature, this modern legend, as David Der-wei Wang argues, has driven "an impulse of imitation," composed of "repetition," "involution," and "derivation,"[4] influencing not only those Wang mentions, such as Wang Anyi (mainland China), Chu Tien-wen (Taiwan), and Sharon Chung (Hong Kong), but others as well. Moreover, Chang's charismatic narratology holds the commercial and artistic potential to be visualized, thus attracting film directors to adapt her works. Starting with Ann Hui's first attempt in 1984 with *Love in a Fallen City*, Fred Tan Hon-Cheung, Stanley Kwan, and Ang Lee also went on to complete *Rouge of the North* (1988), *Red Rose White Rose* (1994), and *Lust, Caution* (2007), respectively.

As the most significant adapter of Chang's work, Ann Hui directed three films, *Love in a Fallen City* (1984), *Eighteen Springs* (1997), and *Love After Love* (2020), and one drama, *The Golden Cangue* (2009). Over more than three decades, Ann Hui apparently bears a cumulative "anxiety of influence," which is not as Harold Bloom classically defined as a compulsion of resisting and avoiding other writers'/competitors' influences,[5] but an ambiguous ambivalence of literally reformatting and creatively reinterpreting Eileen Chang's original texts. The challenge is that the mainstream audience and critics, usually fans of Chang, persistently adopted "normative and source-oriented approaches," in the sense Linda Hutcheon borrowed from Theo Hermans to confirm the impossibility of absolute transmediation,[6] to evaluate the achievement of Hui's adaptations. For instance, the celebrated mainland Chinese film critic Mei Xuefeng's assertion that Hui's genuine character determined her inadequacy in capturing Chang's story apparently supports the generally negative responses based on the author's central position by proposing the necessity of self-modification for optimally recovering the adapted writing.[7]

Problematically, this kind of binary-opposite view that simplistically judges the closeness between transformed texts and source texts not only implicitly impacts on the director's intention but also largely overshadows her independent voice and creativity. Therefore, the following will basically adopt Robert Stam's "intertextual dialogism," regarding adaptation as an interchangeable dialogic/transformative act, rather than an imitative form toward fidelity.[8] Without methodologically displacing "adaptation" with "appropriation," which signifies radical reworking according to Julie Sanders' identification,[9] it interprets Ann Hui's Eileen Chang films as palimpsestic, that is, as layering new meanings onto existing text as Deborah Cartmell and Imelda Whelehan discuss.[10] By neglecting Eileen Chang's sublime aura, a chief focus will be on the represented chronotopes of the three filmic adaptations that reveal how Ann Hui visually, audially, and textually retrieved the fictional worlds set in the 1930s and 1940s and, meanwhile, made deletions, additions, and revisions to contain her (post)colonial thoughts and compromises, such as those related to Hong Kong, the United Kingdom, and mainland China. The main concern here is the concrete background that directs her, because many scholars have profoundly conceptualized the (post)coloniality and Hongkongness of her cinema. For instance, Audrey Yue interprets Hui's use of "postcolonial feminist autobiography" as subverting the "allegory of Hong Kong's utopic homecoming with an alternative narrative of re-turn";[11] Bidisha Banerjee reflects the othered self and the return of the repressed through illuminating the postcolonial identity configured by Hui;[12] and Gina Marchetti highlighted the sexist and paternalistic nature of colonial Hong Kong that is targeted by Hui's post-handover production.[13] Rereading her film adaptations from 1984 to 2020 of a diasporic figure's fiction helps uncover the director's shifting identity, belonging, and filmic strategies beyond Eileen Chang's geographical movement.

Colonial attachment of an imagined war: *Love in a Fallen City*

There are three typically reiterated contexts about Ann Hui's early directorship: (1) the emergence of the Hong Kong New Wave (pushing new directors to "assert their individuality by seeking out new themes, new narrative methods, and a new mise-en-scène"),[14] in which she contributed her first feature film *The Secret* in 1979; (2) the exile of Vietnamese refugees that initiated her direction of political films, such as the Vietnam trilogy, including *Boat People* (1982), screened at the 1983 Cannes Film Festival and winning Best Film and Best Director at the second Hong Kong Film Awards; and (3) the negotiations on the issue of Hong Kong sovereignty that led to the signing of the Sino-British Joint Declaration in 1984 confirming the handover of Hong Kong to China in 1997. Although the third context is not directly represented in Hui's films, many scholars have provided filmic evidence to make the connection between them. In this regard, *Love in a Fallen City* is very controversial, as it was screened in 1984. Against the backdrop of the Japanese invasion of Hong Kong (the fallen city) in 1941, a Westernized bachelor (Fan Liuyuan) changes his mind and decides to marry a divorced Shanghainese woman (Bai Liusu), with whom he would flirt and financially provide for, and the film's narrative hints at a sense of interpersonal and international (British–Chinese) reconciliation. However, there are two points deserving much attention. First, it does not seem to have been Ann Hui's intent to create a national/urban allegory based on Eileen Chang's story of minor history. In an interview with Kwong Po Wei, which was systematically and chronologically included in the monograph *Ann Hui on Ann Hui*, Hui gave a simple reason for making the film without mentioning any political consideration:

> The main reason for shooting *Love in a Fallen City* is because I like Eileen Chang. Over a decade ago, I read Eileen Chang's fiction for the first time. I remember I read the novellas like "Love in a Fallen City" and felt surprised about how this author could write down the Hong Kong that I know. When I was young, the Chinese people and the Westerners lived together. There are many foreigners, including Indian, but the Hong Kong fiction I read never mentioned them. Moreover, her writing is brilliant and sentimental. When she talks about people,

> she does not directly talk about them but does so through a discriminative perspective instead. I was deeply impressed.[15]

In addition, she added that the problems with shooting *Song of the Exile* motivated her to take the fiction she was already acquainted with as the theme.[16] Second, although Hui might still consciously or unconsciously use Chang's Hong Kong story of the 1940s to tell her Hong Kong story of the 1980s, the Sino-British Joint Declaration would not be included in her adaptation as it was drafted on September 26, 1984, and finally signed on December 19, 1984, whereas *Love in a Fallen City* was released on August 2, 1984. Therefore, if political interpretation is possible, it needs to be built upon earlier specific details. However, when Yiu-Wai Chu connected the historical and contemporary contexts and regarded the release as "not just timely but also pointedly metaphoric," one has to notice that the "exile" motif (concerning both the falling and fallen cities) presented throughout Hui's filmic genealogy, including also *Starry Is the Night* (1988), *Ordinary Heroes* (1999), *The Golden Era* (2014), and *Our Time Will Come* (2017),[17] goes beyond a particular political event and maintains a memorial and prophetic transfiguration.

As Ka-Fai Yau's journal article has articulated, some core issues of the film *Love in a Fallen City* include Ann Hui's use of the past to "visualize the contemporary political crisis"; the discordance between the actions of Hui's characters against subordination to the political; Eileen Chang's *cenci* aesthetic (that is, an "uneven, mismatched contraposition" that magnifies the quotidian aspect of mediocre people); and the shift in orientating the space from Shanghai to Hong Kong.[18] In what follows, the focus will be on the representation of war in this adaptation.

Published in Shanghai in 1943 during the Sino-Japanese War, Eileen Chang's version of "Love in a Fallen City" records the Japanese invasion and occupation of Hong Kong in 1941 in a narrative style even more minor than in her ahistorical sardonic prose like "From the Ash" ("Jin Yu Lu", 1944), which recounts her wartime memories. War in Hong Kong, for Eileen Chang, is the "other" of the war in Shanghai (where the "Isolated Period" finally ended in 1943) to please Shanghainese readers, as she expressed that she "always thought about Shanghainese," "utilized a Shanghainese perspective to view Hong Kong," and "loves Shanghainese and hopes Shanghainese love my books."[19] It is also an emptied vehicle, with only escape, simplified marriage, and material shortage related to the war to serve as the plotline toward an ironic happy ending: a philanderer getting married to a traditional woman and starting to flirt with other women instead.[20] (The latter was omitted by the adaptor.) On the contrary, for Ann Hui, war in Hong Kong is an unexperienced subject to retrieve. It is temporally, not geographically, distanced. To recover it, her adaptation strategy is mainly set on duplicating the original setting, dialogues, and interactions. Very precisely, the bombing that marks the outbreak of the war takes place approximately fourth-fifths of the way through the film (at around 71 minutes out of 93 minutes),[21] as in the novella (on page 38 out of a total of 47 pages).[22] However, unlike the novella, which merely mentions the warfare and British soldiers,[23] Ann Hui fills the backdrop of the Hong Kong war with the noise of bombs, bullets, alarms, and aircraft and keeps a British troop onscreen. The noise and fighting scenes that boost the dramatic tension can be interpreted simply as a necessary adjustment to fulfill the expectations of the recipients of the four-dimensional media; however, the consistent display of the colonizer alongside the images of protector, hero, and victim (corpses) seems to imply the auteur's view on contemporary Hong Kong beyond Eileen Chang's text. In fact, during the Sino-British negotiations, there was an important war that probably made an impression on Ann Hui and many Hongkongers: the Falklands War in 1982. As a distant island invaded and occupied by Argentina but finally returned to the United Kingdom, the Falklands were more similar to Hui's Hong Kong than the Hong Kong of forty years prior. The military success of the United Kingdom after seventy-four days seemed to announce the still overwhelming power of the colonizer despite the bloom of post-Second World War decolonization movements. Through the panoramic broadcasting of news and reviews, intellectuals, like the majority, expressed their hope of maintaining the status quo rather than accepting the rule of a post-Cultural Revolution regime. (As a survey conducted by the Reform Club in April 1982 reveals, 93 percent of respondents preferred a British administration after 1997, and a poll later undertaken by the *South China Morning Post* shows a similar result.)[24] Thus, what is significant here concerning the filmic representation of a local war is not simply the auteur's obsession with Hong Kong, Cantonese speaking, and the nostalgic past, in which worries of uncertainty give way to romance, but an ambiguous belonging to and trust in an imperial power that could guarantee political stability and financial prosperity, despite the loss of the Battle of Hong Kong. Before the discussion of identity politics prevailed, Hong Kong elites, perhaps also like those of Gibraltar, where reopening the border with Spain coincidentally happened in 1982, were struggling to safeguard their binary-opposite view. For Ann Hui, who obtained a master's in English and comparative literature from the University of Hong Kong and then graduated from the London Film School, "translating" and "reinscribing" the "social imaginary of both metropolis and modernity" is demonstrated via creating a backward, chaotic, dirty, and crowded cityscape of Chinese locals/refugees in contrast to the well-adorned Repulse Bay Hotel, with an elegant white gentleman playing the piano to calm down others during the war. Without mixing it with "contra-modernity" as Homi Bhabha suggests in relation to postcolonial cultural hybridity,[25] Hui removed Eileen Chang's skepticism about the Westernized male protagonist (perhaps adapted from the image of Clarke Gable in *Gone with the Wind* [1939]) and authorized him to act as the sole savior of a spotlighted Chinese traditional woman at risk as she is without the protection of marital belonging. If one further speculatively interprets the Japanese invaders as future rulers of Hong Kong, their near absence in the film, with only two scenes with junior soldiers clearly seen for few seconds, can be regarded as disempowerment of the PRC government and their Hong Kong lobbyists, such as the tycoons Li Ka-shing, Gordon Wu, Henry Fok, Lee Shau-Kee, and others. The potential collaboration between a suspicious sovereign state and local capitalist powers might form a political belonging that the director ambiguously resisted.

Hongkongless sorrow of the original: *Eighteen Springs*

Asserting that *Eighteen Springs*, as a film screened two months after the handover of sovereignty and one and a half years before *Ordinary Heroes* (1999), is apolitical does not seem compelling. Completed thirteen years after *Love in a Fallen City*, which is close to the narrated time span (fourteen years) of both the original novel and the film, this adaptation usually reminds the audience of the regret, loss, solitude, melancholy, depression, and anxiety that Hong Kong citizens experienced from 1984 to 1997. Surrounding the love, estrangement, and intricacies between Gu Manzhen and Shen Shijun, this poignant story reaches a climax when Gu's sister drives her husband to rape Gu out of jealousy and then deceives Shen by claiming that she has wed another man. The enduring misunderstanding and suffering, as the key device to generate dramatic tension, thus becomes an ideal metaphor to capture the ambivalence of pre-handover locals. Moreover, there are two contexts worth noticing. First, gender is usually deemed allegorical. According to Kim-Soon Sen, when the female protagonist of *Eighteen Springs* said "We cannot return" onscreen, Ann Hui was "reproducing female symbols" with nostalgia and hopelessness against history to "mention the anxiety caused by the loss of identity and subjectivity."[26] Adding that examples like a female ghost's search for her lover in *Rouge* (1987) and the failed satisfaction of homosexual eros in *Happy Together* (1997) might have prominently revealed local directors' collective search for the appropriate means of personalization to signify Sino-British-Hong Kong relations,[27] the tragic end of *Eighteen Springs* (with all characters speaking Mandarin, especially the main actors Leon Lai born in Beijing and then moving to Hong Kong at four due to the Cultural Revolution, and Jacklyn Wu growing up in Taiwan) might prophesize a dystopic Mainlandized Hong Kong.

Second, and trickier, is that Ann Hui took "Eighteen Springs" as the English name for the adaptation, instead of "Half a Lifelong Romance" ("Bansheng Yuan"), the title of Eileen Chang's later version. As *Eighteen Springs* was first published in a Shanghai newspaper *Yi Pao* in 1948,[28] while the Chinese Community Party was triumphing over the Kuomintang, Eileen Chang, under the pen name Liang Jing, sensitively injected some leftist accents into her story. In her later version, *Springs* to *Half a Lifelong Romance*, written after her departure to the United States, she not only reduced the story's duration from eighteen years to fourteen years (ending the narrative in 1944 instead of 1948) but also changed some details politically appreciated in the communist context: Xu Shuhui finally studies abroad in the United States instead of going to Yan'an (the communist headquarters), and the story ends with the two protagonists' reunion, deleting their participation in revolutionary affairs in Northeast China. As a fan of Chang, Ann Hui may well have been aware of these changes and hence utilized a bilingual twist to encode ideology-oriented vicissitudes, in the manner Hong Kong would encounter after 1997. However, overinterpretation here is also possible, because the film mainly accords with the Crown Publishing version of *Half a Lifelong Romance*, without reference to *Eighteen Springs*.

Again, as revealed in interview records, Ann Hui did not express any political intentions concerning *Eighteen Springs*. She mainly just talked about technical issues, such as plot, characters, dialogues, themes, structure, scriptwriting, art direction, sound recording, budget, and market positioning.[29] In relation to her view of Wong Bik-wan's version of the script for *Ordinary Heroes* as "too political," "full of slogans," "advocating democracy," and "propaganda-like," to which she objected,[30] Ann Hui reveals her preference for representing the reality of Eileen Chang's fiction as it is. She not only adjusted it for sense, such as blurring the good/bad polarity in the villain Zhu Hongcai to create a more realistic and less melodramatic effect,[31] but also attempted to decontextualize the story as did Eileen Chang. As she mentioned in another interview, "The other issue we had to consider was how much historical background should be put into the film. Do we need to paste up posters to note that it is a war period? Do we need bombing sound? I don't think it was needed."[32] To adapt *Half a Lifelong Romance*, Ann Hui apparently kept in mind different kinds of spatial representations. As Grace Mak reminds us, for fiction, space is invisible and only through narrative can the imagination of space be aroused, and for film, space is concrete and only through variation of visual space can the impression of time be constructed.[33] As Eileen Chang's *Half a Lifelong Romance* was changed to culminate in 1944, its ahistorical narrative that cut off readers' imagination of occupied Shanghai and Nanjing can be re-historicized by cinematically ordering the necessarily required visual settings. Nevertheless, Hui did not aim to recover the history obscured by Eileen Chang but tended to place more emphasis on striking a balance between aesthetic innovation and audience reception on top of imitating the original work, such as using monologues to deliver the two protagonists' streams of consciousness (an iconic technique of Wong Kar-wai) and poeticizing the rape scene by using the images of caged birds and spiral staircases. Unlike the way in which the British soldiers are highlighted in *Love in a Fallen City*, the film *Eighteen Springs* has no historical identifiers, except for the years, the characters' dress, and the architecture. If Hui adapted *The Rice-Sprout Song* or *Naked Earth*, two anti-communist English novels Chang wrote in the 1950s to cater to American tastes, according to her faithfulness, a more historical and critical space would be constituted. However, checking the details of production, one would discover that she was not judgmental about mainland Chinese history at the moment of production, as she cooperated with Tianshan Film Studio, shot in mainland China, excluded Cantonese speaking, and targeted the Chinese market. This echoes with He Guimei's overview of Hui's cinematic productions as "including 'Chineseness' in her 'Hongkongese narratives'" with a kind of "present absence" (i.e., replacing Chinese history with obscure Chinese spectacle).[34] That means "Chineseness" and "British Hongkongness" are not mutually exclusive in a discourse produced in the colonial context. In other words, the dichotomy of being British Hongkongese and Chinese Hongkongese is not applicable to a chronological understanding of filmic representation, because colonialism could never unify the cultural and self-recognized identity of individuals and variation could turn severe around the transfer of sovereignty. If the previous observation about *Love in a Fallen City* is combined with this, one would notice that, in spite of the potential possibility of political interpretation, Ann Hui, born in Anshan in mainland China and having received a Western education, was either changing her sense of belonging or holding a cosmopolitan view. Overall, the latter appears more plausible as she was dedicated to recording and uncovering the multifaceted reality through drama, reaching a peak with the documentary-like film *The Way We Are* (2008). Places are in any case an obsession in her narrative or re-presentation.

Superficial retrieval of the past/ultimate postcoloniality: *Love After Love*

In 2020, twenty-three years after *Eighteen Springs*, Ann Hui once again adapted Eileen Chang's fiction because a young female director she supervised could not fulfill investors' expectations.[35] Entitled *Love After Love* in English with the same Chinese name as the original, it is a story of an innocent girl indulging in a romantic and erotic relationship with a Portuguese-Chinese playboy and turning into a social butterfly at her aunt's design in order to support his lifestyle. After the screening of this adaptation, and against the backdrop of the Hong Kong Anti-Extradition Movement, Ann Hui similarly presented an apolitical perspective in an interview. Questioned by a foreign scholar, she confirmed the universal value of Eileen Chang's story and prioritized the issues of production, such as "giv[ing] up the multi-language tier of the story" mainly for "distribution purpose."[36] Basically, this film seems to minimize potential references to local political events with a focus on targeting the Chinese market through carefully selecting participants and following a cinematic logic different from that of Hong Kong. First, the director built an international cohort with Ryuichi Sakamoto (the world-renowned Japanese composer), Christopher Doyle (the Australian-Hong Kong award-winning cinematographer), Eddie Pang (the Taiwanese actor who reduces the national hybridity of the film with his purely Chinese appearance), two Hong Kong-based hybrid actors (Isabella Leong and Paul Chun Pui not well-known for their mixed identity),[37] and so on. Among this, mainland Chinese, such as most of the Chinese actors (including the female protagonist Ma Sichun), the scriptwriter (Wang Anyi), the poster designer (Huang Hai), and main production companies (Alibaba Pictures and Hehe Pictures), not Hongkongers, were the majority. Partnering with Eileen Chang's successor for the second time after *The Golden Cangue*,[38] Ann Hui admitted that the additional material of the film is "all Wang Anyi's creations."[39] By trusting in Wang's interpretation of the original story, Hui paid more attention to coordinating between various apolitical sectors toward a level that she could confidently regard as "at least decent" in spite of wide criticism.[40] Hence, the *mise-en-scène* of *Love After Love* is, subjectively speaking, nearly perfect, and commensurate with the caliber of a recipient of a Golden Lion for lifetime achievement. The main reason is that, under the talented direction of Ryuichi Sakamoto and Christopher Doyle, the soundtrack is full of magical twists and turns, revealing relevant scenic spirits and personal emotions, and the shots are not only neat and accurate, with clear hints of connotations, but also intriguingly hazy and colorful. In the scene of a church meeting, the upper-class people of different races and languages, who gather with their flamboyant dress, rhythmic dancing, and lyrical singing, are tremendously eye-catching. This kind of setting sometimes successfully shifts the audience's focus from the content to the representation, obscuring the flaws of overly dramatic acting (such as the actress Faye Yu, a graduate of the Beijing Film Academy who tended to adopt an expressionist style to play the role of Miss Liang in the film) and the mechanically designed narrative, discussed in the next paragraph.

Regardless of the issue of sticking to the original work (such as the common criticism about Eddie Pang being too strong and Chinese-looking), those flaws also appear to have led to the film's box-office failure (only RMB 64 million). A hidden context that resulted in the asymmetry of audiovisual and narrative levels is probably an urge of Hollywoodization-Mainlandization. With reference to what Michael Curtin warns, "national governments are not necessarily the best antidote to globalization, since they too are characterized by unequal structures of power that advance the interests of elites through the fabrication of supposedly indigenous values and cultural artifacts."[41] However, as the Chinese government and film practitioners were copying the globally effective model of the Hollywood film industry, which both determines consumers' preferences and consolidates the imperial spread of American culture, Hong Kong directors who intended to enter the Chinese market increasingly followed the mainstream formulation. Even though a director could resist the temptation of making a main melody film to become a Billion-RMB Film Club member (like Chen Kaige, Tsui Hark, and Dante Lam co-directing *The Battle of Lake Changjin* [2021], commissioned by the Central Propaganda Department, to break the Chinese box-office record of all time), the demands of Chinese investors must still be met. In Ann Hui's case, Stephen Chu recounts in *Main Melody Films: Hong Kong Directors in Mainland China*:

> She accumulated considerable experience in filmmaking in mainland China through her works *The Romance of Book and Sword*, *My American Grandson* (1991) and *Eighteen Springs* (1997). After her first film fully financed by a

> mainland Chinese company, *Jade Goddess of Mercy* (2003), she made *The Postmodern Life of My Aunt* and *The Golden Era*, which primarily targeted the mainland market.[42]

Faced with the conflict between pleasing mainland Chinese audience and delivering a Hong Kong story with allegorical risks, Ann Hui was wise enough to outsource the scriptwriting to Wang Anyi, an elite literary figure whose interests have been advanced by the "unequal structures of power" due to her grasp of "supposedly indigenous values and cultural artifacts." In response to the mainland Chinese public's favors and ideological restrictions, Wang had two strategies. First, she melodramatized the adaptation. As a method ironically opposed by Ann Hui in her making of *Eighteen Springs*, the melodramatization is mainly composed of repeating some common formulas of Chinese black romance: playing hard to get, perpetually suspecting and utilizing others, binding each other with their relationship, feigning innocence to fish for old rich men, repaying disgusting behaviors with disgusting behaviors, and so on. Second, Wang portrays the colonial culture as depraved. Perhaps this does not need any sensitivity to the ant-imperialist and anti-capitalist ideology, because the tragic indulgence delivered by the original text can simply be followed to act as a rejection. But as her novel *The Song of Everlasting Sorrow* (1995), written in the late Deng Xiaoping era with relatively more freedom of speech, took the history between the late 1940s and the 1980s as the background to accumulate the sorrow of the protagonist, Wang Anyi likely chose to cautiously make safe modifications and omit censorable details.

For an audience who is overly acquainted with the melodramatic formulas and restricted representation of history, conceding realist expression to narrative tension might hardly earn appreciation. However, this might become a norm of Hong Kong–China co-production, because Hong Kong, no longer "being the neoliberal exception of China" that Gary Tang and Raymond Hau-yin Yuen assert in 2016,[43] is in the process of internally homogenizing themes and expressions. Although the efforts of Ann Hui and Wang Anyi are unsuccessful, their approach is as Milan Kundera famously stresses in *The Unbearable Lightness of Being*: "*Es muss sein*!" ("It must be!"). If not, *Love After Love* would be either absent or marginalized in the vast mainland, like the current condition of *The Rice-Sprout Song* or *Naked Earth*. From *Love in a Fallen City* to *Love After Love*, Ann Hui crossed from a colonial stage to a post-colonial one. "Post-colonial" is different from "postcolonial" because it does not retain colonial histories and images with nostalgic sensitivity but de-colonially reinterprets the remnants in a new ideological paradigm. In her filmic representation, Hong Kong is becoming Britishless, more blurred than hybrid. The shifting and disappearing representation of colonialism corresponds to Ann Hui's cultural diaspora: studying Western filmology, developing a sense of locality, and then seeking collaboration with mainland China. This somehow reversely matches Eileen Chang's trajectory from basing her work in Shanghai to searching for English readers' acceptance after moving to the United States.

Part Two

Storytelling: Media forms and social change

4

Rescuing humanity

Hong Kong television theory and postrevolutionary intervention in Ann Hui's *The Boy from Vietnam*

Raymond Tsang

The year 1978 marked a pivotal moment in Chinese history. In China, a series of debates unfolded surrounding then-Chairman Hua Guofeng's "Two Whatevers" policy and Deng Xiaoping's vision of "reform and opening up." Ultimately, Deng endorsed the principle that "practice is the sole criterion for testing truth," reshaping the ideological foundation of the Chinese Communist Party. In December of the same year, reformists led by Deng replaced Hua and announced the open-door policy during the third plenary session of the 11th Central Committee of the Chinese Communist Party. This periodization signaled a shift in postrevolutionary national policy, the global rise of neoliberalism, and the emergence of a post-socialist geopolitical condition.

The year also marked a turning point in film and media. In China, a fifth generation of Chinese film directors, including Zhang Yimou, Chen Kaige, and Zhang Junchao, began their studies at the Beijing Film Academy. In Taiwan, Mingji, known as the father of the Taiwanese New Wave, implemented policy changes to enhance publicity and foster international co-productions. Meanwhile, in Hong Kong, the term "New Wave" was coined by the film magazine *Close-Up* to describe a group of young filmmakers transitioning from television to the film industry. This group included Patrick Tam, Tsui Hark, Ann Hui, and Cheuk Pak-tong, many of whom were eager to experiment with new cinematic forms and storytelling techniques.

Such periodization is often viewed as a rupture—an eventful break from previous generations—implying a teleological progression of cinema as a medium superior to other forms of media. Scholars like Hector Rodriguez have not focused on the significance of local television stations in analyzing the cultural fields of the emerging Hong Kong's New Wave.[1] Rather than focusing solely on film, the break can be traced to television as a distinct medium. Practices developed within television stations reveal a transmedia intervention that shaped and echoed the New Wave and the historical conjunctures.

The year 1978 was also a significant one for Hong Kong television. Cultural critic Chengyu described this period as one where the most exciting developments happened behind the scenes rather than onscreen.[2] He referred to the intense ratings wars among the three television companies and the final collapse of Commercial Television (CTV, 1975–8), the third free-to-air broadcast television station in Hong Kong, alongside Television Broadcasts Limited (TVB) and Rediffusion Television (RTV). CTV had invested HKD 1.5 million in publicity, revised its programming policies, and recruited key talent from TVB. In preceding years, the three stations had produced a variety of popular long drama series, such as *Hotel* (1976) and *A House Is Not a Home* (1977) from TVB, *Crocodile Tears* (1978) and *Chameleon* (1978) from RTV,[3] and martial arts dramas like *The Legend of the Condor Heroes* (1976) and *The Gold Dagger Romance* (1978) from CTV and *The Legend of the Book and the Sword* (1976) from TVB. The bankruptcy of CTV, however, was not solely due to a lack of financial support and inadequate facilities. It also stemmed from the negligence of the colonial government and internal conflicts of interest among the station's board members. The collapse of CTV became a major social issue, highlighting the failures of colonial power and broken capitalist promises.

That same year also saw a surge in academic and critical engagement with television. Critics published articles analyzing long drama series, television's social roles, soap operas, and the ideological implications of the medium. Drawing on cultural Marxism, semiotics, and apparatus theory, they launched a wave of cultural criticism, marking 1978 as a landmark year for the development of television theory. Notably, Ann Hui joined Radio Television Hong Kong (RTHK) and contributed three episodes to the *Under the Lion Rock* series that year.

When Ann Hui returned to Hong Kong from London in 1975, she worked as a production assistant, scriptwriter, and director on documentaries and short dramas, including *Wonderful*, four episodes of *C.i.D.*, two episodes of *Social Worker*, and one episode of the *Dragon, Tiger, Panther* series. In 1977, she directed six episodes for the series *Independent Commission Against Corruption*, two of which were banned, before joining RTHK. Hui's early directorial efforts garnered critical attention. Some critics scrutinized the ideological foundations of her work, arguing that "whether reflecting subjective reality or objective reality, they could not avoid following ideology."[4] While the *Under the Lion Rock* series gained popularity for its focus on marginalized communities, critics noted that its perspective often failed to engage with the deeper essence of society. On the other hand, cultural critics like Shu Kei contextualized Hui's television work in relation to her later films, such as *The Story of Woo Viet* (1981) and *Boat People* (1982). Shu Kei praised these works for their critique of "not only a particular government but all forms of totalitarian persecution and corrupt political powers." He also noted the pressures Hui faced while working within bureaucratic institutions, where censorship shaped her television output.[5]

Although Hui often claimed she knew little about politics when creating her Vietnam trilogy—*The Boy from Vietnam*, *The Story of Woo Viet*, and *Boat People*—she emphasized her focus on humanity:

> It is absolutely about humanity, because I know nothing about politics … I've listened to classmates talk about politics all night long, and I still don't grasp much of what they say. I'm not sure if the things they discuss apply to everyday issues like eating, farming, or earning a living. There's a disconnect between their debates and the realities of ordinary life. It's outrageous. I can't see the connection … My focus is on the people who eat and farm, and how they perceive change.[6]

What concerns me about Ann Hui's works is not their politically rebellious or resistant nature, nor the ways her characters fight against government oppression. Instead, I focus on the "missing connection" her works attempt to manifest—the link between the political and the everyday. Much of the critical discourse surrounding her works emphasizes the plight of individuals caught in historical conjunctures, or, as Victor Fan argues, her "doubly—socio-politically and gendered—extraterritorialized position."[7] In particular, many have praised her blending of documentary techniques with a humanist focus on refugees, local villagers, and ordinary people.

This humanism, however, has not gone unchallenged in realist films or documentaries. Structural Marxist theories, such as Louis Althusser's concept of ideological state apparatuses, provided Hong Kong critics with tools to critique the abstractness of humanity and the ideological imprints within Hui's works. I suggest that Hui's intervention does not lie in glorifying oppressed characters but rather in shifting attention from character development to the significance of location. My concern is to shift the focus from characters' position to the everyday location and materiality that condition such positions. While her works may appear apolitical, I argue that her intervention resides in distancing herself from an anti-humanist approach and instead rescuing humanism by highlighting and mediating the everyday material conditions of immigrants' lives. In the postrevolutionary period, realism faced challenges as ready-made heroes, logical narratives, and simplistic solutions proved inadequate to address the transnational plight of humanity. The issue may not be whether Hui's works directly critique the ideology of the colonial government. Instead, the central question is: What kind of humanity did Hui articulate in this postrevolutionary period? How did she respond—or fail to respond—to local critics' ideological critiques of television?

My aim is to demonstrate how Hui's television works respond to the fragmented history of this era and rescue humanism within mainstream media by foregrounding power-laden locations. Her vision of humanity does not glorify humanist heroes in war, but it provides "missing connections" by making invisible locations and homelands visible. In the following sections, I will focus on *The Boy from Vietnam*, the first installment of Hui's Vietnam trilogy. For this work, Hui and her team interviewed more than a hundred Vietnamese refugees and consulted numerous files and books in Hong Kong. In her work, location transcends the role of a mere backdrop and becomes a protagonist—antagonizing, confronting, and arresting characters as mediating nodes. Given the censorship constraints of television, Hui was unable to engage in overt class struggle analysis. However, the immediacy of television allowed her to explore the missing connections between Hong Kong, Vietnam, and the United States; between everyday life and transnational politics; between characters and location; and between media and society. While Victor Fan argues that these transnational communities exercise their respective authorities over the characters as bare life, I begin by historicizing this condition and asking broader questions: How and why did realism and documentary techniques become prevalent in Hong Kong television in the late 1970s? And how was television used to represent "bare life"? What is "Hong Kong television theory," and how might it help us better understand Hui's works? After addressing the specificity of the television medium in Hong Kong during that period, I will examine how location functions in *The Boy from Vietnam* and what it means to rescue humanism through the mediation of everyday materiality.

Hong Kong television and realism

Hong Kong television does not entirely fit Jim Collins' concept of television and postmodernism. Collins contends that the relationship between television and postmodernism is inevitable, impossible, and necessary.[8] Instead, Hong Kong television was characterized by strong modernist and realist concerns. Its development was deeply intertwined with colonial power structures and the interests of transnational capitalists. Film critics such as Law Kar have aptly noted that in the 1970s, Hong Kong films drew significant inspiration from local television shows and lost their social critique function, often transferring this role to television.[9] A brief historical analysis reveals the distinctive forms of realism and modernism that Hong Kong television developed.

Radio Rediffusion transitioned into a subscription-based cable television station in 1957, becoming not only the first television station in Hong Kong but also the first Chinese television station in Sinophone communities. Initially, it primarily imported dramas, documentaries, and newsreels from Britain, many of which were in English and targeted at a middle-class audience. Following the suppression of the 1967 leftist riots, the colonial government tightened control over broadcasting and communications. It centralized radio and television stations in the Broadcast Drive, near a British Army facility, Osborn Barracks. In the same year, Television Broadcasts Limited (TVB), the first free-to-air station, was established, becoming a major competitor to Radio Rediffusion. Rediffusion was renamed as Rediffusion Television Limited and became the second free-to-air television station in 1973, coinciding with TVB's introduction of color television programming. Both TVB and Rediffusion imported shows from Britain and Japan while producing localized adaptations and variety programs, such as *Enjoy Yourself Tonight*, modeled after the Australian show *In Melbourne Tonight*. A range of music and comedy programs also emerged, including *Star Show* by Leung Po-chi and the *Hui's Brothers Show* by Michael Hui. In 1975, Commercial Television (CTV) was founded, sparking intense ratings wars among the three stations, as described in the "Introduction." Before 1967, only 10 percent of households owned television sets. By the late 1970s, however, this figure had risen to 95 percent, with broadcasting hours extending to sixty hours per day.[10] Long drama series became an integral part of everyday life and ratings wars. Television not only reshaped consumption patterns but also influenced media production processes. Stations responded to audience feedback, often altering tragic endings to align with viewer expectations.[11] To better cater to local demands, the three stations implemented a script examination system. Scriptwriters, along with their supervisors, collaborated on script development, program design, and the analysis of foreign shows and formats. Additionally, they rotated program themes every three months to maintain relevance and audience interest.

Before the ratings wars, many television programs consisted of foreign imports, traditional Chinese folklore adaptations, or content aimed at middle-class tastes. During the ratings wars, however, television dramas began focusing more on realism and grassroots communities. This "realist turn" in Hong Kong television can be understood through four key aspects. First, television shows and news programs began to reflect, echo, and even create representations of ordinary life. For example, *Enjoy Yourself Tonight* featured segments that addressed everyday issues in Hong Kong, such as "The Night of Yuen Long," "The Night of Morse Park," and "The Night of Hung Hom Station." Local areas and daily life became central subjects of mass media. Television also played a significant role in addressing social problems through charity shows. These programs raised funds for victims of incidents such as the 1972 Hong Kong landslides, with local philanthropic organizations like Po Leung Kuk, Tung Wah, and Yan Chai collaborating with TVB to organize these events. By directly addressing societal issues, such shows bridged the gap between media representation and reality. News programs gained popularity comparable to that of entertainment shows. For instance, CTV produced investigative news series such as *Bu Ping Ming* (*Crying Against Injustice*) and *Jiaodian* (*Focus*), which invited victims, officials, and other stakeholders to discuss pressing social issues like resettlement challenges and gambling. As Pan Chao-yan, the news manager of CTV, explained in a 1976 interview: "We must use real locations to reflect reality. Whenever we encounter something unjust or pressing, we can expose it through our programs."[12] The most significant media event of this era was the live broadcast of the armed holdup at a Po Sang Bank branch in 1974. Both TVB and RTV provided seventeen hours of continuous coverage, marking a major media moment. This event highlighted the interplay between cinema and real-life crime scenes, with each inspiring the other. The immediacy and sensationalism of such coverage influenced subsequent television productions, including Johnny Mak's TV shows like *Operation Manhunt* (1977), which often featured dramatic gunfight scenes set in urban streets.

To accurately reflect reality, different TV stations established their own research units. For example, when the *Under the Lion Rock* series started in 1972, they had a Program Inquiry Meeting where producer, director, and scriptwriter engaged in collaborative discussions. As the series became popular, a long-term researcher position was created within the department to enhance the show's realism. The researcher's responsibilities included collecting and filing newspaper clippings, consulting with scriptwriters, arranging interviews with relevant individuals, and scouting filming locations. This role played a crucial part in bridging the gap between the show's narrative and real-life cases, ensuring greater authenticity in its storytelling.

In addition to television shows that reflected and created representations of ordinary life, the use of film negatives also contributed significantly to the realist turn in Hong Kong television. By the mid-1970s, several television shows and music videos shot on film negatives achieved notable success. For example, Patrick Tam's *Superstar Specials: Wong Chuen-yu* (1975), produced at TVB, won the Bronze Medal at the New York Festival International TV Awards in 1975. Building on this success, TVB established *fei lin zu* (the Film Negative Group) in the following year. The group recruited future New Wave directors, including Patrick Tam, Ann Hui, Cheung Kwok-ming, and Ng Siu-wan, and produced a series of modernist and realist television dramas, such as *Seven Women*.[13] The use of film negatives allowed directors greater creative flexibility, enabling them to shoot on location and experiment with more dynamic editing and coloring styles. Unlike traditional TV studio setups, which relied on three fixed-position broadcast cameras, hand-painted backdrops, and roofless interiors, film negatives provided a level of authenticity that resonated with audiences. As Ng Siu-wan noted in a TVB interview, the advantages of using film negatives included creating scenes that appeared more realistic and cinematic. Additionally, film negatives facilitated synchronous sound recording on location, eliminating the need for studio dubbing. This practice significantly enhanced the quality of television dramas in three stations such as *Social Worker*, *C.i.D.*, *Youth*, and *Interpol*, produced by TVB, as well as news programs like *Zhen ren zhen shi* (*Real Events*) from RTV. The materiality of film negative enhanced the television storytelling and solidified the realist turn in Hong Kong television history.

The third aspect of the realist turn in Hong Kong television relates to the establishment of the Independent Commission Against Corruption (ICAC) in 1974. Operating independently from the Police Department, the ICAC emerged as a symbol of Hong Kong's stability and prosperity by challenging the presumed impartiality and neutrality of the Royal Hong Kong Police and, by extension, the colonial government. This helped establish a new consensus on moral and ethical boundaries, challenging the previously simplistic black-and-white portrayals of characters. Hong Kong television began to depict more complex and ambiguous characters, reflecting the nuances of real-life situations. To the New Wave directors, this exploration of the "gray area" is where the essence of *renxing* (humanity) resides, highlighting the multifaceted nature of individuals and their moral struggles. However, skepticism about the ICAC persisted even after its establishment, particularly following the 1977 conflict between the ICAC and the police force. Ann Hui's two television dramas addressing police corruption were subsequently banned by the ICAC to avoid exacerbating tensions. Critics questioned the ICAC's motives, arguing that "ICAC is not fighting corruption unreservedly. Their priority is constrained by political reasons—not the severity of corruption." They further posited that the ICAC's establishment was an internal purge aimed at reinforcing the existing power structure, targeting minor offenders such as corrupt civil servants while improving the government's reputation.[14]

What does this have to do with realism? This wavering value directly shaped the realist aesthetics of television dramas. For instance, one episode of Ann Hui's ICAC series, *Gui qu lai zhi* (*Ah, Homeward Bound I Go*), focuses on the civil servant's wife and two mistresses rather than the corrupted civil servant. The criminal recited poetry, and the mistress appeared more humane than the stern and serious ICAC officers. This nuanced portrayal dissatisfied ICAC superiors, who preferred more clear-cut depictions of good and evil.[15] In Hui's banned episode, *Investigation*, two ICAC officers express disillusionment, lamenting public mistrust and their inability to apprehend the criminal. Their dialogue reflects the meta-narrative of ICAC's image-making: "You better shave your beard when you go to investigate Guan's home. Be more polite and look good." "You are right. The image of ICAC is very important." This sarcastic exchange underscores the ambiguity of their positions, where "the good" does not always appear virtuous and "the bad" can seem more humane.

Similarly, TVB's *Interpol*, a drama series adapting international news, tackled taboo subjects such as the Japanese Red Army, the Vietnam War, and the Palestinian struggle. The series' producer, Cheuk Pak-Tong, noted his intent to explore the ambiguous boundaries between law enforcement and criminals. In his view, the villains often had greater vision than the Interpol agents, who primarily served as witnesses rather than active participants in the crimes.[16] These ambiguous characters allowed directors to find spaces to critique and intervene in mainstream media narratives.

The final aspect of the realist turn in Hong Kong television pertains to the ratings wars, which significantly contributed to the flourishing of television realism. In their efforts to boost ratings, the television industry invested substantial resources and recruited talented directors and producers, who employed various techniques to captivate audiences—sometimes pushing boundaries to the extreme. For instance, in *Operation Manhunt* (1977), Johnny Mak directed a scene involving a truck crashing into a police station without prior permission. In another episode, Mak staged a gunfight in front of the

Kowloon Magistracy. By sensationalizing real locations, Mak heightened the sensory experience of television viewers, a practice he extended to his *Long Arm of the Law* (1984) film series. In these productions, Mak went so far as to hire actual criminals as actors and stage dangerous stunts, such as burning a car while an actor was inside, to elicit genuine reactions. These techniques—employing real locations, real characters, real reactions, and real cases—reflect the directors' attempts to capture, confront, and even make sense of the uncertainties of reality. This approach to realism, which Kristof Van den Troost terms "criminal realism,"[17] not only exposes the darker undercurrents of society but also generates its own contradictions: melodrama, sensationalism, and spectacle often emerge in the pursuit of high ratings. The intense competition among the three TV stations during the ratings wars prompted young filmmakers to question the nature of reality and the boundaries between documentary and drama.

Hong Kong television theory

However, not all critics embraced the realist turn that characterized much of Hong Kong television during this period. Works by Johnny Mak and others, known for their sensational and melodramatic style, faced significant criticism. A television critic in 1978 observed, "The weakness of emotionalism is selling cheap sensations. Developing from this, the emotion became gimmicks. Pushing to the extreme, such things became sick."[18] In the mid-1970s, as television underwent a realist turn, local television theories began to emerge. These theories engaged with popular television shows and sought to establish a distinct understanding of popular culture. Hong Kong does, in fact, have its own body of television theories, and without considering these local perspectives, it is impossible to fully grasp Ann Hui's interventions in her early television works. Local television theories provided a critical vocabulary for understanding television as a new medium, enabling nuanced critiques of its content and impact. By contextualizing these theories, we can better understand how Hui negotiated with, distanced herself from, or intervened in the critiques of her contemporaries. Importantly, Hong Kong television theory was not merely a passive recipient of Western critical studies or communication theories. Instead, it actively responded to the unique interplay of commercial media, the colonial government, and the geopolitical shifts of the late 1970s, creating a localized framework for analyzing popular culture.

In many articles analyzing Hong Kong film and media in the late 1970s, one frequently mentioned phenomenon is the decline of the *Zhongguo zhou* (China Week) exhibition. Organized by a group of Maoist students known as the *guo cui pai* (homeland-ist faction), China Week showcased photo exhibitions celebrating socialist China's landscapes, infrastructures, and technological advancements. These events were imbued with a strong ideological agenda, expressing hopes for Hong Kong's reunification with the fatherland and often employing Maoist quotations to analyze political economy while denouncing US imperialism, Soviet revisionism, and British colonialism. During the Cultural Revolution, when travel to mainland China was heavily restricted, these students undertook tours of the mainland to have sightseeing and patriotic lessons. However, China Week ceased operations in 1978, following a series of sociopolitical shifts.

By the late 1970s, radical student movements such as the Defend the Diaoyu Islands Movement (early 1970s) and the Chinese Language Campaign (1964–71) had lost momentum. The arrest of the Gang of Four disillusioned many radical students, undermining the ideological fervor that had sustained China Week. Concurrently, a new initiative, Hong Kong Week, launched in 1975, presented an alternative vision. Advocating for reforms rather than revolutionary changes, Hong Kong Week critiqued the utopian aspirations of China Week. It introduced new content that resonated more with the evolving societal dynamics, drawing an audience of more than 16,000 attendees.

Why did film and media critics mention the decline of China Week? They found the significance of the replacement of China Week by television shows. Television emerged as the dominant medium for showcasing the landscapes and developments of China, rendering the traditional exhibition format of China Week outdated. This shift reflects a broader transformation: students increasingly distanced themselves from socialist China and began to affirm their petty bourgeois status. Here, television realism or television theory is not just an issue of aesthetics; it represents a worldview shaped by the postrevolutionary era. In this context, college students, as well as film and media scholars and critics, sought to develop new critical vocabularies to understand the evolving society and culture of Hong Kong.

Some critics argue that the rise of television marked the end of both classical liberalism and classical socialism.[19] Television, they contend, not only constrained individual creativity and imagination but also reduced the interaction between the medium and its audience to metrics like advertising, ratings, and sponsorship. As local television managers and merchants from Hong Kong were increasingly invited to mainland China to provide advice on the development of Chinese television stations, the classical socialism signals its own end. A cultural critic Q Zai writes,

> China's Four Modernizations project, spearheaded by Deng Xiaoping, was advancing rapidly. Astute merchants, without a doubt, eager to capitalize on the vast market opportunity, sought to secure their share of the profits … Against this backdrop, TVB and RTV were invited to send delegates to mainland China … In addition to touring renowned landmarks, their primary objective was to establish connections with key institutions such as the China Central Public Communication Department, Beijing Central TV Station, Shanghai TV Station, and Guangzhou TV Station. The delegation engaged in discussions on TV technology, program management, and shared experiences.[20]

In response to these developments, local television theory emerged as a critical framework to confront not only the commercialized nature of Hong Kong television but also the outdated ideologies of nationalism, Maoism, and the nascent neoliberalism taking root in China. Interestingly, the intellectual foundation of Hong Kong television theory was grounded in the anti-humanist apparatus theory of French structural Marxist Louis Althusser—whose own theoretical framework was, in part, shaped by Maoist thought. In this translingual and transnational circulation of ideas, Hong Kong television theory reveals the lingering specter of Maoism or, perhaps more aptly, a detour through the anti-humanist lens of ideological critique.

In the late 1970s, numerous cultural magazines published special issues focusing on television culture, including *Close-Up*, *Cultural New Wave*, *City Magazine*, and *Film Biweekly*. These publications reflected diverse research interests in exploring television as a new medium. For instance, in 1978, Cui Yang drew inspiration from Marshall McLuhan to examine the history of television and its potential as an installation art form. Cui discussed television's dual roles in cognitive and technological experimentation, emphasizing its capacity to synchronize sound and image.[21]

Another strand of television studies adopted a sociological and quantitative methodology to analyze audience reception. The Mass Culture Action Team surveys investigated how young people used mass media to fulfill their needs in specific social contexts. Drawing on communication studies from the United States, the team focused not on television content but on its functions in reinforcing societal norms and assessing its social consequences. The findings revealed that TV news and documentary programs ranked among the top-ten most-consumed forms of media, indicating that young people in Hong Kong valued news and information transmission. The survey concluded that

TV culture was emerging as a significant force, capable of articulating and representing public opinion.[22] Building on this sociological approach, Lin Zhiren argued that new media functioned as a form of modern shamanism. He posited that television served as a stabilizing force within communities, helping individuals make sense of the external world and their patterns of life. According to Lin, television, as a formal device, defines the field of relevance and embodies collective consciousness. He writes:

> Remember the sensational news about Godber's release from jail. The news itself was not particularly exciting, but the way it was produced and presented was far more engaging. The notion of "God" is not inherently mysterious; rather, it is the individual who speaks about "God" that creates mysticism. In other words, the form dictates the content.[23]

Television, according to Lin Zhiren, trains our senses by creating an artificial paradise, homogenizing diverse experiences and values, commodifying content through vernacularization, immersing viewers in a spectacle with no escape, and acting as an opiate for the masses. Lin argued that TV news does not help us understand reality; instead, "we are not caring about the news but escaping from the news. In fact, we are being isolated and tricked, settled in an administrated experience of normalcy."[24]

Some critics extended this ideological critique of television, incorporating and translating the works of Louis Althusser and Cultural Studies scholar Marina Camargo Heck. The first issue of *Cultural New Wave* criticized the colonial government and capitalist interests behind the collapse of CTV, describing television as "an effective ideological communication apparatus, controlled by the ruling classes and the government."[25] Beyond translating Althusser's writings on education and reproduction, *Cultural New Wave* also edited and published *Structuralism and Semiotics* as part of its social science series, bringing cultural theories to Hong Kong audiences.

While engaging in ideological critiques, contributors expressed differing perspectives on popular culture, values, and reality. Quan-er, for instance, argued that television production increasingly reflected middle-class tastes. The capitalist goal, Quan-er suggested, was to create a stable society in which ordinary people could engage in controlled conflict within the existing system. He likened television shows to promotional gifts: rewards for enduring TV commercials, comparable to receiving a glass with a bottle of soy sauce or a mahjong tile with a bottle of brandy. Advertising addresses private and practical needs while reinforcing capitalist interests.[26] In this view, television shows reinforced existing power structures, even if audiences found them conservative, repetitive, and cliché.

Q Zai focused on the unconscious aspects of ideology in television. While he praised New Wave directors for their TV productions, his critique targeted the underlying ideological foundations rather than the content itself. He argued that "this ideology goes hand in hand with ruling ideology, sometimes, consciously or unconsciously becoming part of it."[27] To him, television functioned as a tool to reinforce the status quo and existing power structures. He described ideological apparatus as "material, concrete, and objective, rather than superficial, abstract, and subjective."[28] Zhou Zhao-xiang adopted a similarly anti-humanist perspective, emphasizing that television, as a medium, is fundamentally incompatible with pedagogical purposes. Pessimistically, he wrote:

> This tool seems designed for collective self-destruction, and the most alarming reality is that humans cannot erase it, nor do they have the chance to negotiate its existence … For now, the people of Hong Kong are unlikely to accept television as a pedagogical tool.[29]

In contrast, Shen Ming approached the subject through a milder tone, asserting that culture is ordinary and that popular culture serves as a site of conflicting values and struggles. Shen argued that while popular culture may not directly challenge existing realities, it often contains progressive elements, albeit unorganized. He suggested that critics should develop their theories as a form of practice leading to revolutionary change.[30] Chengyu built on this Cultural Studies framework, analyzing the ambiguity of values in the *Under the Lion Rock* series. While the government served as the producer, the filmmakers' expressions were highly individualistic, exposing societal dark sides in an egoistic manner. Chengyu observed:

> These efforts may ultimately change nothing. These scattered, individual acts of resistance might seem futile. However, one thing is certain: television is fully commercialized, and such resistances or efforts in producing the shows are unlikely to be accepted. On the other hand, these efforts might make us pause when critiquing TV shows. Consciously or unconsciously, passionate TV show creators often attempt to dilute the dominant ideology of the entertainment industry or embed their own perspectives. This tension fills the shows with layers of irony.[31]

These critiques and concerns culminated in the Hong Kong Popular Culture Conference held on February 18, 1979. Organized by institutions such as the Film Cultural Center, Art Center, Seal Player Theater, the independent research group Mass Culture Action Team, and magazines like *Close-Up*, *Cultural New Wave*, *City Magazine*, and *Film Biweekly*, the conference marked the emergence of the *xin wenhua ren* (new culture men). This group approached popular culture with seriousness, analyzing it as a critical site of political and economic struggle. The new culture men rejected the frameworks of the "old culture men," criticizing both the outdated cultural nationalist focus on moral high ground and traditional Chinese arts, as well as the fading Maoists, who failed to address a rapidly changing society. In contrast, the new culture men were film critics, TV producers, and scholars who opposed all forms of authority, corruption, and masochistic moralism.[32]

These new cultural theorists directly engaged with commodities and recognized the importance of communication forms and semiotic systems. They adopted structural Marxist and scientific frameworks to understand ideology not as a matter of consciousness but as a structure of the unconscious. In the postrevolutionary era, the "new" in new culture men represented an effort to use scientific social analysis to make sense of the fragmented remnants of Truth, History, and Enlightenment. In parallel, the "new" in New Wave directors like Ann Hui manifested as a deep skepticism toward concrete social analysis, simplistic heroic acts, singular Truth, definitive solutions, and coherent narratives of humanity. This "newness" embodied a broader distrust of grand narratives—whether liberalism, socialism, revolutionary student movements, social movements, or the ideals of History, Enlightenment, and Humanity. Yet this distrust did not entail a wholesale rejection; rather, it involved an attempt to salvage and reinterpret fragments of these grand narratives. Television became a medium through which these historical fragments were mediated, serving as a site for reconstructing meaning. In the following, I will demonstrate how television engaged with fragments of the Vietnam War and the experiences of Chinese Vietnamese, illustrating Hui's capacity to mediate fragmented historical realities.

The making of location

The location serves both a literal and a figurative burst from the context of social movements. Beyond the realist turn in television, which captured, created, and represented everyday life and events in the mid-1970s, the early 1970s witnessed the emergence of spontaneous documentary and experimental filmmaking as tools to document mundane life and social movements. Public spaces and location shooting became not only the subjects of these films but also active sites of participation and action.

Law Kar's experimental film *Routine* (1969) comprises long takes capturing the streets of Kowloon, emphasizing the urban landscape as a protagonist. Similarly, Chiu Tak-hark and Law Kar collaborated with *The 70s Biweekly*, an anarchist publication actively involved in organizing street protests. Together, they filmed the Diaoyudao social movements in 1970. Their documentary eschews a focus on individual characters or activist figures, instead foregrounding the protest locations—Statue Square, the Japanese Consulate, the Community Center, and the Central Police Station—as central protagonists. In 1973, George Chan, a radical associated with *The 70s Biweekly*, collaborated with Granada TV in Britain and the local NGO Society for Community Organization. Drawing on Saul Alinsky's methods and analyses, they documented pressing social issues in Hong Kong such as housing, drug abuse, prostitution, and police corruption.[33]

Ann Hui inherited and expanded upon this documentary tradition. Throughout her career, she has produced several documentaries, including one for the Xinhua News Agency during the challenging production of *Boat People* in 1982, *As Time Goes By* (1997), which explored the lives of her family and friends, and the TV documentary series *Ann Hui with the Famous* (1992). Her most recent documentary, *Elegies* (2023), focuses on Hong Kong poets. Hui has frequently mentioned how documentary techniques influenced her early works, incorporating handheld camera movements in a documentary style.[34] She describes *The Story of Woo Viet* as having a "colorless documentary" aesthetic,[35] and the opening scene of the marching Vietnamese army in *Boat People* as resembling a documentary.[36]

Location, in this context, extends beyond geographical space or the act of location shooting; it also encompasses Hui's approach to reality. Her portrayal of location is both observational and participatory. However, her work lacks overt class analysis, a critique leveled by Q Zai in his review of *The Boy from Vietnam*. He argued that many of the encounters in the film are incidental, stating, "characters in the story seem to be social chances, and we cannot see the root causes of all these social problems."[37] I contend that Hui's approach diverges from the new culture men like Q Zai. While her characters and narratives may appear apolitical on the surface, the locations themselves are imbued with political undertones. For instance, the cabins, Vietnamese Chinese restaurants, customs borders, painters' studios, and war zones depicted in her films seem apolitical yet resist depoliticization. Unlike Johnny Mak's extreme sensational realism—characterized by melodramatic explosions, gunfights, or *Scarface*-

like immigrant narratives—Hui refrains from sensationalizing these locations. Instead, her locations serve as mediating spaces, framing the dynamics of time and space without pointing to utopia or any teleological resolution. In her effort to rescue humanity, Hui compels viewers to witness the interplay of forces within everyday scenes.

In the opening scene of *The Boy from Vietnam*, an off-screen Vietnamese-speaking male voice saying, "The army is coming, let's get back to the house," is superimposed over the film's title (*Lai Ke* in Chinese). This is followed by a series of montages: a close-up of a young child, a close-up of marching feet, a long shot of village houses, and the child knocking on a door. The film then cuts to an extreme close-up of Wen, the main character, lying down. This is immediately followed by a long shot of a large ship, before cutting back to Wen as he rises. A pan shot reveals that he is in the cabin of a ship.

Using only diegetic sound and ambient noise, the scene transitions seamlessly from a premodern Vietnamese village to the interior of a ship bound for Hong Kong. Here, the character serves as a bridge to accentuate the changes of scenes. Locations in this sequence function as mediating force fields, connecting disparate and often infinitesimal flows of power such as the Liberation in Vietnam, the boat people, or the imagination about Hong Kong. Rather than explaining the historical or sociopolitical reasons behind the migration, Hui positions the location as the culmination of these forces. In a one-and-a-half-minute long-take monologue, Ning, a friend of Wen, confides that during the war, faced with either the devastation of war or the uncertainties of life in Hong Kong, many Chinese Vietnamese felt they had no real choice.[38] What compels characters' decisions, I argue, are the power-laden locations that Ann Hui so effectively showcases, which serve as both the backdrop and the driving force of the narrative.

The TV drama's locations captured by Hui underscore the perpetual motion of its characters. Wen, for example, was born in Saigon, defended Tây Ninh during wartime, and moved to Hong Kong after the Liberation. His cousin, who also relocated to Hong Kong after the 1975 Liberation, faced financial difficulties when his family members could not wire money to him. As a result, he turned to prostitution and aspired to start anew in the United States. Ning escaped Vietnam a second time, passing through the Khmer Republic and Macau before eventually arriving in Hong Kong. Other Vietnamese refugees hail from Nha Trang, while Chinese Vietnamese painters express their desire to move to Paris. The characters' transnational journeys are reflected through their constant movement, often depicted in dynamic visual compositions in different vehicles:

a subjective camera inside a car peering through the window, a zooming shot on a refugee boat, a pan shot from the boat, or a tracking shot of a bicycle navigating the streets. These visual elements evoke the ceaseless centripetal and centrifugal flux of migration across locations, evacuated of transformative potential. Rather than directly addressing geopolitical causality, Hui's artistic interventions reveal how state and capital power are inscribed in the built environment. Through mundane, everyday scenes, the TV drama interrogates the meaning of "homeland" within a politicized context.

This tension is further explored in the scene where Wen's cousin applies for a US visa. He faces both identity and bureaucratic challenges, as he seeks to change his ID card from Chinese to Vietnamese citizenship. Without any melodramatic music, the scene is composed of three static shots: a low-angle medium shot showing the cousin through a serrated window, a reverse shot of the immigration officer sternly warning him about canceling his ID card, and a medium close-up of the cousin's disappointed reaction. The absence of voiceover intensifies the coldness of the bureaucratic setting, emphasizing the struggles faced by many Chinese Vietnamese refugees.

Movement itself becomes the central issue in Hui's works, yet it offers no potential for self-revolution, self-transformation, or collective revolution, unlike the leftist Hong Kong films of previous generations. In leftist films such as *Road* (1959) and *Sea* (1963), locations like the open sea serve as challenges that refugees must overcome, while simultaneously functioning as devices to enhance characterization. Refugees are confined to enclosed spaces—such as the hut in *Road* and the deserted island in *Sea*—both of which were filmed in studio settings. These enclosed areas symbolize the "iron house" described by Lu Xun, a key figure in modern Chinese literature and criticism. The "iron house" refers to an indestructible structure in which Chinese people metaphorically sleep, oblivious to their oppression. This spatial theme was central to the May Fourth Movement (1919), where breaking out of the "iron house" collectively symbolized the path to enlightenment, the creation of a new collective, and the emergence of a new nation. In both *Road* and *Sea*, the hope is heralded by the last-minute heroes—the Communist guerrilla forces.

In Ann Hui's *The Boy from Vietnam*, however, the locations shift the focus away from collective transformation and revolution, instead drawing attention to the homogenized landscapes confronting the characters. Hui's films share certain visual and thematic similarities with Jue Fung's *The Mud Child* (1976), a leftist film produced by the Feng Huang Film Company. Adapted from a reportage literature on the 1972 landslide in Hong Kong, *The Mud Child* concludes with a poignant scene: a madwoman who lost her child in the disaster rushes to the cleared site where the landslide occurred. In an extreme long shot, she is shown desperately digging the land with her bare hands. The film ends with a freeze-frame of her helpless reaction alongside those of her neighbors. A subsequent pan shot reveals a large billboard in the background announcing the area's redevelopment. Here, the location is not just a backdrop but a site imbued with capitalist power and the colonial government's negligence. Unlike Jue Fung, however, Ann Hui exhibits a profound reservation of collectivity and simple resolutions. Her works do not place hope in definitive or absolute subjectivities such as working-class heroes or social workers. The locations function as a self-producing system as a whole that cannot break out of their loop. Instead, Hui focuses on observing the mundane and everyday struggles of individuals within specific loops of locations, emphasizing humanity through nuanced perspectives rather than grand revolutionary ideals.

Locations in Ann Hui's works embody multiple perspectives, offering nuanced ways to perceive and interpret change. In *The Boy from Vietnam*, locations function as voices of perspective rather than as overt tools of commentary. The Chinese title of the episode *Lai Ke* (literally translated as "coming guests") provides a lens through which Hong Kong is examined and understood. This title reflects a reevaluation of the dialectics between host and guest. Ackbar Abbas notes that "stories about Hong Kong always turned into stories about somewhere else, as if Hong Kong culture were not a subject."[39] However, I argue the opposite: Hong Kong culture is consistently a central concern for New Wave directors, including Hui, who employ diverse locations and perspectives to explore it. By incorporating various countries—Vietnam, the United States, the United Kingdom, mainland China, and France—and settings such as Vietnamese restaurants, refugee hotels, boats, and Vietnamese painters' studios, Hui reflects on and critiques Hong Kong culture through transnational and localized settings. This interplay of perspectives aligns with what Shu Kei describes as an involvement: "For Ann Hui, an outsider becoming an insider represents a form of involvement that embodies responsibility, emotional attachment, self-critique, and a sense of compensation."[40] Hui's films use the dialectics between viewpoints to interrogate identity, responsibility, and cultural belonging, ultimately exposing Hong Kong's complex cultural landscape.

In the scene where Wen and his friend are walking in the street, Ann Hui employs actuality staging by placing the camera on a moving vehicle, capturing a medium shot of the two characters walking from left to right. Suddenly, they encounter a Mandarin-speaking man asking for directions to Taikoo

Dockyard. Historically, Taikoo Dockyard was a hub for immigrants seeking job opportunities during the first half of the twentieth century. However, by the early 1970s, the land had been redeveloped into a private housing estate. This historical shift renders the dockyard an anachronism for Wen and his friend, who not only fail to understand the man's Mandarin but also struggle to comprehend the historical weight of the site.

As they board a minivan, a medium close-up captures Wen watching that man through the minivan's window. A pan shot follows the man from left to right, alternating between obscured views blocked by the van door and clearer views through the window. The camera then zooms in on Wen's apathetic expression. Melancholic string music fades in as the minivan begins to move, reinforcing the scene's emotional tone. The street and the minivan's interior serve as pivotal locations, echoically marking Wen's initial arrival in Hong Kong. This moment—what Gary Bettinson refers to as pictorial storytelling and staging[41]—signifies Wen's changing perspectives: from being seen as an outsider to becoming someone who now watches other immigrant workers from a distance. Through shifting perspectives within this loop of location, the distortion of time and space becomes palpable. Wen, now fluent in Cantonese, has assimilated into the local culture to the extent that he cannot understand a mainland Chinese immigrant. The alienation experienced by the characters does not stem from personal monologues but rather from the surrounding cityscape, which confronts and antagonizes them.

Ann Hui's approach to location in her films does not center on a class analysis of the Vietnamese Chinese community or a detailed examination of historical causes. Instead, locations become significant protagonists, driving the narrative, connecting isolated characters, and offering viewers multiple perspectives to examine the evolving Hong Kong society. The materiality of these locations in the TV drama continuously reminds viewers of the characters' lived experiences. These include fat pork congee in the refugee cabin, *bánh cuốn* shared by Wen and his cousin in a restaurant, the vegetarian dish eaten by the old soldier in southern Vietnam, and the food delivery on a bicycle overturned by a wedding car. Hui avoids television spectacles by emphasizing the materiality of each location, transcending simplistic binary oppositions such as local versus center, northern versus southern Vietnamese, Vietnam versus Hong Kong, and rural versus urban. This nuanced "dialectical materialism" is reflected in Ning's conversation with Wen: "Sometimes, I feel it is absurd. We Chinese need to help Vietnamese to fight Vietnamese. Now I can escape Vietnam, but so what? I live on making cheap replica paintings." This dialectical perspective rejects the possibility of ascending to an absolute truth. Instead, it remains as a loop and captures a profound sense of emotional attachment and involvement, encouraging viewers to set out on a journey crossing the everyday landscapes into the midst of reflection and re-mediation.

Politics of representation

The reception of *The Boy from Vietnam* was mixed. Critics praised the directorial style and the open ending, which provides no definitive resolution for the boy's fate. However, they questioned the impact of such dramas on the wave of refugees and the ideological underpinnings of the *Under the Lion Rock* series. As one critic noted, "Remember, *Under the Lion Rock* series is a production by RTHK. To many viewers, the episode is like any regular melodramatic TV show they watched."[42] Ann Hui, undeterred by such criticism, continued to employ similar styles in her Vietnam trilogy. In particular, in *Boat People*, she demonstrated a keen self-awareness of the strengths and limitations of her directorial approach, stating: "I don't think I've completely avoided simplifying the characters. In fact, simplifying them can sometimes help convey certain ideas. But in this case, we placed them in particular situations and let them behave naturally, without aiming for a specific goal or resolution. That's both the strength and the weakness of this film."[43] Hui's sensitivity to the forms of representation is evident in *The Boy from Vietnam*, where her critique of mass media went unnoticed by those new culture men. In the following, I focus on her critique of mass media and communication, and how we understand migration of the refugee through the lens of mediation, and what alternative knowledge this episode can create to intervene in the politics of representations.

Hui's television shows for RTHK frequently interrogate the transparency of representation, often breaking the fourth wall. In *Bridge*, villagers and district officers address the camera directly, voicing their perspectives on the destruction of the bridge. In *The Boy from Vietnam*, a switched-off TV set first appears in the cousin's apartment during a scene where the cousin teaches Wen common Cantonese expressions. The next scene opens with a close-up of a TV monitor showing a couple delivering the melodramatic line, "It seems that we are not going to get married." The camera then pans in the opposite direction to zoom in on a mirror reflecting Wen as he writes a letter to his mother, accompanied by his voiceover reading the letter in Cantonese. During this voiceover, a montage sequence unfolds, depicting Wen buying new pants, posting a letter, going to the cinema, eating at a fast-food restaurant, and walking through a nighttime street in Hong Kong. Crucially, Wen states in the voiceover that he is learning Cantonese through television shows. Initially, the television set serves as a decorative object, then as a medium delivering melodramatic spectacle, and finally as a pedagogical tool aiding Wen's assimilation into Cantonese-speaking society. Hui demonstrates that mass media does not serve a singular role in everyday life; instead, it can be instrumental in helping outsiders integrate into a new cultural context. This meta-media sequence underscores how colonial modernity in the cityscape confronts and surrounds him.

Another representation of mass media in the TV drama is the journalist. Journalists first appear in the refugee hotel, interviewing a Chinese Vietnamese couple about their escape from Vietnam. They ask pointed questions such as, "Are you escaping because of political reasons? What do you think about the politics in Vietnam now?" However, as the camera pans away, the couple's response is left unheard, emphasizing either a gap in communication or a political lacuna Hui did not want to fill. Either way, the journalists are portrayed as investigative and politically engaged. Journalists appear a second time when Wen leaves the mortuary after identifying his cousin's body. This sequence is accompanied by Wen's voiceover: "In the following days, many journalists ask me a lot of things about my cousin. I say nothing." The visuals depict journalists rushing toward Wen, followed by a quick pan to their cameras, which are aimed directly at the film's camera, aligning Wen's position with the audience's perspective. The next shot captures Wen, visibly distressed, covering his face as he is surrounded by journalists. These two sequences highlight contrasting aspects of journalism: the first emphasizes investigative reporting, while the second reveals the intrusive, paparazzi-like nature of some journalists. Ann Hui's critique of journalism is evident here and continues in *Boat People*, where the Japanese photojournalist Shiomi Akutagawa becomes disillusioned with the reliability of his medium. Akutagawa realizes that much of what he captures through his camera is orchestrated by the new regime. In a powerful act of defiance and humanity, he sells his expensive cameras to save a Vietnamese girl and her brother, demonstrating his rejection of manipulated narratives and revealing the constructedness of news and reality.

Ann Hui is deeply concerned with the forms of representation and mediation. Extending Marshall McLuhan's notions of "the medium is the message" and "media as the extension of man" to *The Boy from Vietnam* helps illuminate her focus on the "missing connections" in historical transformations. McLuhan's concept emphasizes that the form of media technology, rather than its content, profoundly shapes human relations and our perception of society. As McLuhan argues, thanks to electronic media, "other people are now involved in our lives, as we in theirs."[44] Migration itself can be understood as a form of mediation. John Guillory, in "Genesis of the Media Concept," defines mediation as a process through which two different realms, persons, objects, or terms are brought into relation.[45] In this sense, migration functions as a connective force, transforming relationships through a constitutive process. Hui's *The Boy from Vietnam* explores these complex "connections," or what Victor Fan describes as "alternative kinship" with other "abject figures." Hui highlights multiple layers of mediation, including transborder migration, translation, the TV set as a cultural artifact, the differing currency rates between Hong Kong and Vietnam, and the contrast between modern Hong Kong and war-torn Vietnam.

The idea of "missing connections" is reflected in the motif of fragmented photographs in the story. Wen is forced to hand over a photo fragment to an overseer in the cabin. This fragment is then delivered by a middleman in Vietnam to Wen's mother. A close-up shot of the matching halves of the photograph signifies that Wen has arrived safely in Hong Kong, prompting his mother to pay the remainder of the fee to the middlemen. The photo fragment, originally an ordinary portrait, gains new meaning through the precarious experience of transnational migration. It becomes a message of survival, a tangible representation of Wen's safety for his mother.

Other devices of mediation in the TV drama include letters, flashbacks, and the human body. Wen's first-person Cantonese voiceover narrates his life to his mother, expressing his feelings about his cousin's murder. Wen's flashback memories transport viewers to his sister's funeral and reveal how his brother and sister-in-law failed to board a boat to escape Vietnam. Ning's body, once a disciplined soldier in southern Vietnam, becomes illegitimate after the Liberation. He transforms into an exiled figure, working as a replica painter in Hong Kong before being repatriated to Macau. Wen's cousin, who studied in Vietnam, enters Hong Kong as a mainland Chinese citizen, becomes a sex worker, and ultimately fails to secure a US visa under the status of a Vietnamese refugee. These mediated details shape human relations, changing the forms of human association and action. Ann Hui's intervention lies in her emphasis on the materiality of these mediations—letters, photographs, bodies, TV sets, boats, and food. Through this inventory of mundane objects, Hui illustrates how individuals struggle and adapt to the relentless flux of mediation and migration. As Patricia Zimmermann and Helen De Michiel argue, filmmakers like Hui serve "as community designers who convene people around contradictory, suppressed, and unresolved issues."[46]

Despite criticism that the episode contributes little social impact to the wave of Vietnamese refugees, Hui's work operates as an ongoing process of community understanding and archival knowledge production within the public sphere. While the episode reflects the limited choices available in practical life, it also offers alternative knowledge of the Vietnamese experience in Hong Kong, creating a space for reflection and understanding.

Critics may argue that the episode does not produce alternative knowledge, as it reinforces certain Vietnamese stereotypes. For instance, Yau Ching highlights that in the other two films of the Vietnam trilogy, communist regimes are demonized: Chinese Vietnamese characters idealize the United States as a utopia in *The Story of Woo Viet*, and prostitution in *Boat People* becomes a symbol of moral decadence in Communist Vietnam, perpetuating the association between communism and moral corruption inherited from the 1950s McCarthyism.[47] Similar images can be found in *The Boy from Vietnam*. Wen's cousin becomes a sex worker, serving both female (a Russian woman) and male clients (including his murderer).

However, I contend that the episode examines how bodies in transnational flux become precarious objects rather than simply perpetuating stereotypes. Unlike mainstream media portrayals of Vietnamese refugees in Hong Kong as criminals or rioters, Hui's *The Boy from Vietnam* challenges stereotypes—not only of the Vietnamese but also of Hong Kong and the United States. In the story, Wen's cousin is not the sole figure involved in sex work; there is also a brief scene featuring a female street prostitute. Ning observes policemen checking someone's ID, which heightens his anxiety, and he briefly exchanges eye contact with the prostitute. This chance encounter does not evoke fears of communism but instead highlights a shared sense of vulnerability among immigrant workers in Hong Kong. Additionally, Hui challenges the notion of Hong Kong as a dreamland for refugees. The robbers who target Ning are immigrants with heavy accents, emphasizing the struggles of working-class migrants. The rising modernity of Hong Kong continually confronts, surrounds, and suffocates these transient populations. When Wen's cousin mentions the possibility of applying to the United States, Wen becomes emotional and exclaims in Vietnamese, "I won't go! I won't go!" He then explains in Cantonese, "I hate them so much! They killed my sister!" While Wen's nationalism is diluted into familial unity, his rejection of the American Dream is unequivocal. The three monologues in the episode—Wen's voiceover letters, Ning's soliloquy on the beachside, and Wen's cousin's reflections in a bar—function as testimonies, providing unheard perspectives that connect with Hong Kong television viewers. These narratives offer insights that mainstream media often overlooks, fostering a deeper understanding of the precarious experiences of refugees and immigrants.

The Boy from Vietnam was released in 1978, a year before Hong Kong declared itself the port of first asylum. Vietnamese boat people became a strategic tool for the colonial government to bolster its image at the United Nations, while simultaneously exacerbating tensions between Vietnamese refugees and the local Hong Kong population. This manipulation aimed to create a "crisis of faith" in Communist China as the United Kingdom negotiated with the Chinese government over Hong Kong's future. Consequently, stereotypical portrayals of Vietnamese refugees proliferated in Hong Kong's commercial films and TV shows throughout the 1980s.

The Vietnamese refugee issue transcended the domestic sphere to become a geopolitical concern. As Yau Ching explains:

> The British anticipated the challenges posed by the influx of Vietnamese refugees into Hong Kong, including the social problems that arose as a result. These issues further heightened Hong Kong's fears about potential Communist Chinese rule in the future. This "crisis of faith" among Hong Kong's population became one of the few leverage points for the British government during discussions on the Sino-British Joint Declaration.[48]

After completing three episodes in the *Under the Lion Rock* series, Ann Hui left the television industry and directed her debut film, *The Secret*, in 1979. While some critics argue that her TV works were not overtly political, *The Boy from Vietnam* remains a significant archival document that intervenes in the politics of representation. In contrast to sensational news coverage or depictions of Vietnamese refugees as criminals or rioters in Hong Kong's refugee camps, Hui's work offers a nuanced and humanized perspective, contributing to a broader understanding of the Vietnamese refugee experience.

Conclusion

The bankruptcy of CTV in 1978 led to significant changes in Hong Kong's television industry. With no major competition, TVB disbanded its Film Negative Group in 1979. RTV, however, managed to produce several well-received shows between 1979 and 1981, including the youth romance *I.Q. 100* (1981) and the epic drama *The Fatherland Trilogy* (1982). By 1981, the British capitalists behind RTV sold their shares to Australian investors, and in 1982, Chiu Te-gen acquired the shares, rebranding RTV as Asia Television Limited (ATV). Despite these developments, the television market in Hong Kong became increasingly monopolized by TVB.

By the early 1980s, concerns in Hong Kong's cultural discourse shifted. The focus was no longer on ideological critiques of colonialism or capitalism but rather on questions of identity and cultural standards: What constituted Hong Kong identity? How should popular culture be evaluated? Amid these cultural inquiries, the significance of the New Wave directors persisted throughout the 1980s and 1990s. This chapter has examined the realist turn in Hong Kong's television industry and TV theories during the late Cold War era and explored Ann Hui's contribution in *The Boy from Vietnam*. Hui rescues humanity by distancing it from grand narratives, opting instead to foreground the location and the everyday materiality—letters, food, voiceovers, personal flashbacks, and bodies—as central to her storytelling. By documenting ordinary locations and transforming them into narrative protagonists, Hui intervenes in the politics of representation.

This rescue of humanity by distancing it from grand narratives resonates across the Sinophone community, as seen in the works of mainland China's and Taiwan's New Wave directors. For instance, in *Yellow Earth* (1984), Chen Kaige employs long takes, disproportionate framing, and natural lighting to capture barren landscapes, treating history not as a linear sequence but as something condensed in symbolic and immobile shots.[49] Similarly, Hou Hsiao-Hsien's *City of Sadness* (1989) juxtaposes the silent landscapes of Jiufen with fragmented memories of the February 28 Incident, creating a mosaic of history rather than a coherent narrative. While the French New Wave responded to the sensibilities and traumatic experiences of the postwar and early Cold War period, the New Wave in Hong Kong, China, and Taiwan grappled with the complexities of the late Cold War era. In this postrevolutionary context, space takes precedence over the linear depth of history in the Chinese context. History is no longer portrayed as a teleological progression driven by absolute human subjectivity. Instead, it is spatialized—manifesting through fragmented objects, locations, and the perspectives of observers—thereby challenging coherent narratives and the concrete meanings of autonomous subjectivity.

Acknowledgments

I would like to thank Zhaoyu Zhu for inviting me to contribute to this collection on Ann Hui and for his meticulous copyediting of my references and citations.

I am also grateful for the valuable feedback provided by the reviewers. Special thanks to Tim Teng and his assistant Patrick Koo for helping me access a book from the library at the Chinese University of Hong Kong. Finally, I would like to express my sincere thanks to Ann Hui.

5

Narrative and narrational strategies in Ann Hui's *The Way We Are*

Gary Bettinson

Against a local industry whose auteurs favor stylistic foregrounding, Ann Hui stands out in sharp relief. Several of her films—including *The Way We Are* (2008) and *Summer Snow* (1995)—embrace narrative and stylistic minimalism, a pared-down aesthetic characterized by expressive restraint and subtlety. These are films in which, according to many critics, nothing happens: the uneventful plot substitutes mundane dailiness for dramatic fillips and crescendos. By minifying plot action, Hui poses herself an artistic challenge. How to sustain the viewer's attentional focus and engagement? This chapter explores Hui's strategies of spectator engagement through close analysis of *The Way We Are*, focusing centrally on Hui's approach to narrative plotting and filmic narration.

At the narrative level, *The Way We Are* furnishes a wispy narrative low on dramatic incident. The action centers on middle-aged widow Kwai (Paw Hee-ching) and her teenage son On (Leung Chun-lung), residents of a lower-class neighborhood in Hong Kong's New Territories. While Kwai works as a supermarket grocery clerk, On spends his days running errands, doing chores, and awaiting the results of his high school exam. Kwai befriends the elderly Granny Leung (Chan Lai-wun), a new neighbor and colleague at the supermarket, who grieves for the death of her daughter. Kwai and On help Granny acclimatize to her new milieu. When Kwai's mother (Chan Lai-hing) is taken ill and hospitalized, On tends to her needs, but Kwai puts off visiting her. Instead, Kwai agrees to accompany Granny on a rendezvous: the old woman attempts to reconnect with her young grandson, who fails to attend the scheduled encounter. Dejected, Granny finds solace in the company of Kwai and On. As the narrative winds down, the three protagonists dine together in Kwai's apartment and celebrate the Mid-Autumn Festival.

Critics have variously categorized *The Way We Are* as a woman's picture, a melodrama, and a *wenyi pian* (letters-and-arts film). If the first two labels are broadly synonymous, the fungibility of melodrama and *wenyi* has become a matter of scholarly debate. Emilie Yeh and others caution against treating melodrama and *wenyi* as equivalent forms, partly because to do so risks erasing cultural specificity. For one thing, *wenyi* historically connotes literary prestige and artistic sophistication, qualities that run counter to the soap-opera trappings of melodrama. Still, like melodrama, *wenyi* is a highly protean category. Across Chinese film history, it has evolved a batch of sometimes contradictory traits, including sentimentality, emotional excess, artistic refinement, and expressive understatement. *Wenyi* proliferates, too, in a dizzying array of variants: ethical family drama, romance film, woman's picture, literary adaptation, male melodrama, father-and-son picture, maternal drama, and *wenyi* blockbuster. Notwithstanding the cultural distinctiveness of the *wenyi pian*, Emilie Yeh acknowledges that the genre "share[s] common traits" with melodrama.[1] Li Cheuk-to and Zhen Zhang, meanwhile, perceive much correspondence between the two traditions.[2] Indeed, we can identify salient storytelling tendencies common to both cultural forms.

Whether the viewer's frame of reference is the Hollywood melodrama or the Cantonese *wenyi pian*, a shared cluster of narrative conventions shapes our horizon of expectations. Minimally, we expect dramatic conflict, most likely predicated on familial ruptures: a marriage threatened by a third party (*Eternal Regret*, 1962); filial rifts between parents and children (*Mother's Broken Heart*, 1958); Manichean feuds between in-laws (*Mysterious Murder*, 1951). Goal orientation, too, is a given, though the characters' efforts to attain their goals may be diverted by blind chance, bad luck, or fate. At the center of the tumult is a beleaguered heroine (or, occasionally in the *wenyi*, a male variant). Typically, this figure suffers and sacrifices herself, bending ineluctably to circumstance. Our knowledge of the genre primes us for a drama propelled by sudden twists and *deus ex machina*. And, as with most narratives, we predict modulated arcs of character change.

No stranger to the norms of melodrama, Hui sets out to flout them in *The Way We Are*. As Mirana M. Szeto observes, "There is no dramatic confrontation, no tear-jerking agony, no gripping violence, no event."[3] Hui empties the plot of dramatic crisis. She renders character goals opaque or diffuse: neither Kwai nor On articulate personal goals. Only a loose, tacit objective is assigned to On, oriented around his impending exam results. An explicit goal ascribed to Granny—to forge a close relationship with her estranged grandson—gets roundly thwarted. So the film's plot, if it exists at all, is not motivated by the protagonists' pursuit of substantive goals. Not least, Hui eschews the emotional excess germane to the genre. The lives of the three protagonists—a widowed mother (Kwai), a fatherless teenager (On), a single woman mourning her daughter (Granny)—suggest a melodramatic treatment. Yet in Hui's hands, any impulse toward hyperbole and sentiment is decisively damped down. Nowhere evident is the bitter betrayal, the discovery of a fatal illness, or the grand act of martyrdom that typifies the *wenyi* melodrama. No sudden cataclysm upsets the characters' daily routines. Character change is negligible. As David Bordwell writes, "This is a movie in which, by the standards of traditional dramaturgy, nothing happens."[4]

By implication, *something* can be seen to happen if we apply standards of nontraditional dramaturgy. If "traditional" dramaturgy, in Bordwell's notion, chiefly denotes classical Hollywood plot construction, then *The Way We Are* mobilizes alternative traditions of narrative organization and narration. Specifically, I will argue, the film relies upon norms of plotting long established in Hong Kong cinema. It also embraces a minimalist discourse whose lineage may be traced to popular melodrama in both its Hollywood and Cantonese (and more broadly Asian) variants.

That Ann Hui deploys local storytelling norms in the post-1997 era is no small matter. As mainland Chinese co-productions began to dominate the industry, and as local filmmakers embraced Hollywood-style visual effects, commentators lamented the cultural erasure of Hong Kong film aesthetics. Now, it was claimed, an age of "post-Hong Kong cinema" had dawned, characterized by the twin globalizing forces of Mainlandization and Hollywoodization.[5] In 2003 the Closer Economic Partnership Arrangement (CEPA) ramped up collaboration between the Hong Kong and mainland film industries, and for several years mandated—as a prerequisite for co-production approval—preproduction screenplays, a practice anathema to Hong Kong filmmakers' improvisatory work methods. Similarly, Hong Kong–US co-productions placed an onus on Hollywood-style principles of story construction: tightly woven cause-and-effect, motivated action, three-or-four-act structure, satisfying closure, and so forth. Yet Hui, along with many of her compatriots, clung to local tradition. Launched as a wholly local production, *The Way We Are* testifies to the power and resilience of Hong Kong cinema's dramaturgical principles.

Cohering the quotidian

If the plot of *The Way We Are* is hard to detect, and if the protagonists lack purposeful goals, what glues the action together? Eschewing the tight causality of the Hollywood plot, the film tethers its macrostructure to the traditional principles of Hong Kong dramaturgy: episodic plotting and reel construction. The film's plot episodes are as often connected by chance events as by determinate causal links. And distinct story phases are roughly fitted to reel length, as per local custom. Across the film's first two reels, Hui and screenwriter Lou Shiu-wa introduce the dramatis personae (Kwai, On, Granny) and establish the central locales (Kwai's apartment, Granny's apartment, the supermarket). Reels three and four depict Kwai and On's blossoming friendship with Granny. An unforeseen event—the hospitalization of Kwai's mother—consumes the next two reels, while reels seven and eight coalesce around Granny's abortive reunion with her grandson. The final reel culminates with Kwai, On, and Granny united as a makeshift family. If prima facie the narrative seems aleatory—intentionally so, I suggest, designed to emulate the uncertain rhythms of everyday life—it nonetheless exhibits a unifying structure. A prologue and epilogue flank the major episodes, marked as discrete units by the use of fades (the only occasions on which this device is employed). Such maneuvers seek to endow an ostensibly fragmentary narrative with structural coherence and formal symmetry.

Episodic plots lack the tautness of tight causality, and so *The Way We Are* must marshal a host of cohesion devices to knit its distinct plot phases together. A key tactic is motivic patterning, a favorite principle of Hong Kong dramaturgy. Hui distributes throughout the text a multiplying flurry of motifs—eggs, mushrooms, fruit, soup, mooncake, newspapers, tissue paper—all of which function to unify distinct reels, symbolize themes, and extend Hui's emphasis on the everyday. The quotidian nature of these ordinary domestic items ensures that they never call attention to themselves as symbols—their thematic meaning crystallizes cumulatively throughout the narrative, slowly coming to represent On's growing proficiency in practical matters, the enduring value of cultural customs, and the unspoken emotional bonds among the three protagonists. Scattered across the preceding reels, the major motifs cluster at the epilogue. In lieu of an earth-shattering climax, Hui recalls these recurring items in the final reel, the better to invest an open-ended plot with a formal sense of closure.

Other cohesion devices supply constructive unity. Dialogue "hooks" carry us from one scene to the next, as when, at the end of one scene, On and his classmate discuss a fellowship meeting, which then becomes the locus of the scene that follows. By contrast, dangling causes play a more long-range game of planting and payoff. Consider one of several instances in the film. We first hear of On's school teacher, Ms. Tsui (Idy Chan), in reel three and again in reel four, but not until the closing reel does Ms. Tsui enter the drama. By now, the viewer has been primed for the teacher to make an appearance, but our introduction to Ms. Tsui has been strategically postponed in ways that suspend our curiosity and bolster the final reel's semblance of closure. Then there is the structuring device of deadlines. Classical protagonists operate under the tyranny of the clock: their goals must be accomplished within a certain time frame, lest their efforts come to nought. *The Way We Are* posits the vaguest of deadlines—the publication of On's high school exam results—but Hui and Lou divest the device of its characteristic impetus and suspense. Indeed, the "deadline" in Hui's film does not press the teenager into urgent, goal-oriented activity—On has already completed the exam before the plot begins—but rather serves as a kind of narrative terminus which, arriving in the final reel, helps motivate narrative closure. Tellingly, the epilogue does not disclose the result of On's exam, which functions as both macrostructural device and MacGuffin.

The film's episodic structure gains further unity through the technique of parallelism, another staple of Hong Kong plotting. Each of the protagonists is introduced in their own action line before the narration interweaves their respective trajectories. Subsequently, crisscrossed plotlines set up parallels among the three protagonists, hinting at echoic situations and conferring upon the drama a subtle yet robust architecture. By introducing Kwai and Granny in separate lines of action, and then making these plotlines intersect, *The Way We Are* conjures a simultaneous sense of action motivated realistically by chance or coincidence (a hallmark of both Hong Kong and melodramatic plotting) and purposive narrative design. Episodic reel construction, motivic associations, hook transitions, dangling causes, deadlines, parallelistic plotting—all these constructional features of Hong Kong plotting endow a diaphanous narrative with compositional unity, quietly arousing and sustaining the viewer's interest in the action.

Moreover, when we look closely at *The Way We Are* we find that certain aforementioned norms of Hollywood dramaturgy have not been so much jettisoned as "minified" in accordance with Hui's aesthetic program. Take the Hollywood norm of goal orientation. We noted above that *The Way We Are* frustrates this convention by rendering its characters' goals oblique (On), opaque (Kwai), or fruitless (Granny)—there is no substantive goal formation from which the plot can draw impetus. Yet the protagonists routinely target and achieve small-scale, trivial goals of the everyday variety (fix a lightbulb, install a TV set, buy a newspaper, carve a durian). Such commonplace objectives motivate the characters' actions and maintain the viewer's engagement from one scene to the next. If the characters' workaday pursuits seem subversive against the Hollywood plot's consequential goal-setting and the maximalist stakes of melodrama, we do better to grasp them as a paring down, even a simplification, of goal-based norms traditional to both Hollywood and Hong Kong storytelling.

We can grasp the principle of character change in much the same way. At first blush, On traces no significant arc of personality change across the plot's duration: he is as temperamentally placid at the film's end as he is at the start. Yet Hui and Lou chart the teenager's incremental progress as he acquires and deepens practical and moral knowledge under Kwai's understated tutelage. We find in On neither the startling anagnorisis (*The Sixth Sense*, 1999) nor the steep volte-face (*As Good as It Gets*, 1997) that sometimes qualifies as character change in Hollywood movies but rather a finely calibrated, almost imperceptible arc of psychological growth. Hui and Lou do not reject the character arc altogether, then, but yank it down to earth, rendering it ordinary and undramatic. Nevertheless, as we shall see, *The Way We Are* most typically favors a strategy of character revelation over character transformation.

Critics contend that *The Way We Are* diffuses or discards "plot," but Hui and Lou bestow upon the story action a deceptively rigorous structure. They recruit long-standing norms of Hong Kong dramaturgy to knit scenes, unify reels, and conjure thematic density (for instance, by means of carefully patterned motifs). We might say that Hui is a quintessential Hong Kong filmmaker not just because she explores indigenous social and political subject matter but also because her narrative strategies are firmly rooted in local storytelling practice. In a post-CEPA era supposedly purged of local plot construction—thanks to a preproduction script mandate and CEPA's promotion of Hollywood-style dramaturgy—Hui keeps alive Hong Kong cinema's endangered principles of dramatic composition.

Expect the unexpected

We have seen that the narrative of *The Way We Are*, a film "remarkably bereft of ordinary plotting and dramatic conflict," rests on a stable architecture.[6] Amid an indeterminate plot progression, the viewer finds ballast in the film's narrative patterns and structural integrity. But the question remains: If the plot is minimal, how does Hui compel our investment in the dramatic action? In this section, I turn to Hui's handling of narration, the strategic distribution of story information. I suggest that Hui sustains viewer interest largely through two large-scale strategies of engagement: (1) a shrewd play with genre expectations and (2) an aesthetic of gradual revelation.

I argue that *The Way We Are*'s active play of expectations springs from a purposive clash of generic schemata. The film plays one set of generic expectations off against another, cueing erroneous hypotheses, predictions, and inferences. The deft stroke here is that both sets of generic expectations derive from the same genre: the *wenyi* melodrama.

At first glance, this claim runs counter to critical commentary. Elaine Yee-lin Ho, for instance, writes of Hui's general "aversion to melodrama,"[7] while Yingjin Zhang refers to *The Way We Are*'s "non-melodramatic narrative."[8] Both claims are justified if we conceive of melodrama in its most recognizable form—that is, as a cinematic mode characterized by Peter Brook, Thomas Elsaesser, and others in terms of theatricality, hyperbole, and excess. But there exists in both Hollywood and Cantonese melodrama an opposite impulse. The tendency I have in mind inclines toward expressive restraint, ellipticality, and obliqueness, and a narrative emphasis on trivial everyday reality. Again and again, *The Way We Are* triggers the viewer's default schema for prototypical melodrama only to reveal this schema to be ill-suited to the drama at hand. While the viewer frames expectations appropriate to one genre strain (the melodrama of excess), *The Way We Are* embodies the narrational norms of quite another strain (the melodrama of restraint). Accordingly, the film retards the canonical story schema we standardly apply to "women's pictures." Our pathway through the drama becomes one of correcting faulty inferences, reframing expectations, and acclimating to an alternative set of melodrama norms.

Though a secondary practice, the aesthetic of restraint surfaces throughout the history of Cantonese and Hollywood melodrama. In classical Hollywood, studio directors Otto Preminger and John M. Stahl played down the fraught emotional outbursts prized by contemporaries such as Douglas Sirk and Nicholas Ray. Instead they matched their heroines' quiet stoicism and stifled passion to an atmosphere of subdued emotion. Preminger's *Daisy Kenyon* (1947) and Stahl's *Imitation of Life* (1934), for example, swerve from the paradigmatic melodrama, whose "emotional pattern," according to Elsaesser, "is that of panic and latent hysteria."[9] Early instances emerge in the Mandarin *wenyi pian*, too, most notably Fei Mu's *Spring in a Small Town* (1948), which substitutes a sedate and muted narration for feverish and theatrical affect. More recently, Wong Kar-wai's *In the Mood for Love* (2000) supplants the *wenyi pian*'s crisis-ridden structure with a meditative narrative rhythm, emotionally contained atmosphere, and ornate visual design. And, of course, Asian cinema furnishes many exemplars, ranging from Japan's Ozu Yasujiro to Taiwan's Hou Hsiao-hsien. *The Way We Are* extends this venerable tradition of muted melodrama.

As noted earlier, *The Way We Are* seemingly rejects plot—or at least the sort of plot we expect from *wenyi* melodrama. By foregrounding wholly decent and mutually compatible protagonists, Hui and Lou eliminate the prospect of dramatic conflict. No villain plunges the heroines into turmoil. The story grants its two widows, Kwai and Granny, no romantic opportunities, unlike, say, the affair afforded Cary (Jane Wyman) in Sirk's *All That Heaven Allows* (1955). *The Way We Are* deflects melodramatic sentimentality.[10] And it spurns the genre's narrational communicativeness and omniscience, proving highly suppressive of its protagonists' inner states. Hui avoids the sort of transparent subjective devices that foster spectator sympathy, pity, and pathos. She refuses to funnel character interiority through the internal voiceover device, as Alfred Hitchcock does in *Rebecca* (1940) and Fei Mu does in *Spring in a Small Town*. Moreover, quite unlike the archetypal melodramatic agent who speaks her mind, *The Way We Are*'s three protagonists are almost chronically taciturn. Seldom, if at all, do these characters verbalize their inner states. Consequently, we must infer their interiorities chiefly on the basis of bodily and facial cues. But here, too, the narration obfuscates. Hui mostly abandons what Carl Plantinga calls the scene of empathy, which foregrounds a close facial view of a character so as to make legible her emotions and induce the viewer's empathetic response.[11] As one critic observes, *The Way We Are* sets forth "hardly any emotive close-ups."[12]

Even when framed in legible close-up, the characters tend to be facially impassive, giving little away. When we discover that On's father died some years ago, a frontal close-up of the teenager augurs an explicit emotional display. Yet the boy's laconic visage tamps down the potential for melodrama and skewers sentimentality. What this scene elicits, I think, is something more complex than melodramatic sympathy or pity. On's unselfconscious stoicism, his ability to move forward without complaint or self-pity, triggers the viewer's admiration, even "elevation"—that is, the emotion wrought "by the witnessing of … human beauty or virtue" which spurs in the perceiver "a desire for moral betterment."[13] Without conferring moral sainthood upon On (as a melodrama of excess might do), the scene stirs deep admiration for his fortitude. In sum, *The Way We Are*'s pared-down aesthetic—its repudiation of conflict, bathos, and ingratiating subjective access—differs sharply from the narrational pattern of canonical melodrama. More to the point, the characters' emotional reticence finds an ideal register in Hui's narrational restraint.

One anomalous instance delivers something akin to Plantinga's scene of empathy. Shortly past the midpoint, a single-shot flashback whisks us back to (what we infer is) the funeral of Kwai's husband. A legible medium shot shows Kwai sobbing uncontrollably at her husband's casket. Director Hui holds the shot for a lengthy fifty-five seconds. A plaintive piano cue underscores the action. But the obvious potential for sentimentality is held in check by Hui's oblique visual presentation: the narration refuses to confirm the object of Kwai's anguish. There are no establishing shots of the funeral parlor, the open casket, the assembled mourners. As so often in *The Way We Are*, an equivocating and "gappy" narration roughens narrative comprehension. We must form inferences on the basis of only partial informational cues. And as we shall see, Hui's tricky narration repeatedly sends our inferences awry.

Just as typically, Hui motivates the funeral flashback by oblique means. The present-time action shows Kwai receiving news of a death in the family; subsequently, the narration launches the flashback to her husband's funeral. In the present, the deceased family member is a character absent from the drama, not previously shown onscreen or invoked in dialogue. Yet this character's demise carries causal significance: it triggers not only the flashback but also a later scene in which Kwai, On, and others gather at her funeral. Similarly, an entire chain of events gets initiated by a character who remains entirely off stage—Granny's young grandson, about whom we know little. We come to realize that such characters are but narrative pretexts: they function chiefly to steer the protagonists' spatiotemporal paths, and to illuminate the protagonists' psychologies. They also point toward an overarching formal strategy—namely, the motivation of story action through indirect or diffuse causation. Just as unindividuated or unseen figures shape the protagonists' activity, so mundane "events" supply narrative impetus, as when a broken lightbulb launches a whole suite of actions. Once again, these storytelling stratagems depart from the melodrama of excess. But precedents exist in the restrained *wenyi* melodrama: think of the dramatic causal power accorded the absent spouses of *In the Mood for Love*.

At both narrative and narrational levels, then, *The Way We Are* exploits the viewer's baseline schemas for melodrama while tacitly adopting the norms of another, less dominant strain of melodramatic storytelling. As such, the film throws our default assumptions and expectations into doubt. Hui sets up false expectations from the start. Pregnant with real-world resonance, the film's actual narrative setting—the satellite town of Tin Shui Wai, located in Hong Kong's New Territories—had recently gained media notoriety as a "city of sadness" thanks to a spate of murder-suicides committed therein. The town's recent tragic past doubtless shaped the narrative expectations of the film's original local audience. Likewise, as Esther Cheung points out, the "toponymical reference in the Chinese film title—*Tianshuiwei de ri yu ye*—inevitably reminds Hong Kong viewers of many tragic cases of domestic violence."[14] From the outset, then, Hui readies the audience for a tale of crime and murder. More broadly, she exploits a wider process of social categorization. The locale's public housing estates in which our protagonists reside not only evoke the crowded tenement houses of the classic Chinese *wenyi pian*; they also tap a cultural stereotype linking Hong Kong's housing estates with criminality, as probed in films such as *Made in Hong Kong* (1997) and *Besieged City* (2008). *The Way We Are* thus activates both real-world and genre schemata to misleading effect. Both its Chinese title and its narrative milieu prompt us to expect elements of crime drama, a genre Hui had plied before (*Zodiac Killers*, 1991; *Goddess of Mercy*, 2003).[15]

These misguided expectations are gently reinforced by an erroneous primacy effect. As a function of narration, the primacy effect initiates a set of (more or less reliable) first impressions regarding a character or a situation. In *The Way We Are*, a parallelistic opening reel crosscuts between Kwai and On, the latter of whom we are invited to judge harshly. While Kwai toils at her place of work, On idles the day away in a state of near-constant torpor. Social category attribution, a habitual aspect of film viewing, prompts us to categorize On according to social type, as wastrel, ne'er-do-well, troubled teen. (Later in the first reel, Kwai describes him as "lazy.") Subsequent scenes compound the primacy effect. When the parallel action lines first merge, On and Kwai exchange not a word. At a family celebration, they sit apart and alone: apparently, On spurns his mother's company in favor of solitude. Here social category activation meshes with genre-based expectations. We may surmise that On is a young and dangerous *ah fei* (delinquent youth), a figure common to both Hong Kong's deprived districts and the local cinema's triad genre. And we might forecast a drama of generational conflict within the depleted family unit, a standard trope within *wenyi* and Hollywood melodrama. The narration steers us wrong on both counts.

Through an arc of gradual revelation, On's psychological traits begin to crystallize. We witness him among his male peers, whose rambunctiousness and playful teasing of their friend as "a good boy" qualifies the primacy effect and lays bare On's benign nature. So much for a tearaway delinquent. Mostly, we observe On with his mother. The pair's initially nonverbal interaction, not to say their flouting of demonstrable affection, hints at filial discord or generational rift, but the film reframes their reticence as easy familiarity, debunking any hint of animus. This is no melodrama of teenage revolt. Nowhere evident are the domestic cataclysms of, say, *Stella Dallas* (1937) or *A Mother's Tears* (1953). Rather, *The Way We Are* reveals a tight symbiotic bond between mother and son.

Hui's narration wallows in the intimacy of small moments, as when Kwai teaches On to separate a durian, prepare meals, and execute day-to-day routines. More discreetly, Kwai inculcates in her son not only practical know-how but Confucian moral values. Her knowledge of traditional cultural customs and rituals (such as the preparation and consumption of food) is "handed down" to On along with a humanist ethics of behavior rooted in altruism and compassion. With characteristic docility, On follows Kwai's example, dutifully observing, imitating, and learning—a far cry from the idler implied by the primacy effect. By such means, *The Way We Are* attaches its central relationship to an overarching theme of cross-generational harmony, familial unity, and the preservation of cultural traditions. The viewer, meanwhile, is compelled to correct the faulty inferences cued by an unreliable primacy effect.

Indeed, the spectator's expositional hypotheses, guided by genre expectations and the primacy effect, routinely demand modification. Introduced in the opening reel, Kwai's elderly mother casts an unfavorable first impression: at a birthday celebration in her honor, she grouses and gripes like the ungrateful kin found in so many *wenyi* melodramas. We take the measure of this character immediately, but our negative judgment piggybacks on the fundamental attribution error—we assume that the woman's ornery behavior in the moment amounts to an entrenched personality trait, but later information will reveal that she is not the ingrate we took her for. The primacy effect similarly misdirects our assumptions regarding Kwai's affluent brethren, from whom the heroine seems emotionally detached. Are Kwai's brothers the Machiavellian schemers, the "thankless brutes," of traditional melodrama?[16] To the contrary, the coda belatedly confirms their benevolence, as when one sibling offers to pay On's college tuition fees. Recurrently throughout the film, the primacy effect triggers and undercuts our activity in ways that crystallize a central theme. *The Way We Are* thematizes and affirms familial unity (and, by extension, civic solidarity). By initially hinting at a web of familial disharmonies—between mother and son, mother and daughter, sister and brother—the film drives home its affirmation of family all the more powerfully.[17]

Hui's ludic narration flatly frustrates our expectations. Those expectations spring from the familiar narrative tropes of the prototypical *wenyi* melodrama. The film also exploits our real-world heuristics for comprehending people and events (social category attribution, the primacy effect, the fundamental attribution error, and the like). *The Way We Are*'s narration risks alienating spectators unwilling to play along, but its dynamic of novelty and norm, and its continuous reshaping of knowledge, keeps the motivated viewer engaged.

Moreover, the film's latent appeal to a shadow genre—the melodrama of restraint—challenges our default presuppositions in ways that can generate pleasurable surprise even as our expectations are frustrated.

The primacy effect, for instance, engrosses us partly through a game of gradual revelation. "Revelatory plots," writes Seymour Chatman, "tend to be strongly character-oriented, concerned with the infinite detailing of existents, as events are reduced to a relatively minor, illustrative role."[18] Accordingly, in *The Way We Are* we encounter not so much character change as character revelation, as new information unveils facets of personality formerly concealed by a quietly deceptive narration. Such tactics rivet, rather than slacken, our attention and focus. An ongoing process of inferential elaboration and correction sustains our future-oriented interest. As Todd Berliner and others have shown, the type of narration marked by equivocation, ambiguation, and novelty can yield a richly satisfying experience.[19] The effort to grapple with novelty, to retroactively revise assumptions, to reframe expectations, and so forth is apt to elicit the viewer's "exhilaration," an elated form of pleasure unavailable to viewers of more conventional artworks.

Motifs and misdirection

Misdirection is one of the film's major structuring principles. One short scene in the sixth reel furnishes a devious example. In her apartment kitchen, Kwai cleans a thermos flask and hangs it on a hook on the wall to dry. A ringing telephone lures Kwai into the living room; she thus vacates the kitchen and the camera's field of view. The shot is now apparently an "empty" zone. As we eavesdrop on Kwai's side of the telephone conversation, the camera slowly advances toward the doorway, as if mimicking the viewer's desire to follow Kwai into the living room and observe her reaction to what she hears. Her interlocutor—a family relative—inferably delivers bad news: somebody has died. The camera's grave track forward inclines slightly toward the thermos. The phone call ended, Kwai soon reemerges in the kitchen and resumes her chores, unperturbed, it seems, by news of a death in the family. Now the camera reverses its trajectory and slowly retreats, adopting a characteristically discreet vantage point of the heroine.

This oblique scene launches and reinforces some compelling inferences. Foregoing action has established the thermos as a reiterated motif associated with Kwai's hospitalized mother. Though another of the film's everyday domestic objects, the flask gains a degree of saliency when On first calls on his grandmother in hospital, and again during a subsequent visit. By now, this household item is motivically linked to the ailing elder. True to the film's reserved style, the camera's gradual advance does not isolate the thermos in heavy-handed close-up but rather affords the object a delicate emphasis. In concert with the offscreen dialogue (Kwai's telephone interaction) the shot conjures an unmistakable implication: Kwai's mother has died. Even Kwai's unemotional reaction does not discredit this inference; rather, it seems only to corroborate an earlier hypothesis, sown from Kwai's failure to visit her hospitalized kin, that mother and daughter are estranged. Belatedly, however, the narration springs a surprise. A subsequent funeral scene reveals the deceased family member to be someone other than Kwai's mother, who remains alive and recuperating in hospital.

The narration has hoodwinked us, cueing compelling inferences only to falsify them by means of late-arriving information. The revelation of the true state of affairs keeps us cognitively engaged: we must retroactively revise our initial false impression, plug informational gaps in our knowledge, and shift our expectations regarding the still-unfolding action. Not least, we must adjust our genre schemas. If we expect the thermos scene to adopt the omniscience characteristic of melodramatic narration, we will soon discover that Hui's narration has been stealthily restrictive. The overheard telephone exchange conceals from us the dead person's identity. We (incorrectly) infer this figure's identity thanks to the motivically charged thermos. The camera's track forward, moreover, amounts to a piece of narrational chicanery. Not strictly justified by character movement (Kwai has left the field of action), this unmotivated camera maneuver comes forth as a cunning piece of misdirection, a narrational feint designed to cue faulty inferences.[20] Our discovery of the dead woman's identity—an elderly relative whom Kwai has not seen for many years—also obliges us to reexamine Kwai's lack of distress upon receiving ostensibly tragic news. Likewise, Kwai's presumed apathy toward her mother now needs to be differently construed. In short, the narration engages us in fairly strenuous cognitive activity. It seizes and sustains our interest by activating long-term memory (demanding that we keep track of motifs), planting temporary gaps, triggering inferences, frustrating expectations, generating surprise, compelling retrospective revision, and defying our genre-based schemas at every turn.

This thermos scene delivers in microcosm the film's tendency to lead astray our suppositions and surmisals. From the outset, misleading cues sweep our hypotheses off track. An untrustworthy primacy effect triggers incorrect inferences about the protagonists' traits and relationships. Genre schemata apposite to the melodrama of excess underpin our efforts to forecast the action, often to little or no avail—nowhere to be found, for example, are the "ungrateful wastrels" or "tyrannical" parents of popular *wenyi* melodrama.[21] In the absence of a plot driven by crisis, conflict, and spectacle, the narrational dynamic of inference cueing and correction seizes the viewer's interest. All the while, a strategically gapped narration means that we become cognizant of our inferential errors only gradually, as delayed exposition grants information we did not know we lacked. For the viewer open to an intricate play of schema-and-correction, *The Way We Are* elicits a form of exhilarated pleasure rooted in novelty, curiosity, and surprise.

Moreover, several of the cohesion devices examined earlier in this chapter prove key to Hui's two overarching narrational strategies. The tactic of gradual revelation, for instance, is abetted by dangling causes, which pose lingering questions and then postpone the answers. (When a classmate asks On if he holds a Christian faith, the diffident teen fails to answer; not until three reels later does Hui permit him to supply an answer, belatedly fleshing out characterization.) Further, the narrative's cohesion devices may perform double duty as misdirection devices, not only lending structural reinforcement to loosely connected story events but also fulfilling the narration's governing tactics of duplicity and gradual revelation. Motifs, for example, reveal their connotations incrementally, sprinkled over several reels. Some of these items misdirect the viewer's expectations (as does the deceptive thermos motif), thereby contributing to the film's continual frustration of genre schemata. In such ways, the plot's unifying devices play an important role in bolstering the film's engagement strategies.

My account of *The Way We Are*'s storytelling tactics does not claim to be exhaustive. I have examined elsewhere the way Hui orchestrates visual style and staging to mold the viewer's sense-making activity.[22] Still needed is a poetics analysis of performance in the film—Paw Hee-ching's economical and intricate turn as Kwai, in particular, would repay detailed analysis, such is the emotional eloquence of her minute facial expressions, gestures, and bodily movements.[23] These concerns notwithstanding, I wish to close by briefly clarifying some aspects of the film's narration that I have so far scanted. For one thing, I would stress *The Way We Are*'s enigmatic quality, which critical accounts sometimes play down. As I have tried to indicate, the film often equivocates on narrative information: the narration may confirm or discredit our hypotheses only belatedly; or it may never fully resolve the ambiguities it set forth. There is, for instance, a zone of indeterminacy surrounding On's feelings for Ms. Tsui. Several critics assume that On harbors a schoolboy "crush" on his teacher,[24] but Hui and Lou leave this hypothesis open to interpretation. In fact, Ms. Tsui emerges, like Kwai, as a nurturing figure (as reinforced by her role as youth counselor) rather than as a romantic object. Other equivocations pile up. Opaque facial expressions ambiguate character subjectivity. Narrative lines are left to dangle, as with the unresolved matter of On's exam results. Such elusiveness characterizes much of Hui's filmmaking, laying bare the influence of art cinema narration. This relative complexity further demonstrates Hui's respect for the viewer's intelligence and mirrors the uncertainties, contradictions, and irresolutions of everyday life.

The Way We Are's complexity springs from an aesthetic program rooted in minimalism. Sparse plotting and a refusal of redundancy throw down a challenge to the viewer's attentional focus. By gapping the narration, Hui further attenuates the drama, parceling out suppressed and delayed information in ways that compel the viewer's effortful gap-filling activity. Narrational complexity here is not on the order of a "puzzle film." Hui's narration is far less ostentatious than that of, say, *Mad Detective* (2007) or *Wu Xia* (2011). Nor is its largely linear narrative at all byzantine. Rather, *The Way We Are* swathes its humdrum, even mundane, chronicle of dailiness in tantalizing ambiguity, evincing the ellipticality and open-endedness of art cinema narration. Nor is the film's contemplative style, its penchant for leisurely takes and distant framings, commensurate with the farthest extremes of Asian minimalism. Though Hui's film employs an above-average shot length (16.4 seconds), its editing rate is positively breakneck compared to the sober, meditative work of Hou Hsiao-hsien, Jia Zhangke, Kore-eda Hirokazu, and Hong Sang-soo. No purveyor of slow cinema, Hui pursues a form of Asian minimalism adjusted to the livelier tastes of Hong Kong's art-film audience.

A further critical ambiguity pertains to the narrational point of view. Jing Jing Chang (2016: 732) contends that Kwai functions as "a narrator," such that "the audience shares [her] point of view."[25] Other critics similarly take the film's action to be focalized around the female characters (chiefly Kwai and Granny, but also Kwai's mother). Granted, female-centered focalization dominates the Hollywood melodrama and Chinese *wenyi*. But here again Hui strays from the prototypical generic template. *The Way We Are* displays as much fascination with On as with the female agents. Frequently the narration abandons Kwai and Granny to attach us to the boy's spatiotemporal path; it tethers optical point-of-view shots to neither Kwai nor Granny but rather to On only; and while Kwai undergoes no perceptible character change, On is afforded a subtle arc of improvement. I do not wish to overstate my case—the film does not exhibit a *greater* interest in On than in its women characters—but I do point out that, at the level of narrational point of view, Hui again swerves from dominant melodrama norms. For as much as *The Way We Are* shines forth as a "woman's picture," and notwithstanding Hui's reputation as a feminist filmmaker, the film exemplifies Hui's underappreciated dexterity with male characterization.

It also exemplifies Hui's adventurousness with genre. Famously prone to genre-hopping, Hui in *The Way We Are* plays one genre variant against another, the better to misdirect the viewer's focused effort at narrative comprehension and successful prediction. The film structures our attention through a dynamic pattern of inferential cueing and correction. Character goals, arcs, and interiority stand out against our default schemas for melodrama, yielding complexity, ambiguity, and cognitive surprise. Likewise, Hui's narrational strategies of misdirection exploit schemas rooted in the melodrama of excess. Through such means, Hui mines a minimal drama for quiet surprise and suspense. That drama, in turn, finds coherence from a host of plot devices conventional to Hong Kong dramaturgy. In an era of so-called post-Hong Kong cinema purportedly characterized by the cultural erasure of Hong Kong's storytelling norms, *The Way We Are* shows that, in the post-handover years, local filmmakers did not capitulate to globalizing pressures from mainland China and Hollywood. Like her film's protagonists, Hui lovingly preserves Hong Kong's indispensable cultural traditions.

6

An alternative resistance story

Female subjectivity, theatricality, and the ambiguity of mainland–Hong Kong geopolitics in Ann Hui's *Our Time Will Come*

Han Li

Branded by its major production and distribution company Bona Film Group as a celebratory work for the CCP's 96th anniversary and 20th anniversary of Hong Kong's return to mainland China, Ann Hui's *Our Time Will Come* (2017) narrates a real-life-based story of the CCP-led East River Column evacuating leftist intellectuals out of Japanese-occupied Hong Kong in 1942. The intersection of the film's subject matter, production context, and its positioning within Ann Hui's and her Hong Kong peer directors' post-CEPA oeuvre renders this work a unique text. Ann Hui, one of Hong Kong's most renowned auteurs since the late 1970s, along with some of her New Wave fellow veterans and emerging directors, ventured into making the mainland–Hong Kong co-productions in the new millennium. However, having received mixed reviews and unsatisfactory box-office results with *Jade Goddess of Mercy* (2003) and *The Postmodern Life of My Aunt* (2006), Hui soon "retreated" to telling Hong Kong "local" stories.[1] Her subsequent works, such as *The Way We Are* (2008) and *A Simple Life* (2012), showered with both critical and popular acclaim, are inadvertently hailed as exemplary pieces of "Authentic Hong Kong-flavored" (*chun gangwei*) films. These films were vehemently celebrated and modeled after during the first decade of 2000s, despite the production mechanism and narration of both films suggesting a much more complex picture than what the singular label shows.[2] Viewed in this light, *Our Time Will Come* emerges as an intriguing text in Hui's post-CEPA cinematic genealogy. On the one hand, the film seems to be continuing her record of "telling Hong Kong's own stories" as it uncovers the underappreciated contribution of a Hong Kong indigenous guerrilla force in the grand picture of China's national resistance in the Second World War.[3] On the other hand, as a tributary film, its circulation and reception are inevitably entangled in the ongoing restructuring of the mainland film industry, and its dynamic interplay with the Hong Kong filmmaking landscape further foregrounds the ambiguity of mainland–Hong Kong geopolitics that has been at the core of Hong Kong filmmaking since 1997.

Other than the positioning of the film in Hui's professional trajectory since the new millennium, *Our Time Will Come* also forms a telling juxtaposition with Hong Kong directors' (many of them established players in the industry) "main(land) melody" productions.[4] As scholars have insightfully pointed out, Hong Kong filmmaking veterans play an (un)expectedly instrumental role in the transformation of the mainland film industry, including the reconfiguration of the "main melody" genre (*zhuxuanlü*), a cultural/media infrastructure accompanying China's economic and political rise as a world superpower and its imperative in expanding its soft power influence to both domestic and international audiences. As Zhang Huiyu argues in his illuminating study of what he terms a "mainstream blockbuster" (*zhuliu dapian*), following a series of costume action dramas that kickstarted the restructuring of the mainland film industry in early 2000s, a series of "mainstream blockbusters" began to converge "mainstream value" and "entertainment appeal" contributing to the evolvement of this unique combine genre.[5] Entering the 2010s, Hong Kong filmmakers were increasingly involved in the development of this genre. These "main melody" films share certain distinctive characteristics as they are all (extremely) "masculine"—from creators to cast, from story to theme, from cinematic style to ideology. Viewed in the light of these "mainstream blockbusters," Hui's *Our Time Will Come*, though financed and marketed similarly to a "main(land) melody" film, demonstrates distinctively different traits.

Therefore, while *Our Time Will Come* inherits Ann Hui's long-established sociopolitical concerns and auteurist style, I argue that, although the 1997 factor remains a conducive framework, this work is best understood against a background more pertinent to its production—the intersection of Hui's post-CEPA co-productions (particularly her Hong Kong-themed neorealist works) and Hong Kong filmmakers' (in)voluntary involvement in the redefinition of the "main(land) melody" works. Critics have long agreed that, preoccupied with Hong Kong's colonial status and nationalist belonging, Hong Kong New Waves oeuvres in the 1980s and 1990s are best interpreted through what Abbas calls a "culture of disappearance," a culture "posited on the imminence of its disappearance."[6] However, in the post-1997 era, while the *fin de siècle* is no longer perceived as an ominous prospect but an everyday reality, cultural products as sociocultural responses to Hong Kong's changing identity and mainland–Hong Kong geopolitics are increasingly dealing with "reappearance" rather than "disappearance."[7] For the film industry, the dramatic rise of the mainland film industry and the changing dynamics between the two regions as well as the two film industries constitute a new "appearance." Films produced in the post-CEPA era, both in content and in their very existence, are responding to this "appearance"—regardless of whether they are dealing with or avoiding it.[8] To a certain extent, any films that claim to deal with Hong Kong's "locality" are, without exception, simultaneously dealing with its "interlocal" sensibilities.[9] In this sense, *Our Time Will Come* is an exemplary text on both textual and meta-textual levels.

Adopting a pseudo-documentary style, the film consists of a diegetic 1940s resistance story in color and an enacted present-day interview in black and white. In both diegesis, the film subtly subverts the "center"—a "main melody" masculine narrative. In the 1940s diegesis, *Our Time Will Come* proudly celebrates and resituates "peripheral" Hong Kong in the grand historiography of national resistance in the Second World War. However, Hui's switching of the diegetic focus from the guerrilla sniper "Blackie" to the female protagonist Fong Lan, and her appropriation of narrative elements from underworld legend, spy thriller, and everyday melodrama, further deviates from the cinematic formula prescribed by (overtly) dramatized "neo main melody" epics. In the present-day diegesis, Hui interviews a purported historical witness figure Ben (played by Hong Kong's star actor Tony Leung Ka-fai in old-age makeup), an old taxi driver in contemporary Hong Kong who served as a messenger for the guerrillas as a child. While the *mise-en-scène* of the interview creates an aura of "historicity," the fact that it is (ostentatiously) staged and theatrical simultaneously calls attention to the constructed nature of historiography. Overall, by closely reading *Our Time Will Come* against the aforementioned background, this chapter explores how this film, by presenting an alternative resistance story, offers a prism of Hui's long-standing and newly arisen sociocultural concerns and the ambiguity of mainland–Hong Kong geopolitics in the new millennium.

The departure of the hero(ic)

The wide publicity of *Our Time Will Come* (especially from the mainland media), besides Ann Hui's internationally recognized laureate status, is largely attributed to the subject matter of the film—the heroic rescue of a group of leftist intellectuals following Japan's occupation of Hong Kong in December 1941. The East River Column (*Dongjiang zongdui*) is the CCP-led anti-Japanese armed resistance force active in Guangzhou and Hong Kong from 1939 to 1944.[10] While the guerrillas' historical significance was retrospectively recognized by CCP leaders and historians, its history is less well known by ordinary people. In *Our Time Will Come*, Hui retells this forgotten historical episode, offering a prism for the audience to look into the cultural politics in the film. Ironically, the mission carried out by the East River Column is allegorical to the function this part performs in the overall storytelling in the film—to escort the hero's departure (from the narration). Intentionally or not, the CCP leadership in the rescue action is downplayed and the whole rescuing action is portrayed to be more of a chain of chivalric action.[11] The brevity and the unconventional depiction of this event render the film a "Hong Kong-style variation" of the "main melody."[12]

To further discuss this point, the delineation of the significance and transformation of the "main melody" genre, which *Our Time Will Come* was labeled as by the mainland media, is in order. Originating from the musical term "leitmotif" in the late 1980s, "main melody" initially referred specifically to state-subsidized and propagandistic films that celebrated revolutionary achievements and promoted values aligned with the party's agenda.[13] Exemplary works of this strain, such as *The Birth of New China* (*Kaiguo dadian*, 1989) and *The Creation of a World* (*Kaitian pidi*, 1991), "concentrated mainly on war and biographical events" and upheld "patriotism, collectivism, and socialism in esteem."[14] However, lacking the element of entertainment, these films struggled with commercial appeal. Entering the 2000s, the film industry reform and the influx of foreign investment and private capital into the film industry made it the fastest-growing cultural industry since the beginning of the new century. Scholars observed that several late-2000s films that drew both box-office and critical acclamation suggested a new development in this genre. These films, notably including *Assembly* (Feng Xiaogang, 2007), *The Founding of a Republic* (Han Sanping and Huang Jianxin, 2009), *Bodyguards and Assassins* (Teddy Chan, 2009), and *Aftershock* (Feng Xiaogang, 2010), demonstrated a shift in the production mode and narrative strategy of these "main melody" films, blurring the lines between art, politics, and commerce.[15] In the subsequent decade, Hong Kong directors were increasingly involved in these cross-border collaborations with mainland characteristics.[16] Tsui Hark's Hollywoodized adaptation of the Cultural Revolution model opera *The Taking of Tiger Mountain* (2014) exemplified a convergence of red classic and contemporary blockbuster, and the young, diasporic character Jimmy's return to Northeastern China and his root-searching reunion with his revolutionary kin suggest millennial generations' homecoming to the revolutionary ideas.[17] The next two instalments in the Founding of New China trilogy (respectively *Beginning of the Great Revival*, Huang Jianxin and Han Sanping, 2011, and *The Founding of an Army*, Andrew Lau, 2017) continued to repackage CCP history and its agenda with a star-studded cast to stimulate audience interest. What Chris Berry names as "the action adventure overseas film" such as *Wolf Warrior 2* (2017) and the action-packed Operation series (*Operation Mekong*, 2016, and *Operation Red Sea*, 2019, both directed by Hong Kong director Dante Lam) established new milestones for combining patriotism, nationalism, and the action blockbuster.[18] As Wendy Su argues, this new "Main melody" that the state "has been constantly investing, reinvesting and refining" highlights conflicts and congregation "among official ideology, market demand, and global influence."[19] These "main melody" films form a renewed "masculine" center, combining traditional industrial patriarchal dominance with the state's newly emerged sociopolitical imperatives. Scholars such as Emilie Yeh and Darrell William Davis perceptively point out that the production of these "hyper-national" films "renationalize" the Chinese film industry.[20] In Ka-Fai Yau's study of Ann Hui's film made a decade after the handover, Yau urges the audience to "be aware of the changing present" as "Hong Kong is becoming a very different subject matter."[21] The fact is that not only has Hong Kong cinema changed but "mainland" cinema has also become a different entity during this time. These "main melody" films are no longer one-dimensional propagandist tools as many of them were when the term was first coined. Instead, it is a new multifarious genre that transcends the geographical binary of mainland–Hong Kong and breaks down the barriers between art, politics, and commerce. They represent a new "appearance" in production, content, and the values they seek to deliver.

Within the context of the transformation of the "main melody" genre, the 2009 box-office hit *Bodyguards and Assassins*, a "main(land) melody" produced by fellow veteran Hong Kong director Peter Chan, further reveals the outlier status of Ann Hui's *Our Time Will Come*. *Bodyguards and Assassins* narrates a similar protection story set in Hong Kong, where an assorted group of individuals from different backgrounds unite to safeguard Dr. Sun Yat-sen, the founding father of the Republic of China, during a critical secret meeting in the city. Though both films highlight the contributions of ordinary hero(in)es to grand historical events, two prominent traits in *Bodyguards and Assassins* are noticeably absent in *Our Time Will Come*. Firstly, even though most of the ordinary characters join the protecting mission out of humble, personal reason, *Bodyguards and Assassins* shows that the main protagonists, a father–son duo, are still motivated by the noble national cause. While the son is enlightened by his Western education and revolutionary-spirited mentor, the father, a shrewd businessman who initially is reluctant, eventually commits to the noble idea of revolution (as shown through him reciting the revolutionary teachings that he initially dismisses). Beyond this explicit difference, the narrative rhythm and emotion that the films stir in their audience also diverge significantly between the two films. Told in an intense countdown mode around Dr. Sun's visit, *Bodyguards and Assassins* is a fast-paced, tension-filled tear-jerker that delivers an emotion-packed narrative of the mission. At the end of the film, when the camera glorifies Dr. Sun (both as the historical founding father and the personification of the revolutionary idea) with an emotionally charged low-angle shot accompanied by a list of history-changing uprisings stemming from the meeting, the film invokes a sublime feeling and strong identification with the national cause among viewers. This narrative logic permeates through the new "main melody" films. Whether they deal with historical revolutionary stories or contemporary international rescues, as the characters swear to uphold nationalistic ideologies, the film seeks to invoke a similar identification with these values in the audience.

In contrast, *Our Time Will Come* exhibits caution in this mode. Compared to the dramatic scenes and high energy in *Bodyguards and Assassins*, Hui refrains from portraying the spectacle of sacrifice or the glory of the sublime, steering clear of sensation and drama. The film opens with Mrs. Fong's calculated reaction to her tenants Mao Dun and his wife's early departure. Oblivious to the latter's identities, Mrs. Fong's primary concern over their early departure is the loss of rent. Although branded as a celebratory work, the CCP's leadership in the mission is only vaguely and briefly alluded to without notable acknowledgment in the film.[22] The key events of the rescue mission, other than Blackie Lau single-handedly eliminating a spy while escorting Mao Dun, are portrayed as individual acts of bravery rather than cooperative and collective heroism. Brother Tsang, an underworld "big brother," uses his influence to secure safe passage for the evacuation, adding a layer of underworld lore to the narrative. Piecing these together, the portrayal of the whole mission resembles a tapestry woven from individual daredevil actions and underworld legendary tales. At the end of the rescue mission, when the intellectuals have reached safety, the identity of their savior is not celebrated in the manner typical of a "main melody" film. Instead, the group is simply directed to continue forward and told, "Beyond the mountain is the guerrilla territory." With no personified heroic image or stirring music here, the film only offers an extended take of a winding grove path stretching into the distance, accompanied by the non-diegetic, lightly hummed tune of "We Are All Snipers." In contrast to the high-pitched glorification of revolutionary heroism in "main(land) melody" films such as *Bodyguards and Assassins*, this subdued and anticlimactic portrayal of the rescue mission "was obviously less spectacular and the political narrative less overt."[23] It clearly reflects Hui's deliberate effort to distance her version of the resistance story from the formulaic aesthetics and ideological tenor of the "anti-Japanese war epic" (*kangri shenpian*), a genre known for overly dramatizing resistance stories. Hui's deployment of the evacuation mission is a metaphor for the entire film: less than a third of the way into the film, the East River Column's most celebrated achievement concludes. As the (leftist) heroes leave Hong Kong, so does the glamorized heroism from the storytelling, shifting the narrative further away from "The Great Victory Rescue" (*shengli da yingjiu*) to an alternative resistance story.[24]

Other than the downplayed rescue mission, the espionage subplot in *Our Time Will Come* is treated in a similar fashion. The film parallels Fong Lan's intelligence work with another secret spy warfare plot involving her fiancé Lee Gam-Wing and two undercover female secretaries at the Japanese occupation headquarters. Hui's treatment of this subplot narrative diverges significantly from the "neo-spy films" that have been popular in mainland China since the 2000s. The spy genre, which gained significant popularity in the 1950s and 1960s, reflected national security anxieties of the time and primarily served as political propaganda.[25] Unlike these earlier films characterized by "the idealism of sacred Communists, sloganistic language, and formulaic plots," the neo-spy films and espionage TV series that have flourished since the 2000s probe deep into the characters' psychology and moral ambiguity.[26] Scholars notice that these films, such as Gao Qunshu's blockbuster *The Message* (2009), often feature a sensationalized combination of torture and sexualized bodies. Yanzhong Zhu notes that beyond commercial motives, these scenes are intended to "elicit a sense of identification with the on-screen heroes and empathy for the patriotic narrative of loyalty and self-sacrifice."[27] Interestingly, the espionage storyline in *Our Time Will Come* shares little dramatic intensity or visual spectacle typical of neo-spy films. The subplot, though reflecting another aspect of the underground resistance, is sporadically interspersed throughout the film, requiring considerable effort from viewers to engage with this dimension. This lack of a clear plot or central action aligns with Hui's overall resistance to portraying a master narrative of resistance history. The fragmented plot and genre hybridity serve as Hui's discursive rejection of telling the East River Column history as a main melody master narrative.

The resurgence of the feminine and the quotidian

As discussed, *Our Time Will Come* is structured around the theme of "retreats." In the first part of the film, what could have been depicted as a well-organized, strongly led, and collectively sensational rescue story instead "retreats" into a tale of individual heroic chivalry. As the story progresses, it further "retreats" into the portrayal of a female revolutionary. Alongside this narrative shift, the broad canvas of history and politics is subtly transformed into a milieu focused on familial and everyday life, offering a gendered perspective into Hui's approach to presenting resistance history.

Jack Halberstam's discussion of the relations between masculinity, state, and power offers a telling perspective on these multiple retreats portrayed in *Our Time Will Come*.[28] As Halberstam articulates, "Masculinity … inevitably conjures up notions of power and legitimacy and privilege; it often symbolically refers to the power of the state and to uneven distribution of wealth. Masculinity seems to extend outward into patriarchy and inward into the family."[29] In this light, Ann Hui's cinematic focus on female subject(ivity) in her filmmaking speaks volumes about her views and response to the sociocultural dynamics of Hong Kong and its filmmaking industry. In the early stage of her career, as a filmmaker Hui "quickly established herself as a pioneer in a profession monopolized by men," and as a social critic, her New Wave films "centralized and individualize women subjects in ways that earlier Cantonese cinema had rarely attempted."[30] Later, Hui's post-CEPA co-productions, such as *A Simple Life*, *The Way We Were*, and *The Golden Era*, unambiguously focus on women's history and agency. Therefore, the shift of the narrative focus to the awakening and growth of Fong Lan in *Our Time Will Come* marks a stark contrast to the hypermasculine "main melody" films.

What makes the female subjectivity in *Our Time Will Come* even more special is that, in addition to Fong Lan, the film portrays a constellation of ordinary female heroines: the overcautious but loving mother Mrs. Fong, the muddleheaded courier Ah Si, and the female spies who are infiltrated in the Japanese headquarters. Elaine Ho notes that Ann Hui's films often visualize "a specific bond between women." In *Summer Snow* (1995), the bond between two generations of women—Mrs. Sun and her mother-in-law—showcases women's strength under duress. In *The Way We Were*, the friendship developed between the widowed Mrs. Cheung and her elderly female neighbor illustrates a supportive network among the marginalized in the city.[31] In the second half of *Our Time Will Come*, the resistance efforts are predominantly portrayed as a female fellowship, an alliance where women—mothers, daughters, quasi-sisters, and even strangers—support each other out of kinship, conscience, camaraderie, and humanity rather than a grand (patriarchal or nationalistic) cause.[32] Read in this light, Mrs. Fong's last words become profoundly meaningful. Arrested during a failed intelligence mission and feeling guilty for implicating someone else, Mrs. Fong keeps reiterating "I can't read" in her interrogation and before her execution, which symbolically distances (if not outright rejects) the influence of the grand revolutionary discourse.[33]

Alongside the emergence of female subjectivity in *Our Time Will Come* is a storyline shift from big strokes of war and politics to the milieu of family and mundane life. Critics have long praised the "aesthetics of the quotidian" or "poetics of insignificance" in Ann Hui's films and contend that everyday life in Hui's film carries a unique narrative function and discursive power.[34] In *The Way We Are*, the uneventful, even repetitive, lives of Mrs. Cheung and her son, along with their interactions with friends and relatives, is not just a lifestyle but a symbol of virtue—the externalization of the inner serenity that enables them to face the drastically changing outside world.[35] Similarly, in *A Simple Life*, Ah Tao's seemingly plain interaction with Roger, the young master of the family she has served for more than sixty years, in the latter's small apartment, also creates qualitative time and affective space. In this light, Hui's seemingly out-of-place depiction of a wedding amid war in *Our Time Will Come* also reveals her view about portraying the wartime experience and women's role in it. When Fong Lan, who has begun intelligence work, stops by at her cousin's wedding while on a mission, the film shows the cousin's family still strives to fulfill the rigid customs despite the wartime scarcity and chaos, compromising only when necessary. Firstly, rejecting any singular depiction of the resistance period, Hui aims to recreate the genuine conditions of anti-Japanese wartime life.[36] Secondly, at the beginning of the film, Fong Lan rejects her fiancé's engagement proposal due to the wartime emergency. Therefore, by Fong Lan showing up at her cousin's wedding and letting her explain the rationale for this decision during wartime, Hui also validates the plurality of female choices.

One particularly noteworthy moment in this scene involves detailed attention to food, such as the matchmaker's explanation of the tea-pouring custom (out of respect for the elders) and rice throwing (for prosperity), and the restaurant owner's humble request that guests do not take the tableware due to wartime material shortages. As Mirana May Szeto has observed, food scenes are emblematic of Hui's "cinematics of the everyday life."[37] Whether it is Mrs. Cheung in *The Way We Are* carefully budgeting for groceries, preparing simple meals, and savoring durian and festival treats like mooncakes with her son, or Ah Tao in *A Simple Life* proudly preparing Roger's favorite ox-tongue, these food-related moments serve as Hui's validation of mundane life and female subjectivity. Similarly, in *Our Time Will Come*, the bride's mother and the matchmaker's preoccupation with meticulous wedding etiquette affirms the value of everyday trivialities in contrast to the grand history of war and politics. Hui signals through the scene's playfulness that if the hero's extraordinary deeds in a noble mission are worth recording so too are the everyday experiences of ordinary people.[38] Thus, as Mei Xuefeng contends, "the grand narrative is absolutely dissolved in those quotidian episodes, and those anti-Japanese activities are domesticated and trivialized."[39]

As the narrative focus in *Our Time Will Come* shifts to what might be considered "minor" and "trivial," the settings of these everyday activities similarly move to more peripheral areas. Housing is a recurring and organic narrative component in Hui's films, especially those signaling local consciousness. For instance, in *Summer Snow* the Sun family resides in an old tenement house (*tanglou*). This architectural style, which emerged postwar and is now diminishing, offers an emotive space for families, much like how Mrs. Sun, the female protagonist, perseveres in rapidly modernizing Hong Kong.[40] Another example is Tin Shui Wai in *The Way We Are* and *Night and Fog* (2009). As a satellite town in Hong Kong's New Territories bordering the mainland, the densely packed public housing blocks are home to underprivileged local families and new mainland immigrants. Just as Tin Shui Wai is physically on the edge of Hong Kong, the inhabitants are economically, socially, and emotionally expelled from the center.[41] In the latter half of *Our Time Will Come*, as the resistance efforts are linked with ordinary women and their daily activities, the village houses at the periphery of Hong Kong (in the rural area in the mountains of the New Territories) gain increasing narrative importance. Fong Lan, initially introduced in modern, fashionable attire, begins to wear traditional Hakka ethnic clothes, further embodying the lived experience and daily struggles of the resistance era.[42]

Questioning the "central"

In addition to Hui's deliberate fragmentation of the narrative and centralization of female subjects in contrast to a dominating, central story in the 1940s diegesis, the meta-cinematic structure and her self-reflexive view on historicity further challenge the "masculine" nature of similar stories. In the present-day diegesis of *Our Time Will Come*, Hui underscores her long-standing caution regarding the retrievability of history and the reliability of historiography. This is demonstrated by casting the renowned Hong Kong actor Tony Leung Ka-fai as Ben, an aged Hong Kong taxi driver who, in his youth, served as a junior guerrilla messenger. In a black and white documentary *mise-en-scène*, Ben is presented as though a real historical witness interviewed by Hui. His voiceover, inserted at multiple places in the 1940s diegesis, is presented as both a source and a reference for the 1940s reconstruction.

The effect of designing the present-day diegesis the way it is in the film should be considered within the broader context of the historiography of the East River Column, particularly the Hong Kong–Kowloon Independent Brigade (established in February 1942). The historical memories of the East River Column encompass traditional historiography in written form and materialized/tangible memories such as museums, exhibitions, tours, and oral history. Prior to the 2000s, the majority of contemporary history written about the East River Column, including works such as *The History of the Hong Kong–Kowloon Independent Brigade* (*Gangjiu duli dadui shi*, 1980s), *The History of Armed Struggle of Guangdong Province* (*Guangdong renmin wuzhuang douzhengshi*, 1981), *Historical Materials of the East River Column* (*Dongjiang zongdui ziliao*, 1983), and *The History of Guangdong People's Liberation Army's Anti-Japanese Resistance* (*Guangdong renmin kangri jiefangjun shi*, 1986), were all state-mandated official historiography. The history of the East River Column was often included as part of the CCP's history in Guangdong.[43] After 1997, the history of the East River Column began receiving increased attention and has been viewed as a part of rewriting the history of the Hong Kong–mainland relationship in the special administrative region (SAR). In 2008, the East River Column Historical Society was established in Hong Kong by descendants of its members with the aim to "collect and research the history of the East River Column activities in Hong Kong." Mainly sponsored by the SAR government and the Liaison Office of the Central People's Government, the historical society states its mission is to "continue to tell the story of CCP in Hong Kong, the story of the resistance activities of Hong Kong-Kowloon Independent Brigade, and to deepen Hong Kong people's understanding of the close connection between SAR and the country."[44] In 2022, with support from the SAR government, *The Gazetteer of the Hong Kong–Kowloon Independent Brigade* (*Gangjiu dadui zhi*) was published. Touted as "the most comprehensive military gazetteer of the Hong Kong-Kowloon Independent Brigade," the collection aims to "help Hong Kong people better appreciate the CCP's leadership in anti-invasion and national rejuvenation."[45] Alongside written history, materialized historical records have also been made accessible to the public. This includes the Sha Tau Kok Anti-Japanese Resistance Museum (converted from the Law family village house), which served as an activity base for the Independent Brigade, and a twenty-kilometer Heritage Trail. As Denise Ho and Jie Li insightfully point out, revolutionary museums in China "have been dynamic and vital public spaces that have defined and redefined the past for the present, serving as both a medium and a product of revolutionary culture."[46] Designed as a "patriotic educational base," the Sha Tau Kok Anti-Japanese Resistance Museum and trail aim to "enhance the public's knowledge of the heroic deeds of the Hong Kong-Kowloon Independent Brigade and Hong Kong civilians during the anti-Japanese wartime" as well as the CCP's leadership and contribution to Hong Kong.[47] Additionally, exhibitions, workshops, interviews, and oral history collections of historical witnesses are frequently organized. For instance, at the opening ceremony of the East River Column Historical Images Exhibition at the People's Revolution Military Museum in Shenzhen in 2013, guerrilla veterans, including Liu Cai, Blackie Lau's younger brother, shared their experiences from the resistance period.[48]

The efforts described above constitute only a fraction of the state-endorsed, systematic endeavors to retell the history of the East River Column. This re-narration, following a teleological worldview and an official historiographical formula, is designed to elicit viewers' admiration and identification with historical figures, affirm the role of Hong Kong's anti-Japanese struggle in the CCP's larger resistance campaign, and deepen Hong Kongers' identification with the mainland. While *Our Time Will Come* is marketed as a commemorative work due to its subject matter, the film presents a different view of history than the numerous official historiographies on the East River Column. On the one hand, the *mise-en-scène* of the black and white documentary-style interview creates an aura of truthfulness and authenticity for the 1940s diegesis. However, casting the celebrity star Leung Ka-fai as the interviewee simultaneously reminds the audience of the falseness of this historical witness and the theatricality of the interview. In doing this, Hui reveals the possibility and mechanism of staging truthfulness, ultimately questioning the validity of any historical recounting and cinematic realism.

In fact, it is not rare that Ann Hui states her stance on the irretrievability of historical truth. In her autobiographical documentary *As Time Goes By* (1997), she confesses her skepticism of historical singularity or "absolute truth," influenced by witnessing the contrasting leftists and rightist interpretations of the same event in her childhood. In *Boat People* (1982), the Japanese reporter Akutagawa eventually begins to question the ability to present "reality" through his camera, prompting the audience to rethink the reliability of what they see on screen. The Brechtian moments in *The Golden Era* (2014), where characters directly address the camera to narrate their stories, also underscore Hui's view on the fragmentation of history and subjectiveness of individual lives. Similarly, *Our Time Will Come* employs a meta-cinematic revelation of its own "realist" effect, not merely as a self-reflexive act by the director but also as a disillusioning gesture that highlights the illusory nature of both historical and cinematic realism. In the 1940s diegesis of *Our Time Will Come*, after Blackie Lau says farewell to Fong at the pier, the camera pans to the left and the wartime waterscape is montaged with a glimmering view of the present-day Victoria Harbor. The film concludes elusively when Ben quickly walks out of the community center, drives his taxi, and disappears in the busy metropolitan traffic. The merging of past and present, historical heroism, and everyday mundanity also seems to suggest the indistinguishability of the real and the illusory.

Concluding remarks

Scholars examining Hui's oeuvres through an allegorical perspective claim these films can be read "as political responses to the politics of the construction of Hong Kong's cultural identity."[49] They argue that this type of allegorical cinema carves out "a rhetorical space for Hong Kong filmmakers to continue telling Hong Kong stories … even as the local cityscape rapidly changes under Mainland Chinese influence."[50] *Our Time Will Come* certainly exemplifies this allegorical nature, but its stance on mainland–Hong Kong geopolitics, as some scholars argue, is clearly discernible. Yiu-Wai Chu sees this main(land) melody film as "a Trojan horse" in that it contains complicated messages underneath its seemingly simple and disarming outside/surface and Karen Fang believes this work "astutely fulfills the expectations of her Mainland financing while still upholding local identity."[51] Beneath the façade of a main(land) melody story, Hui elevates women as agents of change, validates the significance of the insignificant, and further subverts the ultimate "center" on a meta-cinematic level, challenging the purported "truthfulness" of historiography and hegemonic "masculine" storytelling. Thus, this alternative resistance story offers an intriguing text where the delicate negotiation between nationalism, localism, and art of cinematic storytelling can be observed.

Part Three

Visualizing Hong Kong females

7

Struggling in between

Hong Kong women as postcolonial subjects in Ann Hui's *Summer Snow*

Yiran Ai

In the context of Ann Hui's filmography, *Summer Snow* emerges as a work of remarkable significance. From the mid-1990s, Hui embarked on a series of films centered on women's lives, including *Summer Snow* (1995), *The Stunt Woman* (1996), *Eighteen Springs* (1997), *Goddess of Mercy* (2003), and *The Postmodern Life of My Aunt* (2006). Amid the lull that Hong Kong cinema was experiencing at the time,[1] characterized by diminishing audiences and decreasing film production, *Summer Snow* was a rare success with both critics and audiences alike.[2] The film won international acclaim, earning a Golden Bear nomination at the 45th Berlin International Film Festival and ultimately winning the Silver Bear Award, while Josephine Siao Fong-Fong won the Silver Bear for Best Actress. Domestically, the film dominated the 32nd Taiwan Golden Horse Awards, winning Best Picture, Best Actress, Best Supporting Actor, and Best Cinematography. The pinnacle of the film's success came at the 15th Hong Kong Film Awards, where *Summer Snow* swept the top categories, including Best Picture, Best Director, Best Actor, Best Actress, Best Supporting Actor, and Best Screenplay—a historic feat that cemented its place as a landmark in Chinese cinema. Its inclusion in the Hong Kong Film Awards Association's list of the "100 Best Chinese Motion Pictures" in 2005 further solidified its standing.[3]

The critical and commercial success of *Summer Snow* can be attributed to its ability to weave intricate storytelling from ordinary lives. Inspired by the Japanese novel *The Twilight Years*,[4] which narrates the experiences of a family caring for an elderly person living with Alzheimer's disease,[5] *Summer Snow* transcends the genre of family drama. It relocates the narrative to pre-handover Hong Kong, where a middle-aged woman—also a daughter-in-law—navigates her father-in-law's Alzheimer's, societal flux, and filial duty. The burden of caregiving falls disproportionately on her shoulders. Despite being overwhelmed, she continues to fulfill the duties imposed by traditional familial roles while simultaneously negotiating her social identity, attempting to reconstruct domestic relationships and claim a space for her own subjectivity. Her experiences serve as a microcosm of a society in transition, as the film examines the complexities of female experience, intertwining personal struggles with the sociopolitical tapestry of the era.

More significantly, as this chapter aims to argue, *Summer Snow* alludes to the "postcolonial situation" in 1990s Hong Kong, as it prepared for and underwent its handover to the People's Republic of China (PRC) in 1997. Specifically, the film explores the complex identity of Hong Kong's society and people, shaped as it is by the interwoven threads of colonial and indigenous cultural influences. Unlike other societies that construct their histories and territorial identities in more autonomous ways, Hong Kong's historical and spatial narrative is deeply entangled with representations of the triangular relationship among the British colonizer, the Chinese motherland, and the territory itself.[6] The film not only showcases the agency of women living amid the interplay of different cultural influences that characterized pre-handover Hong Kong but also forges a distinct female subjectivity, following women who actively seek control over their life choices and autonomy within the social spaces they inhabit. These women are not passive participants but rather architects of their own lives, navigating familial landscapes and redefining societal roles with unwavering resolve. *Summer Snow* depicts a female subject who exists in a constant "in-between" state, torn between societal expectations—such as her role as a daughter-in-law responsible for family care—and her personal ambitions as a woman with her own career.

In this chapter, I explore the film through a postcolonial critical lens. I employ as my main critical framework the 1992 work of cultural critic Rey Chow on Hong Kong's postcolonial identity, particularly in the context of the post-1997 handover.[7] Following Hong Kong's return to Chinese sovereignty, the region entered a postcolonial era. In this new phase, the complexity of its identity became increasingly pronounced. Chow characterizes the handover as a territorial exchange "between two colonizers" (China and Britain), framing it as geopolitical power shift rather than a straightforward decolonization process. Yet, for Hong Kong society, this political transition was far from a simple transfer of authority "from one colonizer to another." I also reflect on Mirana May Szeto's 2006 critique of "a petit-grandiose Hong Kongism,"[8] a kind of inferiority-superiority response to Hong Kong's multiple colonial experiences—a critique that exists in dialogue with Chow's own views on the region's status as a "marginalized entity." When examined within its historical context, Hong Kong's identity—both colonial and postcolonial—emerges as relational, in flux, and shaped by the ongoing triangulation among the British colonizer, the Chinese motherland, and Hong Kong itself. Rather than being fixed or coherent, the territory's cultural identity is marked by its incompleteness and continually shifting form in response to specific political, economic, and social contingencies. As such, the emphasis on Hong Kong's postcolonial identity lies in the state of "becoming"—a way of life and cultural affiliation characterized by transnationality, mobility, and adaptability. I aim to place the aforementioned concept of "in-betweenness" on firmer ground, and in doing so to further the debate on the interplay between feminism and postcolonialism represented in *Summer Snow*. The discussion then turns to the film's portrayal of the predicament faced by women in Hong Kong, who found themselves under the dual influence of the two cultures. Finally, I provide an in-depth analysis of the film's presentation of the female protagonist as a means by which to reflect the cultural status of Hong Kong society during this period of transition, which marked the end of British rule and ushered in a new era of sovereignty and identity for the region.

Hong Kong's postcolonial identity: Rey Chow's "between two colonizers"

Since its establishment as a British colony in 1841 following the conclusion of the First Opium War, Hong Kong's history has undergone significant upheavals, including a period of Japanese rule during the Second World War. The Sino-British Joint Declaration in 1984 confirmed the official transfer of sovereignty over Hong Kong to the PRC on July 1, 1997, marking the commencement of the postcolonial era. Rey Chow's 1992 essay "Between Colonizers" analyzes Hong Kong's complex postcolonial identity shortly before the moment of handover. Chow begins by drawing attention to the often-overlooked status of Hong Kong in discussions on postcoloniality, which have tended to deem the territory "too small to merit attention."[9] Beyond challenging the erasure of Hong Kong in postcolonial studies, Chow repositions the territory in her analysis, framing the 1997 handover as "*a forced return to a 'mother country*'" and positing a "double impossibility" at the heart of Hong Kong's postcolonial predicament.[10] According to Chow, the region's identity defies easy categorization, unable to submit fully to either Chinese nationalist repossession or British colonialism.[11] This perspective resonates with Victor Fan's discussion of Hong Kong as "an extraterritorial space" in his monograph *Extraterritoriality: Locating Hong Kong Cinema and Media* (2019).[12] As Fan observes, the everyday lives of Hong Kong's inhabitants were shaped by two sovereign authorities that were not only mutually conflicting but also mutually collaborating. Both sought to assert political control over Hong Kong and, paradoxically, did so by relegating the city to an extraterritorial position—marginalizing it from the centers of their respective political and institutional systems.[13] This extraterritorial condition underscores the hybridity of both Hong Kong and its citizens, situating their identity in a state of in-betweenness, marked by a detachment from exclusive loyalty to either nation.[14] This resistance stems from a twofold challenge: the need to reclaim a unique cultural identity distinct from both and to navigate the anti-colonial sentiment that resists colonial culture, in particularly the legacies of British rule. Consequently, Chow raises a pivotal question about "the struggle between the dominant and the subdominant within the 'native' culture itself."[15] This internal tension, inextricably tied to the reality of "returning to the motherland," lies at the core of Hong Kong's postcolonial identity, provoking a constant oscillation between native and colonial influences.

While recognizing the "in-betweenness" inherent in Hong Kong's postcolonial identity, Chow specifically characterizes the 1997 handover itself as a straightforward form of "colonization." She argues that Hong Kong's unique position between two colonizers—Britain and China—renders the "mother country" "*as imperialistic as the previous colonizer*."[16] However, she does acknowledge "the fact that a large part of Hong Kong (the Kowloon Peninsula and the New Territories) had been 'on lease' from China to Britain" for ninety-nine years.[17] During this period, China retained *zhuquan* (sovereignty authority) over the territory of Hong Kong, while Britain exercised *zhengquan* (administrative right)—an arrangement that rendered Hong Kong an extraterritorial space.[18] Chow's interpretation of the reunification of Hong Kong with the motherland in 1997 as "colonization" therefore leaves itself open to challenge.

Mirana May Szeto takes issue with Chow's thinking, viewing it as an example of "petit-grandiose Hong Kongism," a paradoxical "inferiority-superiority response to Hong Kong's coloniality."[19] In other words, while acknowledging its own colonial experience, Hong Kong elevates itself above mainland China owing to its economic and cultural distinctiveness. As Chow herself notes, this stance manifests in questions like: "is Hong Kong [as a colony] not in fact a paradigm of

Chinese urban life in the future?"[20] Behind such questions lies a belief that Hong Kong has already achieved a level of modernity that mainland China aspires to reach, placing Hong Kong at "the forefront of 'Chinese' consciousness of 'Chinese' modernity."[21] However, in the pre-handover period, this self-perceived superiority also fueled anxieties. Fear of becoming a special administrative region of China was accompanied by what Szeto describes as an "imagined Chinese cultural snobbery against Hong Kong,"[22] coupled with resentment toward an "imagined threat from an imposing Chinese political regime."[23] These anxieties, Szeto argues, stem from a distorted perception of both Chinese culture and mainland politics.

This internal conflict presents a dilemma for pre-colonized regions, including Hong Kong. On the one hand, Chow acknowledges "the inevitable tendency toward nativism as a form of resistance against the dominance of western colonial culture," as seen in India's postcolonial trajectory.[24] However, Hong Kong's position as a returning territory creates a paradox. Embracing nativism to resist Western influences would, in her view, require compromising its own history. Therefore, Hong Kong's post-handover era demands a new path: a "self-writing" of Hong Kong's identity. This, Chow argues, necessitates moving beyond both British and Chinese historiographical models, transcending the simplistic binary of "foreign colonizer versus native colonized."[25] Echoing this perspective, Yingchi Chu offers a more concrete articulation of Hong Kong's identity, proposing that it "possesses a hybrid identity stemming from British colonization and Chinese society."[26] In a similar vein, Fan contends that this cultural identity occupies an extraterritorial position—constantly caught between opposing political structures and cultural-linguistic forces.[27] This identity claims sovereignty over its own lived experience through the forces that shape it, yet paradoxically remains detached from the sovereign territories to which those forces belong. It is precisely this sense of uncertainty that defines Hong Kong's extraterritorial condition—one that is not merely juridical, political, and legal but also cultural and linguistic.[28] Ultimately, rather than being grounded in clearly delineated national domains, Hong Kong identity remains perpetually situated in an in-between state, negotiating among multiple cultural formations.

Nonetheless, echoing Szeto's cautionary words, "we must ask carefully" whose Hong Kong is the "Hong Kong" that, according to Chow, demands self-writing?[29] By framing Hong Kong as "the forefront of Chinese modernity and modernization [defined by] a cut-throat capitalist economy, a popular culture industry and a managerial technology,"[30] Chow's analysis leans toward a particular version of Hong Kong, one aligned with the petit-grandiose Hong Kongism Szeto critiques. Such a perspective risks eclipsing the nuance and complexity of Hong Kong's postcolonial identity—an indigenous cultural identity that uniquely blends Chinese and British cultures, distinct from the "Chineseness" of mainland China and Taiwan.

To preserve the core of Chow's valuable concept of "in-betweenness"—even as she notes that, within the context of Hong Kong's postcoloniality, this notion implies an idea "of impure origins, of origins as impure"—I propose that any account of Hong Kong's postcolonial identity must seek to assert the existence of an "in-between" space.[31] This identity embraces the influences of both cultures without necessitating exclusive affiliation with either one—the motherland or the colonizer. Instead, it embodies the coexistence of the two cultures in transition. In such a way, Chow's "double impossibility" can be transformed into a possibility: Hong Kong's identity residing in the passage between cultures.

In her essay, Chow argues that popular culture offers a platform from which to articulate Hong Kong's postcoloniality, which she explores through the music of Taiwanese singer Luo Dayou, who achieved success in Hong Kong.[32] Chow emphasizes how Luo's lyrics reflect the territory's postcolonial modernity. However, Szeto argues that Chow's analysis manifests petit-grandiose Hong Kongism, as Chow claims that Luo's songs advocate for Hong Kong's "autonomy" primarily for the sake of its economic and cultural advantages.[33] I concur with Szeto that Luo's work fails to capture Hong Kong's complex postcolonial identity. His Taiwanese origins, along with his self-identification as a mainland Chinese with familial roots in Taiwan, call into question his relevance in representing Hong Kong's identity.[34] Consequently, Chow's focus on Luo provides an abstract and limited exploration of postcolonial Hong Kong identity. A better understanding of Hong Kong's postcolonial "in-betweenness" must consider a broader range of cultural objects. Ann Hui's film *Summer Snow*, set in the 1990s, provides a more localized and grounded representation of Hong Kong's identity by depicting the life of a local family through the lens of a middle-aged woman. The film, directed by a woman from Hong Kong, not only addresses gender issues—absent from Luo's music and Chow's study alike—but also counters the elitist and self-centric tendencies of "Hong Kongism."

Traversing between: Women as postcolonial subjects in Hong Kong

Szeto's critique of Chow's analysis of Luo's lyrics underscores the necessity for context-specific strategies in understanding resistance to political and cultural hegemony through popular cultural forms.[35] *Summer Snow* serves as an exemplar, realistically portraying the struggles of a forty-year-old woman in Hong Kong during the 1990s, before the 1997 handover.[36] The emphasis is placed on the daily challenges faced by the protagonist May (Josephine Siao Fong-Fong), such as routine household tasks. As a full-time accountant at a toiletries company, May juggles her career with the responsibilities of a housewife and carer for her aging parents-in-law, the latter of which are complicated by her father-in-law's cold demeanor. Despite May's traditional domestic responsibilities, the film emphasizes elements of her independence, such as her earning her own livelihood and having her own voice within the nuclear family. In this way, *Summer Snow* portrays its female protagonist as both relatively independent and nevertheless ensnared within the patriarchal currents of 1990s Hong Kong. This dissonance manifests in her suppressed voice within the extended family, as she negotiates conflicting expectations of womanhood amid the tension between individual will and familial responsibilities dictated by entrenched cultural norms.

Two sequences vividly capture May's struggles against the patriarchal order embedded in the traditionalist element of Hong Kong's culture, both of which take place in her extended family's living environments. The film opens with May bargaining with a fishmonger in a bustling market and subsequently preparing her own birthday dinner for the family; meanwhile, her husband (Kar-Ying Law) takes his time getting a haircut at the barbershop. This stark dichotomy establishes the unequal division of labor in the nuclear family, with May taking sole responsibility over caregiving. In the scene of May's birthday celebration, it is revealed that she, her husband, and their son do not live with her parents-in-law. Her mother-in-law shows great affection toward her—she visits their home, cooks May's favorite shrimp dish, personally selects shrimp to feed her before serving the meal, and presents her with a red packet as a birthday gift. However, May discloses that she had an unpleasant past with her father-in-law, who once verbally abused her. His request for May to help him change his slippers during the visit subtly reveals his deeply rooted patriarchal authoritarianism. Later in the film, during the Mid-Autumn Festival celebration at the day center, another sequence visually underscores May's constrained agency. By this point in the narrative, her mother-in-law has passed away, and her father-in-law is now living with May's family. A point-of-view shot portrays May taking her father-in-law for a walk, shielding him from the sun with an umbrella, and almost acting as an instrument of his comfort. In this moment, May's own aspirations appear overshadowed by her seemingly preordained role as the caregiver to the patriarch. As Mrs. Han (Ping Ha), a friend of May's mother-in-law (Sin-hung Tam), performs Cantonese opera—reminiscent of the earlier portrayal where May's mother-in-law sings at the day center—May confronts a potential reflection of her future. Elaine Yee-lin Ho aptly notes that in such moments May becomes "abject, 'colonized' by patriarchal tyranny."[37]

Although May's initial struggles to take control of her life reveal the patriarchal constraints she faces, the film paints a broader and more complex picture. The "colonization" of the female protagonist extends beyond these personal battles, bearing on the complex of traditional values prevailing in a society on the cusp of postcolonial transformation. May's initial resistance to her father-in-law gives way to the weight of filial piety, compelling her to assume responsibility for his care. This cultural norm casts a long shadow, shaping women's lives and circumscribing their autonomy as they are relegated to predefined roles as wives, mothers, or daughters.[38] Her mother-in-law, a constant attendant to her own husband's needs, embodies this subservience. Even Mrs. Han, battling advanced gastric cancer, prioritizes her paralyzed husband's well-being, sacrificing her own comfort without regrets and believing that she has led a fulfilling life. While the selflessness of these women is admirable, it highlights the societal pressures that have already begun to regulate May's life. After visiting Mrs. Han and witnessing her fragility, illness, and continued concern for her husband—who suffers from Alzheimer's and is no longer able to care for himself—May is visibly moved. The emotional weight of caregiving strikes a deep chord with her own experience. This encounter prompts May to quit her job and devote herself entirely to looking after her father-in-law. *Summer Snow* thus illustrates how the attitudes of these two generations of women in 1990s Hong Kong are deeply influenced by the revered traditional values of family devotion. This adherence to tradition emerges as a defining facet of the territory's developing postcolonial identity. As Chu observes, "the cultural identity of Hong Kong is, in the discourse of the true self, always essentially Chinese."[39]

However, the film does not limit itself to a critique of female oppression within traditional Chinese culture. Instead, it carves out a space for female autonomy within this cultural framework. In this way, it depicts another facet of Hong Kong's postcolonial identity, born from the complex interaction between tradition (embodied by traditional Chinese culture) and modernity (represented by contemporary British culture). In the context of "tradition"—typically structured by Confucian ethics and patriarchal cultural logic—a woman's identity is centered around the family. Her primary social roles are defined by her obligations to care for her husband, raise children, and demonstrate filial piety toward her parents-in-law. These responsibilities are collectivist in nature, emphasizing the subordination of individual will to familial ethical structures and prioritizing the interests of the family over those of the self. By contrast, within the framework of "modernity," female identity becomes pluralistic. A woman is no longer confined to the roles of wife and mother but also recognized as an autonomous individual. She is entitled to agency in both the domestic and public spheres. Family responsibilities are no longer preassigned based on gender but negotiated through mutual agreement between partners, highlighting equality and reciprocity. In this tension between traditional and modern models of female identity construction, May becomes an emblematic figure. While adhering to traditional domestic roles, she also maintains a full-time job, reflecting the influence of Western liberal values on Hong Kong.[40] May is contrasted with her brother-in-law's wife (Ching Yee Chong) and Lan (Koon-Lan Law), her husband's sister, neither of whom appear to have careers. Lan's concerns about staying with her parental family in the face of potential disapproval from her in-laws suggest the constraining norms imposed by traditional expectations. Notably, May initially never considers quitting her job despite her domestic burdens, declaring: "My work is the best thing in my life. I warn you that I shall never give it up."[41] Hui's depiction of a woman forging her own path within the confines of patriarchal and cultural expectations represents an innovation within Hong Kong cinema. This aligns with what Ho refers to as "a distinctly feminist turn,"[42] whereby women claim subjectivity and assert their value. Through the character of May, *Summer Snow* suggests the possibility of female agency even within the deeply traditional and colonial context of 1990s Hong Kong.

Caught in the thicket of Hong Kong's postcolonial identity, May negotiates a delicate balance between tradition and modernity, duty and ambition. The film illuminates these conflicts through her workplace battles and demanding family obligations. May harbors a fervent desire for professional success, emblematized in her determination to outshine Isabella, a young mainland Chinese colleague vying for her position; she declares to her father-in-law, "If you were not here, I would have a fight to the death with Isabella." Her ultimate decision to leave the workplace and return to family life therefore underscores the enduring power of traditional Chinese cultural norms. Family remains paramount, even if it means sacrificing personal fulfillment. While May's steadfast pursuit of autonomy represents feminist social gains, Hui's film consistently emphasizes the counteracting domestic pressures faced by average middle-aged women in 1990s Hong Kong, which demand conformism over individual aspiration.

Memory erosion: Female representation as an embodiment of Hong Kong's postcoloniality

In *Summer Snow*, May grapples not only with two clashing cultures (nativist Chinese and colonial British) but also with the theme of "memory erosion." The sudden death of her mother-in-law and her father-in-law's subsequent diagnosis of Alzheimer's disease cast a long shadow on May's life. The last remnants of his fading memory, through which he relives his past as a nationalist air force pilot during the Second World War, become a form of burden for her. May finds herself delving into these fragmented memories in order to ease the difficulties of her own caring responsibilities. Just as she can only identify with a fragmented Hong Kong identity—composed of elements of British colonialism and Chinese ethnicity[43]—she can only construct her female identity through a similar fragmentation. Ho provides a more specific account of the burdens May faces in caring for her father-in-law with Alzheimer's:

> His sense of self, and the patriarchal narrative of history he embodies … is at first difficult for [May] to resist, for only in becoming part of his narrative—and playing along with the fantasies created by his disturbed memory—can [she] access his interiority and contain the disruptiveness of his behavior.[44]

Here, the film employs Alzheimer's disease as a potent metaphor for Hong Kong's own struggle with the historical memory of its colonial past. May's father-in-law's loss of short-term memory symbolizes the lingering vestiges of colonial rule, while his confusion about the present mirrors the challenges of forging a postcolonial identity. This powerful blend of nostalgia and forgetfulness weighs heavily on May, through whom Hui emphasizes the specific weight of historical burdens, pain, fatigue, and moral dilemmas on women during the transitional period. The relationship between May and her father-in-law becomes a microcosm of Hong Kong's internal struggle. Although his fading memories of the past (deep-rooted and familiar) hold a certain power, the intimations of foreign influences (British colonialism) hint at a future in which these two cultures might clash. This tension between past and present, between remembering and forgetting, between tradition and modernity, lies at the heart of May's experience and, more widely, at the heart of Hong Kong's cultural identity. Crucially, the "past–present" dynamic is not merely a source of nostalgia but an integral part of how Hong Kong people negotiate their existence in postcolonial times.

While *Summer Snow* portrays a stark clash of cultures and personal struggles, it also suggests a potential path toward unity in its concluding scenes. The narrative guides the protagonists—the father-in-law and daughter-in-law—toward a reconciliation that transcends generational and gendered conflicts by discovering common ground in life's simple pleasures and the importance of family. The film's penultimate scene returns to the fragmented world of the father-in-law's memory, as May engages in his playful fantasy of secret dates with fairies, once again indulging him. However, their conversation takes an unexpected turn. The old man asks, "Do you know what life is all about?" and answers his own question with the surprisingly simple, "Life is all about fun." This seemingly ordinary exchange carries profound weight, signaling a shift in the film's focus from the confines of family melodrama and gender struggles to a broader contemplation of life in general. The coexistence of memories, with their spatial and temporal variations, prompts a wider reflection on the broader value of individuals within society. The retrieval of the father-in-law's memories and the film's portrayal of cultural adaptation open onto the larger notion of balancing the relationship between man and woman, paving the way for the alleviation of confrontations and power imbalances. As Ho writes, *Summer Snow* "reconciles, through the growing imaginative and emotional empathy between daughter-in-law and father-in-law, the conflict of gendered histories."[45] This reconciliation ultimately offers hope for the family's healing and renewal, representing in miniature a potential path toward a more harmonious future for postcolonial Hong Kong.

The film also investigates Hong Kong's postcolonial identity through a compelling juxtaposition in "memory": the traditional, embodied by May, and the modern, represented by her mainland Chinese colleague. The tension between tradition and modernity is reflected in their contrasting methods of preserving company records. May, who manages the company's stock, orders, and delivery schedules through pen and paper, human connections, and personal memory, reflects the resilience of Hong Kong's indigenous practices. In contrast, her colleague Isabella, reliant on computers, symbolizes the embrace of information technology across mainland China. This conflict reflects the tension between the Hong Kong native's connection to traditional practices and the mainlander's embodiment of the rapid push toward technological modernity.[46] The film's skepticism toward the latter becomes evident through the computer's own lapses in memory, which mirror her father-in-law's illness and suggest a vulnerability within technological progress. The film subtly challenges the notion of Hong Kong's elite modernity proffered in accounts such as Chow's, raising questions about whether a reliance on technology equates to genuine advancement. May's success in safeguarding the company's business through more traditional methods reinforces the value of indigenous culture in shaping Hong Kong's postcolonial identity.

By focusing on the experiences of an ordinary woman, *Summer Snow* sheds light on the intricate ways in which tradition and modernity intertwine with daily life in 1990s Hong Kong. May's story serves as a lens onto the gender issues, identity struggles, and social transformations that characterized the territory in this period. Through her evolving relationship with tradition, technology, and patriarchal structures, the film delivers a potent critique of existing power dynamics while also suggesting the potential of a more inclusive future that honors both tradition and progress.

A sense of loss: Representations of Hong Kong women in 1990s cinema

While Hui offers a fresh perspective on the subjective capacity of ordinary women in 1990s Hong Kong, she simultaneously conveys a sense of loss embedded in their experiences. May epitomizes this duality as she grapples with the challenges of a society caught between different cultures yet rarely raises her voice above a whisper. The women in *Summer Snow* rarely verbalize their exhaustion, and their struggles often remain unspoken and unheard. Hui includes moving moments such as May's passionate declaration about the fulfillment her job brings and her outbursts of grief after her mother-in-law's death, when she is alone on the rooftop and says, "Mum, I miss you so much. I am tired. I do not think I can take it anymore." However, these moments feel fleeting against the backdrop of her silent struggles and seem to fail to capture the whole weight of her burdens. The film presents a network of women who, like May, navigate their lives through selflessness and quiet strength, and thus recognizes them not just as individuals but as integral members of a larger social structure. Characters such as May's mother-in-law and Mrs. Han, who sustain each other through patience, kindness, and shared experiences, paint a picture of resilience and virtue, and yet an unmet need for their voices to be fully heard lingers.

In *Summer Snow*, traces of the "colonization" of women through the reinforcing of gender stereotypes in traditional culture persist. The film unfolds against the backdrop of the traditional Chinese family, with its deeply ingrained values, as women of different generations navigate a precarious balance between familial duty and personal aspirations. Ultimately, the film suggests that family often takes precedence over a career, leaving women in a perpetual state of compromise. The pivotal "summer snow" scene, a surreal blend of reality and fantasy, serves as a prime example of this dynamic. After May brings her father-in-law out of the nursing home, this scene unfolds around the snowfall he imagines, represented by white petals. This act of reconciliation, while seemingly liberating, carries the weight of compromise. The fantastical imagery hints at a utopian ideal of family harmony that contrasts with May's persistent struggles and is soon overshadowed by the harsh realities that persist; the father-in-law's health further deteriorates, exacerbating the burden of care on May's shoulders.

Even after the patriarch's death, the film hints at May's continued "colonization." While its conclusion suggests positive changes in May's family life—her husband taking on domestic responsibilities such as cooking, and their son becoming more supportive—the family structure remains firmly rooted in tradition. Ken Hall reads into the film's ending "a positive vision of life: [the son] and his girlfriend declare their mutual love and May sees the grandfather's 'imaginary' pigeons on the roof."[47] But this optimism overlooks the constraints that still persist. The pigeons that May's amnesiac father-in-law sees on the roof, like the snow, probably exist only in his imagination. Thus, even in his absence, the traditional cultural expectations that he represents continue to confine May, restricting her social mobility and cultural independence. However, as Ho observes,

> [w]hat is equally significant and timely is that [*Summer Snow*] implicitly argues for the endurance in Hong Kong of inherited and quotidian Chinese cultural practices, especially as they relate to women, that have not been erased by colonial history; but it also imagines their renewal in the contemporary moment.[48]

Although individual efforts may be constrained within the family structure, the film proposes the possibility of achieving a more equitable and fulfilling family life. As Ho suggests, Ann Hui's cinema is both socially critical and utopian, realistically portraying women's struggles while simultaneously exploring alternative visions of family life within the Chinese context.[49] Hui's cinematic practice thus exemplifies her distinctive contribution to Hong Kong cinema—merging the sensibility of a seasoned auteur with the conscience of an ethical thinker.[50]

In her work, Rey Chow introduces the concept of a "third space" for postcolonial Hong Kong—a realm that transcends the binary oppositions of colonial and native cultures.[51] This space, unaligned with either extreme, provides a more nuanced framework for envisaging Hong Kong's complex identity. Building on this idea, I suggest envisioning the "third space" as a vibrant "middle ground," drawing inspiration from a TED Talk by the American humorist and writer Emily Levine.[52] This "middle ground" is not a static compromise but a dynamic equilibrium where tensions between cultural traditions, modernity, gender identities, and personal aspirations interact fluidly in search of balance. Both the "third space" and the "middle ground" are notions that emphasize active participation and continuous transformation, where conflict and negotiation fuel creative hybridity rather than leading to fixed binary solutions. In this expanded view, the middle ground of the third space is where individuals actively engage in shaping their identities. Cultures and genders do not merely coexist here—they are continually reimagined and reshaped through open interaction. This space rejects rigid binaries, embracing an ongoing exchange where cultures and genders freely interact, giving rise to new forms of identity and expression. May's journey in *Summer Snow* exemplifies this space. Her struggles to balance traditional family responsibilities with personal desires reflect the challenges of establishing the "middle ground," and her experience highlights the ongoing negotiation and redefinition of social roles within such a space. Although the film provides no easy answers, it hints at a future in which individuals such as May can carve out their own status in an evolving landscape. The middle ground of the third space moves beyond binary thinking, embracing the rich fabric of Hong Kong's postcolonial identity—an identity that is situational, contradictory, and inconsistent by nature.[53] In this space, individuals, cultures, and genders interact and transform each other and themselves, rather than merely clashing in irresolvable antagonisms.

Conclusion

In this chapter, I have explored how Ann Hui's *Summer Snow* positions itself at the threshold of Hong Kong's imminent postcolonial era. I have argued that the film's portrayal of its female protagonist's navigation through the triangular relationship between the Chinese motherland, the British colonizer, and Hong Kong articulates the challenges that defined Hong Kong's transitional postcolonial identity. While navigating the anxieties of the impending postcolonial period, the film refrains from romanticizing a precolonial past. Instead, it prompts contemplation on how external influences have shaped the region and its inhabitants. May's struggles, as she finds herself caught between the family responsibilities imposed by traditional cultural norms and her own individual will, capture the tensions faced by women in a society that is contending with conflicting cultural expectations. While her independence and resilience underline her subjectivity and agency within her family, her delicate balancing act between work and familial responsibilities reflects the traditional social constraints women continue to navigate in this complex postcolonial landscape. *Summer Snow* scrutinizes both nostalgic yearning for local history and the uncritical pursuit of globalized technological modernity, highlighting how both can contribute to the burdens faced by women. Poised at a critical historical juncture, the film weaves a cinematic tapestry from the complex threads of Hong Kong's postcolonial identity, women's agency, and local cultural inheritances. In *Summer Snow*, Hong Kong's postcolonial transition brings with it not only the constraints of traditional society and the challenges of modernization but also new avenues for women to assert their agency and shape their own paths. The film stands as a poignant testament to the way in which Hong Kong's postcolonial identity is not a singular destination but rather a vibrant, ever-evolving process drawing on the territory's diverse cultural histories, at whose forefront stand the voices and experiences of local women.

8

Poeticizing the female body of *qi*

Lyricism and melancholy in Ann Hui's Tin Shui Wai diptych

Weiting Fan

In 2008 and 2009, Ann Hui brought to the global screen two films set in Tin Shui Wai, which is a new town in northwestern Hong Kong famous for its overcrowded public housing estates and issues of social unrest. These two films are *The Way We Are* (*Tianshuiwei de ri yu ye*, 2008) and *Night and Fog* (*Tianshuiwei de ye yu wu*, 2009). Whereas both films center on their female protagonists' life in Tin Shui Wai, they deal with different subject matters with ostensibly different aesthetics. *The Way We Are* revolves around the uneventful everyday life of two elderly women living in the same public housing block, whereas *Night and Fog* bases its plot on a real-life murder case involving an unemployed Hong Kong man slaughtering his young immigrant wife and six-year-old twin daughters in their cramped apartment. While the former film is slow-paced, full of long takes and unexplained ellipsis, the latter is packed with dramatic close-ups, violent camera movements, and an editing style that builds narrative tension. Nevertheless, despite their different themes and aesthetics, both films provide us with a distinct portrayal of female bodies, which is what this chapter will mainly focus on.

There has been a significant lack of scholarship on the portrayal of female bodies in Ann Hui's films. Existing studies on the director generally focus on the intersection between her cinematic representation of women and Hong Kong's overall sociohistorical situation: the significance of her feminist authorship in relation to Hong Kong's postcolonial culture (Gina Marchetti; Audrey Yue); the primitive maternal force in her cinema that confronts Chinese traditions with modern Hong Kong's economic growth and urbanization (Elaine Ho); and ordinary women's mundane lives being the most important anchor for her film aesthetics that renovates the Hong Kong's film industry (Mirana May Szeto).[1] Even in Jing Jing Chang's dedicated discussion of Ann Hui's constitution of a "female subjectivity" in the Tin Shui Wai diptych, the importance of female embodiment is still sidelined.[2]

This chapter seeks to specifically address the understudied topic of how female bodies are presented in Ann Hui's cinema. I argue that, though in divergent ways, both *The Way We Are* and *Night and Fog* accentuate the necessity to demystify the concrete and integrated presence of the female body through nothing but the concrete embodied experience of women themselves. The Tin Shui Wai diptych proposes an alternative form of feminist cinema by highlighting the way in which the exuberant and elusive cultural experience of the female body living in Hong Kong dissipates the concrete form of the body itself as a political and ethical effort to de-classify and de-essentialize the female body.

I will particularly center on the two films' poetic rearrangement of female embodiment. Taking on the Daoist worldview of *qi*, this chapter intends to introduce two poetic concepts in Chinese culture: *shuqing* and *youyu*. The term *shuqing* literally means "to express feelings and emotions." As argued by David Der-wei Wang, *shuqing* is "an old but not necessarily the most conspicuous concept in Chinese literary and cultural discourse," which can be paralleled with *lyricism* or the *lyrical* in modern English, as both generally concern a "poetics of selfhood."[3] Seeking to push back the conceptual norms of both globalization and racialization, Rey Chow has particularly used the idea of lyricism to address the cultural specificity of Hong Kong cinema. As she argues, "[i]n the context of Hong Kong … the capitalist forces of commercialism that undergird colonialization and its aftermath have provided potent grounds for this affective cluster based in mournful lyricism to mutate, and thrive, into a uniquely generative cultural niche."[4] Chow has also specifically located this touch of "residual lyricism and the ambient affect it has been fostering in late-capitalist Hong Kong" in Ann Hui's *The Way We Are*. Under the theoretical framework of traditional Chinese lyricism, Chow reads the film as an expression of "sorrow in human lives touched by loss, transience of human relations, commodified daily living, unexpected opportunities availed by chance encounters, and meanings of coupledom and togetherness."[5] This chapter looks further into the lyrical female bodies portrayed in this film, especially how they dissolve their boundaries and reshape familial relations in the late-capitalist, hyper-consumerist Hong Kong.[6]

While *shuqing*'s most literal meaning is "expressing emotions," this particular form of expression frees not only emotions but also the movement of *qi*. As suggested by Cheng Yu-yu, one of the earliest appearances of the idea of *shuqing* in literature is as both the result and treatment for an illness of *youyu* (忧郁).[7] The Chinese word *youyu* perfectly parallels the English term *melancholy*. While *you* most commonly means *sadness*, *yu* here refers to a stagnant, pent-up status. For Cheng, *youyu* represents the convolving and entanglement of *qi* within the body that necessitates it to be released and unloosed. This necessity originates the idea of *shuqing*, which enables the free mobility of *qi* through the expression of emotions. Therefore, instead of the "mournful lyricism" proposed by Chow, I would like to coin the concept of a *melancholic lyricism* for my discussion of Ann Hui. Indeed, Ann Hui's Tin Shui Wai diptych can be considered a lyrical cinema of *shuqing* with the poetics of *youyu*.

In *The Way We Are*, we are at first confronted with two elderly women's shriveled bodies that are apparently neither the subjective perspectives with which we identify nor the objects of the cinematic gaze. The camera suggests that they are neither looking nor being looked at. Being almost translucent and completely insignificant in their tranquil and content life, their bodies' affective encounters with the external world slowly unfold throughout the film to register their mundane struggles against social stratification and discrimination.

Meanwhile, *Night and Fog* raises an intense awareness of female bodies as both suffering subjects and suffered objects, as both the passive recipients and the active resistance to sexual violence. However, the film also transforms this passionate encounter with destructive violence into an ethical and political effort, manifested as a poetics that vaporizes the concrete presence of the female bodies together with their congealed social significances, breaking their sense of entrapment and isolation and initiating a non-dividing and non-differentiating bond between all beings regardless of common classifications.

As pinpointed by Marchetti, "[w]hile *Night and Fog*, which is based on the truth, rings false on screen for some viewers, *The Way We Are*, a fairytale of domestic tranquility and community cohesiveness appears to be 'real', 'authentic', and 'true'."[8] The aesthetic arrangements of these two films make the effort to keep a balance between presenting an ideal and representing a reality. For my analysis here, I suggest that the ideal emerging in both films is the void body completely vanishing into the immanent flow of *qi*, forming a non-hierarchical plane of immanence. Simultaneously, reality encapsulates the quotidian endurance of and confrontation with the perception of *qi* as accumulated, congealed, and entangled. These modes of perception reveal a social significance and hierarchy that cannot be easily wished away. In both films, the ideal is anchored by and can only be accessed through a poetic rendition of reality.

The body of *qi* and the poetic curing of melancholy

How can the Daoist worldview of *qi* in relation to the poetics of *shuqing* and *youyu* contribute to our understanding of the female bodies portrayed in Ann Hui's Tin Shui Wai diptych, and ultimately to the re-comprehension and reconfiguration of embodied experience in relation to the feminist cinema? Literally, *qi* refers to a gaseous substance, which suggests a status of being that is more than "nothing" but less than what is normally considered as a concrete being. *Qi* as a philosophical term has been a frequent reference in Daoist discussions of the relationship between the human body and the world. In one passage of the Daoist classic *Zhuangzi*, it is suggested that while the world is an undifferentiated whole made of *qi*, the concrete form of our living body is nothing but *qi*'s temporary aggregation:

> Beings are the aggregation of *qi*. *Qi* aggregates, and something comes into being; *qi* disaggregates, and something withers away … Therefore, everything is the same and merges into an undifferentiated One … Therefore, it is said that: "The world under the sky is merged into an undifferentiated One through *qi*."[9]

According to this Daoist worldview of *qi*, the human body is never a sealed-off entity with a clear-cut boundary. The body is constantly formed and deformed through the exchange and flow of *qi* that seamlessly conjoins the body and the world. Hence, our gendered body with all its differences is always subjected to the erosion of *qi*'s fluidity and mobility in every minute cycle of life and death. The female body thus cannot serve as a concrete basis for any essentialist female subjectivity, nor should it be overly fetishized as a stable banner for the reductive agenda of identity politics.

However, this does not mean that the Daoist worldview of *qi* completely dismisses the importance of human embodiment. On the contrary, it is only when we pay special attention to our concrete embodied experience that we can become mindful of the immanent flux of *qi* that connects us to the world. For Cheng, the melancholic feeling of *youyu* represents an embodied experience of the coagulation of *qi* within the body that is yet to be mobilized and released. Cheng quotes from the ancient annotation for the verse where the word combination *shu* and *qing* first appears:

> In this verse, the poet says that he has no place to be within the world around him; with regret and resentment in his heart, his *you* (sadness) entangles together; he thus turns to *zhu* (subdue) the *qing* (emotions) in himself by writing poems, so as to display his *zhi* (ambition). The word *zhu* (subdue) here is interchangeable with the word *shu* (release).[10]

While interchangeable words in ancient Chinese texts are often randomly written mistakes, here, this "mistake" has either deliberately or unwittingly revealed a theoretical coherence. When the *qi* entangled and accumulated in the physical body is released (*shu*), with the coagulated boundary of the Self undermined and dissolved, the closed and interior emotion (*qing*) kept to the Self is thus also subdued (*zhu*) and resolved.

It is also clear here that this poetic release of *qi* is a "display of his *zhi* (ambition)," strongly echoing the Confucian ethical scheme "poetry speaks out ambition" (诗言志 or *shiyanzhi*). Nevertheless, as contended by Cheng, the poetics of *shuqing*, working to let go of the flows of *qi* coagulated in body, clearly suggests more of a disturbance and unsettlement of the body than the Confucian scheme, which references harmony and order educated through poetry.[11] According to Cheng, this disturbance and unsettlement of the body manifest as a form of illness that weakens the body. The normative discourse of such illness in the classical era revolves around an *evil* form of *qi* from the external world that not only invades the physical body but also causes havoc in one's social role and in the harmony of the social order.[12] As cited by Cheng from *Guanzi*, another influential classical text written for the governors in the classical era:

> When the evil form of *qi* invades the interiority, one's physical appearance will become withered and decrepit. The Monarch cannot be a Monarch, and his subservient subject will no longer behave as his subject. The Father cannot be a Father, and his son will no longer behave as his son.[13]

However, as Cheng suggests, the poetics of *shuqing* does not condemn this condition of illness as evil or unethical. Instead, it is preoccupied with how this state of illness, as a manifestation of the body's fixated physical intactness and socialized integrity disrupted by what is essentially a vigorously dynamic flow of *qi*, can raise an acute awareness of our entrapment and entanglement within our bodies and initiates a yearning to achieve a state of openness.[14] This poetic pattern is most prominent in the poetry of Qu Yuan. As a contemporary of Zhuangzi, Qu is also a social and political outcast who operates outside of the rulers' court. Repetitively writing about a death that allows him to fuse into the flows of wind and water, Qu allegedly ended his life by drowning himself in a river:

> I have twisted my longing thoughts to make an ornamental girdle; I have woven my bitter sorrow to make an embellishing stomach band. I broke a branch of the Ruo tree to shade me from the brightness; I would go wherever the wandering wind might carry me.

> . . .
>
> My heart is tied with bands of care that will not be unloosed: the *qi* is twisted up and tied in a knot together. Deep and dim the distance, without a limit; Vast vacant verdancy, sans shape or form.
>
> . . .
>
> My melancholy is quiet and my sadness is constant; even when gracefully moving in the limitless world does not entertain me. Riding the great waves, drifting with the wind, I would go to rest where the water of Peng dwells.[15]

As Cheng argues, what is being described in these poetic verses is how the poet's perception of his own body transforms from a knotted, ensnared, sealed-off accumulation of *qi* to the expansive, nomadic flows of *qi* that merge undifferentiated with the borderless, limitless world. That is, through a poetic expression of *youyu*/sadness, the poet makes the effort to transform his perception of his own body to access the embodied experience of a void body. Accordingly, *youyu* expressed here also manifests as transformation of a sadness that is coiled within the body to a sadness that drifts away with the wind to suffuse the world.

Therefore, when translated as melancholy in English, this specific version of *youyu* productively enriches the existing scholastic discourses concerning melancholy. Resonating with the haunting experience of the unmourned, unprocessed, and thus non-signified loss essential to the psychoanalytic (Freudian) reading of melancholy, the concept of *youyu* redefines the loss as even more fluid, indeterminate, and intricately layered. When *youyu* is manifested as the stagnant entanglement of *qi* in the beginning, what is lost is the interactive openness between the body of *qi* and the world. However, when such a negative loss stimulates the poetic expression of *youyu* and the release and disentanglement of *qi*, it shifts to be a positive loss. What is truly lost in this poetic expression of *youyu* or melancholy is the social hierarchy imposed on the poet, the concrete integrity of their body, and the clear-cut boundary of their self in general: in other words, both the foundations and outcomes for definite, determinate significations itself.

In this sense, the expression of *youyu* suggests an ethical and political effort to access the embodied experience of merging as one with the immanent flow of *qi*, counteracting the body's actual, integrated existence. The lyrical poetics of *shuqing* is the poetic manifestation of such a destructive effort. Regardless, this effort does not deny the concrete embodied experience. It embraces the evil form of *qi* that disturbs and weakens the body. This evil form of *qi* can be paralleled with the form of affect that is also considered evil by Spinoza, as it destroys "the proportion of motion and rest" and hence destroys the body.[16] Through a poetic process, this pernicious and destructive affect ultimately arises when the differentiation between internal and external erodes away with the diminished body rejoining the immanent mobility of *qi*. What collapses along with it are the ethical judgment and the moral signs concerning good and evil, which solely exist to keep intact an existing organism with its fixed proportional order. What arises along with it is a new form of ethics driven by a poetic signifying process that is non-differentiating, non-dividing, and non-hierarchical.

The Way We Are: The lyrical *Qi* of mundane life

The Way We Are foregrounds the ways in which two working-class widows quietly suffer from both the hyper-consumerist modernity and Confucian family values that simultaneously shape Hong Kong's cultural landscape. Kwai (Pau Hei-ching), a mother to high school student Cheung Ka-on (Leung Chun-Lung), works at a supermarket's fruit section. Kwai meets and befriends Granny (Chan Lai-wun), who has recently moved into Tin Shui Wai alone and just started to work in the same supermarket's vegetable section. Without any dramatization, the film shows the mundane lives of both women, who go through their day-to-day life hiding away their misery. Kwai avoids visiting her sick mother in the hospital, seemingly due to her awkwardness around the upper-class families of her two wealthy brothers, as she refuses to become an economic burden to her mother and brothers. Meanwhile, Granny struggles to reconnect with her son-in-law and grandson, who have been estranged from her after her daughter's death.

One specific sequence that first introduces Granny's mundane life stands out with its melancholy. In this sequence, several long takes patiently dwell on Granny after she arrives home from grocery shopping, changes slippers, enters the kitchen, opens her water tap, washes green vegetables, cuts a small piece of beef into slices, cooks her lunch in a large pot, eats her meal alone, and washes the dishes. After finishing all of these routine activities without a word, Granny sits at the table, staring blankly forward, as the camera slowly pans away from her to reveal her tiny apartment with its small window and a set of blurry old family photos sticking to the wall. The film then cuts to her standing in the kitchen again, now in the dim light of dusk. She turns on a flashlight hanging on the kitchen door and sniffs a plate of uncooked food before scraping it into the pot. Then, a close-up reveals the contents of the pot to be the remaining green vegetables and beef from her lunch. The silence throughout the whole sequence is finally broken at this revelation, with a non-diegetic piece of melancholic piano music gently seeping in (Figures 8.1–8.3).

At first glance, this sequence appears to be a perfect parallel to the famous maid sequence in Vittorio De Sica's *Umberto D.*, which is quoted by Deleuze in his discussion of André Bazin to illustrate the "pure optical situation." For Deleuze, the maid in *Umberto D.* does her everyday chores in a sort of "mechanical, weary gestures" with "no response or reaction" to what she sees.[17] Nevertheless, unlike *Umberto D.*, *The Way We Are* manifests a more poetically accentuated affective response to what the camera sees. While Granny's own weary body is numb and irresponsive to her tedious quotidian routines, the camera makes sure to show her entrapment and loneliness by always boxing her within the narrow frames of the public housing apartment's doors and corridors. Together with the music and the selective close-ups, the film emphasizes Granny's melancholic loss: by subtly highlighting her struggle to finish the foods she bought from her morning grocery shopping, the film accentuates Granny's incapability to efficiently survive in a society designed for extravagant consumerism and family households with higher food consumption.

Throughout the film, Granny is shown to repeatedly suffer exclusion from and abandonment by Hong Kong's hyper-consumerist culture and family-oriented society. Nevertheless, it is also at these moments that she is able to temporarily

Figure 8.1 Granny in the kitchen preparing for lunch. *The Way We Are* (2008), directed by Ann Hui.

Figure 8.2 Granny having lunch alone. *The Way We Are* (2008), directed by Ann Hui.

Figure 8.3 Granny in the kitchen preparing for dinner. *The Way We Are* (2008), directed by Ann Hui.

escape the dominant social order and forge strong connections across normative borders. Her friendship with Kwai, her neighbor and co-worker, starts off when she is standing in front of a supermarket shelf, hesitantly pondering a purchase. Kwai starts their conversation by offering to buy the other two bottles from the three-pack so that Granny can get the discount without paying for all three. Kwai ends up giving Granny the oil for free, refusing to take her money. Their second encounter happens when Granny wants to buy a discounted TV set, though she is reluctant to pay the expensive delivery charge. Once again, Kwai helps her by asking her son to carry the TV set to Granny's apartment. Even the burnt-out bulb in Granny's kitchen serves as a bonding mechanism, since Kwai asks her son to repair it.

To a certain extent, just like the melancholic body in Qu Yuan's poetry, Granny's decrepit, dying body also becomes the breaking point of the existing systems and standards for value judgments in Hong Kong's late-capitalist society. Her body is yet to be the signified queer corpse as discussed by MacCormack.[18] However, her fleshly experience of a withering female body becomes the source of her power to act. That is, by living and anticipating the decay and disappearance of her body, she manages to rebel against the social roles and normative value system to which she is assigned. When Granny attempts to return the favor to Kwai, she gifts her with a pack of expensive mushrooms that she originally bought for her grandson. She insists to Kwai that she cannot eat the mushrooms herself because she may pass away before she can finish them all. Ann Hui shoots this conversation in a high-angle long shot, dwarfing both women as they walk down a wide staircase in an open public space (Figure 8.4). When Granny talks about the prospect of her death in a matter-of-fact tone, her body vanishes from the scene as she walks out of the frame from its lower-left corner, with only her voice lingering momentarily in the empty shot (Figure 8.5).

Later in the film, accompanied by Kwai, Granny tries to bond with her son-in-law by offering him a piece of gold jewelry. As Granny confesses to her son-

Figure 8.4 Granny and Kwai. *The Way We Are* (2008), directed by Ann Hui.

Figure 8.5 Disappearance of the bodies and the dialogue on death. *The Way We Are* (2008), directed by Ann Hui.

in-law, her act of giving performs her final duty as a grandmother before her "legs stretch stiff," a euphemism for death in Cantonese. However, her son-in-law rejects her jewelry as well as her wish to fit in with his household. On the bus back home, Granny gives the rejected gifts to Kwai. The two women silently link each other's arms, both looking ahead as if repressing their tears after Granny tells Kwai that she will become a ghost soon and as a ghost she will give her blessing to Kwai's son so that he can receive a good education and have nice manners (Figure 8.6). The camera does not indulge in this sentimental moment. Instead, it cuts to a steady long take of the city road viewed through a bus windshield, again accompanied by the melancholic piano music (Figure 8.7). Granny's body is absent in this shot, yet her pain of being rejected, abandoned, isolated, and denied a place to which she belongs is clearly present. Nevertheless, this moving shot of the industrial highway has poetically processed the pain, as if looking into a future where Granny's body has already been diffused into the air as *qi*, with her unspoken pain merging with the living experience of Kwai, of all those who have fallen into the fissure of Hong Kong's social structure, haunting the neat modern cityscape like a specter. It is through this diffused melancholy immanent to the two women's actual and concrete embodied experience that their differentiative concrete bodies are dissolved, dissipated into the city, capable of passing into the non-differentiative and non-hierarchical plane of immanence shared by all.

Figure 8.6 Alliance between Granny and Kwai. *The Way We Are* (2008), directed by Ann Hui.

Figure 8.7 Hong Kong's modern cityscape. *The Way We Are* (2008), directed by Ann Hui.

Through the film's poetic arrangements, Granny's dying body becomes the crumbled, loose, and fluid site of *qi* where one catches a glimpse of the void body: the social exclusion experienced by her aged body becomes an exemption from her roles and duties. Therefore, this vision of the void body through pain and death fundamentally challenges and dismantles the hierarchical, differentiating system of signification that stratifies society, while not completely sweeping it under the carpet. As shown in another melancholic scene of Kwai throwing away her deceased husband's old trousers, the patriarch's absent body is made ever so palpable by Kwai and her son talking about how he used to wear very tight trousers. Kwai even drags the trousers out of the trash can instantly after throwing them in, carefully folding them up as if someone should still wear them, holding back tears. Afterwards, the film cuts to a faded-color flashback of Kwai wearing white funeral attire, crying uncontrollably over a coffin, the sound of which, once again, is mingled with the same melancholic piano music.

This sequence perfectly exemplifies the lyrical poetics of *youyu*, as it also features a double-layered sorrow in relation to two forms of the body. Through the flashback, Kwai's immediate painful confrontation with her husband's coffin is associated with yet also differentiated from her melancholy over the husband's absent body. When the perished body is still concretely there, Kwai is bound to be a wife ritualistically mourning over her husband, to cry hard for her widowhood and the loss of a normative family. Nevertheless, a different scenario is suggested by the contingent, mundane scene where Kwai shows an affective response to the presence of the absence of her husband's body: now Kwai is reacting to a void body, a body that is finally stripped of all its social significance and merges seamlessly with her own as it flows in and out of her through her breath, tears, and memories.

The ending of *The Way We Are* epitomizes this transition from a sad passion resulting from the normative social structure to a sad action through which all differentiations and boundaries between the internal and the external, the self and the other, are suspended. On the night of the Mid-Autumn Festival, Granny, Kwai, and Kwai's son gather to have dinner together under a warm, antique lamp. The camera slowly tracks over their head to dwell on the night view of Tin Shui Wai across the apartment's window, with their lamplight reflected on the window glass, blending with thousands of lights from different families outside. It is then cut to a series of documentary-like shots from both the present and the past, alternating color and black and white, showing thousands of anonymous families mingling together in a public park, celebrating the festival by lighting candles and paper lanterns. An old song titled "The Moon Delivers My Pining to a Thousand Miles Away ("mingyue qianli jixiangsi") accompanies this footage, its lyrics resembling a traditional lyric poem of *shuqing*:

> The moonlight appears to be murky in the everlasting night, while I am surrounded by loneliness and silence. The cold lamp on my table shines feebly, keeping me company when I am sitting alone in my bitterness. The person is a thousand miles away, with whom I have lost contact; when I want to greet him

> across the distance, there is nothing to carry my message. Please, moon, send the message for me.

The Mid-Autumn Festival famously enshrines the full moon as a symbol of the wholeness of the family. However, this song poetically reappropriates the image of the moon as a signifier of an irretrievable loss: a loss that is painful yet emancipating. Through the effort to express this melancholic loss, the suffering body fluidly intertwines and converges with the moon, the lamp, and its empty surroundings. *The Way We Are* foregrounds such melancholic loss as intrinsic in one's encounter with the normative family values, by contrasting the fixated and determinate family structure with the inevitable fluidity of the mortal human bodies that are bound to disaggregate into immanent flows of *qi*.

Night and Fog: The melancholic *qi* of domestic violence

In *Night and Fog*, women's encounter with violence is much more extreme. The film begins with a news report of the female protagonist's murder, followed by a series of police interviews and flashbacks, through which her tragic life story is gradually fleshed out. Born and raised in an impoverished rural area of mainland China, Ling (Zhang Jingchu) falls in love with Hong Kong construction worker Lee Sum (Simon Yam Tat-wah) when she works as a sex worker. She brings Lee back to her parents, marries him in the village, and gives birth to their daughters. Before long, she moves to Hong Kong as an immigrant, though her life in the metropolis is far from a fairy tale. After a construction accident, her husband Lee Sum is turned into an unemployed alcoholic living off social security, with a fragile ego and a bad temper. Ling's body thus becomes the punching bag to vent his rage. Desperate to escape her harrowing life, Ling attempts to seek help from government officials, social workers, police, and her mother back in mainland China, all of whom respond by encouraging her to stay with her husband, which finally leads to her being brutally murdered.

Despite its social realist elements evident in the critique of institutional indifference to domestic violence, the film's portrayal of violence showcases a poetic touch, particularly in two specific scenes: one featuring Ling's husband raping her in the middle of the night, the other showing his slaughter of Ling and her young daughters. The first scene begins with a dream sequence of Ling, in which a young girl with her back to the camera is wandering alone in a serene and foggy bamboo forest. Beside her is a small creek so clean and unpolluted that one can see the weeds swaying underwater. When the girl finally sits down, slightly turning her head around as if ready to reveal her face, the film suddenly cuts back to Ling turning her head on the small sofa in her cramped Hong Kong apartment (Figures 8.8 and 8.9). She is awoken by her husband, who then drags her into the bedroom by force, binds her hands together with string, threatens her with a knife, and rapes her. This horrifying atrocity is filmed by a handheld camera, with a series of unflinching close-ups of her body, showing nuances like how the thin, transparent strings binding her wrists are cutting

Figure 8.8 Girl in the woods in Ling's dream. *Night and Fog* (2009), directed by Ann Hui.

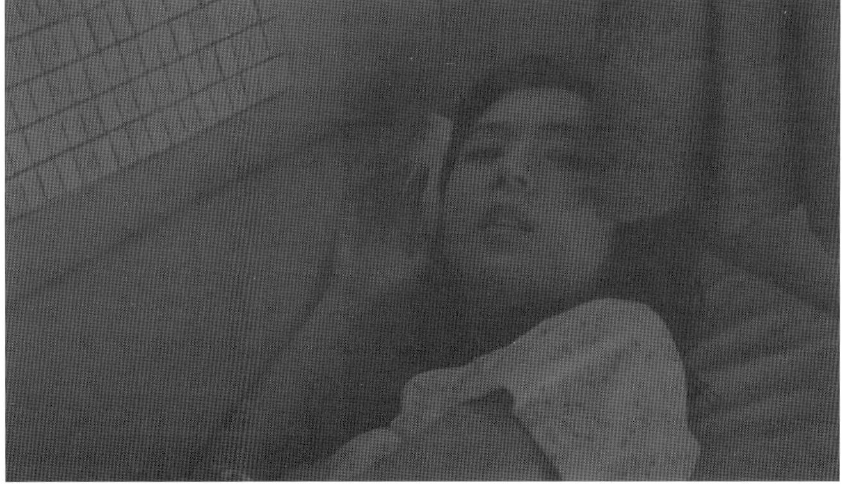

Figure 8.9 Ling waking up to violence. *Night and Fog* (2009), directed by Ann Hui.

deep into her skin. However, in the next shot, the camera quietly retreats to a distant, high-angled perspective, with Ling resting almost peacefully on a curb under a streetlamp, blood vaguely visible down her leg. She strikes up a conversation with a passerby, which leads to an unexpectedly lyrical moment: when she is asked whether she can smell the scent of mud and grass from the wet park of Tin Shui Wai, Ling looks away to locate the scent. At that point, the film suddenly cuts to a floating, disembodied shot, wobbly panning across an obscure night view of Tin Shui Wai's natural scenery under the shadows of urban buildings and their blurry lights in the distance (Figure 8.10).

The first half of this sequence may be hastily read as the tragic destruction of Ling's primitive and innocent body under patriarchal violence, with the dream sequence interpreted as her nostalgia for a natural and uncontaminated self. However, with a similarly composed flashback sequence, the film later reveals that the girl wandering in the bamboo forest is Ling's younger sister. The flashback occurs when the younger sister is interrogated by a policeman after the murder of Ling. In this flashback (the sister's memory), when she turns around to reveal her face, she meets the gaze of Ling's husband, her brother-in-law, who has followed her deep into the forest, aiming to groom her by offering her a pair of earrings (Figure 8.11). This disclosure suggests a demystification of a primitive female body existing prior to its definition by the patriarchal gaze. It also reveals a deep and intertwining bonding between Ling and her sister,

Figure 8.10 From bodily violence to disembodied perspective. *Night and Fog* (2009), directed by Ann Hui.

Figure 8.11 Ling's younger sister as prey. *Night and Fog* (2009), directed by Ann Hui.

forged by sharing the female body that is cursed with the same passivity and vulnerability under patriarchal violence.

However, despite showing the fantasy of an unsocialized, uncultured female body free of hierarchical significances, the film makes an effort to imply a way out *after* the violent rape scene. When the melancholic shot of Tin Shui Wai's natural scenery takes an unfixed, wandering perspective, unlimited to the concrete presence of Ling's body, the camera seems to embody the poetic expression of *youyu* that disentangles Ling from the entrapment of her own body. That is, through this shot, the camera becomes a sensitive organ without the wholeness of a body, which temporarily allows Ling (and the audience) to perceive with a void body, a body purely constituted by immanent flows of *qi* undifferentiated from the world. Regardless, this emergence of the void body is not merely an experimental experience of theoretical potential, or an abstract ideal of the a-subject and a-object merging into the world. Instead, it is triggered and initiated as a poetic and defiant response to the female body's actual encounter with violence that differentiates it, targets it, and threatens to dismantle it.

At the end of the film, when Ling and her two daughters get brutally butchered, a series of muted, slow-motion shots also shift the focus from the spectacle of the incomprehensible atrocity itself to the victims' reactions to it, especially the expressions of their pain and despair. However, following a close-up of Ling's face, which shows that she looks up with sorrowful inertia after she has been stabbed to the ground and witnessed her daughters being slaughtered, the film cuts to a low-angle shot of the bamboo forest. This time around, the forest has completely lost its idyllic charm as it is, instead, imbued with murky lighting and an ominous fog. The sound of Ling's husband beating the family dog to death with a wooden stick echoes through the forest. According to an earlier flashback, this is the first time Ling and her family ever witness his propensity to violence before they return to Hong Kong. While this sequence clearly superimposes Ling's broken body with the dog's, what intertwines them is not the transcendence of their bodies' material objectivity. Like the bamboo forest as an undeveloped natural space disassociated from the myth of its serene transcendence, there are also no transcendent material bodies in their natural state. Instead, Ling's body becomes equal to the dog's body when the film reveals the same contingency of their concrete presence. Their bodies are only marked with a stable visibility and a determinate significance when they are differentiated and targeted. However, when their bodies are targeted by a violence so extreme that the bodies are destroyed, they can no longer carry the definite meanings imposed on them. In turn, their broken bodies become a potential force to render the mechanism of this targeted violence apart. The film makes the poetic effort to linger on this process of destruction, during which Ling's and the dog's bodies are gradually exposed to be nothing but the same accumulation of *qi* ready to disaggregate and ultimately pass into a non-differentiating and non-hierarchical plane (Figures 8.12 and 8.13).

Figure 8.12 Ling's broken body. *Night and Fog* (2009), directed by Ann Hui.

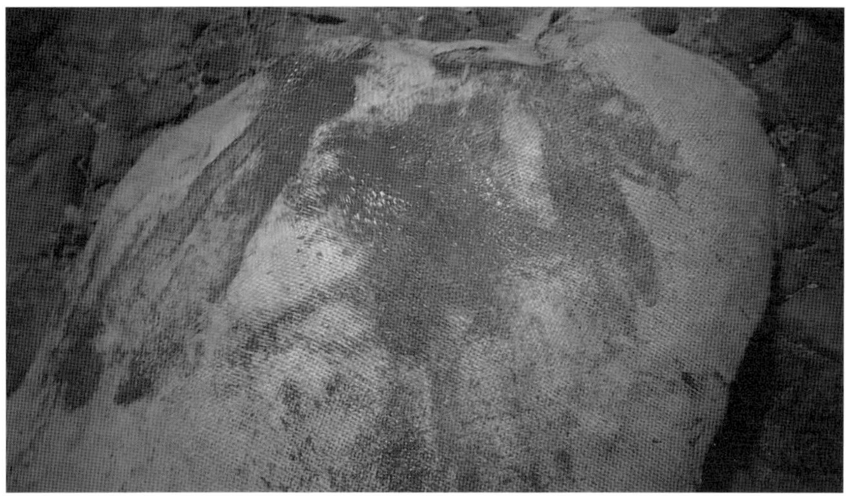

Figure 8.13 The dog's unseen body. *Night and Fog* (2009), directed by Ann Hui.

Conclusion

When we read Ann Hui's Tin Shui Wai diptych as a lyrical cinema of *shuqing* with a melancholic poetics of *youyu*, it becomes clear to us that Hui's cinematic portrayal of the female body valorizes both its socially and culturally situated experience, as well as the poetic effort to vaporize the concrete presence of these bodies and turn them into void bodies and immanent flows of *qi*. Specifically, through such poetic effort, the pain suffered by female bodies in their sociocultural life does not merely diffuse their subjectivity by restoring the bodies to objects and easily accessing a transcendent interobjectivity. Instead, the poetic effort of *youyu* suspends the whole differentiation between subjectivity and objectivity by forcing the bodies to be perceived as immanent flows of *qi* that are yet to concretize. I therefore read the female bodies in this form of cinema as both subjects and objects, yet neither subjects nor objects; both present and absent, yet neither present nor absent; both concrete and abstract, yet neither concrete nor abstract.

Furthermore, the female bodies captured in Ann Hui's films with a dynamic flow of melancholic loss, especially in the Tin Shui Wai diptych, demonstrate how the cinema can transform our perception *of* and *through* bodies into a strategic practice of a power struggle against hierarchical signifying systems of any kind (not only gender but also class, age, nationality, etc.). These mundane female bodies are bodies of *qi* that are simultaneously concretely situated in their sociopolitical milieu and dissolvable into the non-differentiated plane of immanence through the poetic effort of *shuqing*.

9

Postcolonial aging, amah, and diaspora in *A Simple Life*

Jessica Ka Yee Chan

Based on the life story of the Hong Kong film producer Roger Lee, Ann Hui's *A Simple Life* (2011) is a semi-fictional biographical film about the life of Taojie, an amah (Cantonese migrant domestic servant) who served three generations of Lee's family for more than sixty years. The goal of this chapter is twofold. First, the chapter situates *A Simple Life* in the burgeoning but understudied journalistic and documentary discourse on aging as a postcolonial condition in Hong Kong since the 2010s. An intertextuality between the film and its adjacent media productions, such as journalistic reportage and TV documentaries, reveals the social anxiety about the lack of holistic and accessible elderly care in Hong Kong's medical and social welfare system and the profit-driven nursing home industry. Second, *A Simple Life* responds to the postcolonial anxiety of old age by articulating an intergenerational kinship through Roger Lee and Taojie, a diasporic Asian icon of amah that is localized, nationalized, and internationalized under the framework of the 2003 Closer Economic Partnership Arrangement (CEPA) between Hong Kong and the mainland. Multiple imaginaries of home, family, and community—Roger Lee's home, a local nursing home, Roger Lee's transnational family, and a new Hong Kong–mainland cinematic community—coexist in this film as interconnected and interdependent sites of care, demonstrating how a postcolonial, national, and transnational sense of home and belonging are simultaneously articulated under the framework of CEPA.

Cantonese amah, diaspora, and postcoloniality

One of the promotional pictures of *A Simple Life* features the leading character Taojie (played by the Hong Kong actress Deanie Ip) dressed in black trousers and a white blouse with long and neatly braided hair as an amah[1]—a diasporic Asian icon of domestic service in colonial Hong Kong, Malaysia, and Singapore in the 1930s (Figure 9.1).[2] Amahs were a special type of Cantonese migrant domestic servant that included pre-1945 sworn spinsters from Shunde and post-1945 women refugees from Guangdong. Because of the collapse of the silk industry in the 1930s, the Japanese occupation, and the civil war, spinsters, unmarried, or widowed women arrived from the Pearl River Delta to seek other forms of employment, such as domestic service in upper-class Chinese households and European residences in colonial Hong Kong, Macau, Malaysia, and Singapore. As a semi-fictional biopic, *A Simple Life* tells the story of Taojie, a Cantonese migrant from Shunde, who in the 1940s was hired by Roger Lee's family in Hong Kong as a live-in maid at the age of thirteen.[3]

The semi-fictional biopic can be understood in the context of diaspora as a colonial and postcolonial condition. The itineraries of displaced Cantonese amahs point to former colonial cities such as Hong Kong, Macau, Penang, and Singapore, which offered migrant women economic opportunities, freedom of movement, and freedom from marriage as these cities invested in postwar reconstruction and modernization. The invisible domestic labor of Cantonese amahs is a contribution to the postwar economic miracles of East and Southeast Asian cities. In rendering visible the domestic labor and contribution of an aging Cantonese amah, *A Simple Life* engages with Hong Kong's colonial and postcolonial modernity.

Figure 9.1 A promotional picture of *A Simple Life*. *A Simple Life* (2011), directed by Ann Hui.

In *Writing Diaspora*, Rey Chow highlights modernity's fascination with and desire for the authentic native "other": "The production of the native [as an image and a silent object] is in part the production of our postcolonial modernity."[4] Taojie, an illiterate Cantonese migrant domestic servant from the colonial era, can be read as an endangered authentic native "other." Chow reminds us not to place the Third World woman, the native, and the cultural other in an idealized position of an original authentic state, victimhood or powerful resistance, but to interrogate our subject position as an agent in writing the native "other": "The question to ask is not whether we can return the native to her authentic origin, but what our fascination with the native means in terms of the irreversibility of modernity."[5] Telling the story of Taojie as a product of diaspora and (post) colonial modernity in Hong Kong, *A Simple Life* creates Taojie as a quintessential icon of the Cantonese amah.

The production of the film is a postcolonial act of remembering Cantonese amahs, an aging and dying generation that is disappearing in Hong Kong. Ackbar Abbas characterizes Hong Kong's postcoloniality as a "culture of disappearance," whose appearance is "posited on the imminence of its disappearance" after the 1997 handover of sovereignty from Britain to China: "the imminence of its disappearance … was what precipitated an intense and unprecedented interest in Hong Kong culture."[6] *A Simple Life* is a postcolonial attempt to record local family history and to preserve the memory of a passing generation.

The co-production and promotion of the film with mainland finance capital can also be understood in the context of an aging Hong Kong film industry that confronts existential questions about its survival in the post-CEPA era, when low-budget and mid-range films are squeezed out by co-productions with mainland China, with an anxiety over the loss of local flavor. *A Simple Life* is not only about the aging and disappearing Cantonese amahs but also the disappearance of local history and even Hong Kong cinema in what Victor Fan calls a "posthistorical era," when Hong Kong cultural productions after 1997 seek to redefine their existence and invoke "a new sense of community and collective temporality."[7]

That sense of community and collective temporality is invoked by the Hong Kong writer Chip Tsao (pen name To Kit) in his foreword to Roger Lee's memoir, *Taojie and I* (2012). While Tsao describes Taojie as the "collective memory" of a Hong Kong generation, he also praises Taojie's exemplary "virtues" that belong to an earlier "Chinese" generation.[8] The *South China Morning Post*, on the other hand, invokes the "lion rock spirit" (*shizishan jingshen*) in introducing the stage play, *The Amahs* (2015) (co-written by Roger Lee and Wong Wing-sze and commissioned by the Hong Kong Arts Festival): "If we wish to learn about Hong Kong's 'Lion Rock Spirit'—internal jargon for a can-do suggestion—go see an entertainment prolongation *The Amahs*."[9] These promotional endorsements point to the malleability of the diasporic icon of the Cantonese amah in creating cultural identity (Hongkonger or Chinese), collective memory, and a set of shared values within a community.

Journalistic and documentary discourse on aging in postcolonial Hong Kong

A Simple Life can also be read as a text of medical humanities, which explores the human dimension of medical practice, health, and care. In their study of film and Chinese medical humanities, Vivienne Lo, Chris Berry, and Guo Liping highlight "the growing role of audio-visual cultures in the transmission of medical cultures," as well as the "potential therapeutic effects of engagement with the audio-visual."[10] *A Simple Life* must be understood in the context of a burgeoning but understudied journalistic and documentary discourse on aging as a postcolonial condition in Hong Kong since the 2010s. The 1950s witnessed the mainland refugee influx to colonial Hong Kong and the postwar baby boom, which contributed to the rise of the working class and Hong Kong's economic miracle in the 1970s and 1980s. After the 1997 handover, Hong Kong's postcolonial condition intersected with its aging population. In 2011, 13 percent of the Hong Kong population was over sixty-five years old. By 2041, this figure will increase to 30 percent.[11]

Heightened by alarming demographic projections, the 2010s witnessed a burgeoning journalistic and documentary discourse that brought aging and death to the public sphere, increasing cultural literacy about late life in Hong Kong. In 2013, a two-volume work, *Dying in Hong Kong*, was published. The first volume, *Tearing Up*, is about the grieving process and the inadequacy of the Hong Kong medical and social welfare system in handling death. The second volume, *Seeing the Coffin*, is about the funeral industry in Hong Kong and its professionalization. The award-winning author and independent journalist Chen Xiaolei reflects on her decision to take up the project: "There are many guidebooks in bookstores about parenting, how to be successful, and how to improve interpersonal relationship … but when it comes to the last page of life, how should we deal with it?"[12] Su Meizhi, another award-winning author and independent journalist, who serves as a co-author, discusses the taboo of the word "death" in Cantonese: "When we really need to talk about death, the word 'death' disappears mysteriously, takes a detour, and becomes 'passing away' (*guoshen/shiqu*) and 'travelling in the other world' (*xianyou*)."[13]

Similarly, aging and dying are unglamorous and taboo subjects that are usually averted or unrepresentable cinematically because of the "prevailing cultural attitudes" of "ageism and fears of growing old."[14] Calling "age" Hollywood's "nightmare," Sally Chivers uses the term "silvering screen" to refer to a set of Hollywood films that reflect social anxiety about old age: "silvering screen narratives rely on audience members reading such visual markers as grey hair and wrinkles to signify the more obvious decay, decline, and imminent death of the characters … as well as a less obvious social anxiety about identity, self, and meaning."[15] The repeated imaginings about old age on the silvering screen "signify a larger cultural ethic."[16] In locating an intertextuality between *A Simple Life* and its adjacent media productions on aging, this chapter seeks to articulate a social anxiety about old age in postcolonial Hong Kong due to the lack of holistic and accessible elderly care.

An intertextuality between *A Simple Life* and its adjacent media productions, such as journalistic reportage and TV documentaries, reveals the inadequacy of elderly care in Hong Kong due to (1) the lack of end-of-life care programs that facilitate dying in the community and (2) the shortage of government-sponsored nursing homes. The chapter "Dying in a Nursing Home" in *Tearing Up* reveals the lack of end-of-life care programs that provide a possibility for people to die in their familiar beds in nursing homes. In many nursing homes in Hong Kong, a dying person is sent to the hospital and then back to the nursing home if their condition becomes stable, "just like a ball" bouncing back and forth.[17] The journalistic narrator reveals that most nursing homes in Hong Kong do not have the facilities and support that are needed for end-of-life care: pain relief, low-temperature rooms for corpse handling, mortuaries, family counseling, and doctors' presence for the issuing of death certificates. According to Dr. Zhu Weizheng, if mortuaries can only exist in hospitals under the Hospital Authority, it would not be easy to advocate dying in the community:

> Only in Hong Kong would you have so many people dying in hospitals … The Japanese government encourages home care for patients nearing the end of their lives. The United Kingdom established a national end-of-life care program with guidelines on how to die in the community. Hong Kong is unlike anywhere else. The burden on our medical system is too heavy![18]

The anxiety about dying in a hospital in Hong Kong is put in comparative terms: Hong Kong is perceived as an outlier in late-capitalist modernities, where dying in the community is not only possible but encouraged since the hospice movement founded by Cicely Saunders in the United Kingdom in 1967.[19] Saunders' revolutionary concept of "total pain" as having physical, emotional, social, and spiritual components inspired the creation of hospices worldwide, as well as a new branch of medicine called palliative care—the holistic care of individuals with terminal illness.[20]

Although there is end-of-life care in public hospitals in Hong Kong, the demand is too high for patients with chronic illnesses. Private hospitals are not entirely dedicated to patients nearing the end of their lives. Dr. Liang Zhida highlights: "The income of private hospitals is dependent on surgeries, medications and lab tests, rather than rent. People who die of old age rarely use those services. Private hospitals would consider those people occupying the beds for no reason."[21] The less profitable nature of end-of-life care is correlated to the lack of resources and space dedicated to it, indicating the profit-driven model of private hospitals in Hong Kong.

In 2015, about 31,000 elderly were waiting for residency in various Hong Kong government-sponsored nursing homes that provided less than 3,000 beds. Due to the serious shortage, the average waiting time was more than three years. About 40,000 elderly lived in private nursing homes, the quality of which varies due to the lack of caregiving staff.[22] In May 2015, Tai Po Cambridge Nursing Home in Hong Kong was caught up in an elder abuse scandal. The Chinese-language newspaper *Ming Pao* revealed that its nursing home staff had been making elderly residents wait naked on rooftops for showers. The elder abuse scandal was met with harsh criticism and triggered a journalistic and documentary discourse on aging in private nursing homes. Two months after the elder abuse scandal, in July 2015, Radio Television Hong Kong (RTHK) released a documentary titled *Old Age: Where to Turn*. Two more months later, in September, Television Broadcasts Limited (TVB) released a documentary titled *The Choice of Nursing Home*. Both TV documentaries reveal the economic and social anxiety about old age, focusing on private nursing homes as an economic and social choice.

The TVB-produced documentary *The Choice of Nursing Home* reveals the shortage of caregiving staff in private nursing homes in Hong Kong. After the implementation of the minimum wage in Hong Kong in 2011, many caregivers turned to other less demanding professions. In the documentary, Ms. Ng, a head nurse, says:

> If a nursing home fires a caregiver and fails to meet the [Social Welfare Department's] minimum requirement [of caregiving staff], it will be sued. To

> a certain extent, it creates a vicious cycle of caregivers' poor performance … [Interviewer: So even someone who commits errors won't be fired?] Yes, I heard that such cases exist.[23]

Not only is end-of-life care unprofitable for private hospitals; it is also a demanding and undesirable profession, whose compensation cannot compete with the minimum wage in Hong Kong.

The RTHK-produced documentary *Old Age: Where to Turn* discusses the lack of price transparency in private nursing homes in Hong Kong. Some private nursing homes persuade families that their staff can apply for social security assistance on the elderly's behalf to offset the nursing home's monthly charge, but in reality there are hidden miscellaneous costs. With a sense of irony, a similar lack of price transparency is evident in *A Simple Life*, where the nursing home manager takes pride in her so-called "honest" business practice: "There are so many scams out there. In some nursing homes, they do the paperwork for you to claim social security and then give you a rebate of HKD$500 per month. But it's a scam. The rebate they give you is charged back to your bills." When confronted by Roger Lee about the high cost of diapers, the manager says: "It depends on the diaper brand and the quantity. Diapers are charged by piece. That one is water-tight and more expensive." Miscellaneous costs, including diapers, are also conveyed in Roger Lee's memoir *Taojie and I*:

> With my professional accounting background, I began to suspect … I knew that diapers were used during daytime for sure. However, at night, it is possible that diapers were not used because not every resident would need it during their sleep. The staff might take risks, even if that meant cleaning bed sheets, which was more cost-saving than using diapers. Doing so not only saved diapers, but also made a profit because the unused diapers would still go to bookkeeping.[24]

Roger Lee's first-person narration of his experience with the lack of price transparency in a private nursing home provides an instance of intertextuality in multiple media, where Roger Lee's memoir, *A Simple Life*, and the TVB and RTHK documentaries converge to reveal the lack of holistic, humane, and accessible elderly care in a profit-driven capitalist economy. By bringing those issues to the public sphere, the media discourse on aging calls for holistic care that meets the physical, social, and emotional needs of the elderly, echoing Cicely Saunders' hospice movement as a living idea since the 1960s.

A Simple Life as a Hong Kong–mainland co-production under CEPA

A Simple Life is also a meta-cinematic reflection on aging as a postcolonial condition for the individual, the film industry, and the society that is experiencing greater integration with mainland China. The film responds to the postcolonial anxiety of old age by articulating an intergenerational kinship through Roger Lee and Taojie, a diasporic Asian icon of the amah that is localized, nationalized, and internationalized under the framework of CEPA. Signed in 2003, CEPA laid out the parameters for Hong Kong–mainland co-productions: Hong Kong–mainland co-productions are treated as mainland productions after receiving approval from mainland authorities. While CEPA offers the Hong Kong film industry access to mainland finance capital and an enormous market, it presents limitations such as state censorship. Karen Fang presents three modes that characterize the Hong Kong film industry in the contemporary age of co-production and self-censorship: (1) Mandarin-language, big-budget co-productions (e.g., *wuxia* revival film) with epic plots and set in epochal moments of Chinese national history; (2) Cantonese-language, small-budget Hong Kong productions with a local setting that is recognizable as Hong Kong in the tradition of social realism, such as *Echoes of the Rainbow* (Alex Law, 2010); and (3) crime gangster and undercover films, such as *Infernal Affairs* (Andrew Lau and Alan Mak, 2002), that package highly local stories in ways that remain commercially viable with "a loose Hollywood gloss," attracting Hollywood remakes and mainland Chinese cooptation or imitation.[25] After the Umbrella Movement (2014), independent documentaries and fiction films such as *Ten Years* (2015), which features dissent and aspirations for democracy, gained a new audience due to the demand for new genres that proliferated on the internet. After the imposition of the National Security Law in 2020, the future of Hong Kong cinema and Hong Kong–mainland co-productions remains to be seen.[26]

As a Hong Kong–mainland co-production co-presented by Bona Entertainment Co. Ltd., Focus Films Ltd., and Sil-Metropole Organization Ltd. (having the same status as a mainland China state-owned studio), *A Simple Life* tells the story of a Cantonese amah with neither a big budget nor the spectacular imageries typical of a co-produced blockbuster. One of the challenges in situating *A Simple Life* as a Hong Kong–mainland co-production is the potential tendency to perpetuate what Yiu-wai Chu calls the "over-simplified" binary between "co-production (bad)" and "local production (good)": "A third way beyond the 'big budget Mainlandized inauthentic' versus 'small-budget local authentic' dichotomy would prove to be very important for the revival of Hong Kong cinema."[27] Similarly, Han Li situates *A Simple Life* between Hong Kong and mainland China by problematizing the terms "local" and "authenticity," which tend to label Hong Kong cinema as a unique cinema independent from the framework of national cinema.[28]

The goal of this chapter is not to perpetuate the binary between Mainlandized co-production and local production by separating "authentic" Hong Kong elements from what is not. Instead, it locates the ways in which multiple imaginaries of home, family, and community—Roger Lee's home, a local nursing home, Roger Lee's transnational family, and a new Hong Kong–mainland cinematic community—coexist in *A Simple Life* as interconnected and interdependent sites of care. Under the framework of CEPA, a postcolonial, national, and transnational sense of home and belonging is simultaneously articulated.

Gary Bettinson debunks the myth of Mainlandization, suggesting that state censorship is a dynamic process where Hong Kong filmmakers "actively moulded mainland craft practices to Hong Kong work methods" and "innovated stories and styles, adapting local genres to new production conditions."[29] Similarly, Emilie Yeh and Shi-yan Chao highlight the "dual identity" of CEPA films, which "embrac[e] a big mainland market while maintaining a Hong Kong imprint" by "reviv[ing] and extend[ing] signature creative strategies of Hong Kong cinema."[30] *A Simple Life* can be considered as director Ann Hui's creative maneuver, negotiation, and adaptation in representing a diasporic icon of the amah because of the limitations and possibilities offered by CEPA.

In the post-CEPA era of co-production, Hui continues to position herself in the New Wave tradition of social realism in Hong Kong cinema. Hui's rise to prominence as a New Wave filmmaker in the 1980s can be attributed to her early documentary training at RTHK, which emerged as a colonial government-sponsored broadcaster serving taxpayers in the early 1970s. The broadcaster's television documentaries not only serve as a record of social reality, covering important political, economic, and social issues in the city, but also reflect public opinion. As a filmmaker, Hui has a long-standing interest in exploring social issues, "work[ing] within Hong Kong commercial genres while attempting … a more personal approach to subjects often shunned by the mainstream industry."[31] Many of Hui's films are about "ordinary, invisible women in their most mundane contexts, and people marginalized by all the major discourses of Hong Kong."[32] Since *Boat People* (1982), a film that deals with migrants and exile, Hui has positioned herself "on the edge of the mainstream."[33]

Hui sees her work in the "historical strand of realism in Hong Kong filmmaking."[34] In *The Way We Are*, she incorporates documentary footage into the fiction film: "I like to use documentary footage. The footage helps make realist films more believable."[35] Hui's early documentary training at RTHK, as well as her emergence as a New Wave filmmaker on the edge of the mainstream in the tradition of social realism, provides a context for us to understand her adaptive survival and positioning in the post-CEPA era of co-production.

A sensory home

In the film's promotional documentary, Hui describes a "documentary form" (*jilupian xingshi*) of fiction filmmaking as her intentional aesthetic (and marketing) choice for *A Simple Life*, which allowed her to create in the film a "semi-real and semi-fake" (*banzhen banjia*) reality.[36] Documentary is often associated with on-location shooting with its use of long takes and natural light, as opposed to fiction film's use of studio space. In *A Simple Life*, Hui's documentary aesthetic is premised on on-location shooting at Roger Lee's home. Feeling that creating an artificial *mise-en-scène* at a nearby apartment would not capture the "flavour of everyday life" (*shenghuo weidao*), nor would it be possible to find furniture similar to his, Roger Lee concurred with Hui's idea of on-location shooting at his home in the middle-class neighborhood Mei Foo Sun Chuen.[37]

Hui's on-location shooting at Roger Lee's home reconstructs a sensory experience of home as a site of care. I borrow the visual anthropologist Sarah Pink's notion of the "sensory home," which refers to the modern home as a "sensory domain," composed of the "cultural categories of smell, touch, taste, vision and sound, and created by human agents through manipulation of these sensory elements."[38] What Roger Lee refers to as the "flavour of everyday life" includes the flavor, color, and smell of the food that Taojie prepared with care, which exist in the sensory domain and can only be reconstructed visually and verbally in the diegetic world.

Through the lens of domestic labor and service, *A Simple Life* interweaves alimentary images and events of eating to narrate family history. The film introduces Taojie during her trip to the wet market, where she is known to be a picky customer, handpicking garlic. Through Roger Lee's sumptuous lunch that includes a steamed fish and a crab, the audience gets a sense of the master–servant relationship: (1) Taojie, as an amah, eats in the kitchen only after Roger Lee finishes his meal; (2) Roger Lee, who has had heart surgery before, tells Taojie that he is craving ox-tongue. The film later ensues with a close-up sequence of Taojie's cooking ox-tongue: from heating the wok with oil, ginger, and garlic to making a broth to marinate the ox-tongue with onions and spices (Figure 9.2). This sequence of culinary performance renders the domestic labor of Taojie visible: Taojie's domestic labor is not alienated, nor is the relations of production erased by capitalism, for we can get a glimpse of the process of production of the homemade food, as well as the work ethics behind it. Taojie's culinary labor, as a form of homemaking, creates a sensory experience of home as a site of care, bonding various characters as a family or community.

What Roger Lee refers to as the "flavour of everyday life" includes the tactility of material objects in his home. Lee's home, including its furniture and material objects, is an indexical trace of Taojie's presence. In a homecoming sequence, Taojie, as a postcolonial collector, recollects with nostalgia various sensory and material objects from her storage chest, such as an embroidered baby sling (that used to carry Roger Lee), a Lux soap, and a five-dollar bill (her first salary) from the colonial era. These sensory and material objects, some of which are depicted in close-up, are interdependent with other senses beyond the visual, such as smell and touch (Figure 9.3). The family photograph (partially photoshopped and digitally reproduced to include the actors' faces for narrative and promotional purposes) seeks to capture and preserve a moment in time, leaving not so much an indexical trace of the special bond between Taojie and Roger Lee but a digitally reproducible copy of the icon of the Cantonese amah (Figure 9.4). The retrieval of the family photograph under the anthropological gaze of the camera is an illustration of what Rey Chow calls the "modernity of

Figure 9.2 Close-up and extreme close-up shots of Taojie's making ox-tongue, rendering her culinary labor visible. *A Simple Life* (2011), directed by Ann Hui.

Figure 9.3 Close-up shots of touching and smelling sensory and material objects from the colonial past. *A Simple Life* (2011), directed by Ann Hui.

Figure 9.4 The family photograph is digitally photoshopped to reproduce the aura of Taojie as a Cantonese amah, turning the native "other" into a cultural commodity with added value. *A Simple Life* (2011), directed by Ann Hui.

the collector" and their fascination with history and the endangered authentic native.[39] This homecoming sequence digitally reproduces the aura of Taojie as a Cantonese amah, turning her into a cultural commodity with affective value (and star power) for narrative and promotional purposes.

A local nursing home

Xing Lin Nursing Home in the old district of Sham Shui Po is chosen by Hui for on-location shooting because of its environmental resemblance to Taojie's community when her health declined (Taojie did not actually live there in real life). Throughout the film, Hui's on-location shooting navigates in and out of Roger Lee's home and the nursing home, blurring the line between social reality of the nursing home and narrative fabrication. As the narrative ensues, the master–servant relationship at home gradually develops into a new intergenerational kinship at the nursing home.

Cinematic representation of aging uses the trope of "intergeneration"—meaningful interactions between the old and the young—to both reflect and challenge prevailing cultural fears of growing old.[40] *A Simple Life* responds to the postcolonial anxiety about old age by redefining Taojie and Roger Lee in relation to their biological, legal, or social families, necessitating a cultural change in how we think about aging and intergenerational relationships. Socially, the nursing home turns out to be a community that functions as Taojie's new social family. Although Taojie does not know how to play mahjong, she is asked to serve as a substitute when a playmate is missing. Just as Roger Lee's friends are enjoying the ox-tongue delicacy at home, giving Taojie a "miss-you" phone call, Taojie is playing mahjong with her new friends, cutting the phone conversation somewhat short (Figure 9.5). Other than juxtaposing with a graphic match a parallel community of friends at Roger Lee's home and the nursing home, the film depicts food sharing when Taojie generously shares with her friends at the nursing home the bird's nest soup that Roger Lee's mother has made, therefore extending the gesture of care to her new community, which includes the diabetic Uncle Jian, the kidney patient Mei, Aunt Jin, and the headmaster (all played by supporting or veteran actors). As Taojie gains a new social family at the nursing home, her master–servant relationship with Roger Lee is reversed in a new intergenerational kinship that transcends biological and legal ties, for Roger Lee is now the caregiver, taking Taojie for a stroll, to an eatery, or back to his home for his homemade soup.

Hui's intergenerational representation does not always paint a rosy picture. The film's reflection on aging is taken further in the scene when celebrities, schoolchildren, and emotional support animals visit the nursing home residents (played by both veteran actors and actual residents) during the Mid-Autumn Festival season. Some of the gestures of care turn out to be just an entertainment show: the mooncakes gifted to the residents have to be returned rather than shared. With a sense of irony, the scene includes a long shot of a cameraman holding a camera to record the charity singer, who couldn't care less about the elderly audience as objects on display once the recording camera is off (Figure 9.6). This meta-cinematic moment is a creative transgression, considering the ethical challenge of filming actual nursing home residents as authentic objects of representation, with

Figure 9.5 Juxtaposing a parallel community of friends at Roger Lee's home and the nursing home with a graphic match. *A Simple Life* (2011), directed by Ann Hui.

Figure 9.6 A meta-cinematic camera's gaze on the charity performance, with aging residents serving as extras. *A Simple Life* (2011), directed by Ann Hui.

the risk of exoticizing, idealizing, or victimizing them as the aging lonely "other." The meta-cinematic camera's gaze on the charity performance heightens our awareness of the problem of representing nursing home residents, as much as setting out to convince us of the authenticity of representation.

From diaspora to a transnational family reunion

Other than the two imaginaries of home—Roger Lee's sensory home and a local nursing home—*A Simple Life* depicts Roger Lee's extended family—a transnational family which Taojie is a part of. For Taojie, like many other diasporic Cantonese amahs who were displaced by wars, domestic service in colonial cities in Asia was first and foremost a matter of survival—feeding the stomach and having a roof over one's head. On the contrary, for Roger Lee and his middle-class parents, emigrating to the United States (and returning to Hong Kong) was a matter not of diasporic survival but of choice. Both Roger Lee and his father were born in the United States and then moved to Hong Kong when Roger Lee was little.[41] Roger Lee's family moved back to the United States in 1969, so that Roger Lee would not lose his citizenship (Taojie did not emigrate and stayed in the family property in Mei Foo Sun Chuen). After graduating from the University of Oregon, Roger Lee worked as an accountant in San Francisco, followed by other brief stints in New York City, where he was exposed to film, theater, and jazz. He returned to Hong Kong in his late twenties, living with Taojie in Mei Foo Sun Chuen while pursuing a career in the film industry. The difference between Taojie and Roger Lee in social class status and their motivations for migration (diasporic migration vs. choice of citizenship) has profound implications on the growth of the aging family and caretaking in late life.

Taojie's story is a diasporic journey of homemaking—making a home for herself and for her employer. In her lifelong service, Taojie became a part of the Lee family as her adoptive family in essence. As her health declines, Taojie's final wish of witnessing five generations of Lee's family is conveyed in Roger Lee's prayer with the priest (Figure 9.7). The narrative trope of "intergeneration" is linked to the theme of "regeneration," which features older characters who "find closure, resolve significant conflicts, and restore or create some kind of emotional or spiritual wholeness in their lives."[42] The milestone of Taojie's diasporic journey is a transnational family reunion in Hong Kong, where Taojie fulfills her final wish of witnessing five generations of Lee's family as she passes on her jewelry to Jason's Korean wife, who is pregnant (Figure 9.8). By interweaving Roger Lee's sensory home, the local nursing home, and the extended transnational family as interconnected and interdependent sites and networks of care, the film sheds light on how postcolonial aging might necessitate a new form of intergenerational kinship that is transnational and intercultural, rather than biological.

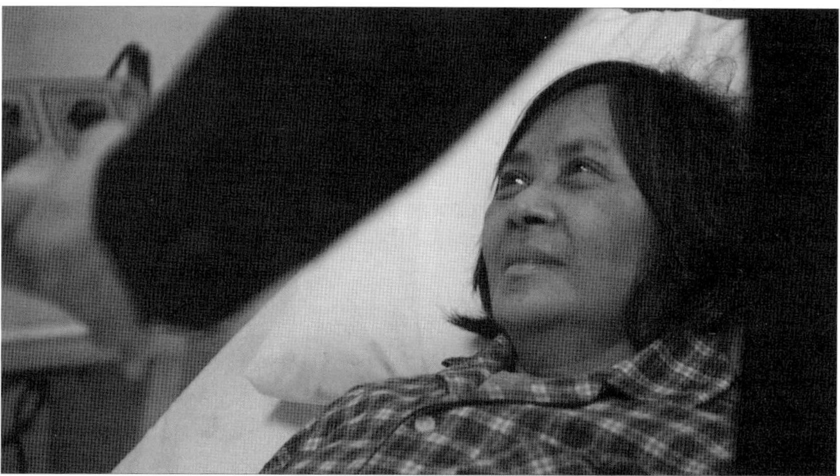

Figure 9.7 A medium shot of Taojie gazing at Roger in his prayer, framed by the arms of the priest and Roger, who are holding hands. *A Simple Life* (2011), directed by Ann Hui.

Figure 9.8 A transnational family reunion in Hong Kong, where Taojie fulfills her final wish of witnessing five generations in Lee's family. *A Simple Life* (2011), directed by Ann Hui.

A Hong Kong–mainland cinematic community

A Simple Life is also a meta-cinematic reflection on the aging Hong Kong film industry and its survival in the post-CEPA era. The film seeks to represent the Hong Kong film industry and invoke a new sense of community with its mainland cinematic counterpart. That new sense of community is created by casting. There are four kinds of actors in the film: (1) professional actors from Hong Kong and the mainland with star power, (2) Hong Kong veteran actors who play supporting roles (mostly in the nursing home), (3) non-actors (actual residents of the nursing home) serving as non-professional extras, and (4) Hong Kong and mainland filmmakers who make a special guest appearance in the film, playing cameo roles in a self-referential way. Hui's casting of professional actors with star power, veteran actors, and non-actors enhances the commercial value of the film, pays tribute to Hong Kong's aging veteran actors, and allows unglamorized subjects to be represented on screen. What results is a collision and symbiosis between the real and the staged, the glamorized and the unglamorized, the Hong Kong film industry in crisis, and the new market potential from the mainland.

Hui originally intended the film to be a low-budget production and had a hard time securing funds for the film. She suggested to producer Roger Lee: "Why not use stars?"[43] For the sake of commercial marketability, Hui cast Andy Lau as the leading character. Andy Lau not only invested RMB 30 million in the film but also served as a narrator of the film's promotional documentary. Hui chose the mainland actress Wang Fuli to play the role of Roger Lee's biological mother not only because of her established star persona in the mainland as a mother but also because of her training in Peking opera. The mainland actress Qin Hailu, who plays the role of Ms. Choi, is selected by Hui for her "unpretentious acting."[44] Hui's deliberate casting choice that created synergy between Hong Kong and mainland actors is a result of the creative opportunity offered by CEPA, which states that "there is no restriction on the percentage of principal creative personnel from Hong Kong, but at least one-third of the leading artists must be from the Mainland."[45]

While the leading roles are marked by star presence from both Hong Kong and mainland China, supporting roles are played by Hong Kong veteran actors, whom Hui regards as a living "treasure" of the Hong Kong film industry.[46] Hui considers veteran actors who are over fifty years old as brilliant actors because they give a "lively performance with professional ethics."[47] Leung Tin (1932–2020), who plays the role of a headmaster in the nursing home, is the first generation of Hong Kong television stars in the 1960s. By using veteran actors for supporting roles, Hui, like a film historian, pays tribute to aging veteran actors for their contribution to the Hong Kong television and film industry. In a daring move, Hui typecasts actual residents in the nursing home as non-professional extras interacting with stars and veteran actors, instilling in her biographical fiction film the unglamorized rawness of a documentary that captures social reality as well as an imaginary of a nursing home.

Because Roger Lee is a film producer, his real life intersects with the lives of many in the Hong Kong film industry and its mainland counterpart. Hui therefore invited more than thirty directors, producers, and actors, such as Raymond Chow, Sammo Hung, Stanley Kwan, Andrew Lau, Ning Hao, Tsui Hark, and Yu Dong, to make a special guest appearance in the film. These special guests became "non-professional" extras, playing cameo roles as directors and producers, negotiating with Roger Lee at work and celebrating with him at the film premiere in the diegesis, which is a meta-cinematic representation of a new Hong Kong–mainland cinematic community. Tsui Hark reflects:

> This film depicts a unique kind of human relationship in Hong Kong. I hope to see more stories about ourselves … There must be a reason why so many of us made a guest appearance. That is because the film portrays the real world of our friend Roger, and we are a part of this real world.[48]

Tsui Hark's so-called "real world" is not only the diegetic world of Taojie and Roger in the film but also the extra-diegetic world of the Hong Kong film industry at large. Sammo Hung's and Tsui Hark's cameo roles are a self-referential and meta-cinematic representation of Hong Kong filmmakers going north to negotiate (with Yu Dong) budgets and deals during all stages of production under CEPA.

Although the majority of the film is shot in Hong Kong, the film includes consistent snippets of mainland geography and train stations through on-location shooting, in order to instill "an atmosphere of exile and displacement" in a metaphorical search for home in postcolonial Hong Kong, where Roger Lee is based as a film producer who frequently goes north because of CEPA.[49] Andy Lau reflects that the mainland gave them "vast geography and room for imagination": even though it is just a few shots of mainland China, the crew would travel far rather than staying close to home, as Hong Kong is too small to offer shots on that geographic scale.[50] The CEPA stipulation that requires the plots or the leading characters to be related to the mainland is not simply a restrictive necessity but a creative opportunity to represent the aging Hong Kong film industry's greater integration with the mainland.[51]

Despite the mainland finance capital and talent that made the film commercially viable, Andy Lau's call for "long live Hong Kong cinema" in the promotional documentary can be read as a postcolonial act of preserving Hong Kong film history as it faces greater integration with the mainland.[52] By casting professional actors (from Hong Kong and the mainland), veteran actors, and non-actors in collaborative interactions and social negotiations, *A Simple Life* represents not only Taojie but also the aging Hong Kong film industry at a meta level as it integrates with its mainland counterpart to form a new cinematic community.

Conclusion

In interweaving family history with Hong Kong film history through the biographical story of an aging Cantonese amah, *A Simple Life* straddles the Hong Kong market, the mainland market, and the rest, while remaining commercially viable, culturally significant, and socially engaged under the limitations and possibilities of CEPA. Echoing journalistic and documentary discourses that challenge a pathologized notion of aging, *A Simple Life*, through the intergenerational kinship between Taojie and Roger Lee, articulates a holistic care that meets the physical, social, and emotional needs of the elderly. If Taojie, an aging Cantonese amah, is a product of diaspora and (post)colonial modernity in Hong Kong, the multiple agents in writing, performing, and remembering the story of Taojie point to the malleability of the diasporic Asian icon of the amah in creating a postcolonial, national, and transnational sense of home and belonging.

An earlier version of Chapter 9 "Postcolonial aging, amah, and diaspora in *A Simple Life*" was first published in Inter-Asia Cultural Studies (June 2023), available online at https://doi.org/10.1080/14649373.2023.2209427

Part Four

Displacement and homeland

10

The position of Hong Kong

On material, space, and memory in Ann Hui's Vietnam trilogy

Siao-Yun Chen

Ann Hui uses material objects in the Vietnam trilogy to explore connections between emotion, identity, and movement. This chapter examines how she utilizes these objects as intermediaries to reflect on Hong Kong's impending postcolonial transition, its role within the Chinese diaspora, and their significance in shaping the imagination of Hong Kong identity, the assurance of identity, the dismantling of power, and the interplay between reality and fiction. In the late 1980s, discussions on new materialism emerged, challenging traditional views of materialism in various ways. Old materialism views humans as the source of all action, treating matter as a static object dominated by human subjects. In contrast, Spinoza and others argue that the material world is not inert but rather a source of movement. Matter is seen as a determinant of action and a source of agency and creativity, serving as a generative force.[1]

Jane Bennett advocates the use of the term "thing-power" to explain the ability of inanimate things to have an impact by combining with other material bodies. She attempts to rethink the traditional distinctions between matter and life, passive objects and active subjects, and emphasizes that agency is not an exclusive property of human beings.[2] Bennett argues that this is not a world of subjects and objects but a world in which various materialities are constantly engaged in a network of relations. It is a world populated less by individuals than by groupings or compositions that shift over time. Attention to things helps to eliminate the opposition between subject and object, and Jane Bennett envisions different kinds of materiality that are constantly involved in relational networks. Instead of imagining individual materialities or isolated things, she advocates that matter tends to make connections and form networks of relations with varying degrees of stability.[3]

Unlike previous analyses of the Vietnam trilogy that view the films as metaphors for Hong Kong through their plots, this chapter, drawing on new materialism and its focus on materiality and relational ontology, examines the objects in the trilogy. This approach opens up new layers of discussion on the relationships between the objects, space, and characters in the films.

In the Vietnam trilogy, these material objects each respond to Bennett's concept of "thing-power" from different perspectives. These objects reveal the agency of matter and open up deeper layers of meaning within Ann Hui's films. It is important to note that when considering the material representations in the Vietnam trilogy, our attention should not be limited to the objects themselves. Rather, we must recognize the assemblage-like qualities of material agency—that is, the agency of matter emerges through its interactions with other things or with human subjects. Photographs, paintings, letters, and cameras do not exist independently within the films; their power derives from their interactions with specific characters and their presence within particular spatial and temporal contexts. These networks of interaction, along with the spatiotemporal conditions and the inherent vitality of the material objects, constitute assemblages that infuse the films' narratives with new reflections on identity and history.

Ann Hui and her films

What sets Ann Hui apart is her role as a pioneer of new Hong Kong cinema, her early adaptations of Eileen Chang's novels, and her prolific output of high-quality films. She consistently explores different ways to depict Hong Kong's story through film. This chapter attempts to rethink Hui's Vietnam trilogy in the context of new Hong Kong cinema. In the past, most discussions of the Vietnam trilogy have centered on political issues, such as Hong Kong's fear of the uncertainty of its future in 1997.

Tony Williams, referring to Hui's earlier film *Boat People*, argued that the director's choice of mainland actors to play the brutal Vietcong was not a coincidence but rather a deliberate political allegory.[4] Many critics have also pointed out similar views on the themes of the Vietnam trilogy, such as pointing out that *The Boy from Vietnam* alludes to the future of Hong Kong through the exile of Vietnamese refugees; *The Story of Woo Viet* reflects the people's fear and dissatisfaction with their political future;[5] and *Boat People* presents North Vietnam from the perspective of Hong Kong people, revealing their fear and criticism of communist rule.[6]

In response to such arguments, Hui has repeatedly objected to such claims. Interestingly, when Hui responds that *Boat People* is a survival story, this denial of politics produces inconsistent evaluations of the film and the audience's perception of it.[7] However, it is essential not to get hung up on whether the Vietnam trilogy is a series of political films or not; it is worthwhile to explore how Hui rethinks the story of Hong Kong through the otherness of Vietnam, as well as the position of Hong Kong and the humanistic concerns revealed in this trilogy. Most critics discussing Hui's Vietnam trilogy emphasize the fear and uncertainty surrounding Hong Kong's handover in 1997, a political discourse rooted in historical reality. However, this focus often overlooks the uniqueness of the three films and Hong Kong's connections with other regions at the time. In *The Boy from Vietnam*, Hui's first film to address the Vietnam subject, she integrates the story of Vietnamese refugees into the Hong Kong narrative. In *The Story of Woo Viet*, she combines the refugee theme with the gangster genre, expanding the representation of Vietnamese refugees and the themes of Hong Kong's genre cinema. These films highlight the refugee and boat people movements, prompting a reimagination of Hong Kong's role as an intermediary and transporter in the 1980s. They also encourage a reexamination of Hong Kong's relationships with regions like Vietnam and the Philippines, showing how these areas collectively confront the global Chinese diaspora. The final installment of the trilogy, *Boat People*, delves deeper into the complex and problematic issues surrounding Vietnamese refugees. Although Hong Kong seems absent from this film, Hui uses it to reflect more profoundly on history and truth.

Tony Williams mentioned that many Hong Kong films have used Vietnam as a metaphor for what might have happened in July 1997, but Hui's films dealing with Vietnam have not. In her films dealing with Vietnam, Hui often deals with transnational and transhistorical issues.[8] The flight and survival of Vietnamese refugees is an issue concerning Vietnam and its domestic politics. However, in the Vietnam trilogy, Hui takes us back to the historical context of the time, bringing out a unique Hong Kong story of the pre-1997 period through the lens of the Vietnam issue. These versions of the story differ from the handover anxieties, instead dealing with Hong Kong's history in the 1980s within a broader context and vision.

Hong Kong position: Interregional relationality and historicity

Hong Kong has always been a port in the literal sense of the word, a door, a threshold, a conduit for the flow of goods, currencies, and information; a nodal point, an in-between state, and as such, Hong Kong is more of an inter-national city than an international one. Abbas has noted that, in contrast to international cities such as New York, London, and Tokyo, which serve as central sites for the production of goods and culture within their respective regions, Hong Kong is primarily a space of facilitation.[9] What new perspectives does Hong Kong offer us as a city on modern urban culture? Hong Kong establishes itself as a city of opportunities, and its portability as a fact of life is one of the crucial factors that place Hong Kong in the world's urban culture.[10]

Whether viewed through historical processes or Abbas's and Chow's perspective of Hong Kong as a seaport city, the roles of mediation, intermediation, and transit were crucial for Hong Kong in the 1980s. These roles highlight an alternative experience and understanding of Hong Kong's sense of time and space during this pivotal period. Hui's Vietnam trilogy provides a lens through which Hong Kong can be viewed from the perspective of the "other," by exploring the spatial and temporal experiences of Vietnam and the movement of refugees. This perspective is a significant aspect of postcolonial Hong Kong. In 1979, the Governor of Hong Kong, Sir Murray MacLehose, went to Beijing with Deng Xiaoping to discuss the issue of Hong Kong's lease of the New Territories in 1997, which was the prelude to the Sino-British talks on Hong Kong. In the 1980s, as China and the United Kingdom began to negotiate the future of Hong Kong, people began to pay attention to the cultural identities of the people of Hong Kong. There was a boom in the discussion of cultural identities around 1997, which led to the exploration of Hong Kong's postcolonial status in the cultural sector. The so-called postcolonial state of Hong Kong refers most directly to the temporal meaning, that is, to the state of Hong Kong after the handover in 1997, but the more profound meaning points to reflecting on and transcending the coloniality of Hong Kong before 1997.[11] In other words, postcolonial Hong Kong has been explored through various discourses or media before 1997. Hui's Vietnam trilogy is one example.

When we talk about Hong Kong's "postcolonial" situation after 1997, we often have to start from the 1980s. This is because the end of the colonial period was already foretold in Hong Kong before the end of the colonial period, hence the term "pre-postcoloniality." In short, as early as the 1980s, during the transitional period, Hong Kong had already begun to think about postcolonial issues, the most obvious of which is the question of cultural identity.[12]

Another critical aspect of Hong Kong's postcolonial identity is that we cannot frame Hong Kong from old binaries, such as the distinctions between East and West, tradition and modernity. Because the local and the global are becoming increasingly intertwined, the so-called binaries are more likely to confuse rather than clarify the question of identity. In other words, we cannot simply and directly think of Hong Kong as a subject; rather, we should try to understand the complexity of its subject formation and pay attention to how Hong Kong's culture has gradually constructed a new kind of subjectivity in the process of negotiating the variations and permutations of colonialism, nationalism, and capitalism. This new subjectivity we are trying to describe is not only a psychological dimension but also an emotional, political, and social one.[13]

Margaret Thatcher's visit to China in 1982 began the process of negotiation and established the moment when Hong Kong's sovereignty would be returned to China in 1984. This Joint Declaration caused a certain degree of anxiety, despite the fact that the article guaranteed that the sociopolitical structure of Hong Kong would remain unchanged for fifty years.[14] In other words, the yet-to-arrive 1997 and the post-colonization of Hong Kong had already begun to fester during this transitional period. As Leung Ping-kwan has mentioned, in the period between the signing of the Sino-British Joint Declaration in 1984 and the return of Hong Kong to China in 1997, some of the anxiety and uncertainty were expressed in films that treat the city allegorically and try to project the mixed and undefined sentiments into a tangible narrative form.[15] Hui's trilogy, at this moment, stitches Hong Kong's postcolonial imagination into her narrative, bringing out the relation between Hong Kong and Vietnam in these images and finding a new subject position for Hong Kong.

The Vietnam trilogy is an imaginative and speculative view of postcolonial Hong Kong before 1997. In the past, when we interpreted the Vietnam trilogy, we often focused on Vietnam itself, but we should further consider how Hong Kong is represented in the Vietnam trilogy. Moreover, it demonstrates how Hong Kong connects and relates to other places in this series of images.

While *The Story of Woo Viet* appears to be a film that focuses on the movement of Woo Viet from Vietnam to Hong Kong, Hong Kong seems to be a temporary place for the Vietnamese refugees, and Hong Kong appears only briefly in the first half of the film. However, the configuration of letters and sounds in the film allows the viewer to imagine Hong Kong's position in more ways than one. Some commentators have pointed out that the movie ends with a voiceover by Woo Viet, who reads a letter to Kwan, telling her of his hopes and plans to create a better future with Ah Sarm and Sum Ching (both of whom are in fact dead). The great hope expressed in the voiceover contrasts sharply with the despair and loneliness seen onscreen as Woo Viet throws Sum Ching's body into the sea and continues his exile alone on the boat. More importantly, this despair is directed at Hong Kong's Kwan, whose absence and silence further trigger the Hong Kong spectator to think about the connection between Woo Viet's destiny and the fate of the people of Hong Kong: What is the future of the people of Hong Kong? She is an invisible, voiceless observer of Hong Kong, powerless in the face of political events.[16]

If *The Boy from Vietnam* and *The Story of Woo Viet* both incorporate images of Hong Kong when dealing with Vietnam, then *Boat People* is a film in which Hong Kong is absent. Hong Kong itself does not appear in the film; it is only mentioned, and only the fact that it is directed by a Hong Kong director and stars Hong Kong actors connects the film to Hong Kong. However, the film suggests that Hong Kong people face a self-reflective dilemma. The Hong Kong audience, for whom this film is primarily intended, will tend to identify with the characters. Although the film does not have an overtly allegorical structure, its self-referentiality may induce Hong Kong audiences to understand the film allegorically and associate Vietnam with their unstable historical and political conditions.[17] From *The Boy from Vietnam* to *Boat People*, Hong Kong's presence in these films diminishes, with a shift from the focus on Vietnamese refugees to Vietnam itself in the latter. However, Hong Kong remains central to Hui's attention. The Vietnam trilogy represents Hui's exploration of the relationship between Hong Kong and Vietnam, and how this relationship can be depicted differently. How do changes in narrative strategy and camera focus provide new ways to explore Hong Kong's role in the context of the Vietnam issue?

The varying visibility of Hong Kong in the trilogy shows Hui's effort to tell a unique Hong Kong/Vietnam story. Rather than just addressing the Vietnamese refugee issue, she uses the trilogy to present different aspects of Hong Kong and Vietnam, highlighting their historical and relational dynamics in the early 1980s.

The film boldly reveals that all "exotic" places may be part of their history. It is essential not to look at Hong Kong alone but to trace how this city, with its complex history and immigrant background, relates to other places, countries, and cultures.[18] Lei once used the Vietnam trilogy as an entry point to discuss Hui's exceptional local articulation. Today, we believe that to be local means to draw a line. Hui suggested in the early 1990s that being local means drawing a map, pointing out many other places, and connecting Hong Kong with these places to understand our history and localities.

Hui's imagination of the locality involves what can be described as a mapping process. If we look back at her Vietnam trilogy, we can see how she redefines the meaning of Hong Kong as a place through spatial narratives in film. From Ah Man's journey from Vietnam to Hong Kong, to Woo Viet's movement from Vietnam to Hong Kong and the Philippines, or the encounters between the Japanese journalist Akutagawa and the Qin Niang family in Vietnam, Hui consistently resists static representations of Hong Kong or Vietnam. Instead, she moves toward a connective imagination of place. Hui places Hong Kong and Vietnam within a transborder context, emphasizing the entanglement of their historical experiences, especially under postcolonial conditions. Rather than portraying places as isolated or self-contained entities, Hui's cinematic mapping foregrounds the dynamic interactions and mutual influences between these spaces. In doing so, she not only challenges the boundaries of local identity but also highlights the ways in which Hong Kong's history and locality are constituted through ongoing connections with other places, peoples, and histories. This mapping process, as enacted in Hui's Vietnam trilogy, offers a powerful lens for rethinking the meaning of locality in a global and postcolonial context, underscoring the importance of mobility, encounter, and historical intersection in the construction of place.

These imaginings and relations of place, as Audrey Yue mentions, critically spatialize and redraw the epistemological field of historical imagination. Critical spatialization remaps the epistemological terrain of historical imagination. It opens up a narrative that triggers a contemporary reconceptualization of space.[19] The Vietnam trilogy tells a different story of Hong Kong/Vietnam, perhaps through the path and process of the Vietnamese refugee movement, the gaze and desire for Hong Kong from the point of view of the Vietnamese refugee as the moving other upon arrival in Hong Kong, and the significance of Hong Kong as an intermediary for Vietnam.

The Vietnam trilogy simultaneously brings out two profound reflections in emphasizing the historicity and relationality between regions. Firstly, Hui universalizes the issue of migrants/refugees. For example, *The Story of Woo Viet* opens a new page of the Chinese diaspora in Hong Kong cinema. As a typical refugee case, Woo Viet involves many fundamental ethnic Chinese problems in Southeast Asia. After docking, these mostly ethnic Chinese Vietnamese boat people are likely to find that these ports are not a place of refuge. However, rather than a place where they fall into another trap, a different kind of struggle for life, their fate may seem like that of orphans with no place to go.[20] Secondly, the Vietnam trilogy shows us how Hong Kong's storytelling is no longer confined within the framework of the China factor. The China factor is prevalent in Hong Kong cinema in the 1980s. Hui's Vietnam trilogy allows us to see the story of

Hong Kong outside of the China factor, that is, to rethink Hong Kong's position in the 1980s and its role in this transnational context through the relations between Vietnam, the Philippines, and Hong Kong.

The Hong Kong position is embedded within the director's narrative, while subtly incorporating a humanist core of care. For example, the release of *Boat People* in Hong Kong, to a certain extent, reflected the political issues of Hong Kong people in terms of box-office revenue. The issue of anti-communism or politics is represented through Hong Kong's position and emotions. However, it is interesting to note that Hui has stated that *Boat People* is not about highlighting the politics of the Communist Party; it is about a sense of life. For Hui, this is a film about boat people from another perspective. *Boat People* was made at a time when the refugee influx had begun to trigger resentment and fears among the local population about limited resources. In general, Hong Kongers did not understand why refugees came to the colony or why they were allowed to stay in the colony. Hui's film provides an important context for this social situation, depicting Vietnamese asylum seekers before they fled and documenting the conditions that led to their exile. The film was made when the majority of those undergoing migration did not yet have a means of self-expression and viewed themselves primarily through news headlines and government policies. Although diasporic Vietnamese writers, visual artists, and filmmakers have begun to tell their own stories over the past few decades, *Boat People* remains a rare and foundational work that depicts Vietnamese refugees as subjects worthy of narrative and ethical contemplation.[21]

In other words, rather than suggesting that Hui's trilogy promotes any particular movement or ideology, it is more likely to highlight how, as a Hong Kong director, Hui's juxtaposition of images of Hong Kong and Vietnam has illustrated the complex relationship between Hong Kong and Vietnam on the one hand, and on the other hand, brought to light Hong Kong's position of mediation and humanity in the 1980s.

The materials in the Vietnam trilogy

As discussed at the outset of this chapter, Bennett's concept of "thing-power" describes how inanimate objects generate force through their connections with other material entities or human subjects. In the Vietnam trilogy, the various objects depicted are not passive or isolated existences; rather, they possess agency within the cinematic narrative and serve to further reveal issues of identity, history, memory, and affect to the audience. The unfolding of these themes not only demonstrates the vital, energetic, and lively qualities inherent in matter itself but also deepens the narrative structure of the trilogy, weaving together the intersecting themes of Hong Kong and Vietnam, migration and the Cold War, as well as colonialism and history. In this way, the agency of material objects in Hui's films does not merely function as a narrative device but actively participates in the construction of meaning, linking disparate historical and geopolitical contexts and enriching the affective and discursive layers of the cinematic text.

Shen Shiao-yin has mentioned that Hui's film style is conveyed through realistic images, structure, and plot details.[22] A key plot detail is the role of material objects in the films. In addition to revisiting Hui's Vietnam trilogy from the perspective of Hong Kong, in this chapter I draw on the discursive space of new materialism to revisit the multiple meanings of matter in Hui's three early works. Matter is not inert, nor simply the background for human activity, but is conceptualized as agentic.[23]

Roland Barthes believes that the photograph is always a certificate of presence. The photograph is special in many ways; as a document, it provides evidence that emphasizes not the restoration of an object but, on chance, opening the image to speculation.[24] Photography produces images that serve as evidence or abstractions; it is special for bearing an indexical trace of the space–time continuum, while the camera itself constructs the nature of the social world, and of feelings that drive people to action.[25]

In the case of Hong Kong, there is an essential relation between architecture and cinema, which involves visual issues. Architecture and cinema are two of the most developed forms of culture in Hong Kong and are also the most market-dependent and visually distinctive. Architecture is often the first visual evidence of a city's perceived identity, and cinema contributes to a critical discussion of colonial space by problematizing visuality itself through architecture.[26] It is necessary to address the complex relation between space and history in Hong Kong, that is, to speak of spatial histories. The new Hong Kong cinema can link history, space, and affectivity.[27]

Architecture, photographs, and paintings in *The Boy from Vietnam*

The Boy from Vietnam depicts the story of Vietnamese stowaways in Hong Kong. The narrative centers on the protagonist, Ah Man, who moves to Hong Kong by boat from Vietnam in search of his cousin, who has been living in Hong

Kong for some time. Ah Man hopes to find a job in Hong Kong and bring his family, who are still in Vietnam, to live in Hong Kong.

The first shot of Ah Man arriving in Hong Kong in the film is a night scene of Victoria Harbour, a skyscraper with flickering lights, where Hui demonstrates the high modernity of Hong Kong through the use of Hong Kong's architectural and lighting objects. The tension in this shot is due to Hui's switching of camera space. As the viewer follows Ah Man, who has been smuggled into Hong Kong by boat, the space of the camera changes from the small and dimly lit cabin of the boat to the night scene of Victoria Harbour in the next shot, which not only allows the viewer to quickly understand that Ah Man has arrived in Hong Kong but also shows the first time that Hong Kong has been presented in the eyes of the Vietnamese refugees. This kind of material space is shown not only at the beginning of the film when Ah Man arrives in Hong Kong but also in the spatial configurations of the streets in Hong Kong, such as streetlamps, taxi cabs, and telephone boxes, which symbolize the modern space and materiality of progress, mobility, and communication.

In *The Boy from Vietnam*, Ah Man writes a letter to tell his family about his life in Hong Kong, revealing that he hopes to earn money and bring his family to Hong Kong. Here, Ah Man describes the contents of his letter through oral narration. The voice of this narration is interspersed with images of the streets of Hong Kong, including a nighttime Hong Kong filled with people, bright lights, and bustling stalls on the street, and the final shot of this narration focuses on the streetlamps, once again symbolizing the modernity that Hong Kong represents.

Hui not only brings out the representation of Hong Kong in physical space but also demonstrates the assurance and revelation of identity through the use of two materials: photographs and paintings. Suppose Ah Man is asked to provide a photograph to identify him before disembarking from the boat, symbolizing the guarantee of identity the photograph provides. In that case, the painting is a material object in the film that symbolizes Ah Man's gradual revelation of his cousin Yau Hing-nin's identity and occupation in Hong Kong. As Ah Man becomes more fluent in Cantonese and adapts to life in Hong Kong, he begins to make money by delivering reproductions of paintings, which ironically leads to Ah Man's discovery of his cousin's dishonorable status as a male prostitute in Hong Kong. It is worth noting that the paintings not only reveal the identity of the cousin in the movie but the audience also learns that the buyers of the reproductions are foreigners living in Hong Kong through the process of Ah Man's delivery of the paintings, indirectly bringing out the unitary image of Hong Kong in Westerners' minds.

Letters in *The Story of Woo Viet*

The Story of Woo Viet has a special status as a turning point and is the one with the most vital internal tension among Ann Hui's works. Tension refers to content, form, and style.[28] Just as in *The Boy from Vietnam*, where Hui brings out the life of Vietnamese refugees in Hong Kong through the oral narratives of the character combined with letters, *The Story of Woo Viet* further reinforces the materiality of the letters with the sound narration, leading the audience into the movement and escape of Vietnamese refugee Woo Viet. From the beginning to the end of the film, there are three central moments in which Woo Viet writes a letter to his pen pal, Kwan, in Hong Kong. The first letter appears at the very beginning of the movie, when the camera captures Woo Viet and a group of people drifting in the sea on a boat, and Woo Viet's confession is shown in the onscreen sound, in which he says that he is about to leave Saigon and go to Hong Kong as a refugee. The letter serves as the material that brings out the connection between Woo Viet and Kwan, whom he has never met, and between Vietnam and Hong Kong.

Shortly after arriving in Hong Kong, Woo gave up moving to Chinatown in the United States to save his girlfriend, Sum Ching, who had been trafficked and went on the run to Chinatown in the Philippines instead. In the Philippines, Woo writes a second letter to Kwan, in which he and his Hong Kong partner Ah Sarm kill a man for Mr. Chung in Chinatown. In the letter, Woo mentions that he is unsure if Ah Sarm has also come to the Philippines with a fake passport like himself. In addition to the materiality of the letter as a continuation of the above, as a link between people and places, the message conveyed in the letter also serves as a questioning of identity, whether it is the Vietnamese Chinese, Woo Viet, or the Hong Konger, Ah Sarm, who are in the same predicament of being separated from the rest of the world.

At the end of the film, Woo Viet kills Mr. Chung, his partner Ah Sarm dies in a car accident, and Sum Ching dies in a Filipino killing spree. Eventually, we see Woo rowing a boat on the river and sinking Sum Ching's body into the river, leaving himself floating alone on the river. Paradoxically, the voiceover at this point, that is, the confession in the third letter that Woo writes to Kwan, reveals that Woo Viet himself, Ah Sarm, and Sum Ching left the Philippines together and traveled to Bantayan Island as refugees, and tells us about their dreams and plans for the future. The break between the voice and the image here reveals the third level of the letter as a material object. That is, the letter constructs fiction and imagination.

Kwan, who observes Woo Viet's story through letters, remains silent throughout the film, and she does not have a chance to establish a personal relationship with Woo, who is in Hong Kong for a short time. On one level, she represents the missing and impotent Hong Kong people; on another level, she is also a blank onto which the desires and potentials of the Hong Kong people and their exile destiny are projected. Her silence invites the spectator to introspect about Hong Kong and its people at this crucial historical moment.[29] In other words, we can say that through the Hong Kong position of Kwan, Hui connects the intermediaries and hopes of the Vietnamese refugees and the Chinese diaspora (e.g., Woo Viet says that he can only be safe if he carries the letters he and Kwan have written in the past).

Camera in *Boat People*

Boat People describes the arrival of Japanese journalist Akutagawa in Vietnam after the end of the Vietnam War. Through his camera, he allows us to see the realities and constructions of Vietnam. Akutagawa sees an entirely different life in Da Nang and the new economic zone. Compared to the real life of the lower class in Da Nang, the new economic zone is filled with two extreme phenomena: the illusion of constructing a better life and the daily routine of dismantling landmines at the risk of one's own life. The story focuses on Akutagawa's acquaintance with Qin Niang's family. Apart from helping them to make a living and photographing the family, he ends up being burnt by petrol while helping Qin Niang escape. Hui once mentioned that the central figure of *Boat People* should be an outsider who can only be guided behind the scenes by these would-be refugees and see what is happening. This protagonist could not be Chinese because it would automatically be assumed that we were commenting on Chinese–Vietnamese political relations. If he had been an American, French, or even just a Westerner, it would have raised the specter of war and dragged in a completely different sensibility.[30]

If Hui uses objects such as buildings, photographs, paintings, and letters to bring out the imagination of Hong Kong, the assurance and revelation of identities, and the connection between people and places in *The Boy from Vietnam* and *The Story of Woo Viet*, then *Boat People* deliberately highlights the camera as a material object to bring out a more profound reflection that involves the reality and fiction of history. Apart from being a tool for Akutagawa to gaze at

Vietnam, the camera also carries complex connotations of witnessing, recording, collaborating in propaganda, deconstructing reality, and debunking the truth of history. At the film's beginning, Hui presents a dual view of Vietnam through the camera, that is, Vietnam under the lens of the film and Vietnam's post-liberation military parade, which is captured by the photographer Akutagawa with his camera. Through Akutagawa's camera, we not only see the procession on the streets after the liberation of Vietnam but also see through Akutagawa's camera a different kind of celebration from that of the procession: a crippled child with a stick in a narrow alley, a backdrop that symbolizes the children who suffered in Vietnam and the reality that the official government wants to hide after the liberation.

Akutagawa's camera is emphasized as a symbol of his visual exploration of Vietnam, and it clearly parallels the film camera itself. The film begins with a scene that explicitly integrates the two cameras. When he clicks the shutter of the camera, the viewer shares his perspective as if looking through his camera. That is to say, the audience and Akutagawa share the same perspective. This opening scene and its representation in this unification of perspectives bring out the fact that the viewer will see Vietnam through it.[31]

Three years later, when Akutagawa arrives in Vietnam again, he brings the contradictions and doubts he had seen through his camera three years earlier and tries to find the reality of Vietnam in the new economic zone. Akutagawa's desire to see the reality of life in postwar Vietnam drove him to photograph. Seeing how the Vietnamese lived or were unable to live was terrifying for Akutagawa, and the brutal reality complicated his innocent desire to see it.[32] In other words, the camera's visibility and gaze complicate reality and contribute to this camera-wielding man's drive with the power to spread the truth by pressing the shutter to reproduce it.

When Akutagawa photographs children singing songs about Ho Chi Minh in the new economic zone, a teacher mentions that Akutagawa's reportage and photographs would allow the world to see the happy, joyful new face of the liberated people of Vietnam. This scene refers to the communication and construction inherent in photography. However, when Akutagawa moves to Da Nang and meets Qin Niang's family, he gradually realizes the reality and fiction of Vietnam through the camera. Qin Niang's mother warns Akutagawa not to photograph the hardship at home, revealing the truth that the Vietnamese government wants to hide. Therefore, Akutagawa switches to being guided by Qin Niang, observing, seeing, and experiencing real Vietnam in the streets of Da Nang. Akutagawa's camera shows a different version of Vietnam's story underneath the camera's gaze. This different reality includes the daily life of Da Nang's grassroots and the brutality and construction of the new economic zone.

After Akutagawa's encounter with Qin Niang, his camera takes on a more complex and dialectical meaning in the film. In contrast to the beginning of the movie, when Akutagawa saw the singing and dancing in Vietnam through his camera, Akutagawa now captures the Vietnamese military government casually taking men on the streets to the new economic zones and the Vietnamese people dying on the chicken farms. The scene where Akutagawa arrives at the chicken farms with Qin Niang and her brother Lok is filled with the absurdity of the Vietnamese reality. Qin Niang and Lok run excitedly toward the bleeding corpses, ready to take whatever they have on their bodies that can be bought and sold, and Lok suggests to Akutagawa that he can capture the scene with the camera.

When Akutagawa is amazed by the scene in front of his eyes, a newcomer, Zu Ming, who has just returned to Da Nang from the new economic zone, also comes to the chicken farm. When Lok sees Zu Ming, he tells him that the camera Akutagawa is carrying is a Nikon camera from Japan, which could be sold for 1,000 dollars if he found a way to get it. To the suffering underclass, the importance of the camera is not to represent reality but to realize the source of money. When Lok first met Akutagawa, he told him, "Nikon, you are Japanese. If you want to sell your camera, I have a way to get rid of it." This remark of Lok's is a prophecy because, in the end, Akutagawa chooses to sell the camera to help Qin Niang's family escape the country.

It is interesting to note that in the film, apart from symbolizing the representation of the construction of a happy life and the reality of the brutal suffering of the underclass after the liberation of Vietnam, and the camera as an exchange of money, the camera reveals a short-lived moment of freedom and happiness in Akutagawa's photographs of Qin Niang smoking a cigarette in a rainstorm, which is preserved eternally in the negative through the camera.

Conclusion

The Vietnam trilogy seems to be about the movement and daily life of Vietnamese refugees. However, the position of Hong Kong flashes from time to time in the images, from Ah Man, who moves to Hong Kong in *The Boy from Vietnam*, or Woo Viet, who corresponds with his pen pal in Hong Kong and goes into exile from Vietnam to Hong Kong and the Philippines in *The Story of Woo Viet*, to the temporary settlement of Vietnamese refugees and the node that connects the history of the ethnic Chinese's movement in exile, or the history of the Vietnam War, which has become an essential part of Vietnam's history. At the same time, Hong Kong is also a place where the history of the Vietnam War has created relations and links with Vietnam in its aftermath. In the Vietnam trilogy, Hong Kong seems absent or only serves as a backdrop for the temporary residence of the refugees/migrants. The theme of the film mainly revolves around Vietnamese refugees. However, through the way Hong Kong is represented in the film, we see the specificity of Hong Kong as a transit, intermediary, and node point. We can say that through the position of Hong Kong in the 1980s, the refugees/migrants opened up a space that activates the pain and memory of the Vietnam War, the reunion of the diaspora, and the double contradiction of having a fresh start and having one's hope dashed.

Through quotidian objects, such as the architecture, photographs, and paintings in *The Boy from Vietnam*, the letters in *The Story of Woo Viet*, and the camera in *Boat People*, Hui problematizes the relationality between material and human, encouraging the viewer, as Abbas puts it in his discussion of Hong Kong's cultural forms, not so much to look at what there is to see but rather to "look again."[33] The new Hong Kong cinema problematizes vision and viewing and offers a critical experience of Hong Kong's cultural space and new visual forms.[34] Through this re-viewing, the Vietnam trilogy invites us to rethink the relationality between Hong Kong and transnational territories and reflect on an alternative story of Hong Kong in the 1980s.

11

Exile or vacation?

Homeland in Ann Hui's *Song of the Exile* and *My American Grandson*

Suk Man Yip

Leave, stay, or reunion?

For most people in Hong Kong, 1990 was a year filled with uncertainty and anxiety. They had just witnessed the Tiananmen Massacre in Beijing the previous June, though most saw it through TV news at home. Still, it shocked the colony's residents, prompting some to consider emigration to other countries once again. For those who had already decided to leave, the incident further strengthened their resolve to depart the city without regret, but sooner. This wave of emigration prompted the British and Chinese governments, as well as the colonial authorities, to become increasingly alert and concerned about the potential loss of foreign investments. In October 1989, then Hong Kong Governor David Wilson proposed urgent infrastructure projects, known as the "Airport Core Programme" or "Rose Garden Project," to encourage citizens and foreign investors to stay. When emigration again became a hot topic in the city, the film *Song of the Exile* was aired on April 27, 1990. In her ninth film, Ann Hui explores the meanings of "home" and "homeland." The film is a semi-fictional autobiography based on the story of Hui and her Japanese mother, who married Hui's father and remained in China after the Sino-Japanese War. After settling in Hong Kong and not returning to Japan for years, she felt estranged from her homeland. Although such diasporic stories have occurred worldwide across many eras, they are akin to a letter home, written by the director to contemporaries, elaborating on the dilemmas faced by the city and its residents.

If we broaden our perspective to include not just Hong Kong but also the Taiwan Strait, we see that a cloud of anxiety and confusion covered both sides following the Tiananmen Incident. When Chiang Ching-kuo lifted martial law and permitted family visits between mainland China and Taiwan in 1987, most Taiwanese Chinese believed that the civil war had come to an end. They looked forward to further economic cooperation with mainland China, although some harbored concerns. However, the June Fourth Massacre shattered these hopes and strained relations once again. Taiwanese people's antipathy was reflected in poor box-office performances and negative reactions to films or TV dramas filmed in mainland China when they were broadcast. The Beijing and Taipei governments planned to hold a meeting to reconcile their relationship and continue economic development. Despite fierce societal controversy, the Nationalist government established the National Unification Council on October 7, 1990, paving the way for talks between the two parties. Meanwhile, Ann Hui was invited to direct a Taiwan-invested film, *My American Grandson*, also known as "The Vacation in Shanghai."[1] The production company engaged Wu Nien-Jen, the screenwriter of *Song of the Exile*, to craft the story. In this second collaboration, Hui and Wu continued to explore themes introduced in their previous film. It revolves around a retired teacher whose teenage grandson returns to Shanghai for a short visit after moving to the United States with his parents as a child. The story of returning home echoed the impending first formal meeting between the Chinese Communist Party (CCP) and the Kuomintang (KMT) after the Retreat to Taiwan in 1949. The film was broadcast on July 11, 1991. As expected, its box-office performance was poor. It earned only half the revenue of *Song of the Exile*, which had already achieved the poorest box-office results in both Hong Kong and Taiwan in 1990. Despite being two years after the Tiananmen Incident, public sentiment had not changed significantly.

Why did the film companies willingly invest in producing these two movies? Notably, there was a consensus that movies filmed in China were unpopular and could not receive the audience's support after 1989. Both films were produced and invested in by Taiwanese film companies and distributed by Hong Kong film companies, with Ann Hui as the director and Wu Nien-Jen as the screenwriter. Although a different company produced the second film, the intention of creating a continuation of the same topic was apparent. However, film companies generally do not invest in another film with the same theme when the first one is unsuccessful, let alone finding the same director and screenwriter for the second one. So why did the companies insist on making two films about returning home/homeland even though a poor box-office result was expected? Did they prepare for the 1992 Hong Kong Meeting, where the 1992 Consensus was addressed, and the later Wang-Koo Summit in 1993?[2] If *Song of the Exile* presents questions about homeland, can we consider *My American Grandson* as a wish to reconcile with the mainland? Is that the meaning the director, the screenwriter, and the Taiwanese film companies wanted to present? Are there other hidden messages behind the story of returning home?

The diaspora is a frequently explored topic in Ann Hui's films from the 1990s and 2000s. Among these works, *Song of the Exile* is a piece that is often studied or cited whenever scholars discuss diaspora, return, and notions of home and homeland in Hong Kong cinema. In her influential and insightful book, *Ann Hui's Song of the Exile*, Audrey Yue offers a comprehensive analysis of this particular work within those themes. She concludes that Hong Kong has already become the mother and daughter's new homeland. Rey Chow examines Hong Kong's postcolonial self-writing and diaspora, while Ackbar Abbas addresses issues of Hong Kong's identity in the postcolonial era. These studies rarely consider the aforementioned concerns in relation to Hui's other works. Although *My American Grandson* was created and produced shortly after *Song of the Exile*, and was written and directed by the same team, previous studies have not treated them as a series of related films or as films sharing relevant content. However, when viewed together, one might observe that the semi-fictionalized autobiographical film only reveals the first part of Hui's narrative about her homeland. In *My American Grandson*, the director suggests that China is frequently a destination after a long journey, as evidenced by Gu Ming, the returning grandson, who transforms from an arrogant American boy into a polite Chinese boy upon returning to Shanghai. We see the full cycle envisioned by the director and screenwriter. After temporarily residing in places like Hong Kong (e.g., Hiu-Yan and her Japanese mother), individuals often return to their homeland and reconnect with their forsaken roots (such as Gu Ming). But is this the conclusion of the Chinese diasporic story? Do Chinese people eventually find their resting place and live happily ever after? Perhaps the Chinese title of the second film, "The Vacation in Shanghai," already offers an answer: returning to China is merely one of many stops, similar to how Gu Ming needs to go home after a brief stay in Shanghai. His story alludes to a line from the theme song of *Song of the Exile*, "The journey in life never ends," a lyric charged with emotion and authenticity. If China is not the final destination but simply a temporary stop, then where is "home"? What constitutes a "homeland"? Is it true that the roots of the homeland can never be severed, even after years of absence? If so, can this bond be transmitted to people's descendants? Can they truly call it their homeland when they know nothing of it? Can someone choose their homeland? Hui repeatedly explores these questions in both films. These are also the key issues this chapter examines.

To reconstruct a comprehensive and clear picture, the chapter analyses the two films as a series (Episodes 1 and 2) under the motif of "homeland" and the issues of the contemporary Chinese diaspora. Three aspects are examined through the parallel reading: (1) the relationship between the content of the films and current political affairs – are they intended solely for entertainment or are they actually propaganda used to convey messages to the other side, and what political metaphors can be identified?; (2) new perspectives on homeland and home, the bond between generations, and the changes in the Chinese diaspora narrative; (3) the messages from Taiwan. What did the Nationalist government and the film companies aim to communicate to the Beijing government? What measures did they take to ensure the films could be broadcast smoothly? Since the Central Motion Picture Corporation (CMPC), an official organ operated by the KMT and the Nationalist government, was one of the production companies that produced *Song of the Exile*, it is inevitable to consider the company's intention in investing in and creating the movie. More details are addressed in the following sections.

Entertainment or propaganda?

Although the two films were produced and broadcast consecutively, the stories within them take place in different periods. The time frame of the first film spans 1945 to 1973. It was around 1972 when Hiu-Yan returned from Britain to attend her sister's wedding. The Cultural Revolution had not yet concluded in mainland China, and negotiations on the sovereignty of Hong Kong between the British and Chinese governments had not yet begun. When Yan had to travel to Guangzhou to see her grandfather, it was the summer of 1973. Before that, she had just finished a news report about police corruption and bribery, focusing on the case of Peter Fitzroy Godber (b. 1922), a chief superintendent of the Royal Hong Kong Police Force who served as deputy district commander of Kowloon, Hong Kong. It was also a period when thousands of people took to the streets for demonstrations and later urged the British colonial government to establish the Independent Commission Against Corruption (ICAC), primarily to investigate corruption within the police force. The story of the second film takes place in the early 1990s, probably after December 1990. In the film, Gu

Ming eats fried chicken at Kentucky Fried Chicken (KFC) on his second day in Shanghai. The first KFC restaurant in China opened in Beijing in November 1987. The first in Shanghai opened in the same building as the Shanghai Dongfeng Hotel in November 1990. As the film was broadcast in July 1991, the story likely occurred between December 1990 and June 1991. Although the time gap between the two stories is nearly eighteen years, the films reveal that the Chinese diasporic story remains ongoing.

Examining the production background of the films and the time they were created, one can see that they were not merely for entertainment but also reflected current affairs.

A child without roots

Song of the Exile was co-produced by two Taiwanese film companies, Kao Shih Film Company and CMPC.[3] When the film was planned and filmed, Koo Chen-fu was the sixth chief executive of the CMPC. He was also the chairman of the Strait Exchange Foundation, which organized the 1992 preliminary talks in Hong Kong that resulted in the so-called "1992 Consensus." In April 1993, he represented the Nationalist government to meet Wang Daohan, the representative of the People's Republic of China (PRC), in Singapore. The meeting, which was called the "Wang-Koo Summit," was the first formal discussion between Taipei and Beijing after 1949.

Although the two parties were still discussing the possibility of a summit when *Song of the Exile* was filmed in Guangzhou in autumn 1989, Taiwanese people were allowed to return to mainland China to visit their families for a period of one and a half years. News about old KMT soldiers reuniting with their families after being separated for forty years kept being reported on TV and in printed media in Taiwan. The film also arranged for the protagonist, Hiu-Yan, to return to her homelands. As a child of a Chinese father and a Japanese mother, she has two homelands. One is her mother's homeland, Beppu in Japan, and the other is Guangzhou in China. She does not know her mother is Japanese until she reunites with her parents in Hong Kong at the age of fifteen. Before that, she lived with her grandparents in Macau and knew nothing of her mother or Hong Kong. This arrangement deliberately made the character into a child unaware of its roots, much like Hong Kong, often described as a "floating city" and a "rootless city." She finally learns more about her mother when she accompanies her to Beppu after her sister's wedding. Even though she is half-Japanese, she does not speak the language or understand the customs, which ultimately allows her to understand her mother's bitterness and sadness as a foreigner who could not speak Chinese but had to live in Chinese communities. Although returning to her maternal homeland pushes her and her mother away from Japan, it also helps reconcile their relationship. She decides to stay in Hong Kong and work at a TV station, giving her the chance to learn more about the city and its people. "It is my first time to look at this place and the people here closely." It shows Yan beginning to build a connection with Hong Kong. As she gradually adapts to life there, she receives terrible news about her grandfather in Guangzhou—he has had a stroke. To see her beloved and respected grandfather, she embarks on a journey to her paternal homeland—China, which was still undergoing the Cultural Revolution at the time. It feels unfamiliar, even though her grandfather told her much about the "motherland" when she was a child. When her grandfather encourages her not to be disappointed with the country, she can only gaze up at the sky, bewildered.

Once again, returning to her paternal homeland distances her from her country (China). However, we do not know her decision this time. Will she stay in China? Or will she return to Hong Kong and make the city her new home, like her mother? The film leaves the ending open, inviting the audience to reflect on the questions raised through their own experiences.

A child regaining their roots

My American Grandson was produced by a single company called Golden Tripod Film Corporation. Although it is not a production of the KMT's official organ, most of the people on its production team were former directors, screenwriters, and producers of CMPC. They were experienced in creating films that address social and political issues. The executive of the film, Pai Ching-jui, was a prominent director of several influential Taiwanese films, including *Fantasies Behind the Pearly Curtain* (1976), *The Coldest Winter in Peking* (1981), and *The Last Night of Madam China* (1984). Before joining Golden Tripod, he served as the director and manager of CMPC. He was one of the representatives of the "Healthy Realistic Films" movement, which the KMT promoted from the 1960s to the 1980s. It is clear that *My American Grandson* follows this style, even though the operational director is Ann Hui. The Taiwanese production team greatly influenced the creation of the film.

Although the film's title is "My American Grandson," both the grandfather and grandson are the protagonists. *Song of the Exile* employs a first-person narrative, in which Hiu-Yan consistently appears as a storyteller with her voiceover audible in the background. *My American Grandson* uses a third-person narrative, with the camera acting as a story presenter from an objective perspective. The grandfather, Gu Dade, is a retired teacher living alone in Shanghai. His wife died at an early age. Their only son and daughter-in-law are scientists and have been residing in the United States for years. He leads a simple, happy life, but it becomes slightly lonely until, one day, a phone call from the United States changes everything. Because his son and daughter are on a research trip to Germany, they must send their son, Gu Ming, Dade's grandson, back to China. Ming was born in Shanghai and moved to America with his parents when he was four, but he has forgotten everything about China and has become Westernized, regardless of his lifestyle and habits. Unlike Hiu-Yan, a child without roots, Ming used to have roots but lost them after leaving his homeland. If Yan represents the people of Hong Kong, Ming's situation is more akin to that of most contemporary Chinese who left mainland China as children and emigrated to other countries with their parents.

Due to the significant differences in eating and living habits, many conflicts occur between them. Still, Dade tries his best to satisfy Ming's demands despite spending almost all his savings. One day, Ming runs away after Dade slaps him. He gets lost and nearly drowns while crossing a river. Fortunately, a farmer couple from a nearby village rescues him. He stays at their house for one night and finally learns to write his name with a Chinese brush and ink, symbolizing that Ming has regained his roots and remembered who he is. Falling into the river and emerging from it feels like a baptism, giving him a new life. The return to his homeland helps him to reconnect with his roots and identity.

From a story of a child without roots to a story of a child regaining roots, Yan's and Ming's stories not only reflect many contemporary Chinese diasporic experiences but also echo the fact that Taiwanese Chinese who left mainland China after 1949 could finally return home to visit their families in 1988.

Hong Kong and China: A floating boat and a weak old man

"The closer we are, the farther we are; the farther we are, the closer we are," Yan's mother says it twice. The first time is after her youngest daughter, Hiu-Wai, leaves Hong Kong and moves to Canada with her husband. It describes her relationships with her two daughters. The second time is when she sits by a riverside and looks at the sunset with Hiu-Yan after staying in Japan for a while. It illustrates her connections with her homeland, Beppu, and her new home, Hong Kong.

Hiu-Yan has maintained a closer relationship with her grandfather than with her Japanese mother since childhood. Although Yan's voiceover at the start of the film attempts to explain the situation due to her mother's silence, it remains challenging for the audience to grasp why Yan and her mother are so estranged. What factors caused the mother and daughter to become strangers to each other initially? The film does not provide a clear answer. Their alienation seems to begin when Yan was born. It would be more appropriate to analyze their relationship based on the character backgrounds and symbolic meanings. Although the film is described as a semi-fictional autobiography based on the story of Hui and her mother, it is understandable that artistic adaptations and changes occur during production. Consequently, applying film analysis techniques remains valid. The screenwriter intentionally portrays Hiu-Yan as being in an unstable state: she was born in Northeast China, moved to Macau at age two, lived with her grandparents until she was fifteen, then relocated to Hong Kong but only stayed with her parents and sister briefly before leaving home to attend a boarding school alone. The story begins when she is pursuing a master's degree in England. Due to her sister's wedding, she eventually returns to Hong Kong. Her living situation constantly shifts—she resembles a boat adrift in the sea, searching for a place to stay yet unable to settle. Whether she chooses to live with her grandparents in Macau, only to be ultimately abandoned, or attempts to find employment in England after graduation but fails, she is perpetually in motion, unable to establish stability. Her experiences vividly reflect the fluidity of Hong Kong's identity.

If Hiu-Yan symbolizes Hong Kong, then Grandpa represents mainland China. If Hong Kong, represented by Hiu-Yan, is like a boat without an anchor, then mainland China, represented by Grandpa, is like a frail old man after a stroke. Near the end, Hiu-Yan says, "Grandpa's body is no longer able to support her granddaughter's weight." Grandpa had a stroke after being tortured by the Red Guard for hours, symbolizing mainland China becoming weak, fragmented, and damaged after the Cultural Revolution. Hiu-Yan's emotional expression implicitly suggests that mainland China was too weak to have Hong Kong. It was the summer of 1973 when Yan returned to Guangzhou. If mainland China was too weak to "carry" Hong Kong in the early 1970s, would it be strong enough to take it over in 1997? It was just a year after the Tiananmen Incident when the film was broadcast; this was a question on many people's minds in Hong Kong.

Inside the films

As the so-called "Deadline of 1997" approached, questions of "home" and "homeland" haunted the people of Hong Kong every day. Given Hong Kong's uncertain situation, the Taiwanese people also felt anxious, especially since the Nationalist government actively opened the country to mainland China. The establishment of the National Unification Council in October 1990 further stimulated the Taiwanese people. They also began to consider the relationships between Taiwan and China, as well as the significance of "home" and "homeland."

Home and homeland

The two films delivered a crucial and advanced message: it is unnecessary to be loyal to the "homeland" forever. Choosing a new one is possible if one no longer loves the original one. The four characters in the two films (Yan's mother, Yan, Yan's sister, and Ming) represent three types of situations in which people face the issues of "home" and "homeland."

Yan's mother represents the people who have already chosen a new home, which may later become their new homeland. We don't know if Yan's mother always wanted to return to her homeland. Perhaps it was a sudden decision after her youngest and closest daughter left Hong Kong and moved to Canada with her husband. She was thrilled upon her arrival in Beppu after being away from her homeland for years. She ordered three meals at a noodle house but forgot to eat them because she coincidentally encountered her teacher and talked with her about the past. She met her old classmates, including her love rival, and sang and danced together happily. Yan suddenly realized that she knew not just a little, but nothing, about her mother. She did not even know her mother's Japanese name. However, her mother felt even lonelier after the first few days of excitement, especially after she learned that her elder brother wanted to sell the ancestors' house in Beppu and move to Tokyo. At first, she rejected her brother's appeal because that meant she would lose her home forever. But the more days she stayed in the homeland, the more loneliness and alienation she had. She found nothing in her homeland that could compare to her memories of Hong Kong, and she began to miss it, including the food and the bathroom at home. She finally realized she had already regarded Hong Kong as a "home" long ago. Maybe after she could speak Cantonese, or after she gave birth to her second daughter, or after she learned how to play mahjong. No matter when she started, we know that she had already chosen Hong Kong as her destination to settle in.

Like most Hong Kong people who are second-generation immigrants from China, Hiu-Yan and her sister Hiu-Wai do not know much about their parents' homelands and lack a strong sense of belonging to the British colony either. They are rootless and still searching for a place to settle, but the sisters' paths are quite opposite—Hiu-Yan decided to return to Hong Kong after years away, while Hiu-

Wai, who has lived in Hong Kong since birth, chose to move to Canada for a new start. We do not know her experience of emigrating to Canada, including how she adapted to a Western country and faced cultural shock. Nevertheless, we can imagine how difficult it must have been, recalling how hard it was when Yan initially sought work in England at the beginning of the film. Instead of returning to Britain, Yan found employment at a Hong Kong TV station, which allowed her to learn about the city and its people. The more she understood them, the stronger her emotional ties became. Although she had not yet decided where her home might be, she was not considering leaving Hong Kong either. However, this temporary stability ended when her beloved grandfather suffered a stroke in Guangzhou. The journey to her homeland did not provide clarity but rather deepened her confusion about the meaning of "homeland." Even though her grandfather encouraged her to have hope for the motherland, her facial expression revealed her uncertainty and hopelessness. Unlike their mother, Hiu-Yan and Hiu-Wai are still searching for a home and feeling unsure about their homeland.

Gu Ming represents those who emigrated to foreign countries with their parents as children and later had the opportunity to choose their home when they grew up. After living and studying in Shanghai for several months, Ming became a polite young boy who loved attending school and playing ball games with friends rather than playing video games alone. He gradually adapted to life in mainland China and enjoyed living with his grandfather, even without a private bedroom. Aside from the obvious symbolic message that Chinese culture can encourage someone to be a better person, the reconstruction of human relationships and family bonds is another important message the film conveys (aligning with the style of "Healthy Realistic Films"). When everything went smoothly, it was also time for Ming to return to the United States. The audience suddenly remembered it was a holiday, echoing the Chinese film title, "The Vacation in Shanghai." On the way to the airport, Dade told Ming, "You are luckier than most others because you have choices, and you can decide where to go and live in the future." Although he had to return to the United States at that moment, he could choose whether to move back to China when he grew up.

All three types of situations point to a conclusion: although people cannot choose where they are born, they can choose their home, which can later be their new "homeland" if they want. When they have time, they can return to their old homeland for a short stay, just as Yan's mother went back to Beppu, Yan returned to Guangdong, and Ming went to Shanghai. Still, they need to go home or go back to their new homeland once the time comes.

The bond between generations

The films give "homeland" another layer of significance—to awaken/to recall/to strengthen the bond between generations, no matter how long one has been away from the place.

The four characters in both films also have problems in their relationships with other family members. Except for Hiu-Wai, who had no chance to learn more about her grandparents because she had already moved to Canada in the first half of the film, the three characters—Yan, Yan's mother, and Ming—significantly change their attitudes toward other family members after the brief visit to the homeland. In *Song of the Exile*, Yan was close to her grandparents but alienated from her parents. After her journey to Japan, she reconciled with her mother. She finally understood her mother's difficulties living in a foreign community without knowing the language and the customs. The unfamiliar homeland surprisingly reconnected her and her mother. Yan's mother eventually realized Hong Kong had already become her new home/homeland after returning to Beppu. The conversation between her and her teacher revealed that she had left Japan for China due to a loss of love. Returning to her old homeland allowed her to reunite with her siblings and old friends, saying goodbye to them and her former identity as a Japanese person. She reconciled not only with her daughter but also with her past. In *My American Grandson*, Ming knew nothing about his grandfather after moving to the United States with his parents for seven years. When the air steward asked him if Gu Dade was his grandfather, his answer showed how alienated they were ("Yes, I guess so"). When his grandfather wanted to hold his shoulders to have a clear look at him, he turned around and hugged the air steward to say goodbye rather than hugging his grandfather. Likewise, he became close to his grandfather after a short stay in Shanghai.

Although the films emphasize the connection between homeland and family bonds, the concept they present is not the traditional idea that people must return to their original homeland and live there until they die, as if a leaf returns to its roots after falling from a tree, or *luoyeguigen*. As mentioned in the previous section, the homeland can be a choice. For example, in the case of Yan and her mother, returning to Beppu allowed them to reconnect. Meanwhile, the place helped her mother see clearly where her new home was. She decided to leave after being healed by her homeland.

The changes in the Chinese diasporic story: From NSN to EWE

The contemporary Chinese diasporic story has never stopped since the beginning of the twentieth century, but it has gradually converted the direction modes from North–South–North (NSN) to East–West–East (EWE). The two films present the changing trend of Chinese migration.

In *Song of the Exile*, Hiu-Yan was born in Northeast China after World War II (after 1945, probably in 1946/7) and followed her parents to move to the south—the Portuguese colony of Macau when she was two (around 1948/9). As her father was a translator for the National Army, the director implicitly informs the audience about their move due to the Retreat to Taiwan. Those low-ranking personnel without air tickets to Taiwan initially moved to Macau and Hong Kong, where they waited for further instructions, although history indicates that no additional instructions were given. There were no more air tickets either. Those left behind by the KMT were stranded in Hong Kong and later settled in Rennie's Mill, whose Chinese name was "A Ridge of Hanging Necks" because many former KMT soldiers felt despair and committed suicide there after being abandoned by the KMT for years and eventually figured out that they would never have a chance to go to Taiwan or return home to see their families. Hiu-Yan grew up in Macau and later moved to another southern city, the British colony of Hong Kong, when her grandparents and uncle decided to return and contribute to the motherland at the age of fifteen (around 1961/2). Mainland China was suffering from the Great Famine. We don't know why her grandparents went back to China at that difficult moment, but we can imagine how chaotic and bitter their lives would be because the Cultural Revolution was about to break out in four years. Probably owing to love and affection, her grandparents did not take Hiu-Yan to Guangzhou with them. This allowed her to live in Hong Kong and study in Britain later, although she initially thought they had abandoned her. She finally returned to China (to the north) to visit her grandparents when she grew up. Her story is a template for many Chinese people's experiences from the 1940s to the 1970s.

Ming's story can be seen as a continuation of the Chinese diasporic narrative in the 1980s, but it shifts the pattern from NSN (within the Sinophone regions) to EWE (across the world). He moved to America with his parents at the age of four (around 1983) and returned to Shanghai at the age of eleven (in 1990). Following the economic reform of 1978, opportunities for Chinese people to travel to the West gradually increased. More Chinese intellectuals studied abroad with government funding in the 1980s. Some returned to China after graduation, but many chose to remain in the West with their families. Ming's parents were among those who had the chance to study for a PhD in the United States and decided to settle there afterwards. Their children, having grown up in foreign countries, learned local languages and customs. Perhaps, like Ming, they only began to experience confusion about their identity and homeland after setting foot on Chinese soil. After the Tiananmen Incident, the number of Chinese intellectuals studying abroad rose rapidly. Since most went to Western countries, cases similar to Ming's continued to occur in the following years.

Messages from Taiwan

As mentioned earlier, *Song of the Exile* was produced by CMPC, an official body operated under the KMT and the Nationalist government. Although another film company produced *My American Grandson*, the production team comprised several former directors, screenwriters, and producers from CMPC. They were familiar with and skilled at creating films that effectively communicated political messages. Therefore, what messages did the film companies and production teams aim to convey through these two films during that critical period (after the Tiananmen Incident and before the first formal meeting between the two sides)?

Taiwan, my new homeland

Both films explore the complex idea of a "new homeland." They suggest that people can choose their new home, which might later become their true homeland. Individuals can break through racial boundaries to select any place or country to live in, even if those groups were once enemies. Yan's mother was Japanese, but she chose to become Chinese and considered Hong Kong her new homeland. Hiu-Wai, a child of Chinese and Japanese descent, was born and raised in Hong Kong but later emigrated to Canada with her husband. The filmmakers and production team expressed views that likely echoed those of many Taiwanese: they had already regarded Taiwan as their new homeland after living there for forty years. The message in *My American Grandson* is even clearer, evident in Dade's words to Ming: "You are luckier than most others because you have choices, and you can choose where to live and where to go." Once Ming is an adult, he can select any place as his home, and that is fortunate! The phrase "most others" refers to those who did not have the chance to leave China. "You" can refer to the newer generations of Chinese who have moved abroad; it can also be interpreted as "Taiwanese Chinese" whose parents moved to Taiwan after 1949. That scene resembles an elder Chinese man speaking to a young Chinese or Taiwanese boy (coincidentally, the young actor playing Gu Ming is from Taiwan), explaining how lucky he is.

"Voice down" to ensure I can speak

Another noteworthy point in both films is the deliberate downplaying of sensitive political events. Unlike the films produced by CMPC in the early 1980s, *Song of the Exile* and *My American Grandson* carefully avoid addressing specific historical incidents that might have provoked the Beijing government, such as the Cultural Revolution and the Tiananmen Incident. For example, when Yan worked at a Hong Kong TV station in 1973, mainland China was still undergoing the Cultural Revolution. Hui adopted a relatively gentle approach to informing the audience about it through TV programs and Grandpa's recollections. The differences are particularly clear when compared to how she portrayed the demonstrations against corruption in the Hong Kong Police, such as the close-up of an angry lower-class woman who complained that the police always asked her for money.

When Gu Ming returned to Shanghai in December 1990, the Tiananmen Massacre had occurred just over a year and a half earlier. However, no mention was made of the events. Similar concealment also took place in the memorial section when Gu Dade had a dream about a night in his twenties in a remote village. That night, the girl he loved married his best friend. The entire village sang and danced in the square to celebrate the newlyweds. He felt sad but could only offer his blessings. It was sorrowful, but what hurt most was the cruel reality behind the joyful wedding. Based on their clothing and the circumstances, the three appeared to be university students sent to the countryside during the Down to the Countryside Movement of the Cultural Revolution. Like thousands of other students, they were forced to live in rural areas and had no opportunity to return to the cities for several years. The political elements in *My American Grandson* were further minimized.

In 1981, two Taiwanese feature films depicting the absurd events of the Cultural Revolution were broadcast. One was *If I Were for Real*, directed by Wang Toon; the other was *The Coldest Winter in Peking*, directed by Pai Ching-jui, produced by CMPC, with Koo Chen-fu as the producer and CEO of the company. Both received significant attention and praise in Taiwan, and they were expected to be banned from mainland China due to their sensitive content and anti-communist messages. Surprisingly, they were also prohibited by the British colonial government on the grounds of "avoiding affecting the relationships with nearby regions." Although they were finally allowed to be shown in Hong Kong in 1989, this did not mean the relevant content could be explicitly presented on screen without consideration in subsequent film production. Some sensitive political events still needed to be "silent" or "voice down" to ensure that the films could be broadcast.

The subtle arrangement of sensitive political incidents in the two films was likely unrelated to their box-office performance, as they were expected to be unsuccessful. Instead, it was probably intended to ensure the films were broadcast so that their messages could reach different audiences during that critical period. Until 1990, Koo had served as the CEO of CMPC for eighteen years. He was well aware of how a film's exhibition could be restricted or permitted in various regions, having experienced this many times since 1972. In 1990, he was appointed to the Committee of the National Unification Council and became chairman of the Straits Exchange Foundation, which later organized the Wang-Koo Summit in 1993. For him, it was essential to prevent reasons for the CCP to reject the upcoming official meeting, while also transmitting their message through the film. Therefore, it was understandable that the film downplayed aspects of the Cultural Revolution while explicitly emphasizing issues of corruption within the Hong Kong Police.

My American Grandson was created by a group of Taiwanese filmmakers who had worked at CMPC. Although the film has no apparent connection to CMPC and the Nationalist government, with no evidence presented, it can be regarded as a production by the Taiwanese people who sought to express their thoughts on the gradually increasing connections between Taiwan and mainland China. Their message was clear: they were lucky because they could choose Taiwan as their home. They were willing to return to mainland China to visit their relatives, but the visit would be brief. After the vacation, they would return home—Taiwan.

Conclusion: "The journey in life never ends"

Many pieces in Tang's poems are about the sorrow of leaving the homeland. Those who had to leave home for examinations or something else were called

"Youzi," which means "a son travelling outside" or "a son leaving home." Poems about "Youzi" often evoke associations with bitterness, sadness, loneliness, and pity. Only when "Youzi" returns home, transforming from "a leaving home son" to "a returning home son," does he become happy and abundant again. However, Ann Hui and Wu Nien-Jen offer a new interpretation of "Youzi" through the two films they collaborated on in the early 1990s: *Song of the Exile* and *My American Grandson*. Leaving home and homeland is no longer a sad experience in the twentieth century. "A leaving home son" is even a lucky person because he has choices and can choose where to live and where to go. The most treasured and crucial experience here is the freedom of selection.

Nowadays, it is no longer challenging to leave home and travel outside due to the invention and popularity of airplanes and high-speed trains. Moving to another place and settling there is not an adventure or a nightmare. The concept of "one becoming valueless once leaving the homeland," or *renlixiangjian*, is no longer applicable. However, when the two films were produced, the issues of "home" and "homeland" caused fierce discussions in Hong Kong and Taiwan. For Hong Kong, the controversy was sparked by the wave of emigration and the 1997 handover. For Taiwan, it was because the Nationalist government was becoming increasingly open to mainland China. When Chiang Ching-kuo lifted martial law and announced that people could visit mainland China for family reasons in 1987, some Taiwanese people worried that the island would eventually be incorporated into communist China. To appease people's anxiety, Chiang frankly expressed his thoughts at a tea party with regional representatives. He said, "I have lived in Taiwan for forty years. I am a Taiwanese, and I am also a Chinese."[4] Chiang's words reflected that he had become Taiwanese after living in Taiwan for years, but he also could not deny his Chinese identity because he was born in China. In traditional Chinese concepts, forgetting one's lineage and ancestors is treasonous. Therefore, the idea of a "new homeland" was bold, advanced, and dangerous when the films were broadcast in the early 1990s, as it meant people could also choose their nationality and identity by changing their homeland. This idea might not have been welcomed by the Beijing government, particularly as an authority that constantly emphasizes the unification of the nations.

The contemporary Chinese diaspora has persisted since the last century. Whether the trend of movement is NSN or EWE, it is foreseeable that the Chinese diasporic story will never truly come to a close. When will contemporary Chinese people find their final resting place rather than a temporary station? The line in the theme song "The journey in life never ends" provides a perfect answer to this question. If we hold on to the traditional notion of "Youzi," the lyrics depict a poignant story of exile. However, if we embrace the concept presented in Hui's two films, it would be a story about a fortunate person having numerous vacations. If one can choose their homeland at any time, it does not matter if there is no fixed destination.

12

Displacement and alienation

Reading Xiao Hong's life of exile through Ann Hui's *The Golden Era*

Chenfeng Wang

This chapter was inspired by a heated online discussion that arose after the 2021 release of Ann Hui's film *Love After Love*. Dissatisfied with this adaptation of Eileen Chang's famous novella *Aloeswood Incense: The First Brazier*, Chang's fans wondered why the talented director Hui had never made a truly successful and well-received adaptation of one of Chang's stories (before *Love After Love*, Hui also adapted *Love in a Fallen City* in 1984 and *Eighteen Springs* in 1997).[1] Although it is not the purpose of this chapter to answer that question, I would agree with some online critics that at least part of the reason can be found in Hui's particular reading—which is affected by her personal aesthetic preference—of Chang's literary works. As Hui herself revealed in an interview, "I came across Eileen Chang's works during the 1970s or 1980s, when I was still at school. Hong Kong, in her depiction, is very vivacious and of spirit, which greatly touched and impressed me. This is exactly the Hong Kong that I know. That's why I adapted two films in succession."[2] We can see that Hui is especially obsessed with literary depictions of place and place-based customs, practices, and individual experience. Unlike Hui's focus on the depiction of Hong Kong, Chang is regarded more as an introverted writer, adept at creating subtle, complex psychological portraits of her ambiguous characters' innermost thoughts and moods; immersed less in large, historical environments than in small, personal affairs.[3]

It might be Hui's aesthetic preferences, which differ from those of Chang, that have prevented her from making a film adaptation satisfying the expectations of Chang's fans. But I argue that it is also precisely these aesthetic preferences—namely, her attention to (and strength in depicting) place and place-based experience[4]—that made her so successful in directing a biopic about another equally legendary and influential female writer: Xiao Hong (1911–42). While Hui once failed to visualize Chang's "wonderful depictions of people's emotions,"[5] in her biopic of Xiao Hong, titled *The Golden Era* (2014), she was able to capture the most important themes in Xiao Hong's life and work: her struggles against displacement and her desires for love and freedom during her years of continuous exile.

In academic discussions of *The Golden Era*, previous scholars, such as Zeng Hong from the City University of Hong Kong, also noticed Hui's distinctive shaping of Xiao Hong's translocal experience. However, while Zeng employs the concept of "translocal subjectivity," coined by Conradson and McKay, her article mainly takes a feminist perspective, focusing on "the sense of female selfhood" drawn from geographical mobility and interactions with different people. Regarding Xiao Hong's migration as an embodied female experience within the socio-spatial dynamics of identity formation, she thus claims Hui's feminist auteurship, arguing that Hui's alternative mode of articulation certifies her work as feminist cinema.[6] Continuing Zeng's emphasis on the translocal mobility of Xiao Hong's life, in this chapter I move on from her particular concern over the female subjectivity of Xiao Hong—which, according to her, is mediated through Xiao Hong's female body. Instead, I argue that besides a feminist auteurship, the more significant motif in this film is Xiao Hong's displacement, and it is exactly her choice to highlight this motif that brings Hui closer to Xiao Hong, connecting and folding together her own life trajectory and artistic pursuits with those of her film subject. Moreover, I argue that along with the persistent state of Xiao Hong's physical displacement, Hui's film also uncovers another important, yet often easily overlooked, aspect of the author's displacement: her alienation from the mainstream literary culture of her time.

In the following sections, I focus on the encounter across historical time and space between Hui and Xiao Hong: two female authors with numerous similarities in their life experiences and works, as well as artistic views and expressions. After that, I explain why Hui chose to devote her film not to Xiao Hong's literary talent and creativity, as many critics would expect, but instead to her frequent migration journeys. I then elaborate on how Hui highlights the instability of Xiao Hong's life of exile from both a spatial and a temporal dimension; and how, through representing Xiao Hong's home-seeking exile ultimately as a homecoming one, Hui crosses the spatiotemporal distance and reaches a mutual resonance with Xiao Hong. On this basis, I illustrate Hui's crucial understanding and empathetic appreciation of Xiao Hong's alienation from the left-wing cultural circle that she was said to belong to, as well as her conscious choice of life path and equally intense pursuit of artistic freedom. Finally, I demonstrate that as Hui's own experience, sentiments, and consistent thematic concern in her career as a director underlie her understanding and film representation of Xiao Hong, the latter's distinctive literary style and perspective, as well as her pursuit of her literary dream, also vividly engage with Hui's filmmaking techniques. This inspires Hui to avoid a linear and unequivocal storyline, to employ an alienation effect, to challenge the expectations of the mainstream film market, and to experiment with and innovate the biopic genre. I argue that with a complex blend of character-narrator-actor narration and a multi-perspective, *Rashomon*-style structure, *The Golden Era*—as Hui's only biopic—aligns with the contemporary trend of engaging with postmodern approaches to representing authors and history, while challenging the conventions of traditional biopics, and contributing to the development of the genre.

Life and work: Parallel translocal experience

When looking at the life experience of Hui's film subject, Xiao Hong, and Hui's own, we can find many parallels. Both Xiao Hong and Hui were born in Manchuria. Xiao Hong's mother died when she was only eight years old. With her father and stepmother always treating her harshly, the only one who offered Xiao Hong familial warmth and love throughout her childhood was her grandfather. Similarly, Hui also experienced the absence of a conventional mother figure when she was young; brought up by her grandparents, she even shared Xiao Hong's memory of learning ancient Chinese poetry from her grandfather. More obvious and profound is the resemblance between Xiao Hong's life of exile and Hui's early experience of diaspora. As Xiao Hong herself once wrote in her suite of poems "Grains of Sand" (1937),

> Go!
> Still, go,
> If life is destined to flow like water,
> Why then, long for peace and rest?

After leaving her patriarchal family at the age of twenty in order to avoid a planned marriage and to pursue further education, Xiao Hong spent her whole life in exile, eventually dying at just thirty-one in a foreign land. During those ten years, she migrated from her hometown of Hulan to Harbin, and then to

Qingdao, Shanghai, Tokyo, Beijing (Beiping at that time), Wuhan, Linfen, Xi'an, Chongqing, and finally to Hong Kong. She migrated to avoid being arrested by the espionage agency in Manchuria, to pursue her dreams of a literary career, to flee from war or her own emotional suffering, to look for a peaceful home, or merely while seeking to survive. Yet, every time, the reality of her displacement would destroy the illusion of peace and stability.

For Hui, though she never experienced war personally, feelings of migration and displacement are likely not unfamiliar. Born to a Cantonese father and a Japanese mother, she moved to the Portuguese-administered Macau with her family at the age of two; her family then moved to Hong Kong when she was five. After graduating from Hong Kong University with a master's degree in comparative literature, Hui spent two years training at the London Film School. During this time, as a member of the Chinese diaspora—and an ethnic minority, especially one from a British colony—she experienced multiple instances of discrimination and marginalization. Hui then returned to Hong Kong to start her career as a director. Since the 1980s, she has frequently traveled from there to different parts of mainland China to shoot films.

As a key figure of the Hong Kong New Wave, it is also Hui who "introduced the themes of displacement and migration that have become key features of the New Hong Kong cinema."[7] While she is a prolific and versatile filmmaker, with works spanning an impressive array of styles and genres, Hui has constantly revisited the same themes of displacement and migration throughout her career, and the tropes of exile, diaspora, and border crossing have always been central to her oeuvre. As film scholar Law Kar points out, "One important motif throughout all of Hui's works is migration and unstableness, or more specifically, people's suffering of displacement and rootlessness caused by their environment. The most appealing characters in her films are also those who have been displaced and repeatedly fail to find a home to return to or a sense of belonging."[8] We can see that *The Golden Era* also explicitly deals with these central themes, tropes, and features, as the life of protagonist Xiao Hong is precisely characterized by migration and unstableness, as well as displacement and rootlessness. I argue that it is Hui's own embodied diasporic experience and her consistent central concern in filmmaking that led her to realize the significance of exile as a theme throughout Xiao Hong's life, and thus to highlight it in this biopic about her.

Since the release of *The Golden Era*, more than a few scholars and critics have criticized the film for its excessive emphasis on Xiao Hong's migration journeys (both for survival and for love), while neglecting her talent and creativity as an influential, prolific writer. As Chinese critic Zhao Yafei observes, the film seldom shows Xiao Hong burying herself in her writing, the publication of her books or essays, or discussions of literature with her friends; instead, it brings to the forefront her migration from place to place and the suffering and illness that ultimately claimed her life. "As a writer, did not Xiao Hong spend most time of her life writing?" Zhao questions. "Yet the film fails to present the development of her literary career and the multifaceted aspects of her life."[9] For her part, Hui insists that she chose carefully when it came to which materials to include in her film and which to leave out. As she claimed in an interview, "Xiao Hong is such a writer whose life and literary works form an integration."[10] Just like Hui—whose life story has profoundly influenced her filmmaking, and whose films also reflect her own subjectivity and personal life experience—Xiao Hong's literary works are autobiographical in nature. Throughout her short but brilliant career, she consciously and continually brought her own life stories and themes of exile into her literary creations. Therefore, although portraying the act of writing and the creative process has become a key characteristic and recurring thematic element of the literary biopic genre,[11] Hui does not need to emphasize this aspect in her film to highlight Xiao Hong's literary creations. In fact, a considerable portion of the film's scenes are drawn directly from Xiao Hong's own works, and Hui even brings large sections of monologues, voiceovers, and character dialogues to the screen without altering a single word.

In a forum about *The Golden Era*, Hui also revealed two things she wanted to convey in the film: "One is that we need to view Xiao Hong's life from various perspectives, and the other is that, in fact, her entire life is all her works."[12] Put differently, for Hui, to depict Xiao Hong's life is to display her works, since the latter is a perfect embodiment of the former. In the same way—as Zhang Yiwu, a literary professor from Peking University, pointed out in another forum—while Hui occasionally inserts writing scenes of Xiao Hong into the film, this is not the main theme of *The Golden Era*. Instead, "the purpose is to imply that what Xiao Hong writes and what this film unfolds (namely, Xiao Hong's life) are mutually integrated."[13] These remarks not only provide sufficient explanation for Hui's choice to focus on Xiao Hong's miserable life of exile but also imply that by sharing parallel translocal experiences and the analogous relationship between her subject's life and work, Hui is emphasizing the most significant aspects of Xiao Hong. In this sense, Hui's crucial understanding, as well as her empathetic appreciation of Xiao Hong, transcends the historical distance between these two female authors and links both their works and their life trajectories.

Home-seeking and homecoming: Spatial and temporal dynamics

In *The Golden Era*, to emphasize the centrality of translocal migration or exile in Xiao Hong's life, Hui's camera obsessively captures emblematic images of travel. Just like in Hui's semi-autographical *Song of the Exile* (1990), "bicycles, ferries, rickshaws, boats, buses, trains and harbours punctuate the film as the protagonists move from place to place."[14] According to Zeng, 80 percent of the production process involved shooting on location, which "took the film crew five months to shoot all of the significant places in which Xiao Hong had once lived."[15] Through location shoots, Hui was able to present drastically disparate landscapes and urban spaces, from the vast snowfield in the northeast to the frozen Yellow River in the northwest, and from the modern metropolis of Shanghai to the ancient capital of Xi'an. In making prominent the distinctions between these places where her subject once lived, Hui calls attention to Xiao Hong's frequent migration journeys.

Within the limited length of this three-hour film, Hui also tries to include as many occasions of departure, arrival, and resettlement as possible, in order to repeatedly intensify the unstable and drifting nature of Xiao Hong's life. Among these, one that is especially impressive is a scene featuring a series of shots and reverse shots between Xiao Hong and pieces of furniture that she has already sold to a ragpicker when leaving Harbin for Qingdao; as an old pot drops to the ground, she shows a painful feeling of reluctance as if seeing off a dear family member.[16] Similarly, we are shocked by the scene in which Xiao Hong, pregnant and fleeing from Wuhan to Chongqing to avoid the war, falls over on a dock along the Yangtze River; she then lies there for a whole night, waiting for someone to help her stand up. Migrating and seeking refuge during wartime are increasingly tough for Xiao Hong, and through her series of forced dislocations, she continues yearning for the settled, stable life of normal people, as represented by trivial daily objects such as the old pot—the thing she once used to cook food and build a family of her own.

The film highlights the motif of migration and instability not only in the spatial dimension but also through the temporal dimension. Like many of Xiao Hong's stories and novels that feature fragmented and nonlinear ways of storytelling, in *The Golden Era* Hui uses frequent flashforwards and flashbacks to interrupt the narrative, allowing it to move freely among the past, present, and future. In this way, Hui creates a sense of anachronism and an intentional displacement in temporality; more importantly, this dynamic and complex narrative, in effect, also serves to make the switching of places in the film more frequent. For example, instead of presenting the process of Xiao Hong's moving from Chongqing to Hong Kong in a chronological sequence, Hui first shows Xiao Hong writing her long essay *In Memory of Lu Xun*, with her husband Duanmu Hongliang at her side, in a house located in Chongqing. While Xiao Hong recounts her memories in a voiceover, the shot cuts to a flashback of Lu Xun's (1881–1936) house in Shanghai, where Xiao Hong's dear mentor is still alive, commenting amiably on her red clothes. But Lu Xun's voice has barely faded away when we abruptly cut back to Xiao Hong's residence in Chongqing, where her neighbor at that time, the writer Jin Yi, tells a servant who usually buys rice for them that "Xiao Hong and Duanmu no longer live here, since they have moved to Hong Kong."

The audience will expect that, as Xiao Hong is already in Hong Kong at present, the film narrative should continue to show what will happen to her in Hong Kong. However, the shot—again unexpectedly—returns to a long-past event in Chongqing, where Xiao Hong visits her old friends, the couple Hu Feng and Mei Zhi. There, she is shown a photo mailed by her former lover Xiao Jun, who has already married another woman, from Lanzhou. After Xiao Hong leaves Hu Feng and Mei Zhi's house, we finally cut to her current residence, Hong Kong; yet, in this shot, Xiao Hong's chief editor Zhou Jingwen is actually talking about a moment in the future, when she is seriously ill and a friend of her younger brother comes looking for her. In this short sequence, we see Xiao Hong in Chongqing, Shanghai, Hong Kong, again in Chongqing, and in Hong Kong. By frequently moving back and forth in various temporalities, Hui makes more manifest the fact that Xiao Hong is constantly changing places. While the audience may be confused by the insertion of Xiao Hong's memory of Lu Xun and her visit to Hu Feng and Mei Zhi, Hui effectively stresses the frequency of migration and the instability of Xiao Hong's life.

After focusing on the theme of exile and framing the narrative of migration and displacement, Hui brings the story of Xiao Hong's whole life back to her hometown, Hulan, in the northeastern region. As Xiao Hong calmly closes her eyes forever at a temporary hospital in wartime Hong Kong, the shot gradually fades into the back garden of her childhood home, where a young Xiao Hong plays joyfully with her grandfather. Moreover, following a series of comments about Xiao Hong's work *Tales of Hulan River*, Hui shows the vast northeastern snowfield again, juxtaposing this shot with one in which the sickly Xiao Hong writes this long, prose-like novel about her childhood and hometown during the final days of her short life. This final sequence of "returning home" parallels the ending of Hui's semi-autographical film *Song of the Exile*, in which all the protagonists "return to rework the roots of their origins as a result of the transformation of diasporic acculturation."[17] It also mirrors Hui's own life choices: after a series of home-finding journeys, Hui eventually confirmed her own place as a film director with cultural roots and local consciousness settled in Hong Kong, the city where she grew up.

Considering that Xiao Hong wrote *Tales of Hulan River*—which interweaves her personal memories with the history of Hulan County—when she was seriously ill and could foresee the end of her life in a foreign land, perhaps we can infer that it is also Xiao Hong's own hope to return to the place that not only nourished her literary creation but also offered her transitory warmth and happiness. After running away from home at the age of twenty and going through constant travels and migrations, Xiao Hong finally returns home in the novel she wrote in her final days. She also does so at the end of Hui's film: just like Hui's semi-autobiographical characters, and like Hui herself. With the story of home-seeking ultimately turning into one of homecoming, the lives and sentiments of Xiao Hong and Hui also intermingle. In the last scene of the film (Figure 12.1), through a medium shot, the character Xiao Hong turns around and looks back toward the camera, as if looking over decades of historical distance to reach a mutual resonance with director Hui. It is also as if the character finally becomes the embodiment of Hui herself, turning around and looking back toward her across decades of vicissitudes. In this sense—as Xiao Hong's life of exile and writing style influence Hui's ideas, concerns, and filmmaking methods, and as the integration of Hui's diaspora experience, sentiments, and aesthetic preference

Figure 12.1 The last scene of *The Golden Era*, in which the protagonist Xiao Hong looks back toward the camera. *The Golden Era* (2014), directed by Ann Hui.

also influences the film representation of Xiao Hong—*The Golden Era* becomes the shared story of these two artists, suggesting that the experience of filming a biopic can enable the filmmaker to discover an embodiment of herself in her subject.

Literary freedom: Alienation from the mainstream

Besides Xiao Hong's persistent state of displacement within her physical surroundings, Hui's film also allows us to see an equally important, yet often easily overlooked, aspect of the author's literary life—namely, her alienation from the mainstream literary culture. This isolation at first seems forced but increasingly becomes more of a conscious literary choice for Xiao Hong. As the film shows, during the Second Sino-Japanese War, Xiao Hong was invited to come to Yan'an, the center of the Chinese Communist revolution and left-wing culture at the time. But she refused, as her relationship with Xiao Jun had deteriorated, and she was afraid that she might meet Xiao Jun again in Yan'an. However, the more fundamental reason for Xiao Hong's refusal to join most of the left-wing literati is that, when faced with a choice between battleground and writing table, Xiao Hong would definitely select the latter. As Zeng elaborates in her article:

> She was faced with two alternatives: either to join mainstream culture, according to which art served political objectives, or to explore her subjectivity as a female writer. The former pathway was well trodden and safe; the latter was risky and lonely. Xiao Hong chose the latter, making her an authentic artist and even a warrior.[18]

Perhaps it is also for this reason that Hui chooses not to place much emphasis on Xiao Hong's activities as a left-wing writer, and—especially in the second half of the film—she tends to increasingly make manifest the divergence of views between Xiao Hong and other mainstream left-wing literati. For example, Hui presents Xiao Hong's view of contemporary politics in a talk she has with the couple Hu Feng and Mei Zhi. In this scene, Xiao Hong admits that she and another famous left-wing female writer, Ding Ling, are actually two very different kinds of people. When Hu Feng asks Xiao Hong why she did not go to Yan'an, she answers, "My only wish is to focus on my writing. I would like to be a person without party affiliation since I do not know much about politics. I'm a layman in this field." In terms of Xiao Hong's view of literature, Hui presents in a similar way a conversation the protagonist has with Duanmu, who later becomes her husband. Xiao Hong says, "They [the mainstream left-wing literati] don't think highly of my novels, simply because I'm not writing in their way. But I don't believe their rules of writing. There should be diverse varieties of novels, since there are different types of writers."

Looking at another aspect of the conversation, Xiao Hong's conscious distancing from the mainstream left-wing cultural center actually suggests her belief in the freedom of literary writing, which for her may have a higher value and significance beyond merely serving political objectives. In this spirit, Hui's film not only expresses her understanding of Xiao Hong's longing for an undisturbed writing environment rather than getting involved in politics but also specifically foregrounds Xiao Hong's intense desire for an unfettered state of freedom on multiple occasions. For example, the film's title is drawn from a letter Xiao Hong wrote to Xiao Jun when she was in Tokyo, which Hui gives special weight to in featuring this half-year sojourn. The content of the letter is presented through Xiao Hong's voiceover:

> Yes, I am in Japan, living in freedom and comfort, peace and leisure, without any economic pressure. This is truly my golden era, but I'm spending it in a cage.

In this letter, Xiao Hong acknowledges that this "comfortable," "peaceful," and "leisurely" time with no money worries should be her "golden era," but she still reveals a hint of disappointment, since she is spending this precious golden era "in a cage." Here, the cage metaphor ruthlessly negates the previous "freedom," implying that even though Xiao Hong lacks financial worries, she does not enjoy true freedom: the ability to live as she likes and to be respected as an independent individual. Furthermore, among Xiao Hong's long, intriguing depictions of her childhood garden in *Tales of Hulan River*, Hui specifically selects the following passage to quote at the end of the film, in order to echo Xiao Hong's burning thirst for freedom throughout her whole life:

> The flowers bloomed it was as though they were awakening from a slumber. When the birds flew it was as though they were climbing up to the heavens. When the insects chirped it was as though they were talking to each other. All these things were alive. There was no limit to their abilities, and whatever they wanted to do, they had the power to do it. They did as they willed in complete freedom … if the cucumber plant wanted to bear a cucumber it did so. If it wanted none of these, then not a single cucumber nor a single flower appeared, and no one would question its decision.[19]

The selection of this passage further demonstrates that Hui fully appreciates Xiao Hong's effort to pursue literary freedom through her voluntary self-alienation from the mainstream culture of her time. Following this quotation from *Tales of Hulan River*, some of Xiao Hong's friends in the film comment on the work. To begin, Luo Feng recalls, "In 1941, when Xiao Hong was writing *Tales of Hulan River*, most other writers in China were writing wartime reportages—short essays, dramas, or anti-war stories. *Tales of Hulan River* did not meet the expectation of people during the War." In spite of that, Hui indicates that Xiao Hong's work, which was marginalized for its divergence from the mainstream at the time, ultimately became a classic of modern Chinese literature. As Jiang Xijin says, "After decades passed by, when we were away from the war-torn, devastated China of that time, people suddenly realized that Xiao Hong's *Tales of Hulan River* was like an immortal flower, hidden in the depths of history." Along similar lines, Shu Qun adds of the author that "it was her self-determined, against-the-current choice that resulted in her lonesome death, but it was also exactly this choice that brought her everlasting fame."

Since she was aware of her displacement and alienation—within both her physical surroundings and the mainstream literary culture—Xiao Hong's feelings of loneliness are no less intense than her sense of constraint, as the "cage" metaphor suggests. Meeting writer Zhang Meilin in Chongqing, she commented, "I always walk alone. From the Northeast, to Shanghai, and then to Japan and back. Now I still walk alone in Chongqing. I seem to be destined to walk alone."[20] In the film, Hui presents a conversation between Xiao Hong and Zhang Meilin on a boat sailing on the Yangtze River. Xiao Hong complains that she does not have true friends, since all of her friends are actually Xiao Jun's friends. Leaving Xiao Jun and distancing herself from the left-wing cultural center, Xiao Hong's loneliness permeates her words and also her later works. Hui's film representation makes clear that she sympathizes with this feeling of isolation, just like she does with Xiao Hong's life of constant exile. From the comments on *Tales of Hulan River* that she selects and presents at the end of the film, however, we can nonetheless see Hui's stronger sense of admiration for Xiao Hong's pursuit of individual freedom and her willingness to challenge the contemporary trends of mainstream literary culture. In this sense, as Hui sees it, Xiao Hong's displacement and alienation certainly caused her to suffer, but it was also a historic opportunity that helped shape her into one of her era's most unique female writers.

Boundary crossings: Challenging the conventions

Situated within a cultural new wave just like Xiao Hong, Hui shares her subject's desire to distance herself from politics, once straightforwardly claiming that "grand politics is a domain that I don't understand."[21] She shares Xiao Hong's sense of loneliness, too; staying single and living with her elderly mother, Hui mocked herself by joking that her life consisted of "making films during the daytime, and returning to a home of old people at night."[22] Because of Xiao Hong's determined pursuit of and insistence on artistic freedom, in tracing her life in *The Golden Era*, Hui intentionally adopts Xiao Hong's stance of eluding or blurring political movements and ideological conflicts. Over and above that, in this biopic, much as Hui projects her own sentiments and concerns onto her distinctive film representation, the latter is also profoundly inspired by Xiao Hong's idiosyncratic style of literary writing.

I have discussed in the second section how Xiao Hong's fragmented and nonlinear ways of storytelling are reflected in the uncustomary temporal movement in Hui's film. Here, I look further into how Xiao Hong's prose-like literary style, which characterizes most of her works, engages with the process of Hui's filmmaking. For example, Xiao Hong's writing is substantially detail-driven and prioritizes the texture of life. To display this tendency, Hui's camera also pays special attention to details of objects. Her film representation of Lu Xun echoes Xiao Hong's literary depiction of him, rendering Lu Xun less like a great serious writer, thinker, and revolutionist than a considerate, fatherly, and humorous mentor. By the same token, compared with narrating a long story, Xiao Hong is more adept at lyrical descriptions. Usually lacking a compelling, central plotline, her novels instead mostly consist of a series of small events—either interconnected or not—being strung together. This feature is made prominent in *The Golden Era* as well, representing Xiao Hong's life not as a monolithic, coherent story but as a lyrical, prose-like montage of fragmented, small events. Interestingly, Hui even remarked that, by experimenting with her cinematic language, she actually opened up "the golden era" of her career as well—although she is already in her old age—with the film becoming her "best picture" from her point of view.[23]

To better represent Xiao Hong's sense of displacement and alienation, Hui intentionally invokes an "alienation effect"[24] in *The Golden Era* to prevent the audience from simply identifying with characters onscreen. One technique that she uses frequently is to let characters in the film look directly into the camera while recounting interactions with Xiao Hong (to the audience). This, at first glance, contributes to the reality effect of the film, evoking documentary footage or an oral account of history. By providing multiple, varied perspectives on Xiao Hong, it seems that Hui is trying to paint a whole picture of her. But upon further scrutiny, we may find that the fundamental difference between interviews in this film and those in a documentary—namely, the interviewees here are just the actors representing the fictional characters in the film—actually serves to remind us continually of the fictionality and artificiality of the cinematic narrative.

One example of this can be found in a scene earlier in the film. After Xiao Hong and Xiao Jun leave Harbin for Qingdao, their friends, the couple Luo Feng and Bai Lang, are drinking with some other left-wing revolutionaries in a dim room (where an underground party usually holds meetings) in Harbin. But suddenly, we cut to a medium shot in which Luo Feng and Bai Lang directly face the camera (Figure 12.2). With Luo Feng still physically beside her, Bai tells the camera that after Xiao Hong and Xiao Jun left, Luo Feng was "arrested and sent to jail," and "two years later," another comrade of theirs was killed by the Japanese. "I sought assistance everywhere," says Bai Lang, "with the hope that I could rescue Luo Feng." As she speaks, Luo Feng looks at her gently; after finishing speaking, she also turns back to look at her husband, eye to eye with him, before the couple smile at each other.

This scene creates a particularly eerie atmosphere. If, as Bai Lang says, Luo Feng has been arrested and is still in jail waiting for her to rescue him, then he should not be sitting with her, together in front of the camera. But if this interview is happening much later, when Luo Feng has been released and the couple can recall their past memories for the camera, it is also contradictory. To begin, the

Figure 12.2 Bai Lang and Luo Feng talk directly to the camera. *The Golden Era* (2014), directed by Ann Hui.

couple still look young, identical to both their earlier and later appearances in the film; further, in the previous shot, they are still in the same room with their other comrades in Harbin. Most paradoxically, as the couple face the camera, we can clearly see that Luo Feng is injured, with many wounds on his face; this implies that he may have just been tortured in the prison. Contrary to what we can infer from Bai Lang's words, everything shown visually onscreen suggests that the characters are situated in the present moment: the year 1934, when Xiao Hong and Xiao Jun leave Harbin, and when Luo Feng is imprisoned. But how can Bai Lang, while she is speaking to the camera, acquire the superpower of foreknowing the future?

This apparent contradiction is easily resolved once we recognize that Luo Feng and Bai Lang are not real individuals but fictional characters played by actors. The scene employs a narrative technique inspired by documentaries, oral histories, and plays, where characters break the fourth wall, speaking directly to the camera to recount events. They reveal the artificial structure of the film and distract the audience from indulging in the representational illusion of reality. The audience are thus alienated from the characters' world yet still provided with the possibility to transcend the fixed boundaries of time and space. Hui often uses this approach throughout the biopic: characters, still within the narrative, shift seamlessly into narrators of Xiao Hong's life. Unlike typical narrators, however, these figures remain as the characters they perform: wearing the same costumes and in the same historical contexts yet narrating future events as if they themselves transcend time and space. As Hui explains in an interview:

> Time and space become entirely blurred. In a single person, they are both the character in the drama and the narrator, with knowledge of both the past and the future. They wear the costume, and the audience sees them as though they are living in 1938, yet they suddenly shift to another era to recount events from a different time.[25]

By merging the roles of character, narrator, and actor—and blending documentary, oral history, and theatrical techniques—the film dissolves the boundaries between past and present, living and acting, as well as reality and fiction. It alienates the audience from the diegesis, prompting them to question the authenticity of what they are seeing and to reflect on the constructed nature of biographical writing and representation. This tension between historical accuracy and dramatic storytelling, alongside questions of truth, reality, and representation, is a long-standing issue in biographical films and academic debates.[26] As *The Golden Era* moves fluidly among the characteristics of a plot-driven feature, the objectivity of oral history, and the theatricality of the alienation effect, we can see that Hui's experimental approach not only stems from her deep understanding of Xiao Hong's literary works; it also signals her skepticism toward the idea of authenticity, which, for her, is not the primary aim of this biopic. Rather than leading the audience to become emotionally immersed in the story, the film continually employs intrusive narrators to remind viewers that this is a life of Xiao Hong pieced together from the memories of various participants, whose reliability remains open to doubt.

Hui further deconstructs the concept of truth in the film through a *Rashomon*-style narrative, presenting multiple, often conflicting, versions of events, such as the breakup between Xiao Hong and Xiao Jun. In an interview about *The Golden Era*, Hui elaborated on her view of "truth":

> To be frank, many so-called realist films aren't truly realistic; they selectively assemble elements deemed "true" and present them as reality. But this is a selective reality, not an absolute one. In this film, we make it clear from the beginning that it's not about the truth—A says one thing, B says another, and she herself says something different. Some versions don't align, and the truth is ultimately elusive. That's the real truth. Memories can be flawed, and even impressions from the time can be deeply subjective. Rather than claiming authenticity, we present various versions and encourage the audience to reflect on what is true or false. We offer one version while signalling that many others exist, leaving it to the viewer to decide.[27]

Therefore, Hui suggested, "In effect, we are opening up a new space, which is the space of the audience."[28] In this space, the audience may critically engage with the various versions from different sources to form their own understanding of Xiao Hong's life and work.

The film's multi-perspective, *Rashomon*-style structure—combined with its nonlinear storytelling; use of the alienation effect; challenge to the idea of a singular, authoritative biographical narrative; and exploration of Xiao Hong's resistance to societal norms—mirrors postmodern concepts surrounding the fragmentation and constructed nature of history, memory, and identity. Hui also deliberately employs anachronisms to connect the past with the present (e.g., the ending sequence on *Tales of Hulan River*, as discussed earlier), highlighting the fluidity of historical interpretation. Through these experimental techniques in her portrayal of Xiao Hong, Hui fundamentally disrupts the conventions of the traditional biopic. As scholar Hila Shachar observes, contemporary literary biopics are increasingly adopting postmodern approaches.[29] Hui's use of these methods to depict Xiao Hong's life aligns with this trend, while also making an innovative contribution to the evolution of the biopic genre. Rather than adhering to strict historical accuracy, her focus shifts toward encouraging deeper critical engagement with the fragmented and subjective representation of personal and historical memory.

By employing these postmodern approaches, Hui's experimental attempts not only challenge the conventional rules and templates of biopic filmmaking;[30] they also echo Xiao Hong's literary choices, which often defied the constraints of the mainstream. Hui was fully aware that making a film about a writer's life—one with complex historical materials, a nonlinear narrative, documentary elements, and the alienation effect—might not appeal to a wide audience and could potentially confuse them.[31] Yet she pressed ahead, driven by a long-held desire to tell Xiao Hong's story, regardless of mainstream market expectations. To bring her vision to life, Hui and screenwriter Li Qiang spent three years tirelessly seeking funding across both Hong Kong and mainland China. Hui recalled, "When we were looking for the money, people were saying that they didn't want to go to school or attend literary class."[32] After three years of effort, they finally secured financing from Stellar Mega Films, allowing her to produce the biopic—an art film—on the scale of a commercial blockbuster.

With a budget of 60 million yuan, *The Golden Era* took three years to develop, culminating in more than 600 scenes shot on location across multiple cities, covering vast regions of China. The film's star-studded cast, featuring Tang Wei, Wang Zhiwen, and Hao Lei, added to its grandeur. Despite the massive investment of resources, however, Hui intentionally avoided including such crowd-pleasing elements as elaborate special effects or large-scale war scenes that are typical of commercial films, simply because they did not align with her vision.[33] As Hui explained:

> We didn't make this film with the audience's reception in mind; we just wanted to make it well. If I were younger, I wouldn't have made this film. When a film doesn't succeed, you may not get another chance to make one. At my age, if I don't take risks now and create something more innovative than before, I won't have the opportunity again … So I poured everything I had into this film—my time, and whatever energy I still have.[34]

In this sense, Hui can be seen as carrying forward Xiao Hong's commitment to individual artistic freedom, particularly through the making of this biopic. Despite the intense competition and commercial pressures in the film industry, she has remained resolute in upholding her creative independence. Therefore, the lives of these two women—Xiao Hong and Hui—intersect and fold into one another within the film. Xiao Hong's journey of translocal migration is extended through Hui's film into a series of transborder interactions: across the mediums of literature and film; across the genres of biography, documentary, and fiction; and between Xiao Hong's and Hui's respective "golden eras," as well as our own time and space.

Conclusion: Two golden eras in dialogue

The Golden Era is not simply a biopic of Xiao Hong's life but a cinematic articulation of shared concerns between two female auteurs—Ann Hui and Xiao Hong—whose experiences, sentiments, and aesthetic visions resonate across different historical and media contexts. Rather than reproducing a conventional literary biopic that traces the development of a writer's creative process, Hui deliberately downplays the act of writing, foregrounding instead the spatial and temporal instability of Xiao Hong's exilic life and her conscious detachment from the left-wing literary mainstream. Through such a focus, Hui highlights displacement—both physical and cultural—not as mere suffering but as a generative space through which Xiao Hong's literary sensibilities and pursuit of freedom are expressed.

It is Hui's own diasporic background and long-standing engagement with themes of migration, exile, and marginality that allow her to establish an empathetic and dialogic connection with Xiao Hong. Their parallel translocal experiences and shared insistence on artistic freedom form the foundation upon which Hui constructs a filmic portrait that is at once historically evocative and formally experimental. As discussed in this chapter, the film's nonlinear narrative, character-narrator-actor layering, and *Rashomon*-style storytelling are not merely stylistic devices; they mirror Xiao Hong's prose-like, fragmented literary voice and emphasize the instability of memory, history, and representation. At the same time, Hui's use of the alienation effect calls attention to the constructedness of the biopic form, resisting emotional immersion and inviting the audience to critically engage with the process of remembering and representing a historical figure.

Through its postmodern narrative strategies and formal innovations, *The Golden Era* challenges the conventions of the biopic genre while paying homage to Xiao Hong's own transgressive and idiosyncratic literary style. It offers a space where literature and film, biography and fiction, history and present intersect—where Hui not only reconstructs the life of Xiao Hong but also reflects on her own cinematic journey. In this sense, the biopic becomes a site of artistic encounter and mutual illumination: Xiao Hong's writing informs Hui's filmmaking, just as Hui's aesthetic vision revives and reinterprets Xiao Hong's life for contemporary audiences. Ultimately, through their boundary-crossing lives—geographically, culturally, and aesthetically—Hui and Xiao Hong offer a powerful meditation on artistic integrity and the reclamation of marginalized voices. *The Golden Era* is not only about Xiao Hong; it is also about Hui, and about the possibilities of authorship itself—where two golden eras interweave and illuminate one another across generations.

Notes

Introduction

1 Audrey Yue, *Ann Hui's Song of the Exile* (Hong Kong: Hong Kong University Press, 2010).
2 Gina Marchetti, "Feminism, Postfeminism, and Hong Kong Women Filmmakers," in *A Companion to Hong Kong Cinema*, ed. Esther M. K. Cheung, Gina Marchetti, and Esther C. M. Yau (Chichester: Wiley-Blackwell, 2015), 240.
3 Mirana M. Szeto, "Ann Hui at the Margin of Mainstream Hong Kong Cinema," in *Hong Kong Screenscapes: From the New Wave to the Digital Frontier*, ed. Esther M. K. Cheung, Gina Marchetti, and See-Kam Tan (Hong Kong: Hong Kong University Press, 2011), 51.
4 Elaine Yee-lin Ho, "Women on the Edges of Hong Kong Modernity: The Films of Ann Hui," in *At Full Speed: Hong Kong Cinema in a Borderless World*, ed. Esther C. M. Yau (Minneapolis: University of Minnesota Press, 2001), 198.
5 Ibid.
6 Patricia Brett Erens, "The Film Work of Ann Hui," in *The Cinema of Hong Kong: History, Arts, Identity*, ed. Poshek Fu and David Desser (Cambridge: Cambridge University Press, 2000), 189.
7 Zeng Hong, "Translocal Female Subjectivity: Notes on Ann Hui's *The Golden Era*," *Asian Cinema* 30, no. 1 (2019): 100.
8 Yue, *Ann Hui's Song of the Exile*, 10.
9 Ibid., 16.
10 Dudley Andrew, "The Unauthorized Auteur Today," in *Film and Theory: An Anthology*, ed. Robert Stam and Toby Miller (Malden, MA: Blackwell Publishers, 2000), 29.
11 David Gerstner and Janet Staiger, "Introduction," in *Authorship and Film*, ed. David A. Gertner and Janet Staiger (New York: Routledge, 2003), xi.
12 Lim Song Hwee, "Positioning Auteur Theory in Chinese Cinemas Studies: Intratextuality, Intertextuality and Paratextuality in the Films of Tsai Ming-liang," *Journal of Chinese Cinemas* 1, no. 3 (2007): 224.
13 Ibid., 225.
14 Ibid.
15 Ibid., 231.

16 Gilles Deleuze and Félix Guattari, *A Thousand Plateaus: Capitalism and Schizophrenia*, trans. Brian Massumi (Minneapolis: University of Minnesota Press, 1987), 5.
17 Ibid.
18 Ibid., 6.
19 Ibid.
20 Ibid., 7.
21 Ibid., 9.
22 Ibid., 10.
23 Ibid., 160.

Chapter 1

1 Ain Ling Wong, "Qingniao yinqin wei tankan—Xu Anhua de dianying zhi lü" [Ann Hui's Journey of Filmmaking], in *Ann Hui: Forty Years of Filmmaking*, ed. Cecilia Wong and Yuet Wah Ng (Hong Kong: Joint Publishing, 2018), 32.
2 Pak-tong Cheuk has discussed Hui's adept use of voiceovers to convey characters' inner thoughts and to structure a multi-perspective narrative in her earlier works, with little critical attention paid to the highly gendered nature of the acoustic aesthetics in Hui's cinema, though. See Pak-tong Cheuk, *Hong Kong New Wave Cinema* (Shanghai: Fudan University Press, 2011), 64–5.
3 Chen Pingyuan, *The Development of Chinese Martial Arts Fiction*, trans. Victor Petersen (Cambridge: Cambridge University Press, 2016), 113.
4 Ibid.
5 Ibid., 96.
6 Chen Pingyuan, *The Establishment of Modern Chinese Scholarship* (Beijing: Beijing daxue chubanshe, 1998), 277.
7 Tang Chenguang, "Lu Xun and the Spirit of Knight Errants" *Lu Xun Studies Monthly* 18, no. 1 (1997): 27.
8 Jun Lei, *Mastery of Words and Swords: Negotiating Intellectual Masculinities in Modern China, 1890s–1930s*. Transnational Asian Masculinities (Hong Kong: Hong Kong University Press, 2022), 20.
9 In her dissertation "Beyond Domesticity: Youth and Chinese Feminism, 1900–1949" (Washington University in St. Louis, 2023), Dou Miao studies the formation of "young women" (*nü shaonian*) as a new sociopolitical category at the turn of the twentieth century and how this new historical agent struggles with the masculinization of the national salvation cause.
10 Lei, *Mastery of Words and Swords*, 64.

11 Man-Fung Yip, *Martial Arts Cinema and Hong Kong Modernity: Aesthetics, Representation, Circulation* (Hong Kong: Hong Kong University Press, 2017), 26.

12 Ibid., 2.

13 Yvonne Tasker, "Fists of Fury: Discourses of Race and Masculinity in the Martial Arts Cinema," in *Race and the Subject of Masculinities*, ed. Harry Stecopoulos and Michael Uebel (Durham, NC: Duke University Press, 1997), 316. Also see David Desser, "Fists of Legend: Constructing Chinese Identity in the Hong Kong Cinema," in *Chinese Language Film: Historiography, Poetics, Politics*, ed. Sheldon H. Lu and Emilie Yue-yu Yeh (Honolulu: University of Hawai'i Press, 2005), 280–97.

14 Gina Marchetti, "Ann Hui: A Well-Connected Auteur Director," trans. Heng Siu, in *Ann Hui: Forty Years of Filmmaking*, ed. Cecilia Wong and Yuet Wah Ng (Hong Kong: Joint Publishing, 2018), 147, 149.

15 Enoch Tam Yee-lok, "Nuxing, shenfen yu zhengzhi—Xu Anhua dianying yanjiu huigu" [Woman, Identity and Politics: A Retrospective Review of Scholarship on Ann Hui's Cinema], in *Ann Hui: Forty Years of Filmmaking*, ed. Cecilia Wong and Yuet Wah Ng (Hong Kong: Joint Publishing, 2018), 119.

16 Ka-Fai Yau, "Looking Back at Ann Hui's Cinema of the Political," *Modern Chinese Literature and Culture* 19, no. 2 (Fall 2007): 132.

17 Poshek Fu discussed Ng's and Mok's social activism and their founding of the influential Trotskyist magazine *The 70's Biweekly* (*70 niandai shuangzhoukan*) in the epilogue of his new book *Hong Kong Media and Asia's Cold War* (New York: Oxford University Press, 2023).

18 In 2003, Evans Chan made a documentary about Mok's theatrical performance. For an in-depth analysis of this documentary, see Gina Marchetti, "Brecht in Hong Kong: Evans Chan's *The Life and Times of Wu Zhong Xian*," in *Postcolonialism, Diaspora, and Alternative Histories: The Cinema of Evans Chan*, ed. Tony Williams (Hong Kong: Hong Kong University Press, 2015), 81–99.

19 Cheung Ka-wai, *Liuqi baodong: Xianggang zhanhou lishi de fenshuiling* [*The 1967 Riots: Post-War Hong Kong's Watershed*] (Hong Kong: Hong Kong University Press, 2012), 4.

20 Hannah Arendt, *The Human Condition* (Garden City, NY: Doubleday Anchor Books, 1959), 45.

21 Chan Sui-jeung, *East River Column: Hong Kong Guerrillas in the Second World War and After* (Hong Kong: Hong Kong University Press, 2009), 9, 10, 17.

22 Lu Yan, *Crossed Paths: Labor Activism and Colonial Governance in Hong Kong, 1938–1958* (Ithaca, NY: Cornell University Press, 2019), 79.

23 Chan Sui-jeung, *East River Column*, 49.

24 Mao Dun, *Tuo xian za ji* [*Escaping from the Fallen City*] (Beijing: Zhongguo shehui kexue chubanshe, 1980).

25 Mao Dun, *Huanghun* [*Dusk*], in *Mao Dun*, ed. Zhuang Zhongqing (Taipei: Bookman, 1992), 162–3. English translation by Jessica Siu-Yin Yeung with minor modifications of mine. Jessica Siu-Yin Yeung, "Ann Hui's Allegorical Cinema," in *Cultural Conflict in Hong Kong: Angles on a Coherent Imaginary*, ed. Jason Poleey, Vinton Poon, and Lian-Hee Wee (Singapore: Palgrave Macmillan, 2018), 99.

26 "A Conversation of Ann Hui with Chen Danjing on *Golden Times*" *The Second Nanjing Film Forum*, May 5, 2014, https://www.bilibili.com/video/BV1Cv411M7n6/?spm_id_from=333.337.search-card.all.click (accessed December 25, 2023).

27 Chan's *East River Column* provides a detailed account of the historical rescue operation.

28 Luce Irigaray, *Sexes and Genealogies*, trans. Gillian C. Gill. (New York: Columbia University Press, 1993), 2. Original italics.

29 Ibid., 188.

30 Michel Chion, *The Voice in Cinema*, ed. and trans. Claudia Gorbman (New York: Columbia University Press, 1999), 17.

31 Lu, *Crossed Paths*, 100.

32 Ibid., 101.

33 In discussing Ding Ling's *Mother*, Tani E. Barlow uses the term "political sisterhood" to depict "a reinvented, politically defined, female identity" embedded in a historicized time-space rather than a universal female identity defined on the anatomical basis of "sexual differentiation and sexual categories." Tani E. Barlow, "Gender and Identity in Ding Ling's Mother," *Modern Chinese Literature* 2, no. 2 (1986): 124.

34 Yip, *Martial Arts Cinema and Hong Kong Modernity*, 75. Akbar Abbas, *Hong Kong: Culture and Politics of Disappearance* (Minneapolis: University of Minnesota Press, 1997), 8–9.

35 Ibid., 84.

36 Arendt, *The Human Condition*, 177.

Chapter 2

1 Carole Hang-fung Hoyan, "Under the Silver Lantern, a Discussion of the Film Adaptation of Eileen Chang's Hong Kong Legend: On Ann Hui's *Love in a Fallen City*," in *Reading Eileen Chang Again*, ed. Liu Shaoming (Shandong: Shandong Pictorial Publishing House, 2004), 103.

2 Luo Jianming, "From Fiction to Film," *City Entertainment Magazine*, November 1984, 34.

3 Li Chaotao, "Ann Hui Talks about *Love in a Fallen City*," *City Entertainment Magazine*, October 1984, 20.

4 Andre Bazin, *What Is Cinema?* (Berkeley: University of California Press, 2005), 142.

5 Hoyan, "Under the Silver Lantern," 115.
6 Lu Weilan and Ann Hui, "Adaptation and Nostalgia: A Discussion Starting from *Love in a Fallen City*," in *The Origin of Images*, ed. Lu Weilan (Beijing: Beijing Publishing House, 2019), 92.
7 Elieen Chang, *Love in a Fallen City* (New York: New York Review of Books, 2006), 121–2.
8 Eileen Chang, "A Few Words to the Reader," in *Eileen Chang Collected Works: Volume Four*, ed. Jin Hongda and Yu Qing (Anhui: Anhui Literature and Art Publishing House, 1992), 308.
9 Wu Hung, *Feminine Space in Chinese Painting* (Beijing: SDX Joint Publishing, 2019), 360.
10 Jonathan Han, *Sensuous Surfaces: The Decorative Object in Early Modern China* (London: Reaktion Books, 2010), 304.
11 Leo Ou-fan Lee, *Shanghai Modern: The Flowering of a New Urban Culture in China* (Cambridge, MA: Harvard University Press, 1999), 295.
12 James Cahill, *Pictures for Use and Pleasure: Vernacular Painting in High Qing China* (Berkeley: University of California Press, 2010), 180.
13 Rey Chow, *Woman and Chinese Modernity: The Politics of Reading between West and East* (Minneapolis: University of Minnesota Press, 1990), 115–20.
14 Chang, *Love in a Fallen City*, 111.
15 Lu Weili, "A Casual Discussion on Ann Hui," in *Xu Anhua shuo Xu Anhua* [*Ann Hui on Ann Hui*], ed. Kwong Po Wei (Shanghai: Fudan University Press, 2010), 351.
16 David Hockney, "A Day on the Grand Canal," last modified June 22, 2019, https://www.bilibili.com/video/BV144411u7cK?spm_id_from=333.337.search-card.all.click&vd_source=385241bd9a8e41b4d90bd9ca7744f8ae (accessed August 29, 2022).
17 Hoyan, "Under the Silver Lantern," 107.
18 Ibid.
19 Eileen Chang, "Writing of One's Own," in *Written on the Water*, ed. Andrew F. Jones and Nicole Huang (New York: Columbia University Press, 2004), 15.
20 Eileen Chang, "Demons and Fairies," *XXth Century*, December 1943, 421.
21 Eileen Chang, "A Chronicle of Changing Clothes," in *Written on the Water*, ed. Andrew F. Jones and Nicole Huang (New York: Columbia University Press, 2004), 65.
22 Chang, *Love in a Fallen City*, 121.
23 Hoyan, "Under the Silver Lantern," 111.
24 Wu Hung, *A Story of Ruins: Presence and Absence in Chinese Art and Visual Culture* (London: Reaktion Books, 2012), 23.
25 Ibid., 34.
26 Shi Qi, "Hong Kong: The Sense of Achievement and Crisis in 1980s Cinema," in *A Comprehensive View of New Asian Cinema*, ed. Peggy Qiao (Taiwan: Yuan-Liou Publishing, 1991), 33.
27 Ibid., 1.
28 Hoyan, "Under the Silver Lantern," 120.

Chapter 3

1 Using the pen name Xun Yu, Fu Lei delivered an essay "Lun Zhang Ailing de xiaoshuo" ("On Eileen Chang's fiction") in 1944. In this very first important review of Chang's works, he appreciates "The Golden Cangue" but mercilessly criticizes "Qingcheng zhi Lian" ("Love in a Fallen City") and "Lianhuan Tao" ("The Chain Lock"). See the full article in Fu Lei, *Fulei Tanyilu* [Fu Lei's Talk about Art] (Beijing: Joint Publishing, 2016), 48–66.

2 According to Wei-chen Su's argument, "The origins of Shanghai cinematography affected Chang's entire subsequent writing career, and yet her own best output in this field was confined to the single year of 1947." See We-chen Su, "Shanghai 1947 Zhang Ailing dianying yuanqi jiantan Buliaoqing Taitaiwansui juben de rensheng canzhao" [Shanghai. 1947. Eileen Chang's Origins of Cinematography—"Unending Love," "Long Live My Wife," Chang's Slice of Life on Stage], *Chungwai Literary* 37, no. 2 (2008): 140. The reason was that the screening of *Long Live the Missus!* on December 14, 1947, originally attracted positive reception but soon resulted in severe criticism against its anti-feminist and regressive consciousness, because the female protagonist finally forgives her unfaithful husband for a comedic effect. This led to Eileen Chang's disappointment with the Chinese market and, adding the drastic change of political situation, her departure to Hong Kong in 1952.

3 C. T. Hsia spent forty-three pages introducing Eileen Chang, a figure rarely related to serious literature before in the history of fiction he compiled. He proclaimed that "Eileen Chang is not only the best and most important writer in Chinese today; her short stories alone invite valid comparisons with, and in some respects claim superiority over, the work of serious modern women writers in English: Katherine Mansfield, Katherine Anne Porter, Eudora Welty, and Carson McCullers." Apparently, he recognized her achievement as excellent not only in Chinese literary history but also in world literary history. The word count and quotation (p. 389) are from C. T. Hsia, *A History of Modern Chinese Fiction* (New Haven, CT: Yale University Press), 1961.

4 See David Der-wei Wang, "Zhang Ailing Zaisheng Yuan-Chongfu, Huixuan yu Yansheng de Xushi Xue" [The Rebirth of Eileen Chang: The Narratology of "Repetition," "Involution," and "Derivation"], *Literary Century*, no. 9 (2000): 53.

5 See details in Harold Bloom, *The Anxiety of Influence: A Theory of Poetry* (Second Edition) (Oxford: Oxford University Press, 1997).

6 See Linda Hutcheon, *A Theory of Adaptation* (New York: Routledge, 2006), 16.

7 See Mei Xuefeng, "'Wentun Zhi Mei' Xu Anhua" [The Beauty of Warm Slowness: Ann Hui], *zhihu*, Posted on September 25, 2021, https://zhuanlan.zhihu.com/p/413813196 (accessed February 6, 2023).

8 See Robert Stam, *Literature through Film: Realism, Magic, and the Art of Adaptation* (Oxford: Blackwell, 2005), 4.

9 Julie Sanders, *Adaptation and Appropriation* (London: Routledge, 2006).
10 Deborah Cartmell and Imelda Whelehan, *Screen Adaptation: Impure Cinema* (New York: Palgrave Macmillan, 2010).
11 See Audrey Yue, *Ann Hui's Song of the Exile* (Hong Kong: Hong Kong University Press, 2010), 85.
12 See Bidisha Banerjee, "What Lies Within: Misrecognition and the Uncanny in Hong Kong's Cityscape," *Inter-Asia Cultural Studies*, no. 4 (2013): 519–37.
13 See the monographic chapter "Brecht in Hong Kong Cinema: Ann Hui's *Ordinary Heroes* and Evans Chan's *The Life and Times of Wu Zhongxian*," in Gina Marchetti, *Citing China: Politics, Postmodernism, and World Cinema* (Honolulu: University of Hawaii Press, 2018).
14 See Hector Rodriguez, "The Emergence of the Hong Kong New Wave," in *At Full Speed: Hong Kong Cinema in a Borderless World*, ed. Esther C. M. Yau (Minneapolis: University of Minnesota Press, 2001), 64. Moreover, a more sophisticated background of the New Wave is offered by his quotation of Law Kar's outline:

> [T]he institutional system of the film culture field in Hong Kong ... includes film pages in cultural magazines (*Chinese Student Weekly*); columns in daily newspapers (*Ming Pao Daily*, *New Life Evening News*, and the *Hong Kong Standard*, among others); screen journals and magazines (*Close Up Film Review* and *Film Biweekly*); film forums and student organizations biased toward auteur and avant-garde cinema (the College Cine Club, the Film Guard Association, and the Phoenix Cine Club); humanities programs in tertiary education institutions (the Chinese University of Hong Kong, the Hong Kong Baptist College, and, more recently, the Hong Kong Academy for the Performing Arts); film and drama courses in independent organizations (the Film Culture Centre and the Hong Kong Arts Centre); events like the Independent Short Film Competition and the Hong Kong International Film Festival; and, especially, the annual publications and retrospectives of the Hong Kong International Film Festival. (Ibid., 54)

15 See Kwong Po Wei, *Xu Anhua shuo Xu Anhua* [*Ann Hui on Ann Hui*] (Shanghai: Fudan University Press, 2010), 33.
16 Ibid. My translation.
17 See Chu Yiu-Wai, *Main Melody Films: Hong Kong Directors in Mainland China* (Edinburgh: Edinburgh University Press, 2022), 59–60.
18 See details in Ka-Fai Yau, "Looking Back at Ann Hui's Cinema of the Political," *Modern Chinese Literature and Culture* 19, no. 2 (2007): 133–45.
19 See Eileen Chang, "Daodi shi Shanghai Ren" [Shanghainese, after All], in *Zhang Ailing Diancang Quanji (Sanwen Juan Yi) 1939–1947 Nian Zuopin* [*The Classical Collection of Eileen Chang (Volume 1 of Prose) Works of 1939–1947*] (Taipei: Crown Publishing, 2001), 8–9.

20 See Eileen Chang, "Love in a Fallen City," in *Zhang Ailing Diancang Quanji (Duanpian Xiaoshuo Juan Yi) 1943 Nian Zuopin* [*The Classical Collection of Eileen Chang (Volume 1 of Short Stories) Works of 1943*] (Taipei: Crown Publishing, 2001), 100.

21 See *Love in a Fallen City*, directed by Ann Hui (1984; Hong Kong: Shaw Brothers, 2002), DVD.

22 See Chang, "Love in a Fallen City," 92.

23 The British soldiers appear two times only. See ibid., 95, 97.

24 See Ian Scott, *Political Change and the Crisis of Legitimacy in Hong Kong* (Honolulu: University of Hawaii Press, 1989), 168.

25 The quotation of the last sentence and this is from Homi K. Bhabha, *The Location of Culture* (London: Routledge, 1994), 9.

26 See Kim-Soon Sen, "Wenben yingxiang yu nvxing fuhao de zaifuzhi, lun Zhangailing de xiaoshuo dianying" [Text, Image and Reproduction of the Feminine Signs: On Ai-Ling Chang's Fiction and Its Cinematic Adaptation], *Chungwai Literary* 33, no. 1 (2004): 54.

27 Concerning *Rouge* and *Happy Together*, see Esther M. K. Cheung, "On Spectral Mutations: The Ghostly City in *The Secret*, *Rouge* and *Little Cheung*," in *Hong Kong Culture: Word and Image*, ed. Kam Louie (Hong Kong: Hong Kong University Press, 2010), 169–92 and Jeremy Tambling, *Wong Kar-Wai's Happy Together* (Hong Kong: Hong Kong University Press, 2003) for details, respectively.

28 See Terry Siu-han Yip, "Fate and Destiny: Yuan as Ming in 'Matrimony Inn' and Eileen Chang's *Half a Lifelong Romance* and 'Love in a Fallen City,'" in *Fate and Prognostication in the Chinese Literary Imagination*, ed. Michael Lackner et al. (Leiden: Brill, 2020), 26.

29 See Kwong Po Wei, *Xu Anhua shuo Xu Anhua* [*Ann Hui on Ann Hui*] (Shanghai: Fudan University Press, 2010), 75–90.

30 See Kwong, *Ann Hui on Ann Hui*, 92.

31 Ibid., 78.

32 See Li Xiaoxian, "Bansheng Yuan de Shijie guan: Xu Anhua Fangtan lu" [The Worldview of *Half a Lifelong Romance*: An Interview with Ann Hui], *The Reading Town*, no. 6 (1998): 9.

33 See Grace Mak, "*Bansheng Yuan* yu *Se, Jie* zhong Dongqing zhi Guanjian: Cong Shijian yu Kongjian Kan Qing'ai zhi xushu" [The Key of Feeling Touched in *Half a Lifelong Romance* and "Lust, Caution": The Narrative of Love from the Perspective of Time and Space], in *Zhang Ailing: Chuanqi. Xingbie. Xipu* [*Eileen Chang: Legend. Sexuality. Genealogy*], ed. Xingqian Lin (Taipei: Linking Publishing, 2012), 246.

34 See He Guimei, "Xu Anhua dianying de xianggang xushi yu zhongguo rentong" [The Hong Kong Narrative and Chinese Identity in Xu Anhua's Movies], *Southern Cultural Forum*, no. 4 (2019): 50–1.

35 See Tom Ue, "Reading Eileen Chang and Filming Hong Kong: An Interview with Ann Hui on *Love After Love*," *Film International* 4 (2021): 101.
36 Ibid., 101–2.
37 It is important to note that these two supporting actors both have a complicated identity. Isabella Leong was born in Macau with Portuguese (one-quarter), British (one-quarter), and Chinese (one-half) heritage. Paul Chun Pui was born in pre-PRC Beijing with the Han (one-half), Manchu (one-quarter), and Mongolian (one-quarter) heritage.
38 For the drama *The Golden Cangue*, Ann Hui and Wang Anyi also played the roles of director and scriptwriter respectively.
39 Quoted from Ue, "Reading Eileen Chang and Filming Hong Kong," 102. Concerning the notion of Wang Anyi as the successor of Eileen Chang, it originated from David Der-wer Wang's article "Haipai Zuojia You Jian Chuanren: Lun Wang Anyi" [*Haipai* Writers Have Another Successor: On Wang Anyi"] which can be found in David Der-wei Wang, *Jishi yu Xugou* [*Fact and Fiction*] (Taipei: Rye Field Publishing, 1996).
40 Quoted from The Culturalist, "(Zhuanfang) Sandu Gaibian Zushi Nainai zhuzuo Xu Anhua" [(Exclusive Interview) Adapting the Grandma's Fiction for the Third Time, Ann Hui Said, "I Do Not Feel Sorry for Eileen Chang."], November 25, 2021, https://www.youtube.com/watch?v=HZv3djXJoM0 (accessed August 15, 2023).
41 See Michael Curtin, "Conditions of Capital: Global Media in Local Contexts," in *Internationalizing "International Communication"*, ed. Chin-Chuan Lee (Ann Arbor: University of Michigan Press, 2015), 109–33.
42 See Chu, *Main Melody Films*, 56.
43 As they declare, "Being the neoliberal exception of China, Hong Kong is positioned to contribute for China by its market economy, as well as the relatively well-established socio-economic institution." Quoted from Gary Tang and Raymond Hau-yin Yuen, "Hong Kong as the 'Neoliberal Exception' of China: Transformation of Hong Kong Citizenship before and after the Transfer of Sovereignty," *Journal of Chinese Political Science* 21, no. 4 (2016): 469.

Chapter 4

1 See Hector Rodriguez, "The Emergence of the Hong Kong New Wave," in *At Full Speed: Hong Kong Cinema in a Borderless World*, ed. Esther C. M. Yau (Minneapolis: University of Minnesota Press, 2001), 53–70.
2 Chengyu, "Tan changshou jiemu" [On Long-Running TV Shows], *Film Biweekly*, no. 2 (January 1979): 49.

3 For more details on the ratings wars, see Derek Lam, "The Left-Wing Legacy in '70s Hong Kong Television: Chameleon (1978) and Lee Sil-hong's Rediffusion (RTV) Tetralogy," *Journal of Chinese Cinemas* 16, no. 2 (2022): 184–200.

4 Q Zai, "Jiao ni di dianshi" [A Lesson on Watching TV], *Cultural New Wave*, no. 4 (January 1979): 12.

5 Shu Kei, "The Television Work of Ann Hui," in *The 17th Hong Kong International Film Festival Changes in Hong Kong Society through Cinema*, ed. Li Cheuk-to (Hong Kong: Urban Council, 1988), 43.

6 Li Cheuk-to, "Survival Zui zhongyao" [The Primacy of Survival], *Film Biweekly*, no. 7 (October 1982): 22.

7 Victor Fan, *Extraterritoriality: Locating Hong Kong Cinema and Media* (Edinburgh: Edinburgh University Press, 2019), 71.

8 Jim Collins, "Television and Postmodernism," in *Film and Theory: An Anthology*, ed. Robert Stam and Toby Miller (Malden, MA: Blackwell Publishers, 2000), 758.

9 Law Kar, "Hou liuqi shidai xianggang dianying de chaoliu bianhua ji shehui ganying yu dianshi zuo hu guan bijiao" [Changes and Social Resonance of Hong Kong Cinema: Comparing to Television], in *When the Wind Was Blowing Wild: Hong Kong Cinema of the 1970s*, ed. May Ng, Oral History Series (7) (Hong Kong: Hong Kong Film Archive, 2018), 43.

10 This information is referenced from the study by the Mass Culture Action Team. For more, see Mass Culture Action Team, "Xianggang qingnian ruhe kandai dianshi de gongyong—wenjuan diaocha baogao shu" [How Hong Kong Youth View the Role of Television: A Questionnaire Report], *Close-up*, no. 56 (April 1978): 4–9.

11 Tian Yan, "Yiyu feizaoju" [Speaking Gibberish on Soap Opera], *Close-up*, no. 51 (February 1978): 13.

12 Li Mo, "Bu ping ming keyi ming dao shenme chengdu" [How Much Can Crying against Injustice Do for Justice?] *Close-up*, no. 9 (April 1976): 9.

13 In *Seven Women*, Patrick Tam paid homage to Jean-Luc Godard by employing many of Godard's signature techniques, including jump cuts, extreme close-ups, and voiceovers, to depict women's lives in Hong Kong.

14 Chen Shouzhen, "Xu Anhua bu zijue de shouhuo" [Ann Hui's Accidental Achievements], *Close-up*, no. 47 (December 1977): 35.

15 Ann Hui, "Ann Hui: Headstrong and Unruly," in *The Quiet Revolution: 40 Years of ICAC Drama Series*, ed. Li Cheuk-to (Hong Kong: Hong Kong International Film Festival, 2014), 27.

16 Cheuk Pak-tong, "Fangwen guoji xingjing de muhuo gongzuozhe" [Interview: The Making of *Interpol*], *Close-up*, no. 56 (April 1978): 13. In another article in the same issue, a local critic Changming argues that the episode "Assassination" from *Interpol* demonizes the Japanese Red Army while portraying the police in a positive light. For more, see Changming, "Shi tan guoji xingjing di er ji cisha de shehui yishi

xingtai" [Let's Talk about the Social Ideology of the Second Episode "Assassination" from *Interpol*], *Close-up*, no. 56 (April 1978): 10–11.

17 Kristof Van den Troost, *Hong Kong Crime Films: Criminal Realism, Censorship and Society, 1947–1986* (Edinburgh: Edinburgh University Press, 2024).

18 Tian Yan, "Speaking Gibberish on Soap Opera," 13.

19 Lusiren, "Huanle jinxiao yu gudian shehui zhuyi de zhongjie" [EYT and the End of Classical Socialism], *Cultural New Wave*, no. 5 (February 1979): 8.

20 Q Zai, "Yishi xingtai dazhan huan le jin xiao zai Guangzhou" [Ideological Warfare EYT in Guangzhou], *Cultural New Wave*, no. 5 (February 1979): 4.

21 Cui Yang, "Tan tan dianshi de ji ge wenti" [A Few Questions about Television], *Close-up*, no. 49 (January 1978): 10.

22 Mass Culture Action Team, "How Hong Kong Youth View the Role of Television," 4.

23 Lin Zhiren, "Dianshi xinwen 1, 2, 3 …" [TV News 1, 2, 3 …], *Close-up*, no. 56 (April 1978): 17. Peter Fitzroy Godber (b. 1922) was a chief superintendent of the Royal Hong Kong Police Force. He was involved in a major bribery scandal just before his retirement in 1973. He fled to the United Kingdom and was later apprehended in 1974 by British police and extradited back to Hong Kong. Godber's arrest became a defining symbol of Hong Kong's turn toward modernity and directly led to the establishment of the Independent Commission Against Corruption (ICAC), which contributed to Hong Kong's later stability and prosperity. This case has been referenced and depicted in many Hong Kong TV shows and films.

24 Ibid.

25 "Jia shi duan ping" [Short Review on CTV], *Cultural New Wave*, no. 1 (October 1978): 29.

26 Quan-er, "Kan qing dianshi, bu yao rang ziji hunmi" [Watch Television Carefully: Avoid Falling into Coma], *Cultural New Wave*, no. 3 (December 1978): 39; Quan-er, "Dianshi minjian xiju weishenme shou huanying?" [Why Are TV Folk Comedy Shows So Popular?], *Cultural New Wave*, no. 9 (June 1979): 15.

27 Q Zai, "A Lesson on Watching TV," 4.

28 Q Zai, "Ideological Warfare EYT in Guangzhou," 4.

29 Zhou Zhaoxiang, "Dianshi jiaoyu zhuding shi zi wo maodun de youxi" [Television Education Is a Self-Contradictory Endeavor], *Cultural New Wave*, no. 8 (April 1979): 16.

30 Shen Ming, "Lun puji wenhua yishi xingtai zai shengchan ji piban" [On Popular Culture Ideological Reproduction and Criticism], *Cultural New Wave*, no. 6 (March 1979): 13.

31 Chengyu, "Fan shangpin hua de nuli" [The Effort of Resisting Commodification], *Film Biweekly*, no. 3 (February 1979): 46.

32 Cheng Siji, "Xin wenhua ren zhongqi baogao shu" [New Culture Men Midterm Reports], *Cultural New Wave*, no. 7 (April 1979): 8.

33 This documentary aroused newspapers' and the government's concerns. For more, see Tom Cunliffe and Raymond Tsang, "The Making and Screening of Independent Films in the Absence of Radical Revolution: An Interview with Augustine Mok Chiu-yu on Social Movements, Technology, and Censorship," *Journal of Chinese Cinemas* 16, no. 2 (2022): 215–30.

34 Kwong Po Wei, *Xu Anhua shuo Xu Anhua* [*Ann Hui on Ann Hui*] (Shanghai: Fudan University Press, 2010), 16.

35 Ibid., 20.

36 Ibid., 26.

37 Q Zai, "A Lesson on Watching TV," 13.

38 Victor Fan appears to make several factual errors in his interpretation of the character Ning in the television drama *The Boy from Vietnam*. For example, Ning's actual journey involved escaping from Vietnam to the Khmer Republic, then to Macau, before entering Hong Kong as an undocumented immigrant. However, Fan claims that Ning was a Chinese Communist soldier in Vietnam who was persecuted by the new government in Vietnam, fled to Macau via mainland China, and made two swimming attempts to reach Hong Kong. Furthermore, Fan misquotes Ning's monologue during a long take. The correct line is not "That's why I can't go back. I can't go back to it" but rather "I don't have a choice. Your cousin doesn't have a choice either. People like us who migrate are all like that." For a full account of Fan's reading, see Fan, "Breaking the Wave."

39 Ackbar Abbas, *Hong Kong: Culture and the Politics of Disappearance* (Minneapolis: University of Minnesota Press, 1997), 25.

40 Shu Kei, "Feng jie Sense and Sensibility" [*The Secret*'s Sense and Sensibility], *Film Biweekly*, no. 95 (September 1982): 33.

41 Gary Bettinson, "Pictorial Storytelling and Staging in Ann Hui's *The Way We Are*," *Jump Cut: A Review of Contemporary Media*, no. 62 (2024), last modified July 30, 2025, https://www.ejumpcut.org/archive/JC62.2024/GaryBettinson/index.html (accessed July 30, 2025).

42 Zhang Zhuoxiang, "Shizi shanxia meiyou zhengzhi yingxiang li" [*Under the Lion Rock* Series Does Not Have Any Political Influence], *Film Biweekly*, no. 1 (January 1979): 51.

43 Li, "The Primacy of Survival," 22.

44 Marshall McLuhan, *Understanding Media: The Extensions of Man* (Cambridge, MA: MIT Press, 1994), 5.

45 John Guillory, "Genesis of the Media Concept," *Critical Inquiry* 36, no. 2 (Winter 2010): 342.

46 Patricia R. Zimmermann and Helen De Michiel, *Open Space New Media Documentary* (New York: Routledge, 2018), vii.

47 Yau Ching, "Xianggang xin langchao ying mei yu xi de xin chengyuan" [Hong Kong New Wave Anglophone New Members], in *Wet Dreams in Paradise*, ed. Yau Ching (Taipei: Lianjing Press, 2024), 416.

48 Ibid., 426.
49 Xiao Liu, *Information Fantasies: Precarious Mediation in Postsocialist China* (Minneapolis: University of Minnesota Press, 2019), 135.

Chapter 5

1 Emilie Yueh-yu Yeh, "Pitfalls of Cross-Cultural Analysis: Chinese *Wenyi* Film and Melodrama," *Asian Journal of Communication* 19, no. 4 (2009): 445. See also Paul Willemen, "Hong Kong Film Festival, 1986: Focus on Melodrama," *Framework* 32 (1986): 193–6; Wimal Dissanayake, *Melodrama and Asian Cinema* (New York: Cambridge University Press, 1993); and Nick Browne, "Society and Subjectivity: On the Political Economy of Chinese Melodrama," in *New Chinese Cinemas: Forms, Identities, Politics*, ed. Nick Browne, Paul G. Pickowicz, Vivian Sobchack, and Esther Yau (Cambridge: Cambridge University Press, 1994), 40–56.
2 Li Cheuk-to, "Introduction," in *Cantonese Melodrama 1950–1969* (revised edition), ed. Li Cheuk-to (Hong Kong: Urban Council, 1997), 8; Zhang Zhen, "Transnational Melodrama, *Wenyi*, and the Orphan Imagination," in *Melodrama Unbound: Across History, Media, and National Cultures*, ed. Christine Gledhill and Linda Williams (New York: Columbia University Press, 2018), 83–97.
3 Mirana M. Szeto, "Ann Hui at the Margin of Mainstream Hong Kong Cinema," in *Hong Kong Screenscapes: From the New Wave to the Digital Frontier*, ed. Esther M. K. Cheung, Gina Marchetti, and See-Kam Tan (Hong Kong: Hong Kong University Press, 2011), 63.
4 David Bordwell, "Modest Doesn't Mean Unambitious," *Observations on Film Art: David Bordwell's Website on Cinema*, March 20, 2008, http://www.davidbordwell.net/blog/category/directors-ann-hui/page/3/ (accessed June 15, 2023).
5 Bono Lee, "The Possibility of China for Hong Kong Directors: The Transformation of Peter Chan's Identity," in *Peter Chan: My Way*, ed. Li Cheuk-to (Hong Kong: Joint Publishing, 2012), 187–95.
6 Bordwell, "Modest Doesn't Mean Unambitious."
7 Elaine Yee-lin Ho, "Women on the Edges of Hong Kong Modernity: The Films of Ann Hui," in *At Full Speed: Hong Kong Cinema in a Borderless World*, ed. Esther C. M. Yau (Minneapolis: University of Minnesota Press, 2001), 190.
8 Zhang Yingjin, "Commentary: The Dynamics of Off-Centeredness in Hong Kong Cinema," in *A Companion to Hong Kong Cinema*, ed. Esther M. K. Cheung, Gina Marchetti, and Esther C. M. Yau (Chichester: Wiley-Blackwell, 2015), 496.
9 Thomas Elsaesser, "Tales of Sound and Fury: Observations on the Family Melodrama," in *Imitations of Life: A Reader on Film and Television Melodrama*, ed. Marcia Landy (Detroit, MI: Wayne State University Press, 1991), 84.

10 By "melodramatic sentimentality," I refer simply to the genre's proclivity toward naked emotional appeals and affective overload. My generic usage differs from the specific sense of sentimentalism theorized by Rey Chow. A key facet of the sentimental, for Chow, is "an inclination or a disposition toward making compromises and toward making-do with even—and especially—that which is oppressive and bearable" (18). Prima facie, *The Way We Are* dovetails with some of the schematic traits Chow identifies within sentimental Chinese cinema: a narrative concern with filiality, domesticity, food, poverty, childhood and old age, physical labor, togetherness and separation, and familial harmony. *The Way We Are* arguably accords, too, with Chow's notion of the sentimental as "idealizing" filiality (22). But crucially, Hui's film lacks the subversive, politically charged undercurrent that characterizes Chow's affective mode—that is, it does not stress the ways "quotidian living itself can take on the weight of imprisonment or assault" (21). See Rey Chow, *Sentimental Fabulations: Contemporary Chinese Films* (New York: Columbia University Press, 2007).

11 Carl Plantinga, "The Scene of Empathy and the Human Face on Film," in *Passionate Views: Film, Cognition, and Emotion*, ed. Carl Plantinga and Greg M. Smith (Baltimore, MD: Johns Hopkins University Press, 1999), 239–55.

12 Maggie Lee, "The Way We Are (Review)," *The Hollywood Reporter*, April 2, 2008, https://www.hollywoodreporter.com/movies/movie-reviews/way-we-are-125594/ (accessed June 15, 2023).

13 Carl Plantinga, *Moving Viewers: American Film and the Spectator's Experience* (Los Angeles: University of California Press, 2009), 96–7; Brian Boyd, *On the Origin of Stories: Evolution, Cognition, and Fiction* (Cambridge, MA: The Belknap Press of Harvard University Press, 2009), 196.

14 Esther Cheung, "The Urban Maze: Crisis and Topography in Hong Kong Cinema," in *A Companion to Hong Kong Cinema*, ed. Esther M. K. Cheung, Gina Marchetti, and Esther C. M. Yau (Chichester: Wiley-Blackwell, 2015), 64.

15 Such predictions, of course, will prove wide of the mark, though Hui would validate those same expectations in *Night and Fog* (2009), whose factual tale of domestic abuse also unfolds in the Tin Shui Wai neighborhood.

16 Szeto, "Ann Hui at the Margin of Mainstream Hong Kong Cinema," 65.

17 I probe this aspect of the film at greater length in Gary Bettinson, "Pictorial Storytelling and Staging in Ann Hui's *The Way We Are*," *Jump Cut: A Review of Contemporary Media*, no. 62 (2024), https://www.ejumpcut.org/archive/JC62.2024/GaryBettinson/index.html (accessed July 30, 2025).

18 Seymour Chatman, *Story and Discourse: Narrative Structure in Fiction Film* (Ithaca, NY: Cornell University Press, 1978), 48.

19 Todd Berliner, *Hollywood Aesthetic: Pleasure in American Cinema* (Oxford: Oxford University Press, 2017).

20 Unmotivated camera movement stands as one of Hui's authorial traits, though the tactic is not always put to deceptive purpose. See for instance *The Secret* (1979), *The Postmodern Life of My Aunt* (2006), and *Night and Fog.*

21 Law Kar, "Archetypes and Variations: Observations on Six Cantonese Films," in *Cantonese Melodrama 1950–1969* (revised edition), ed. Li Cheuk-to (Hong Kong: Urban Council, 1997), 16.

22 Bettinson, "Pictorial Storytelling and Staging in Ann Hui's *The Way We Are*."

23 I call for a poetics approach to performance in the study of Hong Kong cinema in Gary Bettinson, "Commentary: Hong Kong Stars and Stardom," in *A Companion to Hong Kong Cinema*, ed. Esther M. K. Cheung, Gina Marchetti, and Esther C. M. Yau (Chichester: Wiley-Blackwell, 2015), 379–87.

24 See, for example, Gina Marchetti, "Feminism, Postfeminism, and Hong Kong Women Filmmakers," in *A Companion to Hong Kong Cinema*, ed. Esther M. K. Cheung, Gina Marchetti, and Esther C. M. Yau (Chichester: Wiley-Blackwell, 2015), 254.

25 Jing Jing Chang, "Ann Hui's Tin Shui Wai Diptych: The Flashback and Feminist Perception in Post-Handover Hong Kong," *Quarterly Review of Film and Video* 33, no. 8 (2016), 732.

Chapter 6

1 Gina Marchetti, "Gender Politics and Neoliberalism in China: Ann Hui's *The Postmodern Life of My Aunt*," *Visual Anthropology* 22, no. 2–3 (2009): 123–40.

2 Scholars studying this group of "Authentic Hong Kong-flavored" films argue that, although labeled as "pure" or "authentic," the fluidity and circulation of capitals and filmmaking talents in the transnational age "lead to inherent dissonance in the 'purity' of these works." Therefore, the term "Authentic Hong Kong-flavored" does not so much define the "Hong Kong-ness" of these films as it highlights the "multifarious and contesting features, market dynamics, and politics" within this phenomenon.

3 The film Ann Hui made between *A Simple Life* (2012) and *Our Time Will Come* is *The Golden Era* (2014), a biopic of Xiao Hong, China's talented Republican writer with a fate full of twists and turns. The film concludes with Xiao Hong's death in Hong Kong in 1942, coinciding with the start of the narrative timeline of *Our Time Will Time*. Therefore, *The Golden Era* is also viewed by some critics as Hui's continuation in telling the "Hong Kong story" though its focus is not solely about Hong Kong. Please read Jessica Siu-yin Yeung, "Ann Hui's Allegorical Cinema," in *Cultural Conflict in Hong Kong: Angles on a Coherent Imaginary*, ed. Jason S. Polley, Vinton Poon, and Lian-Hee Wee (Singapore: Palgrave Macmillan, 2018), 97 and

Zeng Hong, "Translocal Female Subjectivity: Notes on Ann Hui's *The Golden Era*," *Asian Cinema* 30, no. 1 (2019): 91–107.

4 As the key concept of Yiu-Wai Chu's seminal study of Hong Kong directors' critical engagement in making "main melody" films, "main(land) melody" is specifically used in Chu's monograph to denote "main melody" films made by Hong Kong directors, as opposed to the general film genre referred to as "main melody." See Yiu-Wai Chu, *Main Melody Films: Hong Kong Directors in Mainland China* (Edinburgh: Edinburgh University Press, 2022). This chapter adopts the same usage for clarity and specificity.

5 Zhang Huiyu, "Cong zhu xuanlu yingpian dao zhuliu dapian de shanbian" [From Main Melody Films to Mainstream Blockbusters], *Film Art*, no. 2 (2011): 16–23.

6 Ackbar Abbas, *Hong Kong: Culture and the Politics of Disappearance* (Minneapolis: University of Minnesota Press, 1997), 6.

7 Kwai-Cheung Lo and Pang Laikwan, "Hong Kong: Ten Years after Colonialism," *Postcolonial Studies* 10, no. 4 (2007): 349–56; Yiu-Wai Chu, *Lost in Transition: Hong Kong Culture in the Age of China* (Albany, NY: SUNY Press, 2013).

8 Mirana M. Szeto and Yun-chung Chen, "Mainlandisation or Sinophone Translocality? Challenges for Hong Kong SAR New Wave Cinema," *Journal of Chinese Cinemas* 6, no. 2 (2012): 115–34.

9 Mirana M. Szeto, "Ann Hui at the Margin of Mainstream Hong Kong Cinema," in *Hong Kong Screenscapes: From the New Wave to the Digital Frontier*, ed. Esther Cheung, Gina Marchetti, and See-Kam Tan (Hong Kong: Hong Kong University Press, 2011), 62.

10 The predecessor of the East River Column was the Guangdong People's Anti-Japanese Guerrilla (established in 1937). On December 2, 1943, the Guangdong People's Anti-Japanese Guerrilla was reorganized into the "Guangdong People's Anti-Japanese Guerrilla Team Dongjiang Column," abbreviated as the "Dongjiang Column."

11 Jessica Siu-Yin Yeung, "Xu Anhua de xianggang yuyan: Mingyue jishi you" [Our Time Will Come: Ann Hui's Hong Kong Allegory], *Cinezen*, August 8, 2017, http://www.cinezen.hk/?p=7783.

12 Chan Ping-ting, "Hong Kong-Style Variation beneath a Red Co-production: Ann Hui Did Not Forget Hong Kong," *The News Lens*, July 16, 2017, https://www.thenewslens.com/feature/hk-movies-newwave/73590.

13 The exploration of the "main melody" genre falls outside the focus and purpose of this chapter. This paragraph intends to only provide a brief overview of the genre's development to contextualize the production of *Our Time Will Come*. Further substantial examination of this genre can begin with monographs including Zhang Ying's *Xin shiqi yilai zhu xuanlu dianying yanjiu* [*A Study of Main Melody Films since the New Period*] (Shanghai: Sanlian, 2017); Wendy Su's *China's Encounter with Global Hollywood: Cultural Policy and the Film Industry 1994–2013* (Lexington:

University Press of Kentucky, 2016); Darrell William Davis's article "Marketization, Hollywood, Global China," *Modern Chinese Literature and Culture* 26, no. 1 (2014): 191–241; and Hongmei Yu's "Visual Spectacular, Revolutionary Epic, and Personal Voice: The Narration of History in Chinese Main Melody Films," *Modern Chinese Literature and Culture* 25, no. 2, Special Issue on The Dis/Appearance of the Political Crowd in Contemporary China (Fall 2013): 166–218.

14 Chu, *Main Melody Films*, 5.

15 Huiyu, "From Main Melody Films to Mainstream Blockbusters"; Wendy Su, "It Is Not Just Propaganda: Main Melody Film between the State and Market," *American Review of China Studies* 17, no. 1 (2016): 21–38.

16 Chu, *Main Melody Films*, 14–15.

17 Han Li, "Re-packaging a Cultural Revolution Model Opera: Politics and Commerce in Tsui Hark's *The Taking of Tiger Mountain*," *Theoretical Studies in Literature and Art* 37, no. 5 (2017): 180–93; Zhuoyi Wang, "Transforming the Liminal Hero: Border-Crossing Interconnections in *The Taking of Tiger Mountain* and Its Textual Pedigree," *Chinese Literature Today* 7, no. 1 (2018): 118–28.

18 Chris Berry, "Wolf Warrior 2: Imagining the Chinese Century," *Film Quarterly* 72, no. 2 (2018): 38–44.

19 Su, "It Is Not Just Propaganda," 22.

20 Emilie Yueh-yu Yeh and Darrell William Davis, "Re-nationalizing China's Film Industry: Case Study on the China Film Group and Film Marketization," *Journal of Chinese Cinemas* 2 (2008): 37.

21 Ka-Fai Yau, "Looking Back at Ann Hui's Cinema of the Political," *Modern Chinese Literature and Culture* 19, no. 2 (2007): 145.

22 Li Mei-Ting, "Our Time Will Come: Hong Kong Is the Main Melody," *Cinezen*, July 11, 2017, https://www.cinezen.hk/?p=7713.

23 Chu, *Main Melody Films*, 64.

24 "The Great Victory Rescue" is a term used in historical books about the East River Column to describe this particular rescue operation, often cited as one of the Column's most notable achievements. Interestingly, while English-language histories of the East River Column published in Hong Kong frequently mention the rescue of American pilots as a significant feat, this event is often omitted in many Chinese-language histories and is not covered in *Our Time Will Come*. For English-language accounts of the East River Column's resistance activities during World War II, notable works include Jenny Chan and Derek Pua's *Three Years Eight Months: The Forgotten Struggle of Hong Kong's WWII* (San Francisco, CA: Pacific Atrocities Education, 2019) and Sui-jeung Chan's *East River Column: Hong Kong Guerrillas in the Second World War and After* (Hong Kong: Hong Kong University Press, 2009).

25 Zhu Yanhong, "Bodies in Crisis: Sensuality and the Cinematic Reconfiguration of the Spy Genre in Contemporary Chinese Cinema," *East Asian Journal of Popular Culture* 1, no. 3 (2015): 359–76.

26 Yang Min, "Spy, Abjection, and Post-Socialist Identity: Chinese Neo-Spy Films since 2009," *Studies in the Humanities* 44, no. 1–2 (2019): 92.

27 Yanhong, "Bodies in Crisis," 368.

28 Judith [Jack] Halberstam, *Female Masculinity* (Durham, NC: Duke University Press, 1998).

29 Ibid., 2.

30 Elaine Yee Lin Ho, "Women on the Edges of Hong Kong Modernity: The Films of Ann Hui," in *At Full Speed: Hong Kong Cinema in a Borderless World*, ed. Esther Yau (Minneapolis: University of Minnesota Press, 2000), 177–206.

31 Ibid., 169.

32 Zheng Binghong, "Our Time Will Come: Smuggling Hong Kong Consciousness in Main Melody Films," July 13, 2017, https://opinion.udn.com/opinion/story/10012/2580561.

33 Ibid. Zheng Binghong argues that Mrs. Fong's last words in *Our Time Will Come* are critical for the understanding of this film. In some accounts of Mrs. Fang's life, she is portrayed as a mother who not only steadfastly supported her daughter's involvement in the resistance but is said to have proudly declared "I am Chinese" in her final moments. Therefore, Zheng states that having her reiterate "I can't read" instead of "I am Chinese" in *Our Time Will Come* reveals Ann Hui's interpretation of the common people's motives in the resistance—not necessarily for a grand cause or to become martyrs but more for everyday survival. Similarly, Denise Y. Ho, in "Hong Kong, China: The Border as Palimpsest," *Made in China Journal* 5, no. 3 (2020): 96, also points out that "While later CCP history claimed the work of the East River Column was peasant resistance against imperialism, recent oral histories reveal a patriotism that was far simpler." She cites the example of New Territories villager Zhang Guanfu, who joined the Sha Tau Kok squadron in 1943, and Zhang remarked that joining the guerrillas was a matter of sheer survival. This interpretation challenges grander narratives of patriotic heroism, highlighting the more immediate and practical concerns that drove individuals to participate in the resistance.

34 In terms of the "aesthetics of the quotidian," see Sebastian Veg, "Anatomy of the Ordinary: New Perspectives in Hong Kong Independent Cinema," *Journal of Chinese Cinemas* 8, no. 1 (2014): 84. In terms of the poetics of insignificance, see Szeto, "Ann Hui at the Margin of Mainstream Hong Kong Cinema," 53.

35 Jing Jing Chang, "Ann Hui's Tin Shui Wai Diptych: The Flashback and Feminist Perception in Post-Handover Hong Kong," *Quarterly Review of Film and Video* 33, no. 8 (2016): 722–42.

36 Mei Xuefeng, "Our Time Will Come Has Presented the Most Ordinary Anti-Japanese Heroes," *Wei Wenku*, July 4, 2017, http://weiwenku.net/d/101226524#new.

37 Szeto, "Ann Hui at the Margin of Mainstream Hong Kong Cinema," 54.

38 Chan, "Hong Kong-Style Variation beneath a Red Co-production."

39 Yeung, "Ann Hui's Allegorical Cinema," 98.

40 Szeto, "Ann Hui at the Margin of Mainstream Hong Kong Cinema," 63.

41 Choosing to be "on the edge" is a characteristic that many scholars observe in Ann Hui's work. For example, Elaine Ho observes that "right from the start of her cinematic career in 1979, her films attempted recurrently to distance, dislocate, and disrupt the corporate push toward economic success, Western lifestyles, and technology that characterizes Hong Kong's modernity." See Ho, "Women on the Edges of Hong Kong Modernity."

42 Most of the guerrilla members were local people, many of whom from the local Hakka ethnic community. This enabled them to blend seamlessly into their surroundings, making them less likely to arouse suspicion from the Japanese occupiers.

43 The titles mentioned here were all compiled by the Party History Materials Collection Committee and the Party History Research Committee under the Guangdong Provincial Party Committee.

44 The mission of the East River Column Historical Society can be found in the news report "Establishment of the East River Column Historical Society" on the East River Column official website, http://east-river-column.cn/shouye_zxxw_detail.asp?id=151 (accessed December 13, 2023), and the article "Opening of the East River Column Historical Society's Office," *China News*, November 23, 2022, https://www.chinanews.com.cn/dwq/2022/11-23/9900850.shtml (accessed November 30, 2022).

45 The explanation of the goal of the collection can be seen in this news report "80th Anniversary of the Formation of the Hong Kong and Kowloon Brigade: *The Gazetteer of the Hong Kong–Kowloon Independent Brigade* and *The History of the Hong Kong–Kowloon Independent Brigade* Released in Hong Kong," *South China News*, https://news.southcn.com/node_b710679493/09863327d8.shtml (accessed December 13, 2023). The leading editor of the *Gazetteer* is Professor Liu Shuyong, a senior scholar of Hong Kong history at Lingnan University who was recruited by the university after retiring from Academia Sinica in 2005. With the strong support of the central and SAR government, the United Hong Kong Foundation established the Hong Kong Local History Center in 2019 and launched the comprehensive work of compiling state-endorsed Hong Kong local histories. In 2020, Liu Shuyong and his team published the first volume of the *Hong Kong Gazetteer*.

46 Denise Y. Ho and Jie Li, "From Landlord Manor to Red Memorabilia: Reincarnations of a Chinese Museum Town," *Modern China* 42, no. 1 (2015): 1.

47 The Sha Tau Kok Heritage trail is part of Lingnan University's Hong Kong and South China Historical Research Programme. More information about this program can be found at: https://www.ln.edu.hk/hkschrp/kt/public/sha-tau-kok.

48 In another interview of researchers and witnesses of the East River Column, the 85-year-old Yang Yongguang recollects his memory of the resistance activities when he was a child (Xinhua News Agency, "The Hong Kong Rescue by the East River Column: A True Bond of Loyalty and Courage," May 3, 2021, http://www.locpg.gov.cn/jsdt/2021-05/03/c_1211140069.htm). This news article reveals that real historical witnesses are available to interview should Ann Hui choose to do so, which makes her decision of staging a household name celebrity as a "real" historical witness even more intriguing.

49 Chang, "Ann Hui's Tin Shui Wai Diptych," 4.

50 Yeung, "Ann Hui's Allegorical Cinema," 100.

51 Chu, *Main Melody Films*, 73; Karen Fang, "War Films: Ann Hui's *Our Time Will Come* and Christopher Nolan's *Dunkirk*," in "Writing Hong Kong" issue, *Cha: An Asian Literary Journal*, December 2017, https://chajournal.blog/2017/11/09/our-time-will-come-and-dunkirk/.

Chapter 7

1 According to the "Hong Kong Annual Report," cinema attendance figures declined from 5.7 million in 1990 to 4.5 million in 1993, followed by successive drops to 3.5 million in 1994, 2.8 million in 1995, and 2.7 million in 1996. The decline continued, reaching 2 million by 1999. Annual film production figures depict a similar trend, with more than 230 films produced in 1993, reducing to around 150 films in 1995, and approximately 100 films in 1996. The decline persisted in 1997, with the number dropping to just over 80 films. See Baoxian Zhong, *Xiang gang bai nian guang ying* [*Centennial History of the Hong Kong Film and Television Industry*] (Beijing: Peking University Press, 2007), 372–6.

2 Ann Hui, *Nv ren, Si shi* [*Summer Snow*], in *Xu Anhua shuo Xu Anhua* [*Ann Hui on Ann Hui*], ed. Kwong Po Wei (Shanghai: Fudan University Press, 2010), 69.

3 "The Best 100 Chinese Motion Pictures," Hong Kong Film Awards Association, 2019, https://web.archive.org/web/20191022211054/http://www.hkfaa.com/news/100films.html (accessed October 22, 2023).

4 Sawako Ariyoshi, *The Twilight Years*, trans. Mildred Tahara (Tokyo: Kodansha International, 1987).

5 Yuan Zhao, *Xiang Gang Lao Yin: Xu Anhua de guang ying li cheng* [*Hong Kong Imprint: Ann Hui's Cinematic Journey*] (Beijing: Chinese Film Publication, 2013), 115.

6 Yingchi Chu, *Hong Kong Cinema: Coloniser, Motherland and Self* (London: Routledge Curzon, 2003), 77.
7 Rey Chow, "Between Colonizers: Hong Kong's Postcolonial Self-Writing in the 1990s," *Diaspora: A Journal of Transnational Studies* 2, no. 2 (1992): 151–70.
8 Mirana M. Szeto, "Identity Politics and Its Discontents: Contesting Cultural Imaginaries in Contemporary Hong Kong," *Interventions* 8, no. 2 (2006): 253–75.
9 Chow, "Between Colonizers," 152.
10 Ibid., 153, italics in original.
11 Ibid., 153.
12 Victor Fan, *Extraterritoriality: Locating Hong Kong Cinema and Media* (Edinburgh: Edinburgh University Press, 2019), 11.
13 Ibid., 1.
14 Fei Tang and Raees Calafato, "Transnational Multilingual Families in China: Multilingualism as Commodity, Conflict, and In-Betweenness," *SAGE Open* 12, no. 1 (2022): 4.
15 Chow, "Between Colonizers," 155.
16 Ibid., 153, italics in original.
17 Ibid., 153.
18 "Xuesheng xu renqing Xianggang zhuquan yizhi shuyu Zhongguo" ["Students Should Be Aware That Hong Kong Has Remained under China's Sovereign Authority Throughout"], news.gov.hk, August 2, 2022, https://sc.news.gov.hk/TuniS/www.news.gov.hk/chi/2022/08/20220802/20220802_162403_729.html?type=ticker (accessed July 31, 2025); Fan, *Extraterritoriality*, 1.
19 Szeto, "Identity Politics and Its Discontents," 256.
20 Chow, "Between Colonizers," 158.
21 Ibid.
22 Szeto, "Identity Politics and Its Discontents," 257.
23 Ibid.
24 Chow, "Between Colonizers," 54.
25 Ibid., 156.
26 Chu, *Hong Kong Cinema*, 91.
27 Fan, *Extraterritoriality*, 13.
28 Ibid., 12.
29 Szeto, "Identity Politics and Its Discontents," 261.
30 Ibid.
31 Chow, "Between Colonizers," 157.
32 Ibid., 153.
33 Szeto, "Identity Politics and Its Discontents," 261.
34 Sina Entertainment, "Zhuming yinyue ren Luo Dayou zuoke Xin Lang liaotianshi fang tanshilu (futu)" [Famous Musician Luo Dayou's Interview with Sina Chat Room (with photos)], May 10, 2001, http://ent.sina.com.cn/s/h/42812.html.

35 Szeto, "Identity Politics and Its Discontents," 265.

36 The film's Chinese title is *Nv Ren, Si Shi*, which can be translated into English as *Women at Forty.*

37 Elaine Yee-lin Ho, "Women on the Edges of Hong Kong Modernity: The Films of Ann Hui," in *At Full Speed: Hong Kong Cinema in a Borderless World*, ed. Esther C. M. Yau (Minneapolis: University of Minnesota Press, 2001), 195–6.

38 Rey Chow, "Violence in the Other Country: China as Crisis, Spectacle, and Woman," in *Third World Women and the Politics of Feminism*. ed. Chandra Mohanty, Ann Russo, and Torres Lourdes (Bloomington: Indiana University Press, 1991), 88.

39 Chu, *Hong Kong Cinema*, 92.

40 Ho, "Women on the Edges of Hong Kong Modernity," 195.

41 All translations, unless otherwise stated, are the author's own.

42 Ho, "Women on the Edges of Hong Kong Modernity," 181.

43 Chu, *Hong Kong Cinema*, 98.

44 Ho, "Women on the Edges of Hong Kong Modernity," 181.

45 Ibid., 196–7.

46 Ibid., 197.

47 Ken Hall, "Main Entries: *Summer Snow*," in *Encyclopedia of Chinese Film*, ed. Yingjin Zhang and Zhiwei Xiao (London: Routledge, 2002), 324.

48 Ho, "Women on the Edges of Hong Kong Modernity," 195.

49 Ibid., 198–9.

50 Rey Chow, "Lyricism of the Chance Encounter; or, The Cultural Specificity of Affect in (Examples of) Hong Kong Cinema," *Film-Philosophy* 29, no. 2 (2025): 328.

51 Chow, "Between Colonizers," 158.

52 Emily Levine, "What Does It All Mean? Emily Levine at TEDxDanubia 2014," TEDx Talks, June 10, 2014, 18 min., 21 sec., https://www.youtube.com/watch?v=F4WDlJCO66Y.

53 Chu, *Hong Kong Cinema*, 91.

Chapter 8

1 Gina Marchetti, "Feminism, Postfeminism, and Hong Kong Women Filmmakers," in *A Companion to Hong Kong Cinema*, ed. Esther M. K. Cheung, Gina Marchetti, and Esther C. M. Yau (Chichester: Wiley-Blackwell, 2015); Audrey Yue, *Ann Hui's Song of the Exile* (Hong Kong: Hong Kong University Press, 2010); Elaine Yee Lin Ho, "Women on the Edges of Hong Kong Modernity: The Films of Ann Hui," in *At Full Speed: Hong Kong Cinema in a Borderless World*, ed. Esther C. M. Yau (Minneapolis: University of Minnesota Press, 2001), 177–206; Mirana M. Szeto, "Ann Hui at the Margin of Mainstream Hong Kong Cinema," in *Hong Kong Screenscapes: From the*

New Wave to the Digital Frontier, ed. Esther M. K. Cheung, Gina Marchetti, and See-Kam Tan (Hong Kong: Hong Kong University Press, 2011), 51–66.

2 Jing Jing Chang, "Ann Hui's Tin Shui Wai Diptych: The Flashback and Feminist Perception in Post-Handover Hong Kong," *Quarterly Review of Film and Video* 33, no. 8 (2016): 722–42.

3 David Der-wei Wang, *The Lyrical in Epic Time: Modern Chinese Intellectuals and Artists through the 1949 Crisis* (New York: Columbia University, 2015), 1.

4 Rey Chow, "Lyricism of the Chance Encounter; or, The Cultural Specificity of Affect in (Examples of) Hong Kong Cinema," *Film-Philosophy* 29, no. 2 (2025): 316.

5 Ibid., 325.

6 Ibid.

7 Cheng Yu-yu, *Yingpi lianlei: wenxueyanjiu de guanjianci* [*Quotation, Metaphor, Analogy: The Key Words of Literary Study*] (Beijing: Sanlian shudian, 2017), 47–57.

8 Marchetti, "Feminism, Postfeminism, and Hong Kong Women Filmmakers," 247.

9 Guo Qingfan, *Zhuangzi Jishi* [*The Collection of Interpretation of Zhuangzi*] (Beijing: Zhonghua Shuju, 1961), 733; my translation.

10 Yu-yu, *Yingpi lianlei: wenxueyanjiu de guanjianci*, 53; Wang Yi, *chuci zhangju* [*The Chapters and Sentences of Chuci*] (Taipei: yiwen yinshuguan, 1967), 372.

11 Yi, *The Chapters and Sentences of Chuci*, 52.

12 Ibid.

13 Ibid. Yan Xiaochang, *Guanzi Jiaoshi* [*The Revision and Annotation of Guanzi*] (Changsha: yuelu shushe, 1996), 15.

14 Ibid., 55.

15 Yi, *The Chapters and Sentences of Chuci*, 202–5. Translation adjusted from *The Songs of the South: An Ancient Chinese Anthology of Poems by Qu Yuan and Other poets*, trans. David Hawkes (London: Penguin, 2011), 175–82.

16 Benedict de Spinoza, *A Spinoza Reader: The Ethics and Other works*, ed. and trans. Edwin Curley (Princeton, NJ: Princeton University Press, 1994), 221.

17 Gilles Deleuze, *Cinema II: The Time-Image*, trans. Hugh Tomlinson and Robert Galeta (Minneapolis: University of Minnesota Press, 1989), 1–2.

18 Patricia MacCormack, *Cinesexuality* (Aldershot: Ashgate, 2008), 37.

Chapter 9

1 There are a few origins of the term "amah." The Portuguese word, *ama*, means "nurse" and denotes a nursemaid or maidservant. The Anglicized form of the Chinese term, *ah mah*, means "little mother," whereas *nai mah*, literally, "milk mother," refers to a wet nurse. Chinese household workers of the past were referred to as *ma jie*, literally "mother" and "older sister" (as a form of respect). See Nicole Constable, *Maid to Order in Hong Kong: Stories from Filipina Workers* (Ithaca,

NY: Cornell University Press, 1997), 48. In this chapter, the term "amah" refers to female unmarried Cantonese migrant domestic servants who arrived in colonial Hong Kong in the 1930s and served through the millennium, when many either retired or passed away.

2 For a history of Cantonese amahs, see Kenneth Gaw, *Superior Servants: The Legendary Cantonese Amahs of the Far East* (Singapore: Oxford University Press, 1988). For a history of Cantonese amahs in Malaysia, see Keat Gin Ooi, "From Amah-Chieh to Indonesian Maids: A Comparative Study in the Context of Malaysia, circa 1930s–1990s," in *Proletarian and Gendered Mass Migrations: A Global Perspective on Continuities and Discontinuities from the 19th to the 21st Centuries*, ed. Dirk Hoerder and Amarjit Kaur (Leiden: Brill, 2013), 405–25.

3 Taojie was born in a village in Shunde. She was adopted because of poverty. Her adoptive father owned a hotel but was murdered, leaving behind his wife and Taojie. The hotel's co-owners kicked out Taojie and her adoptive mother, who had no choice but to offer Taojie to serve as a domestic servant in Roger Lee's family when she encountered Roger's grandmother in Macau in the 1940s. See Roger Lee, *Taojie and I* (Hong Kong: Hongtouzi youxian gongsi, 2012), 34.

4 Rey Chow, *Writing Diaspora: Tactics of Intervention in Contemporary Cultural Studies* (Bloomington: Indiana University Press, 1993), 30.

5 Ibid., 36.

6 Ackbar Abbas, *Hong Kong: Culture and the Politics of Disappearance* (Minneapolis: University of Minnesota Press, 1997), 7.

7 Victor Fan, *Extraterritoriality: Locating Hong Kong Cinema and Media* (Edinburgh: Edinburgh University Press, 2019), 158.

8 Lee, *Taojie and I*, 20.

9 Gloria Chan, "The Amahs Explores Hong Kong's 'Lion Rock Spirit,'" *South China Morning Post*, February 11, 2015, https://www.scmp.com/magazines/48hrs/article/1709383/amahs-explores-hong-kongs-lion-rock-spirit. (accessed August 24, 2024).

10 Vivienne Lo, Chris Berry, and Guo Liping, eds., *Film and the Chinese Medical Humanities* (London: Routledge, 2019), 4–5.

11 HKSAR (Hong Kong Special Administrative Region), *Hong Kong Population Projections 2012–2041* (Hong Kong: Census and Statistics Department, 2012), 6.

12 Chen Xiaolei and Su Meizhi, *Dying in Hong Kong: Tearing Up* (Hong Kong: Joint Publishing, 2013), 5.

13 Ibid., 8.

14 Thomas Cole, Nathan Carlin, and Ronald Carson, eds., *Medical Humanities: An Introduction* (New York: Cambridge University Press, 2014), 139.

15 Sally Chivers, *The Silvering Screen: Old Age and Disability in Cinema* (Toronto: University of Toronto Press, 2011), xix, 5.

16 Ibid., xxi.
17 Chen and Su, *Dying in Hong Kong*, 219.
18 Ibid., 225.
19 In the United Kingdom in 2013, 59 percent of all deaths are in hospitals, while 17 percent are in care homes and 18 percent are in the person's own home. See Social Care Institute for Excellence, "Choosing to Die at Home," *SCIE Guide 48: Dying Well at Home: The Case for Integrated Working*, 2013, https://www.scie.org.uk/publications/guides/guide48/choosingtodieathome.asp (accessed April 21, 2023).
20 Mary Baines, "Pioneering Days of Palliative Care," *European Journal of Palliative Care* 18, no. 5 (2011): 225.
21 Chen and Su, *Dying in Hong Kong*, 228.
22 *Old Age: Where to Turn*, aired July 2015, on RTHK (Radio Television Hong Kong).
23 *The Choice of Nursing Home*, aired September 2015, on TVB (Television Broadcasts Limited) News and Information Division.
24 Lee, *Taojie and I*, 68–9.
25 Karen Fang, *Arresting Cinema: Surveillance in Hong Kong Film* (Stanford, CA: Stanford University Press, 2017), 132.
26 The year 2021 witnessed the critical acclaim and box-office success of Hong Kong–mainland co-produced biographical films such as *Zero to Hero* (Jimmy Wan, 2021) and *Anita* (Longman Leung, 2021).
27 Yiu-wai Chu, "Toward a New Hong Kong Cinema: Beyond Mainland–Hong Kong Co-productions," *Journal of Chinese Cinemas* 9, no. 2 (2015): 113, 119.
28 Han Li, "Alternative Locality: Geopolitics and Cultural Identity in Ann Hui's *A Simple Life*," *Asian Cinema* 26, no. 1 (2015): 25–8.
29 Gary Bettinson, "Yesterday Once More: Hong Kong–China Co-productions and the Myth of Mainlandization," *Journal of Chinese Cinemas* 14, no. 1 (2020): 27.
30 Emilie Yeh and Shi-yan Chao, "Policy and Creative Strategies: Hong Kong CEPA Films in the China Market," *International Journal of Cultural Policy* 26, no. 2 (2020): 189, 199.
31 Esther Cheung, Gina Marchetti, and Tan See-Kam, "Interview with Ann Hui: On the Edge of the Mainstream," in *Hong Kong Screenscapes: From the New Wave to the Digital Frontier*, ed. Esther M. K. Cheung, Gina Marchetti, and Tan See-Kam (Hong Kong: Hong Kong University Press, 2011), 68.
32 Mirana Szeto, "Ann Hui at the Margin of Mainstream Hong Kong Cinema," in *Hong Kong Screenscapes: From the New Wave to the Digital Frontier*, ed. Esther M. K. Cheung, Gina Marchetti, and Tan See-Kam (Hong Kong: Hong Kong University Press, 2011), 51.
33 Cheung, Marchetti, and Tan, "Interview with Ann Hui," 68.
34 Ibid., 69.
35 Ibid., 72.

36 *Promotional Documentary: A Simple Life*, directed by Cheung Lai (2011; Hong Kong: Panorama Corporation, 2012), DVD.
37 Zhuo Nan and Wu Yuehua, eds., *Ann Hui: Forty Years in Film* (Hong Kong: Joint Publishing, 2018), 217.
38 Sarah Pink, *The Future of Visual Anthropology: Engaging the Senses* (London: Routledge, 2006), 60.
39 Chow, *Writing Diaspora*, 43.
40 Cole, Carlin, and Carson, *Medical Humanities*, 139, 143.
41 Roger Lee's grandfather is a first-generation Chinese-American who worked in railroad construction in the United States.
42 Cole, Carlin, and Carson, *Medical Humanities*, 143.
43 *Promotional Documentary: A Simple Life*, directed by Cheung Lai.
44 Ibid.
45 Governments of the PRC and the HKSAR (Governments of the People's Republic of China and the Hong Kong Special Administrative Region), "Annex 4: Specific Commitments on Liberalization of Trade in Services," in *Closer Economic Partnership Arrangement*, 2003, 18–19, https://www.tid.gov.hk/en/our_work/cepa/legal_text/fulltext.html (accessed December 6, 2025).
46 *Promotional Documentary: A Simple Life*, directed by Cheung Lai.
47 Ibid.
48 Ibid.
49 Andy Lau, *My 30 Work Days* (Beijing: Zhongguo huaqiao chubanshe, 2012), 66.
50 Ibid., 66.
51 CEPA stipulates: "For motion pictures jointly produced by Hong Kong and the Mainland, … there is no restriction on where the story takes place, but the plots or the leading characters must be related to the mainland." See Governments of the PRC and the HKSAR, *Closer Economic Partnership Arrangement*, 18–19.
52 *Promotional Documentary: A Simple Life*, directed by Cheung Lai.

Chapter 10

1 Charles Devellennes and Benoît Dillet, "Questioning New Materialisms: An Introduction," *Theory, Culture and Society* 35, no. 7–8 (2018): 11.
2 Thomas Lemke, "An Alternative Model of Politics? Prospects and Problems of Jane Bennett's Vital Materialism," *Theory, Culture & Society* 35, no. 6 (2018): 32.
3 Jane Bennett, "The Force of Things: Steps toward an Ecology of Matter," *Political Theory* 32, no. 3 (2004): 354.
4 Shiao-ying Shen, "Politics and Aesthetics of Connection and Splitting: Ann Hui and Clara Law's Love and Loss of Hong Kong," *Chung Wai Literature Quarterly* 29, no. 10 (2001): 48.

5 Ka-yan Ng, "Analyzing the Hong Kong New Wave Cinema through the Stories of Ann Hui" (BA diss., Hong Kong Baptist University, 2008), 31.
6 Chin-pang Lei, "Life's Journey Is Never Flat: Ann Hui's Travel Films and Hong Kong Consciousness," *P-articles*, January 22, 2019, https://p- articles.com/critics/579.html.
7 Ka-fai Yau, "Looking Back at Ann Hui's Cinema of the Political," *Modern Chinese Literature and Culture* 19, no. 2 (2007): 121–2.
8 Tony Williams, "Song of the Exile Border-Crossing Melodrama," *Jump Cut* 42 (1998): 94.
9 Ackbar Abbas, *Hong Kong: Culture and the Politics of Disappearance* (Minneapolis: University of Minnesota Press, 1997), 74.
10 Rey Chow, *Alternative Perspectives on Hong Kong Culture* (Hong Kong: Oxford University Press, 1995).
11 Ping-chiu Chan, "In Conversation with Chan Ping-Chiu: How Long Has It Been since You've Heard the Term 'Postcolonial' in Hong Kong?," *Initium Media*, May 24, 2016, https://theinitium.com/article/20160524-culture-theatre-postcolonialaffairs.
12 Yee-lok Tam, "When We Talk about Post-1997 Hong Kong Cinema, What Are We Talking About: Identity Politics, Theories and Capital-State-Nation," *HKinema* 39 (2017): 12.
13 Abbas, *Hong Kong*, 11.
14 Ibid., 23.
15 Ping-kwan Leung, "Urban Cinema and the Cultural Identity of Hong Kong," in *Between Home and World: A Reader in Hong Kong Cinema*, ed. Esther M. K. Cheung and Chu Yiu-wai (Hong Kong: Oxford University Press, 2004), 388.
16 Yau, "Looking Back at Ann Hui's Cinema of the Political," 125.
17 Ibid., 130.
18 Lei, "Life's Journey Is Never Flat," https://p-articles.com/critics/579.html.
19 Audrey Yue, "Migration-as-Transition: Pre-Post-1997 Hong Kong Culture in Clara Law's *Autumn Moon*," *Intersections: Gender, History and Culture in the Asian Context* 4 (2000), http://intersections.anu.edu.au/issue4/yue.html.
20 Chi-hua Li, "*The Story of Woo Viet*: Confessions of Refugee Fate," in *Six Great Directors of Hong Kong and Taiwan*, ed. Li You-xin (Taipei: Independence Evening Post, 1986), 194–5.
21 Vinh Nguyen, "Ann Hui's *Boat People*: Documenting Vietnamese Refugees in Hong Kong," in *Looking Back on the Vietnam War: Twenty-First-Century Perspectives*, ed. Brenda M. Boyle and Jeehyun Lim (New Brunswick, NJ: Rutgers University Press, 2016), 94–5.
22 Shen, "Politics and Aesthetics of Connection and Splitting," 43.

23 Nick J. Fox and Pam Alldred, "New Materialist Social Inquiry: Designs, Methods and the Research-Assemblage," *International Journal of Social Research Methodology* 18, no. 4 (2015): 400.
24 Abbas, *Hong Kong*, 103–6.
25 Kevin Coleman and Daniel James, "Capitalism and the Camera," in *Capitalism and the Camera: Essays on Photography and Extraction*, ed. Kevin Coleman and Daniel James (London: Verso, 2021), 3–4.
26 Abbas, *Hong Kong*, 64.
27 Ibid., 73.
28 Cheuk-to Li, "A Comprehensive Review of Ann Hui's Four Films," in *Six Great Directors of Hong Kong and Taiwan*, ed. Li You-xin (Taipei: Independence Evening Post, 1986), 181.
29 Yau, "Looking Back at Ann Hui's Cinema of the Political," 124.
30 Karen Jaehne, "Boat People: An Interview with Anne Hui," *Cinéaste* 13, no. 2 (1984): 18.
31 Yau, "Looking Back at Ann Hui's Cinema of the Political," 126–7.
32 Nguyen, "Ann Hui's *Boat People*," 100.
33 Abbas, *Hong Kong*, 103.
34 Ibid., 144.

Chapter 11

1 This is the meaning of its original Chinese title when the film was broadcast in Asian countries.
2 The Wang-Koo Summit in 1993 was the first formal meeting between the CCP and the KMT after the Retreat to Taiwan in 1949. The KMT was represented by Koo Chen-fu (1917–2005), a Taiwanese businessman, diplomat, and film producer. The CCP was represented by Wang Daohan (1915–2005).
3 The credit page of the film shows the company name in Chinese; the English name used here is transliterated with the Wade–Giles system according to its pronunciation in Mandarin. Wade–Giles is a romanization system for Mandarin Chinese. It developed from a system produced by Thomas Francis Wade during the mid-nineteenth century. The Wade–Giles system was used in Taiwan until 2008.
4 The tea party was on July 27, 1987. The original sentence is: "I have stayed in Taiwan for forty years. I am Taiwanese, also I am a Chinese." Kao-ju Chi, *Chiang Ching-kuo's Biography: I Am Taiwanese* (Taipei: Cheng Chung Book, 1998), 244.

Chapter 12

1 See for examples: Tao Chen, "Youzhouyu shuangcheng zhijian: Xun Anhua gaibian Zhang Ailing zuopin shi de 'youyiwudu'" [Wandering between Two Cities: Ann Hui's "Intentional Misreading" in Adapting Eileen Chang's Works], *Peng Pai*, June 16, 2020, https://www.thepaper.cn/newsDetail_forward_7854257; Qiancao, "Xu Anhua weishenme paibuhao Zhang Ailing de xiaoshuo" [Why Can't Ann Hui Adapt Eileen Chang's Fictions Well?], *Zhihu Zhuanlan*, September 19, 2020, https://zhuanlan.zhihu.com/p/255031912; Xiao Q, "Xu Anhua xinpian Diyi luxiang baoshouzhengyi. Zhang Ailing weihe nanyi gaibian" [Ann Hui's New Film *Love After Love* Is Highly Controversial, and Why Is It Difficult to Adapt Eileen Chang's Works?], *Chinawriter*, October 26, 2021, http://www.chinawriter.com.cn/n1/2021/1026/c419388-32264964.html.

2 Shanshan Ren, "Xu Anhua tan huangjinshidai: bubi bawo kancheng wenhuafuhao" [Ann Hui on *The Golden Era*: No Need to See Me as a Cultural Symbol], *National Humanity History*, no. 18 (2014): 122.

3 Kam Louie, "Introduction: Eileen Chang: A Life of Conflicting Cultures in China and America," in *Eileen Chang: Romancing Languages, Cultures and Genres*, ed. Kam Louie (Hong Kong: Hong Kong University Press, 2012), 1–14.

4 Ann Hui's films often open and close with landscape scenes. This approach can be seen in *The Romance of the Book and Sword* (1987) from the 1980s, and *Song of the Exile* (1990) and *Summer Snow* (1995) from the 1990s. It continues into the new millennium with *July Rhapsody* (2002), *The Way We Are* (2008), and *The Golden Era* (2014). As film critic and scholar Mao Jian noted in a review, quoting Dai Jinhua: "Her films are not just a chronicle of Hong Kong's film history, but a collective journey of our generation across China, spanning both sides of the Taiwan Strait and Hong Kong, while portraying a visual gallery of Mainland China's historical transformations." See See Mao Jian, "Liangfeng qiuyue: Xu Anhua dianying zhong de fengjing he Zhongguo shineng" [The Cool Breeze and Autumn Moon: Landscape and Chinese Potential in An Hui's Films], *Southern Cultural Forum*, no. 4 (2019): 54–7.

5 Michael Berry, *Speaking in Image: Interviews with Contemporary Chinese Filmmakers* (New York: Columbia University Press, 2005), 430.

6 Hong Zeng, "Translocal Female Subjectivity: Notes on Ann Hui's *The Golden Era*," *Asian Cinema* 30, no. 1 (2019): 91–107.

7 Audrey Yue, *Ann Hui's Song of the Exile* (Hong Kong: Hong Kong University Press, 2010), 2.

8 Law Kar, "Law Kar shuo Xu Anhua de zaoqi dianying" [Law Kar Discusses Ann Hui's Early Films], in *Xu Anhua shuo Xu Anhua* [*Ann Hui on Ann Hui*], ed. Po wei Kwong (Shanghai: Fudan University Press, 2017), 415.

9 Zhao Yafei, "Huangjin shidai: kunyu laolong zhizhong" [The Golden Era: Trapped in a Cage], *Home Drama*, no. 11 (2016): 115.
10 Ren, "Ann Hui," 122.
11 Hila Shachar, *Screening the Author: The Literary Biopic* (Cham: Springer, 2019), 16–17.
12 Kwong, *Ann Hui*, 282.
13 Yuanying Yang, Yiwu Zhang, Guanping Wu, and Lihua Yang, "Huangjin shidai" [On *The Golden Era*], *Contemporary Cinema*, no. 11 (2014): 52.
14 Yue, Ann Hui's *Song of the Exile*, 17.
15 Zeng, "Translocal," 96.
16 This scene is adapted for the screen from Xiao Hong's autobiographical story "Auctioning Furniture."
17 Yue, Ann Hui's *Song of the Exile*, 17.
18 Zeng, "Translocal," 103.
19 Xiao Hong, *The Field of Life and Death & Tales of Hulan River: Two Novels*, trans. Howard Goldblatt and Ellen Lai-shan Yeung (Bloomington: Indiana University Press, 1979), 180.
20 Meilin, "Yi Xiaohong" [Remembering Xiao Hong], in *Huainian Xiaohong* [*Memory of Xiao Hong*], ed. Guanquan Wang (Shanghai: Dongfang Publishing House, 2011), 161.
21 Ren, "Ann Hui," 124.
22 Yi Zhong, "Xu Anhua: xiang Xiao Hong yiyang gudu you wanqiang" [Ann Hui: As Lonely and Resilient as Xiao Hong], *Times Figure*, no. 9 (2014): 99.
23 Kwong, *Ann Hui*, 281.
24 A term drawn from Bertolt Brecht's theory of theater.
25 "Xu Anhua dui Huangjinshidai de gaobaishu" [Ann Hui's Confession to *The Golden Era*], *CineHello*, October 8, 2014, https://cinehello.com/stream/55074.
26 Deborah Cartmell and Ashley Dawn Polasek, *A Companion to the Biopic* (Chichester: Wiley-Blackwell, 2019).
27 Lv Meijing, "Daoyan Xu Anhua: Yuan nide huangjinshidai si jingzhong laidao xinshang" [Director Ann Hui: May Your Golden Era Arrive Like a Warning Bell to the Heart], *Phoenix Culture*, September 28, 2014, https://culture.ifeng.com/a/20140928/42107198_0.shtml.
28 Kwong, *Ann Hui*, 275.
29 Shachar, "Introduction," 4–9.
30 Belén Vidal, "Introduction: The Biopic and Its Critical Contexts," in *The Biopic in Contemporary Film Culture*, ed. Tom Brown and Belén Vidal (New York: Routledge, 2014), 1–32.
31 An Ying, "Xu Anhua: pi Huangjinshidai paishangle, yinfa Zhengyi shi zuihaode" [Ann Hui: Filming *The Golden Era* Was Exhausting, Sparking Controversy

Is the Best Outcome], *people.cn*, October 8, 2014, http://media.people.com.cn/n/2014/1008/c40606-25784957.html

32 Liz Shackleton, "Ann Hui, *The Golden Era*," *Screen International*, October 3, 2014, https://www.screendaily.com/interviews/ann-hui-the-golden-era/5078265.article

33 Ying, "Ann Hui."

34 Ibid.

Ann Hui's Feature Filmography

1979 *The Secret*

Director: Ann Hui
Producer: Audrey Li; Shu-Ru Hu
Screenplay: Joyce Chan
Cinematographer: David Chung
Editor: Tsan-Feng Yu
Actors (Main): Sylvia Chang; Angie Chiu; Norman Chu
Country: Hong Kong, China
Language: Cantonese

1980 *The Spooky Bunch*

Director: Ann Hui
Producer: Tina Lau; Josephine Siao
Screenplay: Joyce Chan
Cinematographer: Tony Hope
Editor: Yee-Shun Wong
Actors (Main): Josephine Siao; Kenny Bee; Mang-Ha Cheng
Country: Hong Kong, China
Language: Cantonese

1981 *The Story of Woo Viet*

Director: Ann Hui
Producer: Bo-Chu Chui; Teddy Robin Kwan
Screenplay: Alfred Cheung
Cinematographer: Bill Wong
Editor: Yee-Shun Wong
Actors (Main): Chow Yun-Fat; Cora Miao; Cherie Chung; Lo Lieh
Country: Hong Kong, China
Language: Cantonese
Awards: Hong Kong Film Award Best Screenplay 1982

1982 *Boat People*

Director: Ann Hui
Producer: Meng Xia
Screenplay: Cheung Gam Hung; Kang-Chien Chiu
Cinematographer: David Chung; Zong Ji Huang; Chung Kay Wong
Editor: Kin Kin
Actors (Main): George Lam; Season Ma; Andy Lau; Meiying Jia
Country: Hong Kong, China
Language: Cantonese
Awards: Hong Kong Film Award Best Picture and Best Director 1983

1984 *Love in a Fallen City*

Director: Ann Hui
Producer: Mona Fong
Screenplay: Fengcho
Cinematographer: Tony Hope
Editor: Hsing-Lung Chiang; Cheung-Kan Chow; Pao-Hua Fang
Actors (Main): Chow Yun-Fat; Cora Miao; Gerry Barnett; Chiao Chiao
Country: Hong Kong, China
Language: Cantonese

1987 *The Romance of Book and Sword*

Director: Ann Hui
Producer: Fengqi Guo; Minhui Shen
Screenplay: Louis Cha (original novel); Ann Hui
Cinematographer: Bill Wong
Editor: Mok Leung Chau
Actors (Main): Nuo Ai; Shichang Da; Jie Deng
Country: Hong Kong, China; Mainland China
Language: Cantonese

1987 *Princess Fragrance*

Director: Ann Hui
Producer: Fengqi Guo; Minhui Shen

Screenplay: Louis Cha; Tin-Nam Chun
Cinematographer: Bill Wong
Actors (Main): Nuo Ai; Shichang Da; Hachier
Country: Hong Kong, China; Mainland China
Language: Cantonese

1988 *Starry Is the Night*

Director: Ann Hui
Producer: Mona Fong; Feng Hsu
Screenplay: Suk-Wah Leung
Cinematographer: Henry Chan
Editor: Yi-Shun Huang
Actors (Main): George Lam; Brigitte Lin; Derek Tung-Sing Yee; David Wu
Country: Hong Kong, China
Language: Cantonese

1990 *Song of the Exile*

Director: Ann Hui
Producer: King Hu; Jimmy Wang Yu
Screenplay: Nien-Jen Wu
Cinematographer: Zhiwen Zhong
Editor: Yee-Shun Wong
Actors (Main): Maggie Cheung; Siu-Kwong Chung; Tan Lang Jachi Tian
Country: Hong Kong, China
Language: Cantonese
Awards: APFF Awards Best Film 1990

1991 *Zodiac Killers*

Director: Ann Hui
Producer: Lai-Yee Leung;
Screenplay: Raymond To; Nien-Jen Wu
Cinematographer: David Chung
Editor: Ma Kam; David Wu
Actors (Main): Andy Lau; Cherie Chung; Jun'ichi Ishida
Country: Hong Kong, China
Language: Cantonese

1991 *My American Grandson*

Director: Ann Hui
Producer: Chien Kung Fan; Kin-Wah Shum; Fui-Bik Wong
Screenplay: Nien-Jen Wu
Cinematographer: Ping Bin Lee
Editor: Ching-Sung Liao
Actors (Main): Kun-Hsuan Huang; Carina Lau; Peng Sun
Country: Hong Kong, China
Language: Cantonese

1993 *Boy and His Hero*

Director: Ann Hui
Producer: Ann Hui
Screenplay: Hsiao-Ti Wang
Actors (Main): Lung Chin; Hsiao-Wu; Zhoe-Jeh Kao
Country: Hong Kong, China
Language: Cantonese

1995 *Summer Snow*

Director: Ann Hui
Producer: Ann Hui
Screenplay Man-Keung Chan
Cinematographer: Ping Bin Lee
Editor: Yee-Shun Wong
Actors (Main): Josephine Siao; Roy Chiao; Kar-Ying Law
Country: Hong Kong, China
Language: Cantonese
Awards and Nominations: Berlinale Competition 1995
Berlinale Sliver Berlin Bear Best Actress 1995

1996 *Ah Kam*

Director: Ann Hui
Producer: Raymond Man-Wai Chow; Catherine Hun; Ka-Foo Lau

Screenplay: Kin Chung Chan; Man-Keung Chan
Cinematographer: Ardy Lam
Editor: Yee-Shun Wong
Actors (Main): Michelle Yeoh; Sammo Kam-Bo Hung; Wai-Kwong Lo
Country: Hong Kong, China

1997 *As Time Goes By*

Director: Ann Hui; Vincent Chui

1997 *Eighteen Springs*

Director: Ann Hui
Producer: Ann Hui; Jimmy Wang Yu
Screenplay: Kin Chung Chan
Cinematographer: Ping Bin Lee
Editor: Hung Poon; Yee-Shun Wong
Actors (Main): Leon Lai; Chien-Lien Wu; Anita Mui
Country: Hong Kong, China; Mainland China
Language: Cantonese
Awards: Golden Rooster 1998 Best Co-Produced Feature

1999 *Ordinary Heroes*

Director: Ann Hui
Producer: Ann Hui
Screenplay: Kin Chung Chan
Cinematographer: Nelson Lik-wai Yu
Editor: Chi-Leung Kwong
Actors (Main): Kang-sheng Lee; Anthony Chau-Sang Wong; Kwan-Ho Tse
Country: Hong Kong, China
Language: Cantonese
Awards: Hong Kong Film Awards Best Picture 2000

2001 *Visible Secret*

Director: Ann Hui
Producer: John Chang; Thomas Chang; Ann Hui; Abe Kwong; Solon So

Screenplay: Abe Kwong
Cinematographer: Arthur Wong
Editor: Chi Li Kong
Actors (Main): Eason Chan; Shu Qi;Anthony Chau-Sang Wong
Country: Hong Kong, China
Language: Cantonese

2002 *July Rhapsody*

Director: Ann Hui
Producer: Ann Hui; Derek Tung-Sing Yee
Screenplay: Ivy Ho
Cinematographer: Pun Leung Kwan
Editor: Chi-Leung Kwong
Actors (Main): Jacky Cheung; Anita Mui; Karena Ka-Yan Lam; Eric Kot
Country: Hong Kong, China
Language: Cantonese

2003 *Jade Goddess of Mercy*

Director: Ann Hui
Producer: Bolun Li; Buting Yang
Screenplay: Ivy Ho
Cinematographer: Pun Leung Kwan
Actors (Main): Wei Zhao; Nicholas Tse; Yunlong Liu
Country: China
Language: Mandarin

2006 *The Postmodern Life of My Aunt*

Director: Ann Hui
Producer: Wang Zhang
Screenplay: Qiang Li
Cinematographer: Pun Leung Kwan; Nelson Lik-wai Yu
Editor: Ching-Sung Liao
Actors (Main): Siqin Gaowa; Chow Yun-Fat; Wei Zhao
Country: China
Language: Mandarin

Awards: Hong Kong Film Awards Best Leading Actress 2008
HKFCS Award Best Film 2008

2008 *The Way We Are*

Director: Ann Hui
Producer: Shiu-Wa Lou
Screenplay: Jing Wong
Cinematographer: Charlie Lam
Editor: Cheung-Kan Chow
Actors (Main): Hee Ching Paw; Chun-lung Leung
Country: Hong Kong, China
Language: Cantonese
Awards: Hong Kong Film Awards Best Director 2008

2009 *Night and Fog*

Director: Ann Hui
Producer: Ann Hui
Screenplay: King-Wai Cheung; Alex Law
Cinematographer: Charlie Lam
Editor: Chi-Leung Kwong
Actors (Main): Jingchu Zhang; Simon Yam; Audrey Hiu-Yau Chan
Country: Hong Kong, China
Language: Cantonese

2010 *All About Love*

Director: Ann Hui
Producer: Ann Hui
Screenplay: Yee Shan Yeung
Cinematographer: Charlie Lam
Editor: Chi Wai Chan; Chi-Leung Kwong
Actors (Main): Sandra Kwan Yue Ng; Vivian Chow; Eddie Cheung
Country: Hong Kong, China
Language: Cantonese

2011 *A Simple Life*

Director: Ann Hui
Producer: Pui-Wah Chan
Screenplay: Susan Chan
Cinematographer: Nelson Lik-wai Yu
Editor: Chi-Leung Kwong; Manda Wai
Actors (Main): Andy Lau; Deannie Ip; Hailu Qin
Country: Hong Kong, China
Language: Cantonese
Awards: Venice Film Festival Golden Lion 2011
Hong Kong Film Award Best Film 2012

2014 *The Golden Era*

Director: Ann Hui
Producer: Xiaoqing Chen; Sanping Han; Shen Hao; William Kong; Victor Koo; Peikang La; Tit Kwan Tsui; Tiejun Xu
Screenplay: Qiang Li
Cinematographer: Yu Wang
Editor: Manda Wai
Actors (Main): Tang Wei; Shaofeng Feng; Zhiwen Wang
Country: China
Language: Mandarin
Awards: Hong Kong Film Awards Best Picture 2015

2017 *Our Time Will Come*

Director: Ann Hui
Producer: Ann Hui; Stephen Lam; Roger Lee; Zhonghuai Sun; Yiyang Wang
Screenplay: Jiping He
Cinematographer: Nelson Lik-wai Yu
Editor: Mary Stephen
Actors (Main): Xun Zhou; Eddie Peng; Wallace Huo; Deannie Ip; Tony Ka Fai Leung
Country: Hong Kong, China
Language: Cantonese; Mandarin; Japanese
Awards: Hong Kong Film Award Best Film 2018

2020 *Love After Love*

Director: Ann Hui
Producer: Ann Hui
Screenplay: Anyi Wang
Cinematographer: Christopher Doyle
Editor: Chi-Leung Kwong; Mary Stephen
Actors (Main): Sichun Ma; Feihong Yu; Eddie Peng
Country: China
Language: Mandarin

2023 *Elegies*

Director: Ann Hui
Producer: Ken Hui
Cinematography: Mak Chi-kwan
Editing: Salt & Vinegar
Country: Hong Kong, China
Language: Cantonese

Bibliography

"A Conversation of Ann Hui with Chen Danjing on *Golden Times*" [Xu Anhua, Chen Danqing duitan *Huangjin shidai*]. *The Second Nanjing Film Forum*, May 5, 2014. Accessed December 25, 2023. https://www.bilibili.com/video/BV1Cv411M7n6/?spm_id_from=333.337.search-card.all.click.

Abbas, Ackbar. *Hong Kong: Culture and the Politics of Disappearance*. Hong Kong: Hong Kong University Press, 1997.

"Affected by the Bad Box Office/China Shooting Hit Cooling Down." *Lianhe Zaobao*, December 2, 1990, 38.

An, Ying. "Xu Anhua: pi Huangjinshidai paishangle, yinfa Zhengyi shi zuihaode" [Ann Hui: Filming *The Golden Era* Was Exhausting, Sparking Controversy Is the Best Outcome]. *people.cn*, October 8, 2014. http://media.people.com.cn/n/2014/1008/c40606-25784957.html.

Arendt, Hannah. *The Human Condition by Hannah Arendt*. Garden City, NY: Doubleday Anchor Books, 1959.

Ariyoshi, Sawako. *The Twilight Years*, translated by Mildred Tahara. Tokyo: Kodansha International, 1987.

Au, Ben. "Red Co-productions? Don't Underestimate Ann Hui." *HK01*, July 12, 2017. https://www.hk01.com/社會新聞/104168/明月幾時有-影評-紅色合拍片-別太小看許鞍華.

Baines, Mary. "Pioneering Days of Palliative Care." *European Journal of Palliative Care* 18, no. 5 (2011): 223–7.

Banerjee, Bidisha. "What Lies Within: Misrecognition and the Uncanny in Hong Kong's Cityscape." *Inter-Asia Cultural Studies*, no. 4 (2013): 519–37.

Barlow, Tani E. "Gender and Identity in Ding Ling's 'Mother.'" *Modern Chinese Literature* 2, no. 2 (1986): 123–42.

Bazin, Andre. *What Is Cinema?* Berkeley: University of California Press, 2005.

Bennett, Jane. "The Force of Things: Steps toward an Ecology of Matter." *Political Theory* 32, no. 3 (2004): 347–72.

Berliner, Todd. *Hollywood Aesthetic: Pleasure in American Cinema*. Oxford: Oxford University Press, 2017.

Berry, Michael. *Speaking in Images: Interviews with Contemporary Chinese Filmmakers*. New York: Columbia University Press, 2005.

Bettinson, Gary. "Commentary: Hong Kong Stars and Stardom," in *A Companion to Hong Kong Cinema*, edited by Esther M. K. Cheung, Gina Marchetti, and Esther C. M. Yau, 379–87. Chichester: Wiley-Blackwell, 2015.

Bettinson, Gary. “Pictorial Storytelling and Staging in Ann Hui’s *The Way We Are*.” *Jump Cut: A Review of Contemporary Media*, no. 62 (2024). Accessed July 30, 2025. https://www.ejumpcut.org/archive/JC62.2024/GaryBettinson/index.html.

Bettinson, Gary. “Yesterday Once More: Hong Kong-China Co-productions and the Myth of Mainlandization.” *Journal of Chinese Cinemas* 14, no. 1 (2020): 16–31.

Bhabha, Homi K. *The Location of Culture*. London: Routledge, 1994.

Bloom, Harold. *The Anxiety of Influence: A Theory of Poetry*. Oxford: Oxford University Press, 1973.

Bordwell, David. “Modest Doesn’t Mean Unambitious.” *Observations on Film Art: David Bordwell’s Website on Cinema*, March 20, 2008. Accessed June 15, 2023. http://www.davidbordwell.net/blog/category/directors-ann-hui/page/3/.

Boyd, Brian. *On the Origin of Stories: Evolution, Cognition, and Fiction*. Cambridge, MA: The Belknap Press of Harvard University Press, 2009.

Browne, Nick. “Society and Subjectivity: On the Political Economy of Chinese Melodrama,” in *New Chinese Cinemas: Forms, Identities, Politics*, edited by Nick Browne, Paul G. Pickowicz, Vivian Sobchack, and Esther Yau, 40–56. Cambridge: Cambridge University Press, 1994.

Cahill, James. *Pictures for Use and Pleasure: Vernacular Painting in High Qing China*. Berkeley: University of California Press, 2010.

Cartmell, Deborah, and Ashley Dawn Polasek. *A Companion to the Biopic*. Hoboken, NJ: Wiley-Blackwell, 2019.

Cartmell, Deborah, and Imelda Whelehan. *Screen Adaptation: Impure Cinema*. New York: Palgrave Macmillan, 2010.

Chan, Gloria. “The Amahs Explores Hong Kong’s ‘Lion Rock Spirit.’” *South China Morning Post*, February 11, 2015. Accessed August 25, 2024. https://www.scmp.com/magazines/48hrs/article/1709383/amahs-explores-hong-kongs-lion-rock-spirit.

Chan, Jenny, and Derek Pua. *Three Years Eight Months: The Forgotten Struggle of Hong Kong’s WWII*. San Francisco, CA: Pacific Atrocities Education, 2019.

Chan, Ping-chiu. “In Conversation with Chan Ping-Chiu: How Long Has It Been since You’ve Heard the Term ‘Postcolonial’ in Hong Kong?” *Initium Media*, May 24, 2016. https://theinitium.com/article/20160524-culture-theatre-Postcolonialaffairs.

Chan, Ping-ting. “Hong Kong-Style Variation beneath a Red Co-production: Ann Hui Did Not Forget Hong Kong.” *The News Lens*, July 16, 2017. https://www.thenewslens.com/feature/hk-movies-newwave/73590.

Chan, Sui-jeung. *East River Column: Hong Kong Guerrillas in the Second World War and After*. Hong Kong: Hong Kong University Press, 2009.

Chan, Weizhen. “Asking for Xiao Hong: An Interview with Ann Hui.” *Funscreen*, February 12, 2015. http://www.funscreen.com.tw/headline.asp?H_No=553.

Chang, Eileen. “A Chronicle of Changing Clothes,” in *Written on the Water*, edited by Andrew F. Jones and Nicole Huang, 65–75. New York: Columbia University Press, 2004.

Chang, Eileen. “Demons and Fairies,” *XXth Century*, December 1943, 421.

Chang, Eileen. "A Few Words to the Reader," in *Eileen Chang Collected Works: Volume Four*, edited by Jin Hongda and Yu Qing, 307–8. Anhui: Anhui Literature and Art Publishing House, 1992.

Chang, Eileen. *Love in a Fallen City*. New York: New York Review of Books, 2006.

Chang, Eileen. "Writing of One's Own," in *Written on the Water*, edited by Andrew F. Jones and Nicole Huang, 15–22. New York: Columbia University Press, 2004.

Chang, Eileen. *Zhang Ailing Diancang Quanji (Duanpian Xiaoshuo Juan Yi) 1943 Nian Zuopin* [*The Classical Collection of Eileen Chang (Volume 1 of Short Stories) Works of 1943*]. Taipei: Crown Publishing, 2001.

Chang, Eileen. *Zhang Ailing Diancang Quanji (Sanwen Juan Yi) 1939–1947 Nian Zuopin* [*The Classical Collection of Eileen Chang (Volume 1 of Prose), Works of 1939–1947*]. Taipei: Crown Publishing, 2001.

Chang, Jing Jing. "Ann Hui's Tin Shui Wai Diptych: The Flashback and Feminist Perception in Post-Handover Hong Kong." *Quarterly Review of Film and Video* 33, no. 8 (2016): 722–42.

Changming. "Shi tan guoji xingjing di er ji cisha de shehui yishi xingtai" [Let's Talk about the Social Ideology of the Second Episode "Assassination" from *Interpol*]. *Close-up*, no. 56 (April 1978): 10–11.

Chatman, Seymour. *Story and Discourse: Narrative Structure in Fiction Film*. Ithaca, NY: Cornell University Press, 1978.

Chen, Pingyuan. *The Development of Chinese Martial Arts Fiction*. Cambridge: Cambridge University Press, 2016.

Chen, Pingyuan. *Zhongguo xiandai xueshu zhi jianli* [*The Establishment of Modern Chinese Scholarship*]. Beijing: Beijing daxue chubanshe, 1998.

Chen, Shouzhen. "Xu Anhua bu zijue de shouhuo" [Ann Hui's Accidental Achievements]. *Close-up*, no. 47 (December 1977): 34–5.

Chen, Xiaolei, and Su Meizhi. *Dying in Hong Kong: Tearing Up*. Hong Kong: Joint Publishing, 2013.

Chen, Xiaolei, and Zhou Rongrong. *Dying in Hong Kong: Seeing the Coffin*. Hong Kong: Joint Publishing, 2013.

Cheng, Siji. "Xin wenhua ren zhongqi baogao shu" [New Culture Men Midterm Reports]. *Cultural New Wave* (April 1979): 8–12.

Cheng Yu-yu. *Yingpi lianlei: wenxueyanjiu de guanjianci* [*Quotation, Metaphor, Analogy: The Key Words of Literary Study*]. Beijing: Sanlian shudian, 2017.

Chengyu. "Fan shangpin hua de nuli" [The Effort of Resisting Commodification]. *Film Biweekly*, no. 3 (February 1979): 46.

Chengyu. "Tan changshou jiemu" [On Long-Running TV Shows]. *Film Biweekly*, no. 2 (January 1979): 49.

Cheuk, Pak-tong. "Fangwen guoji xingjing de muhuo gongzuozhe" [Interview: The Making of *Interpol*]. *Close-up*, no. 56 (April 1978): 12–13.

Cheuk, Pak-tong. *Xianggang xin langchao dianying (1978–2000)* [*Hong Kong New Wave Cinema (1978–2000)*]. Shanghai: Fudan University Press, 2011.

Cheung, Esther M. K. "On Spectral Mutations: The Ghostly City in *The Secret*, *Rouge* and *Little Cheung*," in *Hong Kong Culture: Word and Image*, edited by Kam Louie, 169–92. Hong Kong: Hong Kong University Press, 2010.

Cheung, Esther M. K. "The Urban Maze: Crisis and Topography in Hong Kong Cinema," in *A Companion to Hong Kong Cinema*, edited by Esther M. K. Cheung, Gina Marchetti, and Esther C. M. Yau, 51–70. Chichester: Wiley-Blackwell, 2015.

Cheung, Esther M. K., Gina Marchetti, and Tan See-Kam. "Interview with Ann Hui: On the Edge of the Mainstream," in *Hong Kong Screenscapes: From the New Wave to the Digital Frontier*, edited by Esther M. K. Cheung, Gina Marchetti, and Tan See-Kam, 67–74. Hong Kong: Hong Kong University Press, 2011.

Cheung, Ka-wai. *Liuqi baodong: Xianggang zhanhou lishi de fenshuiling* [*The 1967 Riots: Post-war Hong Kong's Watershed*]. Hong Kong: Hong Kong University Press, 2012.

Cheung, Koon Fu. "Hong Kong Voices." Oral History Archives, November 26, 2011. http://www.hkmemory.hk.

Chi, Kao-ju. *Chiang Ching-kuo's Biography: I Am Taiwanese*. Taipei: Cheng Chung Book, 1998.

Chivers, Sally. *The Silvering Screen: Old Age and Disability in Cinema*. Toronto: University of Toronto Press, 2011.

Choi, Sin-Yee. "Our Time Will Come: The Secret Message underneath the Main Melody." *MP Weekly*, July 8, 2017. https://www.mpweekly.com/culture/明月幾時有-許鞍華-建軍大業-41950.

Chow, Rey. "Between Colonizers: Hong Kong's Postcolonial Self-Writing in the 1990s." *Diaspora: A Journal of Transnational Studies* 2, no. 2 (1992): 151–70.

Chow, Rey. "Lyricism of the Chance Encounter; or, The Cultural Specificity of Affect in (Examples of) Hong Kong Cinema." *Film-Philosophy* 29, no. 2 (2025): 312–28.

Chow, Rey. *Sentimental Fabulations: Contemporary Chinese Films*. New York: Columbia University Press, 2007.

Chow, Rey. "Violence in the Other Country: China as Crisis, Spectacle, and Woman," in *Third World Women and the Politics of Feminism*, edited by Chandra Mohanty, Ann Russo, and Torres Lourdes, 81–100. Bloomington: Indiana University Press, 1991.

Chow, Rey. *Woman and Chinese Modernity: The Politics of Reading between West and East*. Minneapolis: University of Minnesota Press, 1990.

Chow, Rey. *Writing Diaspora: Tactics of Intervention in Contemporary Cultural Studies*. Bloomington: Indiana University Press, 1993.

Chu, Yingchi. *Hong Kong Cinema: Coloniser, Motherland and Self*. London: RoutledgeCurzon, 2003.

Chu, Yiu-Wai. "Hybridity and (G)Local Identity in Postcolonial Hong Kong Cinema," in *Chinese-Language Film: Historiography, Poetics, Politics*, edited by Sheldon Lu and Emilie Yeh, 312–28. Honolulu: University of Hawaii Press, 2005.

Chu, Yiu-Wai. *Lost in Transition: Hong Kong Culture in the Age of China*. Albany, NY: SUNY Press, 2013.

Chu, Yiu-Wai. *Main Melody Films: Hong Kong Directors in Mainland China*. Edinburgh: Edinburgh University Press, 2022.

Chu, Yiu-Wai. "One Country Two Cultures? Post-1997 Hong Kong Cinema and Co-productions," in *Hong Kong Culture: Word and Image*, edited by Kam Louie, 131–45. Hong Kong: Hong Kong University Press, 2010.

Chu, Yiu-Wai. "Toward a New Hong Kong Cinema: Beyond Mainland–Hong Kong Co-productions." *Journal of Chinese Cinemas* 9, no. 2 (2015): 111–24.

Chua, Lawrence, and Ann Hui. "Ann Hui." *BOMB*, no. 36 (Summer 1991): 28–30.

Cole, Thomas, Nathan Carlin, and Ronald Carson, eds., *Medical Humanities: An Introduction*. New York: Cambridge University Press, 2014.

Coleman, Kevin, and Daniel James. "Capitalism and the Camera," in *Capitalism and the Camera: Essays on Photography and Extraction*, edited by Kevin Coleman and Daniel James, 1–27. London: Verso, 2021.

Collins, Jim. "Television and Postmodernism," in *Film and Theory: An Anthology*, edited by Robert Stam and Toby Miller, 758–73. Malden, MA: Blackwell Publishers, 2000.

Constable, Nicole. *Maid to Order in Hong Kong: Stories from Filipina Workers*. Ithaca, NY: Cornell University Press, 1997.

Cui, Yang. "Tan tan dianshi de ji ge wenti" [A Few Questions about Television]. *Close-up*, no. 49 (January 1978): 10–11.

The Culturalist. "(Zhuanfang) Sandu Gaibian Zushi Nainai zhuzuo Xu Anhua: 'Wo Duidezhu Zhang Ailing'" [(Exclusive Interview) Adapting the Grandma's Fiction for the Third Time, Ann Hui Said, "I Do Not Feel Sorry for Eileen Chang"], November 25, 2021. Accessed August 15, 2023. https://www.youtube.com/watch?v=HZv3djXJoM0.

Cunliffe, Tom, and Raymond Tsang. "The Making and Screening of Independent Films in the Absence of Radical Revolution: An Interview with Augustine Mok Chiu-yu on Social Movements, Technology, and Censorship." *Journal of Chinese Cinemas* 16, no. 2 (2022): 215–30.

Curtin, Michael. "Conditions of Capital: Global Media in Local Contexts," in *Internationalizing "International Communication"*, edited by Chin-Chuan Lee, 109–33. Ann Arbor: University of Michigan Press, 2015.

Davis, Darrell William. "Marketization, Hollywood, Global China." *Modern Chinese Literature and Culture* 26, no. 1 (2014): 191–241.

Deleuze, Gilles. *Cinema II: The Time-Image*. Translated by Hugh Tomlinson and Robert Galeta. Minneapolis: University of Minnesota, 1989.

Desser, David. "Fists of Legend: Constructing Chinese Identity in the Hong Kong Cinema," in *Chinese-Language Film: Historiography, Poetics, Politics*, edited by Sheldon H. Lu and Emilie Yueh-yu Yeh, 280–97. Honolulu: University of Hawaii Press, 2005.

Devellennes, Charles, and Benoît Dillet. "Questioning New Materialisms: An Introduction." *Theory, Culture and Society* 35, no. 7–8 (2018): 5–20.

Dissanayake, Wimal. *Melodrama and Asian Cinema*. New York: Cambridge University Press, 1993.

Dou, Miao. "Beyond Domesticity: Youth and Chinese Feminism, 1900–1949." PhD diss., Washington University in Saint Louis, 2023.

Elsaesser, Thomas. "Tales of Sound and Fury: Observations on the Family Melodrama," in *Imitations of Life: A Reader on Film and Television Melodrama*, edited by Marcia Landy, 68–91. Detroit, MI: Wayne State University Press, 1991.

Erens, Patricia Brett. "The Film Work of Ann Hui," in *The Cinema of Hong Kong: History, Arts, Identity*, edited by Poshek Fu and David Desser, 176–96. Cambridge: Cambridge University Press, 2000.

Fan, Victor. *Extraterritoriality: Locating Hong Kong Cinema and Media*. Edinburgh: Edinburgh University Press, 2019.

Fang, Karen. "War Films: Ann Hui's *Our Time Will Come* and Christopher Nolan's *Dunkirk*," in "Writing Hong Kong" issue, *Cha: An Asian Literary Journal*, December 2017. https://chajournal.blog/2017/11/09/our-time-will-come-and-dunkirk/.

Fei, Tang, and Calafato, Raees. "Transnational Multilingual Families in China: Multilingualism as Commodity, Conflict, and In-Betweenness." *SAGE Open* 12, no. 1 (2022): 1–14.

Fox, Nick J., and Pam Alldred. "New Materialist Social Inquiry: Designs, Methods and the Research-Assemblage." *International Journal of Social Research Methodology* 18, no. 4 (2015): 399–414.

Fu, Lei. *Fulei Tanyilu* [Fu Lei's Talk about Art]. Beijing: Joint Publishing, 2016.

Gaw, Kenneth. *Superior Servants: The Legendary Cantonese Amahs of the Far East*. Singapore: Oxford University Press, 1988.

Governments of the PRC and the HKSAR (Governments of the People's Republic of China and the Hong Kong Special Administrative Region). "Annex 4: Specific Commitments on Liberalization of Trade in Services," *Closer Economic Partnership Arrangement*, 2003, 18–19. Accessed December 6, 2025. https://www.tid.gov.hk/en/our_work/cepa/legal_text/fulltext.html.

Guillory, John. "Genesis of the Media Concept." *Critical Inquiry* 36, no. 2 (Winter 2010): 321–62.

Guo, Qingfan. *Zhuangzi Jishi* [*The Collection of Interetation of Zhuangzi*]. Beijing: Zhonghua Shuju, 1961.

Halberstam, Judith [Jack]. *Female Masculinity*. Durham, NC: Duke University Press, 1998.

Hall, Ken. "Main Entries: *Summer Snow*," in *Encyclopedia of Chinese Film*, edited by Yingjin Zhang and Ziwei Xiao, 323–4. New York: Routledge, 2002.

Han, Jonathan. *Sensuous Surfaces: The Decorative Object in Early Modern China*. London: Reaktion Books, 2010.

Han, Li. "Alternative Locality: Geopolitics and Cultural Identity in Ann Hui's *A Simple Life*." *Asian Cinema* 26, no. 1 (2015): 23–41.

Han, Li. "Re-packaging a Cultural Revolution Model Opera: Politics and Commerce in Tsui Hark's *The Taking of Tiger Mountain*." *Theoretical Studies in Literature and Art* 37, no. 5 (2017): 180–93.

He, Guimei. "Xu Anhua dianying de xianggang xushi yu zhongguo rentong" [The Hong Kong Narrative and Chinese Identity in Xu Anhua's Movies]. *Southern Cultural Forum*, no. 4 (2019): 50–3.

HKSAR (Hong Kong Special Administrative Region). *Hong Kong Population Projections 2012–2041*. Hong Kong: Census and Statistics Department, 2012.

Ho, Denise Y. "Hong Kong, China: The Border as Palimpsest." *Made in China Journal* 5, no. 3 (2020): 94–101.

Ho, Denise Y., and Jie Li. "From Landlord Manor to Red Memorabilia: Reincarnations of a Chinese Museum Town." *Modern China* 42, no. 1 (2015): 1–35.

Ho, Elaine Yee-lin. "Women on the Edges of Hong Kong Modernity: The Films of Ann Hui," in *At Full Speed: Hong Kong Cinema in a Borderless World*, edited by Esther C. M. Yau, 177–206. Minneapolis: University of Minnesota Press, 2001.

Hockney, David. "A Day on the Grand Canal." Last modified June 22, 2019. Accessed August 29, 2022. https://www.bilibili.com/video/BV144411u7cK?

Hong Kong Film Awards Association. "The Best 100 Chinese Motion Pictures." 2019. Accessed October 22, 2023. https://web.archive.org/web/20191022211054/http://www.hkfaa.com/news/100films.html.

Hong Kong Movie Database. "Zodiac Killers (1991)." Accessed October 15, 2024. https://hkmdb.com/db/movies/view.mhtml?id=7445&display_set=big5.

Hsia, C. T. *A History of Modern Chinese Fiction*. New Haven, CT: Yale University Press, 1961.

Hui, Ann. "Ann Hui: Headstrong and Unruly," in *The Quiet Revolution: 40 Years of ICAC Drama Series*, edited by Li Cheuk-to, 24–9. Hong Kong: Hong Kong International Film Festival, 2014.

Hui, Ann. *Nv ren, Si shi* [*Summer Snow*], in *Xu Anhua shuo Xu Anhua* [*Ann Hui on Ann Hui*], edited by Kwong Po Wei, 67–70. Shanghai: Fudan University Press, 2010.

Hung, Wu. *Feminine Space in Chinese Painting*. Beijing: SDX Joint Publishing, 2019.

Hung, Wu. *A Story of Ruins: Presence and Absence in Chinese Art and Visual Culture*. London: Reaktion Books, 2012.

Hutcheon, Linda. *A Theory of Adaptation*. New York: Routledge, 2006.

Irigaray, Luce. *Sexes and Genealogies*. New York: Columbia University Press, 1993.

Jaehne, Karen. "Boat People: An Interview with Ann Hui." *Cinéaste* 13, no. 2 (1984): 16–19.

"Jia shi duan ping" [Short Review on CTV]. *Cultural New Wave*, no. 1 (October 1978): 29. "Our Time Will Come: A Dialogue between Ann Hui and Mit Chan [aka Chi-tak Chan]." *Initium Media*, July 25, 2017. https://theinitium.com/article/20170725-culture-dialogue-xuanhuachenmie.

Jianming, Luo. "From Fiction to Film." *City Entertainment Magazine*, November 1984, 34.

Kwong, Po Wei. *Xu Anhua shuo Xu Anhua* [*Ann Hui on Ann Hui*]. Shanghai: Fudan University Press, 2010.

Lam, Derek. "The Left-Wing Legacy in '70s Hong Kong Television: Chameleon (1978) and Lee Sil-hong's Rediffusion (RTV) Tetralogy." *Journal of Chinese Cinemas* 16, no. 2 (2022): 184–200.

Lau, Andy. *My 30 Work Days*. Beijing: Zhongguo huaqiao chubanshe, 2012.

Law, Kar. "Archetypes and Variations: Observations on Six Cantonese Films," in *Cantonese Melodrama 1950–1969* (revised edition), edited by Li Cheuk-to, 15–20. Hong Kong: Urban Council, 1997.

Law, Kar. "Hou liuqi shidai xianggang dianying de chaoliu bianhua ji shehui ganying yu dianshi zuo hu guan bijiao" [Changes and Social Resonance of Hong Kong Cinema: Comparing to Television], in *When the Wind Was Blowing Wild: Hong Kong Cinema of the 1970s*, edited by May Ng, 32–43. Oral History Series (7). Hong Kong: Hong Kong Film Archive, 2018.

Law Kar. "Law Kar shuo Xu Anhua de zaoqi dianying" [Law Kar Discusses Ann Hui's Early Films], in *Xu Anhua shuo Xu Anhua* [*Ann Hui on Ann Hui*], edited by Kwong Po wei, 413–22. Shanghai: Fudan University Press, 2017.

Lee, Bono. "The Possibility of China for Hong Kong Directors: The Transformation of Peter Chan's Identity," in *Peter Chan: My Way*, edited by Li Cheuk-to, 187–95. Hong Kong: Joint Publishing, 2012.

Lee, Leo Ou-fan. *Shanghai Modern: The Flowering of a New Urban Culture in China*. Cambridge, MA: Harvard University Press, 1999.

Lee, Maggie. "*The Way We Are*." *The Hollywood Reporter*, April 2, 2008. Accessed June 15, 2023. https://www.hollywoodreporter.com/movies/movie-reviews/way-we-are-125594/.

Lee, Roger. *Taojie and I*. Hong Kong: Hongtouzi youxian gongsi, 2012.

Legislative Council (Hong Kong government). "Legislative Council Meeting Record (1989.10.11)." Accessed October 15, 2024. https://www.legco.gov.hk/yr89-90/chinese/lc_sitg/hansard/h891011.pdf.

Lei, Chin-pang. "Life's Journey Is Never Flat: Ann Hui's Travel Films and Hong Kong Consciousness." *P-articles*, January 22, 2019. https://p-articles.com/critics/579.html.

Lei, Jun. *Mastery of Words and Swords: Negotiating Intellectual Masculinities in Modern China, 1890s–1930s*. Hong Kong: Hong Kong University Press, 2021.

Leisure and Cultural Services Department (Hong Kong government). "The American Grandson." Accessed October 15, 2024. https://mcms.lcsd.gov.hk/FAMS_ipac/cclib/search/showBib.jsp?oai=Y&f=e&id=6553718662405.

Lemke, Thomas. "An Alternative Model of Politics? Prospects and Problems of Jane Bennett's Vital Materialism." *Theory, Culture & Society* 35, no. 6 (2018): 31–54.

Leung, Ping-kwan. "Urban Cinema and the Cultural Identity of Hong Kong," in *Between Home and World: A Reader in Hong Kong Cinema*, edited by Esther M. K. Cheung and Chu Yiu-wai, 369–98. Hong Kong: Oxford University Press, 2004.

Levine, Emily. "What Does It All Mean? Emily Levine at TEDxDanubia 2014." TEDx Talks, June 10, 2014. Video, 18 min., 21 sec. https://www.youtube.com/watch?v=F4WDlJCO66Y.

Li, Chaotao. "Ann Hui Talks about *Love in a Fallen City*." *City Entertainment Magazine*, October 1984, 20.

Li, Cheuk-to. "A Comprehensive Review of Ann Hui's Four Films," in *Six Great Directors of Hong Kong and Taiwan*, edited by Li You-xin, 173–93. Taipei: Independence Evening Post, 1986.

Li, Cheuk-to. "Introduction," in *Cantonese Melodrama 1950–1969* (revised edition), edited by Li Cheuk-to, 8. Hong Kong: Urban Council, 1997.

Li, Cheuk-to. "Survival Zui zhongyao" [The Primacy of Survival]. *Film Biweekly*, no. 7 (October 1982): 19–23.

Li, Chi-hua. "*The Story of Woo Viet*: Confessions of Refugee Fate," in *Six Great Directors of Hong Kong and Taiwan*, edited by Li You-xin, 194–6. Taipei: Independence Evening Post, 1986.

Li, Han. "Alternative Locality: Geopolitics and Cultural Identity in Ann Hui's *A Simple Life*." *Asian Cinema* 26, no. 1 (2015): 23–41.

Li, Mei-Ting. "Our Time Will Come: Hong Kong Is the Main Melody." *Cinezen*, July 11, 2017. https://www.cinezen.hk/?p=7713

Li, Mo. "Bu ping ming keyi ming dao shenme chengdu" [How Much Can Crying Against Injustice Do for Justice?]. *Close-up*, no. 9 (April 1976): 9.

Li, Xiaoxian. "Bansheng Yuan de Shijie guan: Xu Anhua Fangtan lu" [The Worldview of *Half a Lifelong Romance*: An Interview with Ann Hui]. *The Reading Town*, no. 6 (1998): 8–9.

Liu, Xiao. *Information Fantasies: Precarious Mediation in Postsocialist China.* Minneapolis: University of Minnesota Press, 2019.

Lo, Kwai-Cheung, and Pang Laikwan. "Hong Kong: Ten Years after Colonialism." *Postcolonial Studies* 10, no. 4 (2007): 349–56.

Lo, Vivienne, Chris Berry, and Guo Liping, eds. *Film and the Chinese Medical Humanities*. London: Routledge, 2019.

Louie, Kam. "Introduction: Eileen Chang: A Life of Conflicting Cultures in China and America," in *Eileen Chang: Romancing Languages, Cultures and Genres*, edited by Kam Louie, 1–14. Hong Kong: Hong Kong University Press, 2012.

Lu, Min. "Hong Kong History Expert Liu Shuyong: Bringing History into Reality." *People's Daily Overseas Edition*, December 24, 2022. http://paper.people.com.cn/rmrbhwb/html/2022-12/24/content_25956028.htm

Lu, Weili. "A Casual Discussion on Ann Hui," in *Xu Anhua shuo Xu Anhua* [*Ann Hui on Ann Hui*], edited by Kwong Po Wei, 330–51. Shanghai: Fudan University Press, 2010.

Lusiren. "Huanle jinxiao yu gudian shehui zhuyi de zhongjie" [EYT and the End of Classical Socialism]. *Cultural New Wave*, no. 5 (February 1979): 8.

Lv, Meijing. "Director Ann Hui: May Your Golden Era Arrive Like a Warning Bell to the Heart" [*Daoyan Xu Anhua: Yuan nide huangjinshidai si jingzhong laidao xinshang*]. *Phoenix Culture*, September 28, 2014. https://culture.ifeng.com/a/20140928/42107198_0.shtml

Ma, Nannan. *Cultural Hong Kong: A Study of Ann Hui's Film* [*Renwen xianggang: xuanhua dianyingyanjiu*]. Nanjing: Nanjing University Press, 2019.

MacCormack, Patricia, *Cinesexuality*, Aldershot: Ashgate, 2008.

Mak, Grace. "*Bansheng Yuan* yu *Se, Jie* zhong Dongqing zhi Guanjian: Cong Shijian yu Kongjian Kan Qing'ai zhi xushu" [The Key of Feeling Touched in *Half a Lifelong Romance* and "Lust, Caution": The Narrative of Love from the Perspective of Time and Space], in *Zhang Ailing: Chuanqi. Xingbie. Xipu* [*Eileen Chang: Legend. Sexuality. Genealogy*], edited by Xingqian Lin, 243–56. Taipei: Linking Publishing, 2012.

Mao, Dun. *Huanghun* [*Dusk*], in *Mao Dun*, edited by Zhuang Zhongqing. Taipei: Bookman.

Mao, Dun. *Tuo xian za ji* [*Escaping from the Fallen City*]. Beijing: Zhongguo shehui kexue chubanshe, 1980.

Mao, Jian. "Liangfeng qiuyue: Xu Anhua dianying zhong de fengjing he Zhongguo shineng" [The Cool Breeze and Autumn Moon: Landscape and Chinese Potential in Ann Hui's Films]. *Southern Cultural Forum*, no. 4 (2019): 54–7.

Marchetti, Gina. "Brecht in Hong Kong: Evans Chan's *The Life and Times of Wu Zhong Xian*," in *Postcolonialism, Diaspora, and Alternative Histories: The Cinema of Evans Chan*, edited by Tony Williams, 81–99. Hong Kong: Hong Kong University Press, 2015.

Marchetti, Gina. *Citing China: Politics, Postmodernism, and World Cinema*. Honolulu: University of Hawaii Press, 2018.

Marchetti, Gina. "Feminism, Postfeminism, and Hong Kong Women Filmmakers," in *A Companion to Hong Kong Cinema*, edited by Esther M. K. Cheung, Gina Marchetti, and Esther C. M. Yau, 237–64. Chichester: Wiley-Blackwell, 2015.

Mass Culture Action Team. "Xianggang qingnian ruhe kandai dianshi de gongyong—wenjuan diaocha baogao shu" [How Hong Kong Youth View the Role of Television: A Questionnaire Report]. *Close-up*, no. 56 (April 1978): 4–9.

McLuhan, Marshall. *Understanding Media: The Extensions of Man*. Cambridge, MA: MIT Press, 1994.

Mei, Xuefeng. "'Wentun Zhi Mei' Xu Anhua" [The Beauty of Warm Slowness: Ann Hui]. *zhihu*, September 25, 2021. Accessed February 6, 2023. https://zhuanlan.zhihu.com/p/413813196.

Meilin, "Yi Xiaohong" [Remembering Xiao Hong], in *Huainian Xiaohong* [*Memory of Xiao Hong*], edited by Guanquan Wang, 152–162. Shanghai: Dongfang Publishing House, 2011.

News.gov.hk. "Xuesheng xu renqing Xianggang zhuquan yizhi shuyu Zhongguo" [Students Should Be Aware That Hong Kong Has Remained under China's Sovereign Authority Throughout], August 2, 2022. Accessed July 31, 2025. https://sc.news.gov.hk/TuniS/www.news.gov.hk/chi/2022/08/20220802/20220802_162403_729.html?type=ticker.

Ng, Ka-yan. "Analyzing the Hong Kong New Wave Cinema through the Stories of Ann Hui." BA diss., Hong Kong Baptist University, 2008.

Nguyen, Vinh. "Ann Hui's *Boat People*: Documenting Vietnamese Refugees in Hong Kong," in *Looking Back on the Vietnam War: Twenty-First-Century Perspectives*, edited by Brenda M. Boyle and Jeehyun Lim, 94–109. New Brunswick, NJ: Rutgers University Press, 2016.

Ooi, Keat Gin. "From Amah-Chieh to Indonesian Maids: A Comparative Study in the Context of Malaysia, circa 1930s–1990s," in *Proletarian and Gendered Mass Migrations: A Global Perspective on Continuities and Discontinuities from the 19th to the 21st Centuries*, edited by Dirk Hoerder and Amarjit Kaur, 405–25. Leiden: Brill, 2013.

Pearson, Veronica. "The Past Is Another Country: Hong Kong Women in Transition." *The Annals of the American Academy of Political and Social Science* 547 (1996): 91–103.

Pink, Sarah. *The Future of Visual Anthropology: Engaging the Senses*. London: Routledge, 2006.

Plantinga, Carl. *Moving Viewers: American Film and the Spectator's Experience*. Los Angeles: University of California Press, 2009.

Plantinga, Carl. "The Scene of Empathy and the Human Face on Film," in *Passionate Views: Film, Cognition, and Emotion*, edited by Carl Plantinga and Greg M. Smith, 139–255. Baltimore, MD: Johns Hopkins University Press, 1999.

Q Zai. "Jiao ni di dianshi" [A Lesson on Watching TV]. *Cultural New Wave*, no. 4 (January 1979): 12–13.

Q Zai. "Yishi xingtai dazhan huan le jin xiso zai Guangzhou" [Ideological Warfare EYT in Guangzhou]. *Cultural New Wave*, no. 5 (February 1979): 3–7.

Qi, Shi. "Hong Kong: The Sense of Achievement and Crisis in 1980s Cinema," in *A Comprehensive View of New Asian Cinema*, edited by Peggy Qiao, 30–46. Taiwan: Yuan-Liou Publishing, 1991.

Quan-er. "Dianshi minjian xiju weishenme shou huanying?" [Why Are TV Folk Comedy Shows So Popular?]. *Cultural New Wave*, no. 9 (June 1979): 15.

Quan-er. "Kan qing dianshi, bu yao rang ziji hunmi" [Watch Television Carefully: Avoid Falling into Coma]. *Cultural New Wave*, no. 3 (December 1978): 39.

Ren, Shanshan. "Xu Anhua tan huangjinshidai: bubi bawo kancheng wenhuafuhao" [Ann Hui on *The Golden Era*: No Need to See Me as a Cultural Symbol]. *National Humanity History*, no. 18 (2014): 120–5.

Rodriguez, Hector. "The Emergence of the Hong Kong New Wave," in *At Full Speed: Hong Kong Cinema in a Borderless World*, edited by Esther C. M. Yau, 53–70. Minneapolis: University of Minnesota Press, 2001.

RTHK (Radio Television Hong Kong). *Old Age: Where to Turn*. July 2015.

Sanders, Julie. *Adaptation and Appropriation*. London: Routledge, 2006.

Saunders, Cicely, Dorothy H. Summers, and Neville Teller, eds., *Hospice: The Living Idea*. London: Edward Arnold, 1983.

Scott, Ian. *Political Change and the Crisis of Legitimacy in Hong Kong*. Honolulu: University of Hawaii Press, 1989.

Sen, Kim-Soon. "Text, Image and Reproduction of the Feminine Signs: On Ai-Ling Chang's Fiction and Its Cinematic Adaptation." *Chungwai Literary* 33, no. 1 (2004): 41–59.

Shachar, Hila. *Screening the Author*. Cham: Springer, 2019.

Shackleton, Liz. "Ann Hui, *The Golden Era*." *Screen International*, October 3, 2014. https://www.screendaily.com/interviews/ann-hui-the-golden-era/5078265.article

Shen, Ming. "Lun puji wenhua yishi xingtai zai shengchan ji piban" [On Popular Culture Ideological Reproduction and Criticism]. *Cultural New Wave*, no. 6 (March 1979): 11–13.

Shen, Shiao-ying. "Politics and Aesthetics of Connection and Splitting: Ann Hui and Clara Law's Love and Loss of Hong Kong." *Chung Wai Literature Quarterly* 29, no. 10 (2001): 35–50.

Shu, Kei. "Feng jie de Sense and Senibility" [*The Secret*'s Sense and Sensibility]. *Film Biweekly*, no. 95 (September 1982): 29–35.

Shu, Kei. "The Television Work of Ann Hui," in *The 17th Hong Kong International Film Festival Changes in Hong Kong Society through Cinema*, edited by Li Cheuk-to, 42–52. Hong Kong: Urban Council, 1988.

Sina Entertainment. "Zhuming yinyue ren Luo Dayou zuoke Xin Lang liaotianshi fang tanshilu (futu)" [Famous Musician Luo Dayou's Interview with Sina Chat Room (with photos)], May 10, 2001. http://ent.sina.com.cn/s/h/42812.html.

Social Care Institute for Excellence. "Choosing to Die at Home." *SCIE Guide 48: Dying Well at Home: The Case for Integrated Working*, 2013. Accessed April 21, 2023. https://www.scie.org.uk/publications/guides/guide48/choosingtodieathome.asp

Spinoza, Benedict, *A Spinoza Reader: The Ethics and Other works*. edited and translated by Edwin Curley, Princeton, NJ: Princeton University Press, 1994.

Stam, Robert. *Literature through Film: Realism, Magic, and the Art of Adaptation*. Oxford: Blackwell, 2005.

Su, We-chen. "Shanghai 1947 Zhang Ailing dianying yuanqi jiantan Buliaoqing Taitaiwansui juben de rensheng canzhao" [Shanghai. 1947. Eileen Chang's Origins of Cinematography—"Unending Love," "Long Live My Wife," Chang's Slice of Life on Stage], *Chungwai Literary* 37, no. 2 (2008): 139–81.

Su, Wendy. *China's Encounter with Global Hollywood: Cultural Policy and the Film Industry, 1994–2013*. Lexington: University Press of Kentucky, 2016.

Su, Wendy. "It Is Not Just Propaganda: Main Melody Film between the State and Market." *American Review of China Studies* 17, no. 1 (2016): 21–38.

Szeto, Mirana M. "Identity Politics and Its Discontents: Contesting Cultural Imaginaries in Contemporary Hong Kong," *Interventions* 8, no. 2 (2006): 253–75.

Szeto, Mirana M. "Ann Hui at the Margin of Mainstream Hong Kong Cinema," in *Hong Kong Screenscapes: From the New Wave to the Digital Frontier*, edited by Esther M. K. Cheung, Gina Marchetti, and Tan See-Kam, 51–66. Hong Kong: Hong Kong University Press, 2011.

Szeto, Mirana M., and Yun-chung Chen. "Mainlandization or Sinophone Translocality? Challenges for Hong Kong SAR New Wave Cinema." *Journal of Chinese Cinemas* 6, no. 2 (June 2012): 115–34.

Taiwan e-Learning and Digital Archives Program, Academia Sinica. "A Long Way Home: Veterans Returning Home and Visiting Family Movement." Accessed October 15, 2024. https://ndweb.iis.sinica.edu.tw/TWM/Public/pdf/old_soldier.pdf.

Tam, Yee-lok. "When We Talk about Post-1997 Hong Kong Cinema, What Are We Talking About: Identity Politics, Theories and Capital-State-Nation." *HKinema* 39 (2017): 12–17.

Tam, Yee-lok, Enoch. "Nuxing, shenfen yu zhengzhi—Xu Anhua dianying yanjiu huigu" [Woman, Identity and Politics: A Retrospective Review of Scholarship on Ann Hui's Cinema], in *Ann Hui: Forty Years of Filmmaking*, edited by Cecilia Wong and Yuet Wah Ng. Hong Kong: Joint Publishing, 2018, 110–19.

Tambling, Jeremy. *Wong Kar-Wai's Happy Together*. Hong Kong: Hong Kong University Press, 2003.

Tang, Chenguang. "Lu Xun yu moxia jingshen" [Lu Xun and the Spirit of Knight Errants]. *Lu Xun yanjiu yuebao* [*Lu Xun Studies Monthly*] 18, no. 1 (1997): 22–6.

Tang, Gary, and Raymond Hau-yin Yuen. "Hong Kong as the 'Neoliberal Exception' of China: Transformation of Hong Kong Citizenship before and after the Transfer of Sovereignty." *Journal of Chinese Political Science* 21, no. 4 (2016): 469–84.

Tasker, Yvonne. "Fists of Fury: Discourses of Race and Masculinity in the Martial Arts Cinema," in *Asian Cinemas: A Reader and Guide*, edited by Harry Stecopoulos and Michael Uebel, 437–56. Durham, NC: Duke University Press. 1997.

Taylor, Jay. *The Generalissimo's Son: Chiang Ching-kuo and the Revolutions in China and Taiwan*. Cambridge, MA: Harvard University Press, 2000.

"The Hong Kong Rescue by the East River Column: True Brotherhood and Loyalty." Xinhua News Agency, May 3, 2021. http://www.locpg.gov.cn/jsdt/2021-05/03/c_1211140069.htm.

"The Significance of the East River Column Historical Photo Exhibition." China Radio Network, November 11, 2012. http://mil.news.sina.com.cn/2013-11-11/1741748977.html.

The Songs of the South: An Anthology of Ancient Chinese Poems by Qu Yuan and Other Poets (Penguin Classics), translated by David Hawkes, London: Penguin, 2021.

Tian Yan. "Yiyu feizaoju" [Speaking Gibberish on Soap Opera]. *Close-up*, no. 51 (February 1978): 12–13.

TVB (Television Broadcasts Limited) News and Information Division. *The Choice of Nursing Home*. Aired September 2015.

Ue, Tom. "Reading Eileen Chang and Filming Hong Kong: An Interview with Ann Hui on *Love After Love*." *Film International* 4 (2021): 99–103.

Van den Troost, Kristof. *Hong Kong Crime Films: Criminal Realism, Censorship and Society, 1947–1986*. Edinburgh: Edinburgh University Press, 2024.

Veg, Sebastian. "Anatomy of the Ordinary: New Perspectives in Hong Kong Independent Cinema." *Journal of Chinese Cinemas* 8, no. 1 (2014): 73–92.

Vidal, Belén. "Introduction: The Biopic and Its Critical Contexts," in *The Biopic in Contemporary Film Culture*, edited by Tom Brown and Belén Vidal, 1–32. New York, London: Routledge, 2014.

Wang, David Der-wei. *Jishi yu Xugou* [*Fact and Fiction*]. Taipei: Rye Field Publishing, 1996.

Wang, David Der-wei. "Zhang Ailing Zaisheng Yuan: Chongfu, Huixuan yu Yansheng de Xushi Xue" [The Rebirth of Eileen Chang: The Narratology of "Repetition," "Involution," and "Derivation"]. *Literary Century*, no. 9 (2000): 53–8.

Wang, David Der-wei.*The Lyrical in Epic Time: Modern Chinese Intellectuals and Artists through the 1949 Crisis*. New York: Columbia University, 2015.

Wang, Yi. *chuci zhangju* [the chapters and sentences of chuci]. Taipei: Yiwen yinshuguan, 1967.

Wang, Zhuoyi. "Transforming the Liminal Hero: Border-Crossing Interconnections in *The Taking of Tiger Mountain* and Its Textual Pedigree." *Chinese Literature Today* 7, no. 1 (2018): 118–28.

Weilan, Lu, and Ann Hui. "Adaptation and Nostalgia: A Discussion Starting from *Love in a Fallen City*," in *The Origin of Images*, edited by Lu Weilan, 92–156. Beijing: Beijing Publishing House, 2019.

Willemen, Paul. "Hong Kong Film Festival, 1986: Focus on Melodrama." *Framework* 32 (1986): 193–6.

Williams, Tony. "*Song of the Exile* Border-Crossing Melodrama." *Jump Cut* 42 (1998): 94–100.

Wong, Cecilia, and Yuet Wah Ng, eds. *Xu Anhua: Dianying Sishi* [*Ann Hui: Forty Years of Filmmaking*]. Hong Kong: Joint Publishing, 2018.

Xi, Xi. *Flying Carpet*. Hong Kong: Su Yeh Publisher, 1996.

Xi, Xi. *Marvels of a Floating City*. Hong Kong: Renditions Paperbacks, 1997.

Xiao, Hong. *The Field of Life and Death, and, Tales of Hulan River: Two Novels*, translated by Howard Goldblatt and Ellen Lai-shan Yeung. Bloomington: Indiana University Press, 1979.

Xiao, Hong. *Xiaohong quanji* [*The Complete Works of Xiao Hong*]. Harbin: The North Literature and Art Publishing House, 2018.

Xiao, Liu. *Information Fantasies: Precarious Mediation in Postsocialist China*. Minneapolis: University of Minnesota Press, 2019.

Xingfeng, He. "Under the Silver Lantern, a Discussion of the Film Adaptation of Eileen Chang's Hong Kong Legend: On Ann Hui's *Love in a Fallen City*," in *Reading Eileen Chang Again*, edited by Liu Shaoming, 99–131. Shandong: Shandong Pictorial Publishing House, 2004.

"Xu Anhua dui Huangjinshidai de gaobaishu" [Ann Hui's Confession to The Golden Era]. *CineHello*, October 8, 2014. https://cinehello.com/stream/55074.

Yan, Lu. *Crossed Paths: Labor Activism and Colonial Governance in Hong Kong, 1938–1958*. Ithaca, NY: Cornell University Press, 2019.

Yan, Xiaochang. *Guanzi Jiaoshi* [*the Revision and Annotation of Guanzi*]. Changsha: yuelu shushe, 1996.

Yang, Min. "Spy, Abjection, and Post-Socialist Identity: Chinese Neo-Spy Films since 2009." *Studies in the Humanities* 44, no. 1–2 (2019). https://link.gale.com/apps/doc/A587877317/AONE?u=anon~8520f830&sid=googleScholar&xid=9b5934ab.

Yang, Yuanying, Yiwu Zhang, Guanping Wu, and Lihua Yang, "Huangjin shidai" [On *The Golden Era*], *Contemporary Cinema* 224 (November 2014): 49–57+98.

Yau, Ching. "Xianggang xin langchao ying mei yu xi de xin chengyuan" [Hong Kong New Wave Anglophone New Members], in *Wet Dreams in Paradise*, edited by Yau Ching, 394–447. Taipei: Lianjing Press, 2024.

Yau, Ka-fai. "Looking Back at Ann Hui's Cinema of the Political." *Modern Chinese Literature and Culture* 19, no. 2 (2007): 117–50.

Yeh, Emilie Yueh-yu. "Pitfalls of Cross-Cultural Analysis: Chinese *Wenyi* Film and Melodrama." *Asian Journal of Communication* 19, no. 4 (2009): 438–52.

Yeh, Emilie Yueh-yu. "*Wenyi* and the Branding of Early Chinese Film." *Journal of Chinese Cinemas* 6, no. 1 (2012): 65–94.

Yeh, Emilie Yueh-yu, and Darrell William Davis. "Re-nationalizing China's Film Industry: Case Study on the China Film Group and Film Marketization." *Journal of Chinese Cinemas* 2 (2008): 37–51.

Yeh, Emilie Yueh-yu, and Shi-yan Chao. "Policy and Creative Strategies: Hong Kong CEPA Films in the China Market." *International Journal of Cultural Policy* 26, no. 2 (2020): 184–201.

Yeung, Jessica Siu-yin. "Ann Hui's Allegorical Cinema," in *Cultural Conflict in Hong Kong: Angles on a Coherent Imaginary*, edited by Jason S. Polley, Vinton Poon, and Lian-Hee Wee, 87–104. Singapore: Palgrave Macmillan, 2018.

Yeung, Jessica Siu-Yin. "Xu Anhua de xianggang yuyan: Mingyue jishi you" [*Our Time Will Come*: Ann Hui's Hong Kong Allegory]. *Cinezen*, August 8, 2017. http://www.cinezen.hk/?p=7783.

Yip, Man-Fung. *Martial Arts Cinema and Hong Kong Modernity: Aesthetics, Representation, Circulation*. Hong Kong: Hong Kong University Press, 2017.

Yip, Terry Siu-han. "Fate and Destiny: Yuan as Ming in 'Matrimony Inn' and Eileen Chang's *Half a Lifelong Romance* and 'Love in a Fallen City,'" in *Fate and Prognostication in the Chinese Literary Imagination*, edited by Michael Lackner et al., 17–45. Leiden: Brill, 2020.

Yu, Hongmei. "Visual Spectacular, Revolutionary Epic, and Personal Voice: The Narration of History in Chinese Main Melody Films." *Modern Chinese Literature and Culture* 25, no. 2, Special Issue on The Dis/Appearance of the Political Crowd in Contemporary China (Fall 2013): 166–218.

Yue, Audrey. *Ann Hui's Song of the Exile*. Hong Kong: Hong Kong University Press, 2010.

Yue, Audrey. "Migration-as-Transition: Pre-Post-1997 Hong Kong Culture in Clara Law's *Autumn Moon*." *Intersections: Gender, History and Culture in the Asian Context* 4 (2000). http://intersections.anu.edu.au/issue4/yue.html.

Zeng, Hong. "Translocal Female Subjectivity: Notes on Ann Hui's *The Golden Era*." *Asian Cinema* 30, no. 1 (2019): 91–107.

Zhang, Huiyu. "From Main Melody Films to Mainstream Blockbusters" [Cong zhu xuanlu yingpian dao zhuliu dapian de shanbian]. *Film Art*, no. 2 (2011): 16–23.

Zhang, Ying. *Xin shiqi yilai zhu xuanlu dianying yanjiu* [*A Study of Main Melody Films since the New Period*]. Shanghai: Sanlian, 2017.

Zhang, Yingjin. "Commentary: The Dynamics of Off-Centeredness in Hong Kong Cinema," in *A Companion to Hong Kong Cinema*, edited by Esther M. K. Cheung, Gina Marchetti, and Esther C. M. Yau, 489–98. Chichester: Wiley-Blackwell, 2015.

Zhang, Zhuoxiang. "Shizi shanxia meiyou zhengzhi yingxiang li" [*Under the Lion Rock* Series Does Not Have Any Political Influence]. *Film Biweekly*, no. 1 (January 1979): 50–1.

Zhao, Yafei. "Huangjin shidai: kunyu laolong zhizhong" [The Golden Era: Trapped in a Cage], *Home Drama*, no. 11 (2016): 115.

Zhao, Yuan. *Xiang Gang Lao Yin: Xu Anhua de guang ying li cheng* [*Hong Kong Imprint: Ann Hui's Cinematic Journey*]. Beijing: Chinese Film Publication, 2013.

Zheng, Binghong. "*Our Time Will Come*: Smuggling Hong Kong Consciousness in Main Melody Films." July 13, 2017. https://opinion.udn.com/opinion/story/10012/2580561.

Zhong, Baoxian. *Xiang gang bai nian guang ying* [*Centennial History of the Hong Kong Film and Television Industry*]. Beijing: Peking University Press, 2007.

Zhong, Yi. "Xu Anhua: xiang Xiaohong yiyang gudu you wanqiang" [Ann Hui: As Lonely and Resilient as Xiao Hong]. *Times Figure*, no. 9 (2014): 98–9.

Zhou, Zhaoxiang. "Dianshi jiaoyu zhuding shi zi wo maodun de youxi" [Television Education Is a Self-Contradictory Endeavor]. *Cultural New Wave*, no. 8 (April 1979): 14–16.

Zhu, Yanhong. "Bodies in Crisis: Sensuality and the Cinematic Reconfiguration of the Spy Genre in Contemporary Chinese Cinema." *East Asian Journal of Popular Culture* 1, no. 3 (2015): 359–76.

Zimmermann, Patricia R., and Helen De Michiel. *Open Space New Media Documentary*. New York: Routledge, 2018.

Index